WILD BRITAIN

OVER 1,000 OF THE BEST WILDLIFE SITES AROUND BRITAIN

Edited by Kath Stathers
Assistant Editor: Tania Adams

Supported by

SWAROVSKI
OPTIK

THINK
BOOKS

First published 2007 by Think Books
an imprint of Pan Macmillan Ltd
Pan Macmillan, 20 New Wharf Road, London N1 9RR
Basingstoke and Oxford
Associated companies throughout the world
www.panmacmillan.com
www.think-books.com

ISBN 978-1-84525-039-3

Editor: Kath Stathers
Assistant Editor: Tania Adams
Sub-editors: Victoria Chow and Rica Dearman
Think Books: Emma Jones, Mark Searle and Malcolm Tait
Editorial research: Erin Heavey, Amaan Hyder, Jessica McSweeny, Gillian Parker,
Sundus Pasha, Lauren Priest, Man Tsuey Tse and Daniel Warnock
Design: James Collins
Cartography: John Plumer

1 3 5 7 9 8 6 4 2

A CIP catalogue record for this book is available from
the British Library.

Printed and Bound in Italy by Printer Trento

Visit www.panmacmillan.com to read more about all our books and to buy
them. You will also find features, author interviews and news of any
author events, and you can sign up for e-newsletters so that you're
always first to hear about our new releases.

Cover image: European Otter, *Lutra lutra*, Simon Litten/FLPA

THANK YOU

· ·

This book would not have been possible without the help and co-operation
of the following organisations and their excellent websites:

Countryside Council for Wales
Environment and Heritage Service Northern Ireland
Forestry Commission
Natural England
Plantlife
RSPB
Scottish Natural Heritage
Wales and Dolphin Conservation Society
Waterscape
Wildfowl and Wetlands Trust
The Wildlife Trusts
The Woodland Trust
Zoological Society of London

With special thanks to Howard Park at The Wildlife Trusts.

Help us to help them..

Wildlife Aid is a charity dedicated to the rescue, rehabilitation and release of sick, injured or orphaned British Wildlife. Dealing with over 20,000 wildlife incidents each year, the centre receives no corporate funding and relies entirely on donations and legacies from the public to keep its doors open.

All the animals on this page were orphans and were hand-reared and cared for by Wildlife Aid. They were successfully released back into the wild to live a healthy and natural life.

For further information visit
www.wildlifeaid.com

As seen on TV's
wildlife SOS

Wildlife Aid - registered charity no. 297610 . 24hr Helpline 09061 800132 (50p per minute) . www.wildlifeaid.c

Contents

Absolutely Watertight

Pocket-Sized Long-Distance Viewing

Due to its sophisticated interior focusing system the Pocket 8x20B from Swarovski Optik is the smallest watertight, dustproof, pocket-sized binocular on the market. The world's most intricate optical system, for this category of binocular, guarantees perfect vision. Astonishingly light and compact – the true greatness lies in the detail.

SWAROVSKI
OPTIK

Swarovski U.K. LTD., Perrywood Business Park, Salfords, Surrey RH1 5JQ, Tel. 01737-856812, Fax 01737-856885

www.swarovskioptik.com

There is one place that will remain in my top 10 favourite wildlife hot spots. It's a cluster of small islands in north-west Europe, known as the British Isles.

Foreword
by Simon King

I am hugely lucky, travelling the world as a wildlife film-maker, documenting many of the greatest natural spectacles on Earth. My journeys have taken me to see many of the planet's most astonishing natural events, and yet, there is one place that will remain in my top 10 favourite wildlife hot spots. It's a cluster of small islands in north-west Europe, known as the British Isles.

Wildlife Britain sounds like a bit of an oxymoron; how can a country so small and so heavily populated possibly have anything wild about it?

Yet the truth is, these islands are among the most wildlife rich in the whole region, despite the people, the traffic, the tarmac and the housing developments. If you were to travel from the south of England to the most northerly point of mainland Scotland, you would pass from the lush leafy forests and fields of the south, into the rolling meadows of the midlands, skip sideways into the mountains and moors of Wales, then on to the hills and moors of northern England and on past the mountains and uplands of the Scottish highlands and finally into the near Arctic moors of the far north. In short, Britain's got the lot. And to compliment such a wide variety of habitats there's the wildlife to match.

And that's just the mainland. With the thousands of islands that make these shores some of the richest in the world for seabirds and other wild spirits, Britain really does have a tremendous amount to offer for anyone wanting to get in touch with reality. I use the phrase with purpose, since for many, the idea of spending a bit of time away from the office, walking in the hills, taking a stroll through a park or simply gazing out of the window and onto the garden is interrupted by what is frequently described as a 'reality check'. But I would argue that the 'real' world lies outside your window.

My own passion for the wild world kick-started in Kenya (where I was born), but only truly bloomed in the UK when I moved here as a toddler. The tiny garden adjoining the house in Bristol where I was raised hosted nesting blackbirds, song thrush and wrens among others, and each evening foxes would come to feed on scraps we proffered on the patio.

As my horizons broadened I found lesser spotted woodpeckers and kingfishers in my local woods and streams and further afield started to explore the lakes and coastline of Somerset. I had the enormous benefit of being shown these new territories by friend and mentor Mike Kendall, a man whose knowledge opened the door to new places and creatures.

I am certain, that if this book had been available 35 years ago, it would have accompanied us on our wildlife-watching trips, and with it the magic that may be found in every region and neighbourhood would have been all the broader.

So, explore the pages, then the recommended spots to visit, and welcome to the real world.

How to use this guide

There are probably as many ways people will want to use this guide as there are species of butterflies on the South Downs. So what we have tried to do is group the different sites firstly by geographical region – 12 in all, and we've included Northern Ireland in our title of *Britain* – and then by the nature of the reserves. For example, if you're in Chester and in the mood for a woodland wander, you'll find all the forests and woodlands in the North West grouped under one heading whether they're managed by the Forestry Commission, The Woodland Trusts or English Nature.

However, when it comes to trying to neatly organise wildlife into different categories, problems come from the fact that everything is, well, a bit wild and the boundaries between the categories can be less than clear. The system we've chosen is to put entries under these headings:

● **National Parks** – these huge swathes of land take in all sorts of habitat and wildlife. There are 14 in all, in England, Scotland and Wales. Roads cross them, villages and farms are in them, but the emphasis is always on conservation and promoting their enjoyment to the public.

● **AONBs** – Areas of Outstanding Natural Beauty gain their status for just that reason, they are beautiful and so need to be safeguarded. They are usually smaller than National Parks and their primary aim is always to conserve and enhance the natural beauty of the landscape.

● **Nature Reserves** – These are protected reserves of all different types of habitats, from chalky grassland to wet heathland, that are being managed by different organisations such as Natural England or The Wildlife Trusts to preserve their particular nature. All the ones in this book offer access to the public.

● **Bird Reserves** – Although many of these reserves might look and feel much like those in the previous category, they are managed by the RSPB with an emphasis on the birdlife and good viewing opportunities for visitors.

● **Forests & Woodland** – Many of these sites are those that are managed by the Woodland Trust or the Forestry Commission, but others are woodland reserves managed by other organisations that just seemed to fit better here. If a reserve has a mix of habitats in it, it has been left in the Nature Reserves category.

● **Coasts, Wetlands & Waterways** – Many of these aren't protected by any reserve status, but still offer wonderful wildlife-viewing opportunities. Others are reserves with a predominantly watery feel, so exceptionally good for wildfowl in the winter.

The CLUB WITH AN INTERNATIONAL DIMENSION

Royal Over-Seas League

Special membership rates for readers of Wildlife Britain

The Royal Over-Seas League (ROSL) has a long history of welcoming members from the UK and overseas to its London and Edinburgh clubhouses and providing a network of reciprocal clubs, branches or honorary representatives around the world.

The London clubhouse, comprising two period houses, is in a prime location bordering Green Park and near the Ritz Hotel. Over-Seas House has a private garden, al fresco dining, restaurant, buttery for light meals, bar, drawing room, 80 bedrooms and seven conference and private dining rooms. The Edinburgh clubhouse is centrally situated at 100 Princes Street.

Benefits of membership include economical central London pricing*, varied events programmes, quarterly journal, discounts on certain cruises and tours, in-house art exhibitions and concerts, evening speakers and short term access to over 90 other clubs around the world in Canada, Australia, New Zealand, Singapore, Hong Kong, Malaysia, India, Pakistan, South Africa, Kenya, Gibraltar, Spain, USA and elsewhere.

Specially discounted joining fees for *Wildlife Britain* readers range from £26 (resident overseas) to £59 (resident within 50 miles of Charing Cross, London). 2007 annual subscriptions range from £74 to £228 and are halved for new members joining after 1 July. The joining fee is waived for those aged 17-25.

For further information please contact the Membership Department, remembering to quote WILDLIFE BRITAIN.

Over-Seas House, Park Place, St James's Street, London SW1A 1LR
Tel: 020 7408 0214   Fax: 020 7499 6738
(Enquiries: 9.00am-5.00pm Monday-Friday - exts. 216 and 315)
Website: www.rosl.org.uk   E-mail: info@rosl.org.uk

London clubhouse: gin & tonic £3.70; pint of beer £2.80; house wine £2.95; three course lunch/dinner in the restaurant £26.50; in the garden £19.95; afternoon cream tea in the garden £5.95; evening events from £4.00; bedrooms £85 - £170; complimentary e-mail and computer facilities in Central Lounge, broadband internet connection in bedrooms. Prices correct at time of design, March 2007.

● **Not so Wild** – There is wildlife in Britain that's not found out in the countryside – urban farms, butterfly houses, zoos – and it seemed only right to include a selection of these slightly more controlled environments, especially as wildlife viewing here is virtually guaranteed, something the natural world can never offer.

The entries

In a book with over 1,000 entries, there isn't the space to give you detailed directions to car parks and where to find the nearest cream tea, but we have tried to make listings information as comprehensive as possible.

Each entry lists its nearest town and points you to its location on a map at the back of the book as well as to a website where you can find more detailed information of how to get there. If places aren't permanently open, we've listed their opening times and if places charge an entry fee we've listed the price for children and adults. (We've simplified this rather than given in-depth details of all the different family tickets and concessions that are available, but we've printed the more expensive options so that any surprises in prices should be pleasant ones.) We've also included various icons so that you can know what to expect when you visit a site, the key is in the box to the right.

Then, finally, there are the individual write-ups about the reserves themselves. If an area is well known for a particular species it will say so, but there will always be other species to see, too, and we won't have been able to include them all. Also, this is nature, so don't forget that things can change.

To help give a brief overview of what you can expect to see where, the next few pages are all written by the organisations that have helped to compile this book… the RSPB tells you

about Britain's birds, the Woodland Trust about woodlands, etc.

If you're starting from scratch, it might seem like there's a lot to take in – and in part there is, that's what makes wildlife watching such a fascinating pastime – but you'll soon find that the more you see, the more you understand how nature works and the more the world around you makes sense. A couple of field guides might help with this, such as the RSPB's *Birdwatching* or Collins' *Complete British Wildflowers*; more recommendations are listed at the back.

So, now that you're holding the book that can lead you to all of Britain's best nature reserves in your hands, all you have to do is make some time in your diary to get out there and start spotting wildlife.

KEY

P	Car park
P	(££) Car park with charge
ⓘ	Information/visitor centre
	Information panels
WC	Toilets
	Disabled toilet facilities
♿	Disabled access (only limited where indicated)
	Binocular hire
	Picnic tables
	Pushchair friendly
	Café
	Hides

Getting out there

Advice from The Wildlife Trusts

Wildlife is a little like music: you don't really need to know much about it to be able to enjoy it. The difference with wildlife, however, is that the more you understand it, the greater your delight will be in the behaviour that you see.

Many people would like to know more about Britain's wildlife, but often feel they don't know where to start. The Wildlife Trusts have an easy answer to this: your local patch. Don't feel you have to venture out alone, either. There is an army of dedicated conservationists out there; they are incredible sources of information and most of them will be delighted to share their knowledge and passion for the natural world with you. Contact your local Wildlife Trust (www. wildlifetrusts.org) to find out about events on reserves in your area: join a bat walk or a dragonfly course and, as well as sharing the spotting duties with others, there will also be somebody to answer any questions you might have about the difference between a vagrant darter and a hairy hawker.

At The Wildlife Trusts we are often asked which is the best season to watch wildlife. While spring and summer are of course buzzing and abundant, there is something to see at any time of the year. Woodland walks in autumn are unbeatable for enticing sights, sounds and smells – make the most of them by joining a fungus foray or a local bird walk. Even in the depths of winter, major wetland reserves never let you down for an array of birds. Land near the coast can be transformed by, for example, thousands of pink-footed geese from Iceland. They arrive in great skeins making a terrific cackling as they go to roost.

The key about venturing out in all seasons is just to be realistic and make sure you are well equipped for bad weather. It is certainly worth getting kitted out with some good quality outdoor clothing. And if you are thinking of investing in your wildlife watching or, indeed, planning some birthday present hints, top of the list should be:

● Binoculars. They seriously increase your enjoyment of birdwatching and are more or less mandatory to stand a chance of getting a good look at many wild mammals. Although you don't need to buy the top-of-the-range, thousand-of-pounds sets, a bit of an outlay can pay dividends. There are some excellent outlets in some of the big reserves; if you buy from these you'll be supporting conservation work in the area and should be able to get some sound advice on the spot. One tip: don't forget to consider the weight – a heavy pair can become quite a drag after being around your neck for two hours.

● Field guides on your favourite species. Dedicated wildlife watchers all have their own individual favourite books. More accessible to the beginner, though and excellent in bad weather, are laminated FSC

(Field Studies Council) unfolding field guides on any given species. Do bear in mind the natural law that states that if you choose to take out your 'Butterflies of Britain' you will invariably happen across a squadron of the most beautiful damselflies you have ever seen. That's wildlife. More guides are recommended at the back of this book.

The more you get out there and enjoy wildlife the more passionate you'll become about protecting it. Key to this is to be aware of the sensitivities of the area. Most fundamental is to avoid trampling rare plants and key habitats. Stick to the paths or, if venturing further, take local expert advice. If you are asked to keep dogs away or, indeed on a lead, there will be good reasons, such as ground-nesting birds nearby. (There is a copy of the Countryside Code on page 37 with more advice.)

Wildlife is increasingly under great pressure from everything from insensitive development to climate change, so sustainable living is vital to preserve our wildlife heritage for the future. We can all make a difference: look at saving energy in your house, take up composting and wildlife-friendly gardening if you haven't done so already. And think about food miles – buying seasonal produce and supporting nearby businesses can have a big impact on cutting carbon emissions. Finally please do join a conservation charity if you can – support from our members is vital to protect wildlife for the future.

Most importantly of all, however you get involved with wildlife, do get involved. You won't regret it.

PICTURED
Far left: Red squirrel
Top left: Dragonfly at sunset
Top right: A badger

The Wildlife Trusts
www.wildlifetrusts.org

● There are 47 local Wildlife Trusts across the whole of the UK, the Isle of Man and Alderney.

● The Wildlife Trusts are committed to an environment rich in wildlife for everyone.

● It is the largest UK voluntary organisation dedicated to conserving the full range of the UK's habitats and species, with 670,000 members.

● The junior branch, Wildlife Watch, has 108,000 members, mainly between five and 14, who receive information and magazines and many join local Wildlife Watch groups where they learn more about their wildlife while having fun.

Britain's birds
by the RSPB

For its size, the UK has one of the richest varieties of landscapes of any country in the world. From the almost subtropical Scilly Isles to the subarctic Cairngorm plateau, the British Isles are crammed with different habitats. This sheer diversity – which can be appreciated on any lengthy rail journey – is reflected in the range of birds that can be found either nesting, passing through on migration or spending the winter here.

Five hundred and seventy-three species of birds have been sighted in Britain. Although some of these are only rarely spotted, around 280 species can be seen regularly, and in any year there are reports of over 350 varieties. Although coastal areas see the most birds, even inland counties will regularly boast more than 200 species a year.

Wherever you are in Britain, you are rarely far away from interesting birdlife. Have a look out of your window for 10 minutes. Almost every garden and park will have a blackbird and a robin, and if you put out food for garden birds, the variety will increase enormously. Blue, great and coal tits will be quick to appear and, in some parts of Britain, other colourful birds, such as the nuthatch and great spotted woodpecker,

will become regular visitors to larger gardens, especially ones near woodland.

It is in woodland, and especially in springtime, that you will hear the best chorus of songbirds. Among the earliest each morning is the nightingale which, as its name suggests, is really a part of the nightshift. As the notes of this sweetest of songsters fade, the orchestra is joined by other birds: garden warblers and blackcaps; song and mistle thrushes; and even woodpigeons and stock doves all adding their voices – either grand or humble – to the chorus. Most people will have a bird-rich forest within a few miles of their home, allowing easy access to a world-class wildlife experience.

Coasts in Britain are busy all year. A trip in the summer to a seabird colony will be rewarded with a cacophony of gulls, guillemots, possibly even puffins and terns. The UK is the best location in the world for some seabirds: gannets, Manx shearwaters and great skuas live in greater numbers in the UK than anywhere else on the planet.

Far from going quiet in the autumn and winter, this is when Britain receives bird visitors from northern Europe, northern Asia, the Arctic and Canada. Birds like the Brent goose and knot undertake lengthy migrations to spend the winter on the UK's relatively mild and sheltered coastline. The muddy ooze of estuaries is hugely popular with hungry birds as it contains billions of worms, shellfish and crustaceans and they are always a good place to head to for watching birds – sometimes in their thousands.

Wetlands also gain greater bird populations in the colder months. Every winter, a multitude of water birds descend on Britain's reservoirs, gravel pits, lakes, marshes and reedbeds. Colourful ducks, such as the male pochard and goldeneye, migrate from harsher conditions in other parts of Europe to large bodies of open water, where they join year-round birds, such as the great crested grebe, coot and moorhen.

Arguably, there has never been a better time to see birds in Britain. Sadly, some birds, such as our native partridge and lapwing, have declined hugely in number, but other birds like the magnificent red kite and osprey are enjoying a resurgence in numbers thanks to intense conservation efforts following centuries of persecution.

The RSPB offers unrivalled opportunities for anyone wanting to see and know more about birds in their local area. It has a network of more than 200 nature reserves across the UK, including many which have access for members and the public. In addition, there are extremely popular viewing schemes – staffed by bird experts with a good range of binoculars and telescopes – to help people get a close-up view of some of the UK's most interesting and charismatic birds. Log on to find a site near you: www.rspb.org.uk.

All about the RSPB
www.rspb.org.uk

● The RSPB is the largest wildlife conservation organisation in Europe with over one million members, including 150,000 young people. It works to secure a healthy environment for birds and other wildlife.

● Founded in 1889 to fight the trade in birds' feathers, the RSPB is a leading member of BirdLife International.

● The RSPB owns and manages more than 200 nature reserves, which welcome more than 1.5 million visitors each year. The Society has land in every part of the UK, from Fetlar in the Shetlands to Marazion in Cornwall and from the Lower Lough Erne Islands in County Fermanagh to Berney Marshes in the far east of Norfolk.

● The charity also runs more than 60 'Aren't birds brilliant!' sites across the UK giving members of the public the opportunity to get close to birds including red kites, peregrines, ospreys and seabirds.

● You can help secure a better future for birds and other wildlife by joining the RSPB, making a donation, getting involved as a volunteer or by buying from the RSPB webshop www.rspbshop.co.uk where 100 per cent of profits go directly into the charity's conservation work.

PICTURED
Main: Robin
Left: Osprey
Above: Blue tit

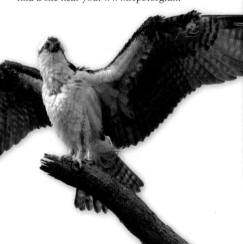

Explore
Lee Valley Regional Park

With an incredible eight Sites of Special Scientific Interest and the Lee Valley Special Protection Area and Ramsar site, Lee Valley Regional Park is a key regional wildlife destination serving London, Hertfordshire and Essex. Green spaces, nature reserves, heritage sites and country parks run both sides of the beautiful River Lee, making the 26 mile Regional Park the perfect place for bird watching, fishing, cycling and walking.

Offering visitors a wide range of rich flora and fauna throughout the seasons, there are plenty of opportunities to see wildlife up-close, such as orchids in the summer or rare water birds like the elusive Bittern in the winter. Why not take a visit to the unique WaterWorks Nature Reserve to see its different wetland habitats or experience the stunning scenery and wildlife of River Lee Country Park?

Lee Valley Regional Park also offers excellent recreation opportunities, including golf, horse riding and ice skating - all allowing you to combine sport and nature for a great day out. There is a range of accommodation within the Regional Park, including a top class youth hostel and ideally situated caravan and campsites, providing reasonably priced accommodation for a fantastic weekend away.

For more information about Lee Valley Regional Park and what you can do and see there, call 01992 702 200 or visit **www.leevalleypark.org.uk**

1967-2007 celebrating 40 years

Lee Valley Park

Open spaces and sporting places

Places to go
by Natural England

Many of the nature reserves you will find in this book are designated NNRs – National Nature Reserves. These areas are places where wildlife comes first. This does not mean they are 'no-go areas' for people, it means that protecting the wildlife of these fragile places is the prime concern.

There are 222 NNRs in England, from Lindisfarne in Northumberland to The Lizard in Cornwall. Within them you'll find populations of rare flowers, ferns and mosses, butterflies and other insects, and nesting and wintering birds. Every type of vegetation is found, from coastal saltmarshes, dunes and cliffs to downlands, meadows and the subtle variations of our native woodlands. Scarce and threatened habitats such as chalk downs, lowland heaths and bogs and estuaries are all conserved in NNRs.

The reserves are looked after either by Natural England or an approved body such as a The Wildlife Trusts. They are often very beautiful areas with a greater range of plants and animals than you'd find in the wider countryside. The ground might be covered in a rich carpet of wildflowers or thousands of birds might be seen on the wetlands as well as many unusual species. They are important for study and research, and also help maintain historical and cultural features.

About Natural England
www.naturalengland.org.uk

● Natural England works for people, places and nature to conserve and enhance biodiversity, landscapes and wildlife in rural, urban, coastal and marine areas.

● We conserve and enhance the natural environment for its intrinsic value, the wellbeing and enjoyment of people, and the economic prosperity it brings.

● We promote access and recreation, and contribute to the way natural resources are managed so they can be enjoyed now and by future generations.

● We promote sustainable solutions to environmental problems to increase the social and economic value of the natural environment.

PICTURED: Bassenthwaite Lake NNR, managed by the Lake District National Park Authority

Caring for the Countryside
by the Countryside Council for Wales

Since May 2005, with the new rights of access, almost a quarter of all existing Welsh countryside has been open to the public. The Countryside Council for Wales (CCW) looks after much of this land, including more than 60 National Nature Reserves, from the dunes of Merthyr Mawr to the summit of Snowdon.

Wales has enjoyed a number of success stories in recent years: the red kite has been brought back from the brink of extinction, and Cardigan Bay is a sanctuary for grey seals and bottlenose dolphins. Current action plans are in place for the wellbeing of animals such as the brown hare and otter, and lesser-known creatures such as the glutinous snail and black bog ant.

CCW is also working with the Welsh Assembly Government to increase and improve access to the coast of Wales, with all the health, social and economic benefits that come from enjoying the great outdoors.

PICTURED
Top left: Grey seals
Above left: Snowdonia
Right: Red Kite
Below: Hiking Crib Goch in Snowdonia

Wildlife watching in Scotland
by Scottish Natural Heritage

Much of Scotland is a wildlife paradise. About 20 per cent of its land receives some special protection because its wildlife or landscape is particularly rare, fragile or distinctive.

The body in charge of safeguarding and enhancing these areas is Scottish Natural Heritage, a government agency that was set up in 1992.

Scottish Natural Heritage and partner bodies manage National Nature Reserves (NNRs) around Scotland which include some of the country's best-known natural assets such as Beinn Eighe, the Isle of Rum, the Cairngorms and St Kilda. From the delicate beauty of mountain plants on the wintry slopes of Ben Lawers in Perthshire to the whirling cries of seabirds on the island of Noss in the Shetland Isles at the height of summer, NNRs offer inspirational sights and sounds at any time of year.

Nature comes first on NNRs, but they are also places that people are very welcome to visit and enjoy. Careful management of the land, continual research, and the promotion of responsible access are vital to the future of these special places for the benefit of both wildlife and people.

National Scenic Areas (NSAs) are other areas you'll read about in this book. NSAs are nationally important areas of outstanding natural beauty, particularly lochs and mountains, which also provide a wide range of social and economic benefits to local communities. Explore them at your leisure, and gain some of those benefits for yourself.

SCOTTISH NATURAL HERITAGE

PICTURED
Top: Loch Lubnaig **Above:** Fulmar on the Isle of Skye
Below: Highland Cattle

Wildlife watching in Northern Ireland
by the Environment and Heritage Service

Northern Ireland has many impressive wildlife spectacles in magnificent settings. Though boasting fewer species than the mainland, the Irish races of stoat and mountain hare are distinct and Réal's wood white butterfly and the Irish damselfly are unknown in Great Britain.

Environment and Heritage Service (EHS) is the government agency for conserving wildlife and the countryside. It manages most of the 50 statutory nature reserves (NRs) covering some 8,303 acres of coast, wetland, grassland, woodland and upland. The Forest Service, National Trust, RSPB, Wildfowl and Wetlands Trust, Ulster Wildlife Trust and some councils also manage properties for nature conservation. Access to many is free.

The finest wildlife spectacles are on wetlands. Lough Neagh attracts vast numbers of wintering diving duck, with great flocks of whooper swans in nearby fields. Thousands of great crested grebe breed in the reedbed fringes. Oxford Island NR has hides and a visitor centre.

The five sea loughs also attract important numbers of wintering waterfowl including most of the pale-bellied Brent geese which breed in north-east Canada. Castle Espie (WWT), lough-side lay-bys and the Quoile Pondage NR provide fine birdwatching around Strangford Lough, as does the RSPB's Belfast Harbour Reserve near the Belfast City Airport.

Four species of tern breed on sea lough islands. Tens of thousands of auks, fulmar, shag and kittiwake line the sea stacks at Kebble NR on Rathlin Island (a ferry ride from Ballycastle). Watch out for Irish hares here and at Belfast International Airport, and for Manx shearwaters from the Irish Sea ferries. Coastal promontories provide good sea-watching with sightings of basking sharks, whales and dolphins. Seals haul out in the Strangford Narrows, whose waters and the undersea cliffs around Rathlin Island attract divers interested in the colourful marine invertebrates. See marine life up close at the Exploris aquarium in Portaferry and The Coastal Zone and in Portrush.

Salmon can be seen leaping up weirs and waterfalls at Roe Valley Country Park in autumn. Peatlands Park supports many species of dragonfly and Ireland's only wood ant colonies, and Killard, Murlough, Magilligan and Umbra NRs, are good butterfly sites.

Environment & Heritage Service
www.ehsni.gov.uk

An Agency within the Department of the
Environment
www.doeni.gov.uk

PICTURED: Giant's Causeway

STAY AT PARTICIPATING HOTELS FOR **FREE**

FREE Hotel Accommodation - All year roun

Treat yourself to a break

Do you enjoy getting away from it all?
With a Privilege Hotel Pass from Travel Offers Ltd, you and a partner can stay for free at over 320 hotels and sample their culinary delights without paying for your room.

How it works

For only £29.95, your Privilege Hotel Pass gives you the freedom to enjoy as many hotel breaks as you wish over 12 months. All you have to do is pay for your meals - dinner and breakfast - your accommodation is absolutely free! Twin or double rooms are available and meal prices range from £19 to £30 and over per person for award-winning dining.

With your pass you will also receive the Travel Offers Hotel Directory which provides details

on each of our featured hotels. With so many to choose from, you'll be spoilt for choice!

Stay for just 1 night or more – however long you stay, just pay for your meals and any additional items you choose to purchase, e.g. drinks and spa treatments.

Where you can stay

We have an extensive range of hotels in a wide variety of impressive locations across the UK and Ireland.

Choose from over 320 hotels:	
England	192
Channel Islands	6
Wales	26
Scotland	71
N.Ireland & Ireland	29

Whether you're looking for a relaxing break by the coast, a weekend away in the country or fancy exploring a new town, we have the perfect break for you. Many of our featured hotels have won awards for their cuisine, boast top leisure facilities and have a stunning selection of attractions and amenities close by - all you have to do is decide where you want to go!

TRAVEL OFFERS ★ LTD

£29.95
for as many hotel breaks as you wish over 12 months*

To Order Call:
0871 282 2882
Lines are open
Mon-Fri 8.30am-9pm, Sat 10am-4pm, Sun 2pm-6pm
www.travel-offers.co.uk

Take a woodland wander
by the Woodland Trust

After the last Ice Age, wild woodland covered much of Britain. Now however, woodland accounts for only 12 per cent of our land cover – a figure that is on average 44 per cent in many of our European neighbours.

Ancient woodland, land which has been continuously wooded since the 1600s, is our closest link to this original forest, but now covers only about two per cent of Britain. The vast majority of this has no legal protection.

Most of the native woodland in Britain is broad-leaved, consisting of trees that drop their leaves in winter such as beech, birch, oak, ash or lime wood. Although it is the trees that are the dominant feature and often used to describe woodlands, they are not the only plants. You'll find shrubs, too, such as hazel, hawthorn and holly, while some of the prettiest plants in the woodland are the wildflowers that appear throughout the year starting with snowdrops from January through to carpets of wood anemone and wood sorrel in March to the magnificent bluebell in May. The wonderful colours and textures provided by mosses, lichens, liverworts, ferns and fungi all add to a woodland's own particular appeal.

Animals that live in woodlands include badgers, bats, deer, dormice, stoats, shrews, squirrels, mice, hedgehogs, foxes, weasels and voles. Many of them will hear you and head for cover long before you catch a glimpse of them, but it's not too much to hope to see deer between the trees from time to time or a mouse scurrying in the autumn leaves. Dusk is the best time to spot badgers, bats and hedgehogs. ▶

PICTURED
Below: Wormley Wood
Right: Tawny Owl

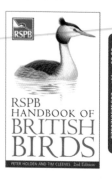

Woodlands attract many birds, too, including three species of woodpecker, wren, nuthatch, willow tit and tawny owls. Other wildlife includes reptiles and amphibians; thousands of insects and other invertebrates, such as butterflies, beetles, centipedes and millipedes.

The almost magical, mystical quality of woods makes them a great place for relaxation and recreation. A walk in the woods can give anyone a feeling of peace and tranquillity, and most of us have fond childhood memories of playing on and around trees.

Sadly, however, the value of Britain's woodland resource is not reflected in the way we treat it. Nearly 50 per cent of the ancient woodland that still remained in the 1930s has been lost or damaged. The decline in woodland began with the arrival of man and the first clearance of the forest for basic agriculture and the keeping of animals. Deforestation continued at an alarming rate, as Britain's population grew and more land was turned over to agriculture and development.

Unless something is done to halt the decline, Britain risks losing what is left of its precious woodland heritage.

The Woodland Trust
www.woodlandtrust.org.uk

The Woodland Trust is a UK-wide charity working to protect and restore Britain's native broad-leaved woodland. Established in 1972, the Trust is now the UK's leading woodland conservation charity, with four main aims:

1. To protect ancient woodland
2. To improve and restore woodland biodiversity
3. To increase new native woodland
4. To promote people's awareness and enjoyment of woodland

The Woodland Trust cares for more than 1,000 sites, covering more than 50,000 acres, and access to them is free. It is funded by a range of sources including grants, legacies, donations and membership. The support of over 160,000 members is especially vital to continuing its work.

About the Forestry Commission
www.forestry.gov.uk

The Forestry Commission manages more than two million acres of public land, including some of the country's oldest and finest woodlands such as the New Forest, Forest of Dean and parts of the Loch Lomond Trossachs National Park.

Visit and you could find places to go walking or cycling, thousands of species of wildlife to see, the finest mountain biking in the world, visitor centres, horse-riding trails, barbecue and picnic sites. All in beautiful scenery, with clean, fresh air, and most of it free for all to enjoy.

The woodlands are managed to FSC environmental standards, provide a valuable timber resource for the country, help combat climate change, provide jobs and more for local communities and redevelop brownfield sites.

They are managed on behalf of the governments of England, Scotland and Wales.

Loch Lubnaig, near Callander, Trossachs, Scotland

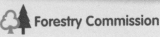

Where to see plants
by Plantlife

There is barely a place in Britain where you won't find wild plants: purple drifts of rosebay willowherb cover train embankments in late summer, and old walls burst into life with maidenhair spleenwort and ivy-leaved toadflax. These plant names, evolved from ancient English, may be unfamiliar, but the plants won't be.

You don't need much to enjoy the UK's extraordinarily diverse plants and flowers: a good pair of eyes and the ability to pick out the fleck of colour in a field which might just turn out to be an orchid. If you want to find out more, there are many excellent books (see page 326), but even without these, there is endless enjoyment to be had from finding a strange-looking fungus, a particularly fragrant flower or even the skeletal remains of an autumn leaf on the ground.

The seasonal nature of our weather ensures that barely a fortnight will be characterised by the same vegetation. Woodlands tend to come into their peak in late April, as wood anemones and early purple orchid struggle to reproduce before the tree canopy closes; pasture and meadows are generally at their best in mid-summer; and heathlands are at their best at the end of August when heather is in full bloom.

Britain enjoys a staggering diversity of plants; in well-managed grassland, you could find up to 80 species in a single square metre and there are around 3,500 flowering plants, ferns and mosses in Britain in total. In addition to these, there is the incredible world of fungi and lichens to be explored, which means there is always something to look out for, whatever the season.

There are a wealth of societies and botanical groups to help you learn more about plants, but first, just get out there and start enjoying the countryside.

About Plantlife
www.plantlife.org.uk

● Plantlife is the leading charity working to protect wild plants in Britain with offices in England, Scotland and Wales.

● It was established in 1989 after a meeting of conservationists and botanists, led by Professor David Bellamy, called for a new organisation to champion plant conservation.

● Plantlife believes that we should conserve wild plants as an intrinsic part of our countryside, rather than in gardens or national seed banks. By working alongside farmers and landowners, local volunteers and councils, and in partnership with the government and other conservation organisations, Plantlife identifies sites of botanical importance, rescues plants on the brink of extinction and works to ensure that common plants don't become rare in the wild.

● Plantlife manages 4,500 acres of wildflower nature reserves which are open to the public.

PLANTLIFE

help give them a safe landing

The Wildfowl & Wetlands Trust (WWT) is a leading UK conservation organisation saving wetlands for wildlife and people across the world. WWT is the only UK charity with a national network of nine specialist wetland visitor centres.

Join WWT today and enjoy the following benefits!

- Unlimited entry to all nine WWT centres – FREE
- Quarterly 'Waterlife' magazine (£3.75) – FREE
- Discounts at special events... and best of all, you will be making a positive contribution to the conservation of wetlands and their wildlife.

membership pack

JOIN WWT TODAY!

Please return completed application form below, or a photocopy, to: WWT Membership Office, Wildfowl & Wetlands Trust, FREEPOST GR1228, SLIMBRIDGE, GLOUCESTER GL2 7BR

Category of membership Please tick ✔

1 Adult	£31.50
2 Adults	£47.00
Family 2 Adults + Children (aged 4–16)	£54.00

Prices correct until December 2007

Call us on (01453) 891198 or visit us at www.wwt.org.uk

PAYMENT DETAILS

Name (Mr/Mrs/Miss/Ms)

2nd Adult Name

Address

Postcode

Phone (incl. area code)

Email

For **Family Membership** - please supply name and D.O.B for each child on a separate note.

DIRECT DEBITING INSTRUCTION (Originators ID: 852644)

Please pay WWT Direct Debits from the account detailed in this instruction subject to the safeguards assured by the Direct Debit Guarantee. I understand that this instruction may remain with WWT and, if so, details will be passed electronically to my Bank/Building Society.

To the Manager Bank/Building Society

Address

Postcode

Name(s) of Account Holder(s)

Account No   Sort Code

Signature   Date

giftaid it New Gift Aid legislation allows us to reclaim basic rate tax on your subscription and additional donations. Please state that you are happy for us to do this by signing the Declaration below. If you are a UK tax payer, for every pound that you give, WWT is able to reclaim 28p tax (this allows us to claim an additional £15.12 on a family membership worth £54).
I wish WWT to benefit from the Gift Aid legislation. This Declaration applies to all subscriptions/donations I make on or after 6 April 2000.

Name   Address

Signature

Date

Postcode

Saving wetlands for wildlife and people   Wildfowl & Wetlands Trust Registered charity no. 1030884   WB2007

All about wetlands
by WWT

Wetlands are essential to all life on Earth. They are found from the poles to the tropics, from mountains down to the sea, and are as diverse as the wildlife they support. They include ponds, lakes, rivers and their floodplains, marshes, swamps and coastal waters.

Wetlands provide habitats for a wealth of animals and plants from flamingos to swans, from marsh marigolds to mangroves, from water voles to dragonflies. They also store and clean our water, and provide protection from floods and storms.

Millions of people depend directly upon wetlands for their livelihood and, in an increasingly urbanised and frenetic world, many millions more enjoy wetlands as places to walk, relax and get closer to nature.

Unfortunately, wetlands are threatened as never before. Reclaimed for building or agriculture, increasingly polluted and degraded, wetlands are often the first casualty of human development.

Half the world's wetlands have been lost over the last century and with them their unique wildlife.

The Wildfowl and Wetlands Trust (WWT) was founded in 1946 by a keen birdwatcher, Sir Peter Scott. He had been to Slimbridge and spotted two lesser white-fronted geese among a crowd of thousands of white-fronted geese. He wanted to set up an organisation that could keep track of sightings and studies such as these.

Today, WWT is a global leader in the management, development and protection of wetland habitats, endangered species and conservation education.

About WWT
www.wwt.org.uk

● WWT researches and raises awareness of the wildlife living in and around wetlands including swans, geese, ducks, flamingos, otters, beavers, water voles, dragonflies, frogs and rare plantlife.

● WWT manages nine wetland visitor centres in the UK. They are an extremely enjoyable way to get up close to birds and other wetland wildlife.

Big planet, small turtle. Please help.

Marine turtles face countless threats - from illegal trade in meat, eggs and shells to marine litter, indiscriminate beach development and fishing bycatch.

Act now to ensure that endangered marine turtles do not soon disappear from our seas forever.

Adopt-a-Turtle

Adopt online: www.mcsuk.org
or telephone: 01989 566017

The Marine Conservation Society is supporting vital research and conservation projects in the UK and abroad. You can help us protect marine turtles by adopting an endangered turtle species.

Marine
Conservation
Society

Registered charity no: 1004005

On Britain's waterways
by Waterscape.com

Britain's canals and rivers support a range of wildlife – from common sights such as mallards and moorhens to the more shy and retiring residents of the riverbank, such as the otter and water vole. Half of the UK's population lives within five miles of a waterway – so you don't have to travel miles to take a walk or a bike ride along a towpath.

On both rivers and canals, swans glide by, coots flap and splash, and herons stand motionless at the water's edge. Grass snakes often like to bask on the towpath and toads can be spotted making their spring pilgrimages to their breeding ponds.

The slow-flowing nature of canals offers a different habitat and hunting ground to fast-flowing rivers. Kingfishers favour this slower pace. Similarly, water voles prefer the slow-moving water as they don't have webbed feet to swim with.

Otters are spotted on quiet stretches of canals, but lakes and rivers are their more natural habitat. Once widespread throughout the UK, otters are now most often sighted in Scotland, Wales and the South of England.

Over the years, bats have had to expand their roosting areas from hollowed-out tree trunks, to encompass old buildings, including canal bridges and tunnels up and down the country. Greywell Tunnel on the Basingstoke Canal is a well-known roost for a number of species of bats.

The landscape and wildlife of the waterways change with the seasons and different plants are found throughout the year.

You can find your nearest canal or river quickly and easily on Waterscape.com, a comprehensive internet site with details of all the UK waterways.

About Waterscape
www.waterscape.com

Waterscape.com is the official online leisure guide for Britain's canals, rivers and lakes. The website includes information on:

- Waterway wildlife species and habitats, including an annual online spotters' survey
- How to hire a canal boat or book a waterside holiday cottage
- Where to walk, cycle, jog and fish beside the water
- Best waterside bars, pubs and restaurants
- Waterway guides with information on wildlife, visitor attractions and local history.

Waterscape.com is owned by British Waterways. British Waterways is the public corporation that cares for the nation's 2,200-mile network of historic canals and navigable rivers. Waterscape.com also works in conjunction with the Environment Agency and The Broads Authority.

waterscape.com

PICTURED: The Falkirk Wheel, Scotland, the world's only rotating boatlift between two canals – the Forth and Clyde Canal and the Union Canal.

Adopt Me!

Will you adopt Rainbow or one of her friends?

When you do you will be helping WDCS, the Whale and Dolphin Conservation Society, to protect your dolphin and his or her friends and family.

These dolphins live off the east coast of Scotland where man-made threats have driven them to the brink of extinction.

Please will you help us save them?

For just £4 a month you will form a special link with an individual dolphin and help us in our fight to protect whales and dolphins all over the world.

To adopt **your** dolphin **just call our adoption hotline today on 0870 870 5001 or go to www.adoptadolphin.com**

Please quote Wildlife Britain.

WDCS is the global voice for the protection of whales, dolphins and their environment.

Whale and Dolphin Conservation Society

Company Registration No: 2737421   Reg Charity No: 1014705   Photo: © Mark Carwardine

Whale watching around Britain
by the Whale and Dolphin Conservation Society

Many people are amazed to learn of the variety of cetaceans (the collective name for whales, dolphins and porpoises) which may be seen off the British coastline, often imagining that they must go overseas to go whale watching. Yet, around two dozen cetacean species have been recorded in British waters over the years.

Many of the sightings are very infrequent visitors and just the occasional record exists. However, other species are much more reliably seen.

There are three known resident populations of bottlenose dolphin in the UK. One off Cardigan Bay in West Wales; one off the Moray Firth in north-east Scotland, and one along the coastline of Cornwall, Devon and Dorset. Usually seen in pods of between two to 15, bottlenose dolphins are renowned for their friendliness and will often approach vessels to bow-ride or body-surf in the wake. These robust dolphins, which can grow up to four metres long, are great acrobats and will frequently leap and somersault.

The harbour porpoise is widely distributed around the British coast and may be seen year-round. The smallest cetacean in our waters (1.5 metres), the harbour porpoise is timid and unobtrusive. Most sightings consist of a brief glimpse of a small triangular dorsal fin. Harbour porpoises usually travel alone or in small groups.

The minke whale (8.5 metres max) is the smallest and most commonly encountered baleen whale (filter feeder) in the North Atlantic. Its preference for inshore waters makes it the whale species most likely to be observed from land. The vast majority of sightings occur off west Scotland and the Western Isles during the summer months when inquisitive minkes may follow boats for

hours and may 'spyhop' repeatedly – poking their head above the surface of the water as if to check out the occupants of a boat.

Other species encountered with reasonable regularity include the Risso's dolphin with its characteristic heavy scarring, short-beaked common dolphins, sometimes numbering dozens or even hundreds of animals, and dramatic-looking killer whales (orcas) which are most abundant off the north and west of Scotland.

About WDCS
www.wdcs.org

- WDCS, the Whale and Dolphin Conservation Society, is the global voice for the protection of whales, dolphins and their environment.

- We take action to stop the threats facing whales and dolphins, to protect these animals and the places they live, and to reach out to as many people as possible.

- Established in 1987, WDCS is staffed by over 70 people, along with many more volunteers. We have offices in Argentina, Australia, Austria, Germany, the UK and the US, plus a worldwide network of consultants, researchers and supporters. In addition, The WDCS Wildlife Centre in the Moray Firth, Scotland – home to the Moray Firth bottlenose dolphins – brings the world of whales and dolphins alive to thousands of visitors every year.

WDCS
Whale and Dolphin Conservation Society

UNBEATABLE SUBSCRIPTION OFFER FOR WILDLIFE BRITAIN READERS

3 FREE ISSUES

That's 12 issues for the price of 9 when you subscribe today

BBC Wildlife Magazine is your essential guide to the natural world. Each issue you'll enjoy stunning photography, top-quality writing and the latest environmental news.

YOUR FANTASTIC SUBSCRIPTION PACKAGE...

» **3 FREE ISSUES** – that's 12 issues for the price of 9*

» **SPREAD THE COST** and pay just £14.50 every 6 issues when you subscribe by convenient Direct Debit.

» Every issue **DELIVERED FREE** to your door (UK only)

» **NEVER MISS AN ISSUE** of the world's best natural history magazine.

*Direct Debit customer saving is based on receiving 12 issues (12 issues for the price of 9).
Non-Direct Debit saving is based on receiving 13 issues (13 issues for the price of 10)

And, by getting every fantastic issue delivered to your door every month, you'll not only guarantee yourself a copy of the world's best natural history magazine, you'll also save money.

OFFER MUST END 30 DECEMBER 2007

The importance of captive breeding
by the Zoological Society of London

Most people know that lions and tigers are facing extinction, some know there are less than 300 Sumatran rhinos left in the world, but few realise the threat to the red-barbed ant here in the UK.

Animals found in the United Kingdom are an important part of our towns, countryside and our national heritage. Their ecological roles are vital and as well as contributing to the biodiversity and variety of life in the UK, they also provide an important resource for recreation and tourism.

But the news for some of these species is just as bad as it is for polar bears and pandas because of changes in land use, agricultural and fishing practices, and the development of urban areas and roads.

More than 40 British species including nine whales are internationally threatened, and in the last century 170 species of plants and animals became extinct in the UK.

The red-barbed ant has declined to just one same-sex colony in mainland Britain because of the loss and degradation of British heathland. The only chance the red-barbed ant has for survival on mainland Britain is through captive breeding and reintroduction.

Because so many native British species are under threat, ZSL sites are increasingly being managed as refuges for native wildlife, with great thought going into planting and the developments of good habitats including a woodland walk, a butterfly garden and a pond.

But perhaps the real crux of native species conservation is educating people and raising awareness so they can take action themselves. It is vitally important that people understand the threats facing our native wildlife and the kind of steps they can take to stop them. Everyone can get involved in native species conservation because it's happening on our doorstep. Creating suitable habitats like log piles for stag beetles, green or brown roofs on garden sheds or attaching boxes for bats and nesting birds to trees and buildings are all ways people can get involved without even leaving their gardens.

About ZSL
www.zsl.org

● Founded in 1826, the Zoological Society of London (ZSL) is an international scientific, conservation and educational charity: our key role is the conservation of animals and their habitats. ZSL runs ZSL London Zoo and ZSL Whipsnade Wild Animal Park, carries out scientific research in the Institute of Zoology and is actively involved in field conservation in other countries worldwide.

● Our Native Species Conservation Programme is one of seven comprehensive conservation programmes going on around the world. Its focus is on action and education regarding the threats to Britain's native species and includes a number of captive breeding and reintroduction programmes.

PICTURED:
Wart-biter

ZSL
LIVING CONSERVATION

The Countryside Code

- **Be safe, plan ahead and follow any signs**
Even when going out locally, it's best to get the latest information about where and when you can go. For example, your rights to go onto some areas of open land may be restricted while work is carried out for safety reasons, or during breeding seasons. Follow advice and local signs, and be prepared for the unexpected.

- **Leave gates and property as you find them**
Please respect the working life of the countryside, as our actions can affect people's livelihoods, our heritage, and the safety and welfare of animals and ourselves.

- **Protect plants and animals and take your litter home**
We have a responsibility to protect our countryside now and for future generations, so make sure you don't harm animals, birds, plants or trees.

- **Keep dogs under close control**
The countryside is a great place to exercise dogs, but it's every owner's duty to make sure their dog is not a danger or nuisance to farm animals, wildlife or other people.

- **Consider other people**
Showing consideration and respect for other people makes the countryside a pleasant environment for everyone – at home, at work and at leisure.

For more information visit:
www.countrysideaccess.gov.uk

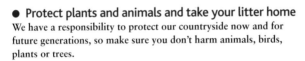

Where to see wildlife

Greater London

Britain's bustling capital city might not be the most obvious destination for wildlife spotting, but if you know where to look, you'd be surprised at the variety of wildlife that you can find.

There are eight royal parks in Greater London which vary hugely in character, from the long-grassed, large expanses of Richmond Park – that has a healthy population of deer, fungi, many different species of bird and more than 500 species of butterfly – to the more clipped lawns of Kensington Gardens, where you're likely to spot green woodpeckers who nest in the park's magnificent trees, as well as up to 170 different species of birds at different times of the year. Whichever part of London you're in, you're never too far from one of these parks.

Kew Gardens, in the south-west of the Greater London area, is internationally renowned for its vast collection of flora, both native and exotic, while in its grounds there also live bats, badgers, weasels, hedgehogs, woodmice and foxes, as well as many species of birds who enjoy the rich pickings offered by the different trees. Its ponds, too, are full of waterfowl to watch. Kew Gardens is one of several sites in London (along with Bushy Park and Richmond Park) where it is quite common to see a large flock of ring-necked parakeets flitting from tree to tree.

Birds also abound at the London Wetland Centre, which is well known as one of the best urban locations in Europe for watching wildlife. Bittern, Cetti's warbler and peregrine falcon return to the site every year, as do hundreds of wetland birds, along with various dragonflies, amphibians and other bank-dwelling creatures.

Not all of London's wildlife is found in such controlled areas, though. The canals and waterways that were once the business hub of London, are now often quiet and secluded spots where a walk along a towpath will reveal kingfishers and herons, butterflies flitting among the cow-parsley and willowherbs, and moorhens and ducks bobbing on the water.

Further out from the centre, there are pockets of woodland that are home to fungi, birds, and a wide variety of tree types. Most boroughs have a city farm of one sort or another that allows visitors to get up close to pigs, mice, chickens, rabbits and other small animals.

The more you explore the capital, the more you'll discover that there is wildlife to be seen everywhere you look.

PICTURED: Stag in Richmond Park, with the towers of the city behind it

Not to be missed

- **Camley Street Natural Park**
  On the banks of the Regent's Canal, just by King's Cross, is this treasure trove of a park. A pond, a meadow and woodland that are left wild for bees, butterflies and birds to enjoy.

- **Epping Forest**
  Take a walk in this ancient coppiced woodland and marvel at how you're never far from a view over central London.

- **London Wetland Centre**
  It's not just the 180 species of wild birds that make this urban wetland such a must-see for the wildlife enthusiast, it also has eight species of bats, seven species of reptiles and amphibians, and hundreds of damselflies and dragonflies.

- **Mudchute Park and Farm**
  Almost in the shadow of the skyscrapers of Canary Wharf are the open fields of this city farm that offers green space to local residents and London's visitors alike.

- **Richmond Park**
  Take a mini walking safari in this large and wild park, where you can spot two types of deer, woodpeckers, all sorts of wildfowl and frequent parakeets.

- **Royal Botanic Gardens, Kew**
  The cultivated formality of Kew doesn't stop wild animals from making it their home. Birds love the berries and the ponds, foxes and badgers like the quiet woodland and butterflies flit around the wildflowers.

ROYAL PARKS

Bushy Park
Near: Hampton, near Sunbury
Map: 1, C2
Web: www.royalparks.org.uk
Open: daily, 5am to 10.30pm
(6.30am to dusk for vehicles)

Red and fallow deer wander
among the trees at Bushy Park.
Birdlife includes warblers,
woodpeckers, tits and herons
which come to Leg of Mutton
pond to catch fish. There are
also unusual species of flora.

Green Park
Near: Kensington and Chelsea
Map: 1, C2
Web: www.royalparks.org.uk

Green Park is the smallest of
London's Royal Parks and it
adjoins St James's Park. The
landscape is dominated by trees
such as lime, London plane
and hawthorn, and squirrels
are common.

Greenwich Park
Near: Lewisham
Map: 1, D2
Web: www.royalparks.org.uk
Open: daily

There is a variety of wildlife
in Greenwich Park. A large
grassland enclosure covering
13 acres serves as a sanctuary
for fallow deer, foxes,
waterfowl, starlings, sparrows,
song thrushes, warblers,
woodpeckers, tree creepers and
tawny owls. The park is also
home to a variety of flowers,
shrubs and trees.

Hyde Park
Near: Kensington and Chelsea
Map: 1, C2
Web: www.royalparks.org.uk
Open: daily, 5am to midnight

Hyde Park covers 350 acres.
There are many fantastic
flower-bed displays, as well

as the fragrant rose garden
and a wide variety of native
and non-native trees.

Kensington Gardens
Near: Kensington and Chelsea
Map: 1, C2
Web: www.royalparks.org.uk
Open: daily, 6am to dusk

Since records began 100 years
ago, 178 species of bird have
been identified in Kensington
Gardens. Green woodpeckers
nest in the trees, which is a rare
occurrence in central London.
The Round Pond is the home
of three-spined sticklebacks,
roach, gudgeon and eel.

Regent's Park
Near: Camden
Map: 1, D2
Web: www.royalparks.org.uk
Open: daily, 5am to dusk

Regent's Park has a wide
variety of wildlife, with its
lake and copse land providing
a home to an abundance of
animals. This is also where
you'll find ZSL London Zoo,
which houses a good number
of animals.

Richmond Park
Near: Richmond, Hammersmith
and Fulham,
Map: 1, C2

Greenwich Park

Web: www.royalparks.org.uk
Open: daily; summer, 7am to dusk; winter, 7.30am to dusk
🅿 ♿ ☕

Richmond is a sanctuary for wildlife. Its acid grassland, grazed by deer, is excellent for plants and insects, and more than 500 species of butterfly and moth have been identified. Rural bird species include reed bunting, skylark, meadow pipit, kestrel, little owl, ducks and songbirds. More than 1,000 beetle species live in Richmond alongside endangered fungi and small rodents. The woodland setting of the Isabella Plantation is carpeted with bluebells in spring and azaleas and rhododendrons in summer.

St James's Park
Near: Westminster
Map: 1, C2
Web: www.royalparks.org.uk
Open: daily, 5am to midnight
♿ ♿ ☕ ☕ 🚫

Duck Island is home to many wild breeds of ducks and other birdlife including gulls, swans, geese and pelicans. Some rare winged visitors are golden eyes, carrion crows, grey wagtails and shovelers.

NATURE RESERVES

Bramley Bank Local Nature Reserve
Near: Croydon
Map: 1, C3 and D3
Web: www.wildlondon.org.uk
Common violet and enchanter's nightshade are among the interesting flowers at this woodland reserve in Croydon. The wood is predominantly oak, ash and sycamore and has wonderful springtime displays of bluebells. Yellow flag and flote grass surround the margins of the large woodland pond, and a small clearing of acidic grassland is alive with a wealth of species, including sheep's fescue, heather and heath bedstraw. Birds include woodpeckers and nuthatch, and you'll also find the purple hairstreak butterfly and the yellow meadow ant here.

Camley Street Natural Park
Near: King's Cross, near Camden
Map: 1, C2
Web: www.wildlondon.org.uk
Open: Monday to Thursday, 9am to 5pm; weekends 10am to 4/5pm
♿ ℹ

In spring, look out for frogspawn and coots building their nests on the pond at Camley Street Natural Park, as well as the bright yellow flag iris. Summer brings bees, butterflies, pond dippers and minibeast hunters, and in autumn there is fungi to be seen. In winter, creatures to be spotted include squirrels, wood pigeons, swans, Canada geese, kestrels, moorhens and herons.

The Chase
Near: Romford, Elm Park
Map: 1, E2
Web: www.wildlondon.org.uk
There are shallow wetlands, reedbeds, horse-grazed pasture, scrub and woodland in this large reserve. These harbour an impressive range of animals

Wildlife Britain **43**

St James's Park

and plants, including the rare black poplar tree. This site is a haven for birds, with around 200 different species recorded here over the years – from teal and shoveler in winter and woodpecker and kingfisher all year to a range of scarce and rare bird.

Crane Park Island
Near: Twickenham
Map: 1, C2
Web: www.wildlondon.org.uk

Once the old Hounslow Gunpowder Mills, this island is now a peaceful haven. It is a mosaic of woodland, scrub and reedbed, which provides a home for the increasingly scarce water vole. The island welcomes visitors throughout the year.

Fox Wood
Near: Walthamstow
Map: 1, D1
Web: www.wildlondon.org.uk
The hoot of the tawny owl can often be heard in Fox Wood,

and cheerful blooms of bluebell and lesser celandine can be seen in the woodland in spring. Summer attracts butterflies and insects to the small wildflower meadow in the upper cusp of the reserve, while autumn brings dramatic colours. Winter is a good time to see the shape of the woodland set against the steep sides of the old reservoir. There is a winding path through the wood, which is a popular walking route.

Frays Island and Mabey's Meadow
Near: West Drayton
Map: 1, B1
Web: www.wildlondon.org.uk
Alive with insect life, the flower-rich Mabey's Meadow is astonishingly colourful in the summer and orchids thrive in an adjoining area outside the reserve. Frays Island, which is only accessible by footbridges, is next to this meadow. This willow woodland, set between the Colne and Frays River,

provides a perfect spot to see the beautiful River Colne. The river ripples with rich aquatic life – banded demoiselle damselflies and the brilliant blue flash of the kingfisher in flight can sometimes be seen.

The Grove
Near: Hillingdon, near Uxbridge
Map: 1, B2
Web: www.wildlondon.org.uk
A sequence of shaded ponds – homes for frogs and toads – run the length of this reserve surrounded by lush grassland and woodland. Cheerful blooms of yellow flag, soft rush and meadowsweet can be seen alongside these ponds, with reed sweet grass in the adjacent marshy areas. Once the grounds of a large house, from which the reserve takes its name, The Grove has developed into a wide variety of semi-natural habitats. The woodland harbours woodpecker and tawny owl, while the grassland is rich

in herbs and grasses, such as meadow foxtail which provides ample nectar for feeding butterflies.

Gunnersbury Triangle

Near: Chiswick, near Ealing
Map: 1, C2
Web: www.wildlondon.org.uk
ⓘ
Cut off from the surrounding area by railway tracks in the late nineteenth century, Gunnersbury Triangle became one of The Wildlife Trusts' first reserves when it was saved from development following a campaign run by local people. Since the end of World War II, the woodland here has grown up naturally and the reserve has become a sheltered birch and willow woodland with attractive pond, marsh and meadow. Hidden away, the reserve opens up before you – follow the nature trail, listening out for birds or the rustle of a hedgehog, and look for tunnels of field voles or interesting spiders and ladybirds.

Hampstead Heath

Near: Hampstead and Highgate
Map: 1, C1
Web: www.cityoflondon.gov.uk
🚻 🚏 📷
More than 10 million people visit Hampstead Heath every year to enjoy this beautiful green space in the heart of the city. Wildlife thrives in the large areas of meadows, woodlands, 25 main ponds and the small reinstated areas of the exceptionally rare heathland habitat that give Hampstead Heath its name. Breeding kingfishers made a welcome return in 2001, making use of a sandbank specially constructed to offer them a suitable nesting site. The magic of Hampstead Heath lies not only with its wildlife interest, but also with its proximity and accessibility to millions of people.

Hutchinson's Bank, Chapel Bank and Threecorner Grove

Near: Croydon
Map: 1, C3 and D3
Web: www.wildlondon.org.uk
The steep grassland slope of Hutchinson's Bank hosts wonderfully diverse butterflies, plantlife and birds. Pyramidal, common spotted and man orchid are among the flora, with grasses, kidney vetch and the nationally scarce greater yellow-rattle. More than 100 species of moth have been recorded here and in a good year, 28 species of butterfly can be seen, including small blue and dark-green fritillary. Following the chalk walk around Hutchinson's Bank brings you to Chapel Bank. This is an area of ancient woodland, scrub and chalk grassland, spiked with orchids including common twayblade and white helleborine. Threecorner Grove is found between the two banks and is a small stand of ancient woodland of oak, wild cherry and hazel, with moschatel, wild garlic and carpets of bluebell in spring.

Oakhill Wood

Near: Barnet
Map: 1, C1
Web: www.wildlondon.org.uk
Tall oaks have stood in Oakhill Wood since medieval times, shedding their golden leaves among the reds and yellows of hornbeam and ash. Bright

woodland flowers appear each spring. Both pipistrelle and brown long-eared bats roost here, and noctule bats have also been recorded. On a summer's evening you can watch them swoop over adjacent meadows.

Saltbox Hill SSSI

Near: Biggin Hill
Map: 1, D3
Web: www.wildlondon.org.uk
Over the years, many rare species of wildflower and grasses have been recorded on Saltbox Hill – a surviving fragment of original downland – including pyramidal orchids, wild basil and quaking grass. Sunny, west-facing slopes provide ideal conditions for more than 20 species of butterfly to breed on the site, including the increasingly scarce chalkhill blue, grizzled skipper and dark-green fritillary. Adjacent woodland provides homes for woodpeckers, nuthatches and treecreepers. Visitors will appreciate the peace and tranquillity of this special place.

Totteridge Fields

Near: Barnet
Map: 1, C1
Web: www.wildlondon.org.uk
Ancient hay meadows are criss-crossed by hawthorn and blackthorn hedgerows, bright with blossom in spring; these provide excellent nesting

Britain's best-named wildlife

- Edible dormouse
- Purple hairstreak (butterfly)
- Corky-fruited water dropwort (wildflower)
- Chimney sweeper (moth)
- Comma (butterfly, pictured)

and feeding sites for birds. The fields are a riot of colour in the summer, when grasses and flowers – including meadowsweet, hardheads and buttercups, bloom. Butterflies are abundant and sedges occur in the ditches, which provide valuable shelter for amphibians.

The Warren
Near: Bromley
Map: 1, D2
Web: www.wildlondon.org.uk
Dragonflies can be seen flitting over two woodland ponds at The Warren and common blue, comma and peacock are among the butterflies seen in the meadow. The woodland has a dense, shady canopy of beech, oak and sycamore with hornbeam and field maple, which support birds including warblers, finches and woodpeckers. In autumn, numerous fungi can be seen when the cool, damp atmosphere allows spore development and dispersal – look out for the characteristic fly agaric with its brilliant red-and-white spotted cap.

The Yeading Valley Reserves
Near: Hillingdon, near Uxbridge
Map: 1, B2
Web: www.wildlondon.org.uk
Four reserves link up along the Yeading Valley to form this site: Gutteridge Wood, with its oak and hazel coppicing; Yeading Brook Meadows, which blossom with wildflowers each summer; Ten-Acre Wood, whose hawthorn and blackthorn provide copious berries for birds in the autumn and winter; and Ickenham Marsh, a low-lying site dominated by tussocks of soft rush and tufted hair grass close to the river. Together they form a green valley that is a valued wildlife treasure for locals and visitors alike.

Who needs Latin?
Fungal names, like most species names, were traditionally in Latin. The recent creation of English alternatives has led to some very descriptive naming: orange peel fungus, tripe fungus, beefsteak fungus and porcelain fungus, for example.
PICTURED: Tripe fungus

BIRD RESERVES

Rainham, Wennington and Aveley Marshes
Near: Purfleet, Essex
Map: 1, E2
Web: www.rspb.org.uk
Open: daily, 9.30am to 5pm
Admission: £1/£2.50

The reserve is well known for its variety of breeding birds (especially breeding waders) and the numbers of wintering wildfowl, waders, finches and birds of prey. The reserve supports the region's largest population of breeding lapwing and redshank, all of which are in serious national decline. Keep an eye on the banks, too, as the reserve boasts one of the highest densities of water voles in the UK.

FORESTS & WOODLAND

Blackbush and Twenty-Acre Shaw Woods
Near: Cudham, near Biggin Hill
Map: 1, D3
Web: www.wt-woods.org.uk

Blackbush and Twenty-Acre Shaw are two adjacent woods. There is a whole range of wildflowers in the area: moschatel, scarlet pimpernel, blue form, wood anemone, lords and ladies, white bryony, traveller's joy, broad-leaved helleborine, spindle, autumn gentian, toothwort, bird's-foot trefoil, twayblade, bee orchid, fly orchid, cowslip, primrose, goldilocks, buttercup, hairy violet and dog violet.

Epping Forest
Near: Walthamstow and Loughton
Map: 1, D1
Web: www.cityoflondon.gov.uk

Covering 6,000 acres, Epping Forest is the largest open public space in London. Its woodlands are full of fantastic examples of ancient pollarded and coppiced trees, and there are more than 650 species of plants found here – and that's not counting the wonderfully diverse fungi that pops up in the autumn. Birds include treecreepers, woodpeckers and skylarks and many wildfowl make their homes on the area's 80 ponds and lakes.

Pot Kiln Wood

Near: Upminster, Havering
Map: 1, E2
Web: www.wt-woods.org.uk

Pot Kiln Wood is in the Thames Chase Forest. Its four meadows are species-rich with a total of 88 species of flora recorded. The hedgerows are believed to be ancient in origin, with the most common species being field maple, midland hawthorn, common hawthorn, ash, blackthorn, oak, wild rose and elder.

Ruffet and Big Wood

Near: Coulsdon, Croydon
Map: 1, C3 and D3
Web: www.wt-woods.org.uk
Ruffett Wood is made up of ash, wild cherry and beech trees and has wildflowers, including bluebell, sanicle, dog's mercury and nettle-leaved bellflower. Big Wood has mainly sycamore trees.

Ruislip Woods NNR

Near: Ruislip Common, Harrow
Map: 1, B1
Web: www.ruislipwoods.co.uk

Ruislip Woods consists of four principal areas: Mad Bess Wood, Bayhurst Wood, Park Wood and Copse Wood. As well as foxes and squirrels, the woods are home to a number of different birds such as the nuthatch, crow, jay, magpie, blue tit, great spotted woodpecker, sparrowhawk, robin, redwing, starling, collared dove, wood pigeon, grey heron, rook and song thrush.

Heron hunting

Sydenham Hill Wood

Near: Dulwich, near Wandsworth
Map: 1, C2
Web: www.wildlondon.org.uk
Combined with the adjacent Dulwich Wood, Sydenham Hill forms the largest remaining tract of the old Great North Wood. Today, the wood is a unique mix of recent woodland, Victorian garden survivors and older oak and hornbeam woodland. Sydenham Hill is home to more than 200 species of trees and plants, including wild garlic, early dog violet and bugle. A multitude of fungi, rare insects, birds and elusive woodland mammals are also present, particularly in summer when the woods are surprisingly full of insects and birds, a hotspot particularly for stag beetles. Cox's Walk, an avenue lined with oaks, supports nuthatch and green woodpecker.

Whitings Wood

Near: Barnet
Map: 1, C1
Web: www.wt-woods.org.uk

Whitings Wood is found within Watling Chase Community Forest. Its trees are mixed native broad-leaves – mainly oak, ash, field maple and some woody shrubs.

COASTS, WETLANDS & WATERWAYS

Bow Back Rivers

Near: Stratford, near Hackney
Map: 1, D1
Web: www.waterscape.com

Bow Back Rivers attract pondlife such as hornworts, floating water lilies, branched bur-reed, sponges and molluscs. Wildlife that can be spotted includes kingfishers, white-clawed crayfish, dragonflies and herons – and even the occasional otter and water vole. Bats love the seclusion of the bridges and tunnels, and all sorts of amphibians and reptiles – such as frogs, toads, newts and grass snakes – dip in and out of the waters. Moorhens, ducks and mute swans glide along the waters, and swallows, thrushes and tits nest in trees along the verges.

Grand Union Canal

From: Central London to the Chilterns (continues to Coventry)
Map: 1 and 14, B4
Web: www.waterscape.com
On the towpath of the Grand Union Canal, you will find clover, willowherbs, buttercups, cow-parsley and cuckoo-pint. Butterflies abound, in the form of meadow brown, cabbage white, tortoiseshell and peacock. Waterfowl include common coots, moorhens, and mallards, but also swans, herons and kingfishers. You might even spot water voles.

Hertford Union Canal

From: Grand Union Canal to the Lee Navigation, near Hackney
Map: 1, D1
Web: www.waterscape.com
Though the wildlife along the Hertford Union Canal is not exceptional, it provides a rare 'green lung' for wildlife among the built-up surroundings of east London.

Limehouse Cut

From: River Lee at Bromley-by-Bow to the Thames at Limehouse, near Hackney
Map: 1, D1 and D2
Web: www.waterscape.com
Plants on the water of the Limehouse Cut include

sponges and pondweed. Moorhens and ducks can be seen on the channel, and swallows, thrushes and tits nest in the trees and verges.

Little Venice

Near: Paddington, near Westminster
Map: 1, C2
Web: www.waterscape.com
Just minutes from Paddington station is Little Venice, the area where the Grand Union Canal and Regent's Canal meet. The waterway winds peacefully through a very

urban landscape, with swans and ducks enjoying the tranquillity.

London Docklands

From: Southwark to Greenwich
Map: 1, D2
Web: www.waterscape.com
The old docks provide an oasis for wildfowl in an otherwise heavily built-up environment, but don't come expecting much in the way of riverbanks and plants – these were, after all, London's working docks for many years.

London Wetland Centre

Near: Hammersmith
Map: 1, C2
Web: www.wwt.org.uk
Open: daily, 9.30am to 5/6pm, last admission 4/5pm (except 25 December)
Admission: £4.50/£7.25

The London Wetland Centre is the best urban location in Europe to watch wildlife. It has a diverse range of breeding wetland birds and winter flocks of shoveler and gadwall duck. In addition to attracting more than 180 wild bird species each year (including regular rarities such as bittern, Cetti's warbler, peregrine falcon and a breeding colony of sand martins), the reserve is a safe haven for eight species of bat, seven species of reptile and amphibian, and more than half of all the UK's dragonfly and damselfly species.

PICTURED: The main lake as a storm clears

Thames Estuary

Near: Gravesend and Gillingham, Kent, and Southend, Essex
Map: 5, B1 and C1
Web: www.thamesweb.com

The Thames Estuary is one of the UK's most important wildlife habitats. Due to the abundance of invertebrates in the mudflats – including shrimps, molluscs, minute snails and worms (of which there are more than 350 species) – the area attracts an estimated 200,000 wildfowl and waders, including avocet, knot, dunlin, dark-bellied brent geese, curlews, redshanks, oystercatchers, water rail, black-tailed godwit, ruff and hen harrier. Other birds include the short-eared owl and the tree sparrow. There are oysters also, as well as saltmarsh plants, such as sea arrowgrass, scurvey grass, sea lavender and glasswort plants. You can see rare ants, bees and wasps in the surrounding land, and grey seals offshore. There are also 121 species of fish in the waters.

PICTURED: A dunlin grazes for food

Regent's Canal

From: River Thames at Limehouse, City to Paddington, Westminster
Map: 1, C1 and D1
Web: www.waterscape.com

Regent's Canal provides a haven for wildlife in an otherwise built-up environment, with native and migrating birds using the waters. Bats have also been seen feeding over Battlebridge Basin on the canal. The Camley Street Natural Park, created on the banks of the Regent's Canal, features a pond, meadow and woodland. It provides a natural environment for birds, bees, butterflies, amphibians and a rich variety of plantlife.

River Lee

From: Hertford to Central London
Map: 6, C4 and 1, C2 and D2
Web: www.waterscape.com

Many wildflowers, such as cowslips, marsh marigolds, ragged robin and Indian balsam, can be found along the River Lee. Several species of wetland birds can be found on and around the river including the tufted duck, shoveler, gadwell, great crested grebe, grey heron, cormorant and kingfisher.

River Roding

From: Ilford Bridge to the Thames
Map: 1, D2
Web: www.waterscape.com

Roding Valley Meadows Reserve is found on the banks of the River Roding. The meadows are rich in flowers, including sneezewort and pepper saxifrage, with southern marsh orchid, ragged robin, marsh marigold and several rare sedge species in the wetter areas. Sedge warbler and reed bunting frequent the marshy areas, while kingfisher and sand martin occasionally nest in the riverbank. Grey heron, little grebe, snipe, green and common sandpiper are regular winter visitors.

River Thames

From: Lechlade-on-Thames, near Witney, to the Thames Estuary
Map: 7, E5, 1, and 5, C5,
Web: www.waterscape.com

The Thames is now at its cleanest in living memory: kingfishers and otters can be glimpsed on certain sections of the river and more than 20 species of freshwater fish can be found here. The river is a haven for swans, ducks, great crested grebe, coots, moorhens, herons and kingfishers. Water voles and squirrels can also be seen along its banks.

Welsh Harp/Brent Reservoir

Near: West Hendon
Map: 1, C1
Web: www.waterscape.com

The reservoir has high numbers of wintering and nesting wildfowl, as well as one of the largest breeding colonies of great crested grebes in the country. It also has a wide diversity of wetland and marginal plants. The land habitats support a wide variety of species, from greater spearwort and fringed water lily to sedge warblers, reed bunting, kingfishers, sparrowhawks and even kestrels. More than 40 species of invertebrate, such as butterflies and dragonflies, reside here.

West Reservoir Centre

Near: Stoke Newington, near Hackney
Map: 1, D1
Web: www.wildlondon.org.uk
Open: daily, with limited access

Just off the Green Lanes, two old reservoirs have been turned into an environmental education and watersports centre. In winter, visiting birds arrive and in summer there is a population of damselflies. There are grasslands and hedgerows on the site and a special wildlife garden. The Wildlife Trusts runs education projects at the centre.

NOT SO WILD

Battersea Park

Address: Battersea, near Wandsworth, London SW8
Map: 1, C2
Web: www.batterseapark.org
The most obvious wildlife in Battersea Park are the birds living on or around the lake. You can often see herons, cormorants, grebes and black swans. Plants include foxglove. There is also a small zoo.

Brooks Farm

Address: Skeltons Lane Park, Skeltons Lane, Walthamstow, London E10 5BS

Map: 1, D1
Tel: 020 8539 4278
Web: www.farmgarden.org.uk
Open: daily, April to October, 10.30am to 5.30pm; November to March, 9.30am to 4.30pm
Admission: £1

You can see sheep, pigs, goats, chickens, ducks, calves, shetland ponies and llamas at Brooks Farm. There are also small animals, such as guinea pigs, rabbits and pygmy goats.

Centre for Wildlife Gardening

Near: East Dulwich, Lewisham
Map: 1, D2

Web: www.wildlondon.org.uk
Open: Tuesdays, Thursdays and Sundays, 10.30am to 4.30pm (except December 25)

Wildlife you can see includes newts, damselflies, grasshoppers, wolf spiders swifts and blue tits. In March, there are frogs and toads spawning and you can find speckled wood, red admiral and other butterflies in July.

Coram's Fields

Address: 93 Guilford Street, London WC1N 1DN
Map: 1, C2
Tel: 020 7837 6138
Web: www.coramsfields.org.uk

A riverside scene in London

Open: daily, 9am to 7pm/dusk (except 25 December)
Admission: free

ℹ️ ☎ 🚻

Coram's Fields has a wide variety of activities including extensive lawns and a pets corner with sheep, goats, ducks, hens and much more.

Deen City Farm
Address: 39 Windsor Avenue, Merton, London SW19 2RR
Map: 1, C2
Tel: 020 8543 5300
Web: www.deencityfarm.co.uk
Open: Tuesday to Sunday, 10am to 4.30pm
Admission: free

♿ 🚻 📷 ☎ ↖

Deen City Farm has a wide range of farm animals, including red poll and dexter cattle, Gloucester old spot pigs, anglo nubian, toggenburg and golden Guernsey pigs, pure breed poultry, jacob, poll douset and texel sheep, geese, ducks, donkeys, an aviary, rabbits, chinchillas and guinea pigs.

Freightliners City Farm
Address: Sheringham Road, Islington, London N7 8PF
Map: 1, D2
Tel: 020 7609 0467
Web: www.freightlinersfarm. org.uk
Open: Tuesday to Saturday and Bank Holidays, 10am to 4/5pm
Admission: free

🚻 ☎ 🚻

A long-established working city farm with poultry, pigs, cattle, sheep, goats, ducks, geese and a vegetable garden.

Hackney City Farm
Address: 1a Goldsmiths Row, London, Bethnal Green E2 8QA
Map: 1, D2
Tel: 020 7729 6381
Web: www.hackneycityfarm.co.uk
Open: Tuesday to Sunday and Bank Holidays, 10am to 4.30pm

Admission: free
🅿️ (££), ☎

Animals on the farm include the duroc, British saddleback and Vietnamese pot-bellied pigs, donkeys, goats, calves, sheep, chinchillas, rabbits, rats, degus, ducks, chickens and turkeys.

Hammersmith Community Gardens Association
Address: 59 Godolphin Road, London W12 8JF
Map: 1, C2
Web: www.hcga.org.uk
Hammersmith Community Gardens Association manages two community gardens and two glasshouses in Hammersmith. Loris Garden is a mature garden with a grassy, hilly area and wildlife pond. Godolphin Garden has a few specimen trees, a pond, a wildlife area and herb beds.

> ### DID YOU KNOW?
> Foxes have only lived in urban areas since World War I when suburban areas with large gardens were created.

Hounslow Urban Farm
Address: Faggs Road, Feltham, Middlesex, Hounslow TW14 0LZ
Map: 1, C2
Tel: 020 8751 0850
Web: www.hounslow.info/urbanfarm
Open: Tuesday to Sunday and Bank Holidays, 10am to 4pm
Admission: £1.50/£3

ℹ️ 🚻 ☎ 🚻

Hounslow Urban Farm was set up in 1990 and it has cattle, sheep, pigs, poultry, goats, rabbits, waterfowl, guinea pigs and horses.

Kentish Town City Farm
Address: 1 Cressfield Close, off Grafton Road, Camden, London NW5 4BN
Map: 1, C2

Tel: 020 7916 5421
Web: www.aapi.co.uk/cityfarm
Open: Tuesday to Sunday and Bank Holidays, 9.30am to 5.30pm
Admission: free

🚻 🚻

Kentish Town City Farm provides animals, gardening space, horse-riding and a focus for youth and community work. It has cattle, sheep, horses, goats, pigs and assorted poultry.

London Aquarium
Address: County Hall, Westminster Bridge Road, London SE1 7PB
Map: 1, C2
Tel: 020 7967 8000
Web: www.londonaquarium.co.uk
Open: daily, 10am to 6/7pm (except 25 December)
Admission: £9.75/£13.75

♿ 🚻 📷 ℹ️ ☎ ↖

The London Aquarium is one of Europe's largest displays of aquatic life and home to more than 350 species and more than 50 displays, from sharks, stingrays and clownfish to moray eels, lionfish and crabs. You can watch rays and native British sharks being hand-fed.

London Butterfly House
Address: Syon Park, Brentford, near Ealing, Middlesex TW8 8JF
Map: 1, C2
Tel: 020 8560 7272
Web: www.londonbutterflyhouse. com
Open: daily, 10am to 3.30/5pm (except 25 and 26 December)
Admission: £3.95/£5.25

🅿️

In the glasshouse at the London Butterfly House you can walk among hundreds of free-flying tropical butterflies. At any time there will be 1,000 butterflies on display with up to 50 species visible. There is also The Tropical Aviary – home to the whydah, bulbul, Japanese waxwing, quail, munnia and black-bibbed

Boom boom

It is very difficult to see a bittern: not only are they limited to a few healthy reedbeds mainly in the south of England, they are also very shy and stealthy. However, even if you never see one, to hear a male in the spring is a thrill with its huge booming sound that echoes across still waters. They are found at Cley Marshes and Hen Reedbeds in Norfolk, Oare Marshes in Kent, Arnside and Silverdale in Cumbria/Lancashire and the London Wetland Centre near Barnes.

Royal Botanic Gardens, Kew

Address: Royal Botanic Gardens, Richmond, Surrey TW9 3AB
Map: 1, C2
Tel: 020 8332 5922
Web: www.rbgkew.org.uk
Open: daily, winter, 9.30am to 4.15pm; summer, 9.30am to 6.30pm
Admission: £6.50/£9.50

The beautiful setting of Kew Gardens is well known for its diverse range of plants that come from all over the world, but the grounds are also home to a wide variety of wildlife, including brown long-eared bat, badger, weasel, fox, woodmouse, pipistrelle and hedgehog. Birds include the jay, mistle thrush, tit, green woodpecker, sparrowhawk, ring-necked parakeet, heron, reed bunting, kingfisher, osprey and grey wagtail. There are mosses, liverworts, ferns and algae, as well as various species of fungi. The gardens host an annual tropical flower and orchid festival.

thrush – and the Tropical Mini-Beasts Area, which has spiders, beetles, stick insects, praying mantis, toads, cockroaches, frogs, lizards, snails and millipedes.

ZSL London Zoo
Address: Regent's Park, near Camden, London NW1 4RY
Map: 1, C2
Tel: 020 7722 3333
Web: www.zsl.org.uk
Open: daily, 10am to 4/5.30pm (except 25 December)
Admission: £9.50/£12

ZSL London Zoo has more than 600 species of animals, including lions, tigers, primates, giraffes, penguins, pelicans, meerkats, tapirs, sloth bears, Komodo dragons, bearded pigs, painted dogs, zebras and tamarins. There are different habitats, such as the rocky outcrops or the ponds and waterfalls, and a range of indoor enclosures. There is also the chance to see farmyard animals.

Mudchute Park and Farm
Address: Pier Street, Isle of Dogs, near Greenwich, London E14 3HP
Map: 1, D2
Tel: 020 7515 5901
Web: www.mudchute.org
Open: daily, 9am to 5pm
Admission: free

Mudchute was created from the mud and silt removed from the surrounding docks towards the end of the nineteenth century. There are herbs and wildflowers in the park and horses, cattle, sheep, poultry, goats, pigs and llama are kept on the farm.

Newham City Farm
Address: Stansfeld Road, Beckton, near Ilford, London E6 5LT
Map: 1, D2
Tel: 020 7474 4960

Web: www.farmgarden.org.uk
Open: Tuesday to Sunday and
Bank Holidays, 10am to 4/5pm
Admission: free

The farm has a wide collection
of farm animals with an
emphasis on rare breeds.
It also has birds of prey, a
pheasant aviary and a small
foreign finch collection.
There are three wildlife areas
with a dipping pond and
boundary hedgerows outside
the farm. Animals include a
working shire horse, milking
red poll cow, sheep, pigs,
poultry and goats.

Spitalfields City Farm

Address: Weaver Street, Bethnal
Green, London E1 5HJ
Map: 1, D2
Tel: 020 7247 8762
Web: www.spitalfieldscityfarm.org
Open: daily, 10.30am to 5pm
Admission: free

Animals on Spitalfields City
Farm include horses, pigs,
donkeys, cows, goats, sheep,
poultry (miniature call ducks
and light Sussex cockerel),
rabbits and guinea pigs.

Stepping Stones Farm

Address: Stepney Way, Stepney,
Bethnal Green, London E1 3DG
Map: 1, D2
Tel: 020 7790 8204
Web: www.farmgarden.org.uk
Open: Tuesday to Sunday,
9.30am to 5/6pm
Admission: free

Stepping Stones Farm has
cows, sheep, goats, pigs,
donkeys, poultry, rabbits,
guinea pigs and small pets.

Surrey Docks Farm

Address: Rotherhithe Street, near
Westminster, London SE16 5EY
Tel: 020 7237 6525
Map: 1, C2
Web: www.surreydocksfarm.
org.uk
Open: Tuesday to Thursday,
10am to 5pm
Admission: free

Surrey Docks Farm is sited
on the edge of the River
Thames. There are herb, dye
and vegetable gardens and an
animal yard that has a herd
of milking goats, cows and
Gloucester old spot pigs.

Thameside Park City Farm

Address: 40 Thames Road, Barking
near Ilford IG11 0HH
Map: 1, D2
Tel: 020 8594 8449
Web: www.farmgarden.org.uk
Open: daily, 9.30am to 4.30pm
Admission: free

The farm was founded in
1982 and around 20,000
visitors each year come
to see the animals. The
farm has a sensory garden
and a pets' corner for small
animals, and is planting
an orchard.

Vauxhall City Farm

Address: 165 Tyers Street, London,
near Westminster SE11 5HS
Map: 1, C2
Tel: 020 7582 4204
Web: www.vauxhallcityfarm.
org.uk
Open: Wednesday to Sunday,
10.30am to 4pm
Admission: free

Vauxhall City Farm has cattle,
goats, sheep, ducks, horses
and a donkey.

South East

Spanning the breathtaking Kent Downs, the serenity of the New Forest and encompassing the natural beauty of the Isle of Wight, the South East is truly a fascinating mosaic of habitats and diverse wildlife.

There are many woodlands in the region, home to grey squirrel and fox, and an abundance of other animals, too. Badgers, bats and deer, both muntjak and roe, frequent the glades, while owls perch up in high branches and all three species of woodpecker make their homes here. Those with a sharp eye may be lucky to spot the rare goldcrest amidst the mixed conifers. Although red squirrels can, on occasion, be seen on the mainland, a trip to the Isle of Wight provides a much greater chance of spotting this British native.

In springtime, carpets of bluebells, wood anemone and primrose flourish across many of the area's woodland floors, where daffodils and wild garlic are also found.

Take time to explore the expanses of heathland, beautiful in purple in the summer months, and the place to spot any of Britain's six reptile species. Adders and grass snakes inhabit the heaths, while frogs, newts, toads and the sand lizard are attracted to ponds.

The New Forest boasts the largest remaining area of lowland heath in Europe, plus of course its famous wild ponies that graze the meadows and are a hit with both adults and children. Move closer to the area's watering holes to spy on the rare water vole or take advantage of an ever-expanding population to glimpse the otter in action.

An area with dominant chalky undertones, the South East provides ideal conditions for many grassland flowers and their associated wildlife. A very rich bryophyte and lichen flora can dominate in places, accompanied by an impressive range of orchids, including the purple, bee and pyramidal. Attracted by the sheer diversity of such grassland, butterflies abound, among them the Duke of Burgundy fritillary, the purple emperor and the lovely chalkhill blue.

There are plenty of wetland and waterways in the area that attract the kingfisher and sandshank, as well as migrators including the osprey, and breeding wildfowl and waders.

A visit to the South East is full of opportunities for watching wildlife – as you head out into the countryside, it's hard to believe that this is Britain's most densely populated area.

PICTURED: The New Forest

Not to be missed

● **Blean Woods**
Enjoy a walk in these splendid oak woodlands with their sunny glades and openings of heathland and see just how many different bird species you can spot.

● **Kingley Vale**
Butterflies love this place, and so will you – there are panoramic views, herds of deer and one of the oldest yew forests in western Europe.

● **New Forest**
See the famous wild ponies and soak up the atmosphere of this huge expanse of national park that has many, many habitats and a wide variety of wildlife – if you're lucky enough to disturb a wild boar, climb up a tree.

● **Old Winchester Hill**
Right on the South Downs Way, these chalky slopes have a wonderful display of wildflowers – especially for the orchid fan.

● **Pulborough Brooks**
In winter, the flooded River Arun is chock-a-block with wading birds, ducks and geese who visit in their thousands.

● **Reculver Country Park**
Combine wildlife and history here with a cliff-top walk past an old Roman fort and a hunt for fossil shells and sharks' teeth down on the beach.

Wild pony in the New Forest

NATIONAL PARK New Forest

Hampshire
Map: 3, C2 and D2
Web: www.newforestnpa.gov.uk

The New Forest national park is a unique landscape of ancient woodland, heather-covered heath, wide lawns, boggy mires, farmland and coastal saltmarsh. Set aside by William the Conqueror as a hunting forest more than 900 years ago, today the forest is a wonderful area to explore, by walking, cycling or on horseback. The forest offers walkers and cyclists a huge choice of circular and linear routes of varying lengths. A living and working place, ponies and cattle graze freely, and deeper in the forest, wild boar is said to browse. As the largest remaining area of lowland heath in Europe, the forest is ideal for adders and grass snakes, while the dotted pools attract frogs, toads and lizards. The New Forest Reptile Centre is also a fantastic place to observe such creatures, located just south of Lyndhurst. The forest is most atmospheric at dusk, encouraging deer, bats and nightjars to emerge. Home to a collection of trees from around the world, some of the tallest and oldest Douglas firs in Britain can be seen at the Rhinefield Ornamental Drive, while redwoods are also abundant.

AONB

Kent Downs
Kent
Map: 5, B1, C2, D2
Web: www.kentdowns.org.uk

Stretching from the White Cliffs of Dover to the Surrey and London borders, the Kent Downs offer a diverse and vibrant landscape of dramatic chalk escarpments, dry valleys, ancient woodlands and historic hedgerows. The central chalk ridge is the most important geological feature of the area, designated an AONB in 1968. One of south-east England's highest points is situated on the Sevenoaks Greensand ride, while three main river catchments – the Darent, Medway and Great Stour – cut through the Downs, draining in a south to north direction.

NATURE RESERVES

Ashford Hangers NNR
Near: Petersfield, Hampshire
Map: 3, E2
Web: www.english-nature.org.uk
♿ (ltd)

Ashford Hangers NNR is part of a mainly wooded escarpment where the Hampshire chalk plateau meets the lower Weald. These 'hangers' (woods growing on the sides of steep hills) are an important landscape feature of the Petersfield area in east Hampshire. Rare and unusual species characteristic of the hangers include sword-leaved helleborines and herb paris. Various fungi, insects and nesting birds also thrive here along with roe deer, badgers and foxes. There is also a 21-mile path running south from Alton railway station through the Hangers to the South Downs at Queen Elizabeth Country Park.

Aston Rowant NNR
Near: High Wycombe, Buckinghamshire
Map: 2, C3
Web: www.english-nature.org.uk

Aston Rowant NNR sits on the steep west-facing scarp of the Chilterns. It comprises flower-rich chalk grassland together with beech woodland and juniper scrub. A number of scarce plants can be seen at the reserve, including Chiltern gentian and a wide variety of orchids. In the summer, the site is home to many species of butterfly such as the silver-spotted skipper and chalkhill blue. It is one of the best places in England to see red kites.

Beacon Hill NNR
Near: Petersfield, Hampshire
Map: 3, E2
Web: www.english-nature.org.uk

Beacon Hill NNR is a prominent chalk hill at the western end of the South Downs. The reserve contains high-quality chalk grassland, with small areas of scrub and woodland. The NNR's rich downland flora is characterised by sheep's fescue grass, rock rose, scabious, yellow-rattle, eyebrights and several species of orchid. Round-headed rampion, field fleawort and hairy-rock cress are also found on the site. The woodland is mainly mature beech and hazel coppice, with ash found in gaps that have been created by 'windblow'. Several butterfly species occur in the area, including chalkhill blue, brown argus, silver-spotted skipper and Duke of Burgundy fritillary.

> ### DID YOU KNOW?
> The Arctic tern makes the longest migration of any bird. It travels from the Arctic to the Antarctic and back each year, a distance of 35,000km.

Bough Beech
Near: Tonbridge, Kent
Map: 5, B2
Web: www.kentwildlifetrust.org.uk

Bough Beech covers the northern part of the Sutton and East Surrey Water Reservoir. High winter water levels attract numerous waterfowl. Waders, including little ringed plover and green sandpiper, are visible in the summer and autumn, as are rarities such as the little crake – a first for Kent. Reedbeds on the North Lake increasingly attract grey wagtail and kingfisher. Woodland and willow scrub attract warblers and finches, while floating islands accommodate nesting terns, and a small orchard provides a bird-feeding area in the winter. Ospreys are regular passage visitors and it is probably the best place in the UK to see mandarin ducks. A permit is needed for access to the reserve.

Burnham Beeches NNR
Near: Slough, Berkshire
Map: 2, C4
Web: www.english-nature.org.uk

Burnham Beeches NNR is an area of beech and oak wood pasture with small areas of hazel coppice, dry and wet heathland and sphagnum bog. One of the best examples of ancient woodland in Britain, it is home to a variety of wildlife. Birds, bats, fungi and other wood-living organisms thrive through careful habitat management. Livestock has been reintroduced, including pigs, sheep, cows and ponies. Recent experiments with pollarding – an ancient technique that aims to provide a regular crop of timber without damaging the trees – has raised hopes that woodpeckers, tawny owls, foxes, dragonflies and some of Britain's rarest invertebrates have an assured future at Burnham Beeches.

Butser Hill NNR
Near: Petersfield, Hampshire
Map: 3, E2
Web: www.english-nature.co.uk
(££), – all at Queen Elizabeth Country Park

Butser Hill NNR is a large area of chalk grassland in Hampshire. The site consists of improved and unimproved calcareous grassland with scattered scrub, chalk heath, yew woodland and semi-ancient broadleaved woodland. The site has a very rich bryophyte and lichen flora with more than 200 lichen, moss and liverwort species being recorded in the chalk grassland. More than 30 butterfly species have been sighted here including the Duke of Burgundy fritillary, silver-spotted skipper and chalkhill blue. As the highest point on the South Downs, Butser Hill dominates the surrounding landscape. A large area is designated as a scheduled ancient monument, reflecting its historical significance, particularly in the Iron and Bronze Ages.

Species-rich grassland in Chimney Meadow

Castle Bottom NNR

Near: Camberley, Hampshire
Map: 3, E1
Web: www.english-nature.org.uk
P (ltd)

Castle Bottom NNR is a stunning lowland area in northern Hampshire, containing one of the most important valley mires in southern England, with associated heathland habitats. There are also some areas of woodland, including aspen, which is home to a number of scarce invertebrates. The reserve has recently been designated a Special Protection Area (SPA), recognising its status as a site of European importance for bird populations. Visitors can enjoy Castle Bottom by following a network of footpaths, while the reserve is also close to a major trail, the Three Castles Path.

Chimney Meadows NNR

Near: Witney, Oxfordshire
Map: 2, A3
Web: www.english-nature.org.uk

Chimney Meadows benefits from 618 acres of wildlife-rich land along the banks of the River Thames. The reserve consists of six wildflower meadows with large populations of characteristic plants, such as adder's tongue, pepper saxifrage and meadow rue, while also providing a vital refuge for waders. Butterflies, including gatekeepers, meadow browns, ringlets and common blues, are frequent visitors. The site can only be accessed on foot, by walking the Thames Path National Trail and access is restricted to public rights of way (access to other parts of the reserve is by permit only).

Chinnor Hill

Near: Thame, Oxfordshire
Map: 2, B3
Web: www.english-nature.org.uk
P

Chinnor Hill combines chalk grassland and woodland, with fine views over the Vale of Aylesbury. At its summit, imposing beech woodland includes old, weathered trees, and the ancient trackways that lead down the slope meander through beech and yew. In spring, hairy violets thrive on the grassland, where the cocoons of dark-green fritillary butterflies can also be found. Dormice are known to live among the trees, but you're more likely to find the rare Chiltern gentian or a glow worm in the open grassland. In summer, redstarts visit and thyme provides nectar for common blue butterflies, while the winter foods of the juniper attract redwing and fieldfare.

Chobham Common NNR

Near: Woking, Surrey
Map: 4, B1
Web: www.english-nature.org.uk
P

The largest NNR in south-east England, Chobham is a fine example of lowland heath. Expanses of heather, valley bogs and grassland create a patchwork of mini-habitats. Regarded as the premier site for ladybirds and spiders, the variety of birdlife spans more than 100 species, including the rare Dartford warbler. In the heathland and deep in the ponds live frogs, newts, adders and sand lizards. Foxes and deer are occasionally seen and rare water voles may be glimpsed feeding by the heathland ponds. More than 300 species of wildflower grow, including rare marsh gentians, present in the wetlands. Open country species that have disappeared elsewhere, such as skylarks and tree pipits, are seen here.

College Lake Wildlife Centre
Near: Tring, Hertfordshire
Map: 6, A4
Web: www.wildlifetrust.org.uk/herts

P   WC   i   🚻   🔦

This worked-out chalk quarry has been restored as a wildlife centre with a mosaic of wetland and grassland habitats. The reserve is particularly interesting for its birdlife, and is an addition to the famous birdwatching Tring reservoirs. A variety of waders, terns and other species are regularly seen on migration, while breeding birds include lapwing, redshank and little ringed plover. Kingfisher, red kite and buzzard are present throughout the year, and the rare whooper swan and goosander emerge in bad weather. In addition to its wonderful wildlife and spectacular views, the reserve is excellent for fossils; remains of marine life, mammoths and even lions have been found.

Cothill NNR
Near: Abingdon, Oxfordshire
Map: 2, B3
Web: www.english-nature.org.uk

🚻

Cothill NNR is one of the most species-rich lowland calcareous fen systems in the UK. The reserve includes a full transition from open water and short fen, through to oak and alder woodland. A large number of scarce invertebrates have been recorded here, including southern damselfly and Desmoulin's whorl snail. Several uncommon plants typical of alkaline fen are found at the site, including narrow-leaved marsh orchid, marsh helleborine, bog pimpernel, black bog-rush and marsh valerian. Grass snakes and lizards can often be seen and the reedbeds provide cover for sedge warblers and reed warblers.

Dancersend
Near: Aylesbury, Buckinghamshire
Map: 2, C2
Web: www.bbowt.org.uk

P

Nestling in a hidden Chiltern valley, Dancersend is a wonderfully rich nature reserve combining mixed woodlands and chalk grasslands. Adder's tongue fern and Solomon's seal abound among the more common cowslips and primroses of spring, while green hairstreak and grizzled skipper butterflies can be seen along the rides and scrub. Chiltern gentian and meadow clary can be found in summer, accompanied by ringlet and dark-green fritillary butterflies. In autumn, numerous fungi emerge, including the remarkable earthstar, while you may spot the edible dormouse fattening up for the winter.

Furnace Meadow and Brick Kiln Rough
Near: Midhurst West Sussex
Map: 4, A2
Web: www.plantlife.org.uk

P

This reserve is split into two parts: Furnace Meadow, the 10-acre area of unimproved grassland, and Brick Kiln Rough, six acres of ancient semi-natural woodland. The single field of Furnace Meadow incorporates a warm slope that supports a real mix of species, including the rarer hawkbit, pepper saxifrage and musk mallow. In and alongside the stream a different suite of plants can be found, such as yellow iris, hemlock and brooklime. The woodland of Brick Kiln Rough is oak dominated with an interesting ground flora, including daffodil, bird's nest orchid and bluebell.

Hertford Heath SSSI and Balls Wood
Near: Hertford, Hertfordshire
Map: 6, C4
Web: www.wildlifetrust.org.uk/herts

🚻

Hertford Heath SSSI is a rare open heathland, with

Brownish in colour with a dark zigzag down its back, the adder is the only poisonous snake native to Britain. From November to February it hibernates underground, but from March to October it is frequently spotted basking in sunshine in woodland clearings or on open heathland. Its poisonous bite is only used as a last means of defence – usually if it's caught or trodden on. No one has died in Britain from an adder bite for more than 20 years. Look out for them at Wye, Cannock Forest, Blacka Moor, Bedford Purlieus, Old Wood and Flanders Moss.

Snakes and adders

woodland and several heathy pools. The reserve is in two sections, Goldington's and Rounding, with the adjacent Balls Wood. In the woodland, hazel and blackthorn are scattered among hornbeam coppice and secondary oak, while heather and petty whin grow on the open heathland. Spreading healthily since The Wildlife Trusts took the invasive scrub and trees in hand, the pools are filled with sphagnum mosses and rushes, while the largest pool provides impressive yellow flag iris. Birds commonly seen here include little owl, long-tailed tit and lesser spotted woodpecker.

Kingley Vale NNR

Near: Chichester, West Sussex
Map: 4, A3
Web: www.english-nature.org.uk

Kingley Vale contains one of the finest yew forests in western Europe, including a grove of trees that are among the oldest living things in Britain. This reserve is also an important archaeological site, boasting Bronze Age burial mounds at the top of Bow Hill, where stunning panoramic views can be enjoyed. The reserve has recorded 39 species of butterfly, while breeding birds have included nightingale and green woodpecker. In recent years, the mewing of buzzards has been increasingly heard, and other observable birds of prey are kestrel and tawny owl. Of the mammals, rabbits, herds of roe deer, stoats, foxes and badgers are all visible.

Kingston Great Common NNR

Near: Ringwood, Hampshire
Map: 3, C2
Web: www.english-nature.org.uk

Kingston Great Common is regarded as an outstanding example of mire habitat. Alongside the mires are associated heathland habitats with areas of pine woodland and, although the NNR can be visited at any time of year, the mires become waterlogged and dangerous to cross in winter. Birdlife on the site includes woodlark, nightjar, Dartford warbler and, occasionally, hobby. The reserve is home to an important invertebrate population, including 20 species of dragonfly.

Lewes Down (Mount Caburn) NNR

Near: Lewes, Sussex
Map: 4, C3
Web: www.english-nature.org.uk

Mount Caburn is a hill and valley clothed in grassland with a scattered scrub and a good example of ancient, traditionally managed chalk downland. As well as the fragrant and pyramidal orchids typical of these downs, the site has the largest British population of burnt-tip orchid. The rare small-leaved sweet-briar can also be found among the downland scrub. Invertebrates include chalkhill blue butterflies and the scarce forester moth. The cultural history of the reserve mirrors its wildlife value. The Caburn is one of the best-preserved Bronze Age hillforts in Sussex and, although now rare, the internationally famous South Downs sheep were developed on this downland.

Long Herdon and Grange Meadows

Near: Marsh Gibbon, near Bicester, Buckinghamshire
Map: 2, B2
Web: www.plantlife.org.uk

Long Herdon and Grange Meadows are two adjacent hay meadows, lying alongside the River Ray. They have never been ploughed, drained or had fertilisers added, and are now full of wildflowers. Regular winter floods provide the ideal habitat for flora, such as great burnet, meadowsweet and tubular water-dropwort. However, it is not just plants that prosper at Long Herdon and Grange – these wet meadows are also noted for their numbers of wintering birds, including curlews, redshanks and lapwings. A number of butterflies are also present,

750-year-old yew tree in Kingley Vale NNR

including marbled white, meadow brown, small heath and small skipper.

Lower Test

Near: Southampton, Hampshire
Map: 3, D2
Web: www.hwt.org.uk

🅿 ♿ ⓘ ⌂ 🔦

Lower Test is one of the last sites in Britain where there remains a natural graduation from saltmarsh through brackish grassland to neutral grassland. During the warmer months, saltmarsh plants, such as English scurvy grass, can be found, while further inland, colonies of hairy buttercup are observable. The reedbeds support scarce species such as Cetti's warbler, while the old wet meadows have many flowering plants, including green winged orchids. An important winter refuge for wildfowl, up to 25 water pipits have been found over-wintering here. Passage visitors include marsh harrier and osprey, while waders are often seen feeding in the scrapes.

Lullington Heath NNR

Near: Eastbourne, Sussex
Map: 4, D3
Web: www.english-nature.org.uk

🅿 🚻

The slightly acid, fine soil of Lullington Heath has allowed the development of an intimately mixed chalk and heath plant community. Acid-loving heathers and tormentil grow among plants such as thyme, salad burnet and dropwort, which have adapted to the chalk. The nature trail allows you to see some of the 98 species of bird or the 34 species of butterfly recorded here. Welsh beulah sheep and New Forest ponies graze the heath, and help to maintain its condition. Access to the reserve is limited to public rights of

Norbury Park SSSI

Near: Leatherhead, Surrey
Map: 4, B1
Web: www.surreywildlifetrust.co.uk

🅿 ♿ 🚻 ⌂ 🖼 🔦

Norbury Park lies within the Surrey Hills AONB and is an attractive mixture of woodland, grassland and farmland. Its varied, well-managed landscape, combined with its free-draining geology, means good walking is possible throughout the year. Yew and box occur across the park, combining with other species to give the site its SSSI status. Spring carpets the woodland floors with bluebells, while summer brings orchids and chalk grassland flowers, and the coniferous and deciduous trees of autumn add colour. Numerous walking trails and cycle routes allow you to leave the beaten route and glimpse the roe deer or perhaps a badger, kingfisher or woodpecker.

way, but guided walks organised by English Nature's Sussex and Surrey team allow for wider access.

Malling Down

Near: Lewes, Sussex
Map: 4, C3
Web: www.sussexwt.org.uk

🅿

Malling Down is a superb example of chalk grassland, within easy walking distance of Lewes town centre. Until around 40 years ago, sheep and cattle closely grazed the whole area, and the grass was among the richest in downland flowers, orchids and butterflies anywhere in Sussex. Since then, scrub has spread over much of the site – thickly in some areas. However, much rich grassland remains, notable for its wild orchids and such chalk specialities as wild thyme, round-headed rampion, dropwort and autumn gentian. The yellow horseshoe vetch attracts the chalkhill blue butterfly and the rare Adonis blue.

North Solent NNR

Near: Southampton, Hampshire
Map: 3, D2

Web: www.english-nature.org.uk

⌂

North Solent comprises the lower reaches of the Beaulieu River where it drains into the Solent. Diverse habitats range from open shore to saltmarsh, grassland, woodland, valley mire and heathland. Plants include dwarf spike-rush and slender hare's-ear. Moths and butterflies recorded include the pearl-bordered fritillary and orange footman, while the reserve is also home to the rare Roesel's bush cricket. North Solent is internationally important for its populations of over-wintering and migratory waterfowl, and is of national importance for its populations of breeding gulls, terns and wading birds. Due to the sensitivity of many habitats, access is restricted to public rights of way.

Old Lodge

Near: Uckfield, East Sussex
Map: 4, C2
Web: www.sussexwt.org.uk

🅿

Combining vistas of heather with pine woodland, Old Lodge is set in the middle of Ashdown Forest. The heathland attracts stonechat and tree pipit, while the sparrowhawk has been seen coursing the woodland. Grazing has been restored to Old Lodge, and, in conjunction with birch and bracken control, is steadily improving the reserve for heath and acid grassland species. The boggy pools provide a breeding ground for dragonflies, and hawkers may be seen in summer, searching the pines for prey. The views, relatively free from development, form a lasting impression, while the reserve is one of the few places left in Sussex where the redstart breeds regularly.

Old Winchester Hill NNR
Near: Petersfield, Hampshire
Map: 3, E2
Web: www.english-nature.org.uk

There is a range of habitats here, with distinct differences between the plants found on the warm, dry, south-facing slopes and those on the steep north-facing areas – and in hollows – which are much damper. Flower-rich grasslands have developed on the thin chalky soils. In May and June, several species of orchids appear on the slopes around the hillfort. These are followed by oxeye daisies and round-headed rampion in July. Insects and butterflies, including the chalkhill blue, flit among the grasses on this popular site.

Queendown Warren
Near: Chatham, Kent
Map: 5, B1
Web: www.plantlife.org.uk

Queendown Warren is a fine example of unimproved chalk grassland. Orchids thrive in these dry, nutrient-poor conditions, particularly the fragrant orchid, scattered

A mute swan nesting in The Swale NNR

with groups of early-spider, bee and man orchids. Summer welcomes chalk grassland butterflies, including the Adonis blue. The short sward required to maintain the orchid populations is assured by a colony of rabbits and cattle. Native broad-leaved trees are also prevalent, while some sweet chestnut coppice is managed by traditional methods. The southern woodland is on chalk and is especially good for observing adders.

St Catherine's Hill SSSI
Near: Winchester, Hampshire
Map: 3, D2
Web: www.hwt.org.uk

Combining more than 350 species of flora with archaeological features including a hillfort and burial grounds, St Catherine's Hill is a remaining tract of unimproved chalkland. Spring brings carpets of cowslips and the first sightings of small blue and green hairstreak butterflies, while summer welcomes chalkhill blues accompanied by brown argus and influxes of clouded yellow. The grassland is dotted with flowers such as rockrose and kidney vetch, along with a range of orchids, and recorded birds include yellowhammer and skylark, while green woodpeckers feed on the anthills. Redwing and fieldfare flock in the winter months, while stonechat and linnet are regulars in the adjacent Plague Pits Valley.

Stodmarsh

Near: Canterbury, Kent
Map: 5, D2
Web: www.english-nature.org.uk
P WC 🏠 🏠

This reserve is made up of reedbeds and lagoons and supports large populations of waders and wildfowl. In the autumn and spring, large flocks of martin, swallow and wagtail use the reserve as a stopover. The rare shining ram's-horn snail is found here, as well as a number of rare plants, including the greater spearwort and bog-bean.

The Swale NNR

Near: Sheerness, Kent
Map: 5, C1
Web: www.english-nature.org.uk
P 🏠 🏠

This coastal reserve is predominantly a grazing marsh, supporting significant wintering populations of waterfowl. It has an outstanding assemblage of scarce plants, including narrow-leaved and dwarf eel grass on the mudflats and Ray's knotgrass and white sea kale on the beach. The saltmarsh supports glassworts and golden samphire. Gargany and short-eared owl have been known to breed, and the area provides a hunting ground for barn owl and Montagu's harrier. Many rare and uncommon migrant butterflies and moths have been recorded, including the clouded yellow butterfly and the convolvulus and bedstraw hawkmoths. Macro-moths, such as shaded pug and obscure wainscot, have also been known to breed or visit.

Swanscombe Skull Site NNR

Near: Gravesend, Kent
Map: 5, B1
Web: www.english-nature.org.uk
P WC 🏠

Swanscombe Skull is a small geological site of national importance. The name of the site refers to a fossilised human skull, pieces of which were discovered here in the 1930s and 1950s. These skull fragments are some of the oldest human bones ever found in the UK. Research has revealed that tropical animals, such as hippos, rhinos and elephants, once roamed the Medway's shores. Even today, the site is home to very rare and interesting wildlife. There are 238 species of invertebrate living in the area and more than one third of the species listed in the park are rare.

DID YOU KNOW?

Grass snakes are good swimmers and feed mainly on toads, frogs, newts and small fish.

Thursley NNR

Near: Godalming, Surrey
Map: 4, B2
Web: www.english-nature.org.uk
P

Thursley NNR is one of the largest remaining fragments of Surrey heath and includes areas of lowland heath, mire and woodland. The site supports a range of typical heathland wildlife, including large invertebrate populations. The best time to visit is between May and September to see birds and flowers.

Wildmoor Heath

Near: Bracknell, Berkshire
Map: C4
Web: www.bbowt.org.uk
P ℹ

This valuable remnant of Berkshire heathland and bog, provides a wildlife refuge that is very much alive today. Wildmoor combines dry and wet heath, acid grassland, pine plantation and scrub. From spring onwards, the heath is busy with songbirds and reptiles, the wet heath attracting dragonflies and damselflies. In the evening, you might see pipistrelle bats and glow worms. In August, flowering heathers provide nectar for butterflies and in autumn fungi can be found in the woodland fringing the heath. The rare Dartford warbler resides throughout the year and may be spotted in patches of gorse.

Wisley Common, Ockham and Chatley Heath

Near: Leatherhead Surrey
Map: 4, B1
Web: www.surreywildlifetrust.co.uk
P ♿ WC 🚻 ℹ 🍴 🚰 🔦

These three areas combine to create a fascinating mix of habitats, including heathland, ancient woodland, conifer woodland, grasslands, ponds and a large lake called Boldermere. Coal tit and sparrowhawk frequent the pine and birch woodlands, while the heathland is spectacular in the summer, when insects abound. By June, nightjars have returned to breed on the scrub and, although autumn and winter are quieter, redwing continue to visit the fields on the edges of the common. As well as a wealth of wildlife, the Semaphore Tower on Chatley Heath provides a point of historical interest.

Wye NNR

Near: Ashford, Kent
Map: 5, C2
Web: www.english-nature.co.uk
P 🏠

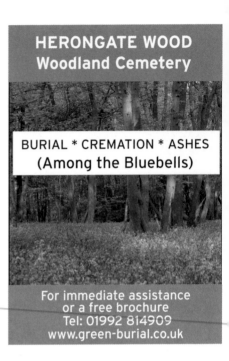
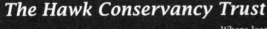

Warburg

Near: Henley-on-Thames, Oxfordshire
Map: 2, B4
Web: www.wildlifetrusts.org

Warburg extends across a winding chalk valley with a mosaic of woodland, scrub and grassland. Glades entice woodland butterflies, such as the purple emperor. Shady woodland encourages violet helleborines and remnant patches of conifer plantation support goldcrest in the winter. Chiltern gentian grow in the older grassland areas, while grazing sheep keep scrub short, allowing chalk grassland plants to flourish. Artificial ponds attract amphibians and reptiles, including grass snakes, while adders and common lizards also reside. Winter attracts marsh tit and redpoll and nesting birds include sparrowhawks and woodpeckers. Rabbits are common but hares can also be seen on open ground near woodland. Fallow, muntjak and roe deer roam in the woodlands, and there are dormice too.

Wye's steep coombes of chalk grassland and woodland provide spectacular views over the Romney Marsh and Weald. The site is also widely known for landscape features such as the Devil's Kneading Trough, a dry, steep-sided valley formed by peri-glacial action towards the end of the last Ice Age. The grassland supports more than 21 species of orchid, including lady orchid, fly orchid and the rare late and early-spider orchid and man orchid. The habitats of scrub woodland and hedgerows support around 50 species of breeding birds, including nightingale, lesser spotted woodpecker and kestrel. Reptiles found here include adder, grass snake, slow worm and common lizard.

BIRD RESERVES

Brading Marshes
Near: Sandown, Isle of Wight
Map: 3, D4
Web: www.rspb.org

Acquired in 2001, Brading Marshes is the only RSPB reserve on the Isle of Wight. Combining low-lying wet neutral grassland with a network of lagoons and a fringe of woodland, access is currently restricted to footpaths from Brading Town and Bembridge Harbour, which provide attractive views across the wetlands. Spring and summer attract lapwing, herons and shelduck, along with marsh harriers and peregrines. In autumn and winter, migrating waders join ducks, geese and resident wading birds feeding in the pools. While the RSPB is currently managing the site for its populations of over-wintering waders and wildfowl, there is much planned work to develop the reserve over future years.

Cliffe Pools
Near: Rochester, Kent
Map: 5, B1
Web: www.rspb.org

The 568 acres of Cliffe Pools are a mix of saline lagoons, freshwater pools, grassland, saltmarsh and scrub, developed on old clay diggings and river dredgings. Acquired in 2001, the reserve already attracts thousands of birds. It is renowned as a site for waders, with massed flocks moving from the Thames Estuary onto the pools in winter high tides, a wide range of passage birds in autumn and spring, and breeding avocets, redshanks, lapwings and ringed plovers. It is also a good place to see water voles, harvest mice and an array of insects.

Dungeness NNR
Near: Lydd, Kent
Map: 5, D3
Web: www.rspb.org.uk
Open: daily, 9am to sunset/9pm (except 25 and 26 December)
Admission: £1/£3; RSPB members free

This RSPB reserve occupies nearly 2,500 acres of the Dungeness peninsula, the largest shingle formation of its kind in Europe. The shingle is made largely from material eroded during the last Ice Age and is the major habitat at the reserve, together with natural and artificial wetlands and grazing marsh. Dungeness has important breeding colonies of gulls and terns and attracts migrating birds, including Bewick's swans and gadwalls. Dungeness also has an important population of medicinal leech. In the past these were used to treat a variety of ailments and were collected in such numbers that they became extinct in many parts of the country.

Elmley Marshes
Near: Sittingbourne, Isle of Sheppey, Kent
Map: 5, C1
Web: www.rspb.org
Open: 9am to 9pm, closed Tuesdays

🅿 (inc ♿), 🚾
🛗 (inc ♿ access), 🔭

The wet grassland of Elmley Marshes is a nationally important area of coastal grazing marsh, comprising smaller areas of saltmarsh, brackish water pools and fleets. Winter attracts ducks, geese and waders, along with hen harriers, merlins, peregrines and short-eared owls. The marshes are also one of the best sites in the UK to see wintering raptors. In the summer, many wading birds, including the elegant avocet, breed here. The grazing marsh supports the highest density of breeding lapwing and redshank in south-east England. Elmley also supports 12 rare invertebrates, including nine species that are listed as being under threat.

Fore Wood
Near: Hastings, East Sussex
Map: 4, E3
Web: www.rspb.org

🅿

Fore Wood, one of the larger blocks of semi-natural ancient woodland remaining in East Sussex, is managed by coppicing, which provides a home for many colourful insects, including silver-washed fritillary and white admiral butterflies. The areas of high forest hold green, greater and lesser spotted woodpeckers, alongside nuthatch and treecreeper, while the coppices and scrub support marsh tit and migrant warblers, such as blackcap. Moorhen and mallard, plus the occasional kingfisher and grey heron, visit the large pond, which also supports large numbers of dragonflies and damselflies. Bluebells, wood anemones and early purple orchids are abundant in the spring.

Fowlmere
Near: Royston, Hertfordshire
Map: 6, C2
Web: www.rspb.org.uk

🅿 🚾 📷 🏤
🛗 🔭

From each of the reserve's three hides, birds such as kingfishers, water rails and up to nine species of warblers can be seen flitting around the chalky stream that runs through this special wetland habitat. Natural chalk springs feed Fowlmere's reedbeds and pools which, in turn, feed the old watercress beds on the site.

Langstone Harbour
Near: Havant, Hampshire
Map: 3, E2
Web: www.rspb.org

🅿 🏤

The RSPB reserve here occupies one third of Langstone Harbour, incorporating a group of saltmarsh islands and the surrounding inter-tidal mud. Terns, gulls and wading birds descend to breed on the islands in spring and summer, while black-tailed godwits and Brent geese migrate from the Arctic to feed and roost in safety here. Winter wading birds, such as dunlins, oystercatchers, grey plovers and curlews, form spectacular roosts at high water, the majority on the RSPB islands.

Nor Marsh and Motney Hill
Near: Gillingham, Kent
Map: 5, C1
Web: www.rspb.org
Open: 8.30am to dusk

🅿 ♿ 🚾 📷 🏤 🔭

Nor Marsh is a saltmarsh island in the Medway Estuary and to the east is Motney Hill, another area of mud and saltmarsh. In the winter, both sites attract large numbers of wildfowl, including Brent geese, pintails, shelducks and goldeneyes along with grey plovers, knots and avocets. In the spring and autumn, look out for black-tailed godwits. In recent years, small numbers of little egrets have taken to roosting on Nor at high tide. Motney Hill is a good area to look for the rarer grebes, occasional divers and sea duck such as red-breasted merganser, goldeneye and common scoter.

Tiny as a bird

Britain's smallest resident bird isn't in fact the wren, as many think, it's the goldcrest which is mainly dull green in colour with a white chest and a distinctive orange or yellow stripe on its crown. Its favourite habitat is coniferous forest, particularly where there are spruce and silver fir. If you're lucky, you might see them at Lower Lough Erne, Wolves Wood, Blean Woods or Nidd Gorge.

Northward Hill

Near: Rochester, Kent
Map: 5, B1
Web: www.rspb.org
P (inc ♿)

The Northward Hill woodland has been in RSPB ownership since 1956 and recent marsh management has been successful in encouraging the return of breeding species, including lapwing, redshank, avocet and marsh harrier, and also wintering waterfowl like wigeon and teal. The ditches offer a wealth of other wildlife including water voles, dragonflies and a multitude of beetles. The wood is still the site of the UK's largest heronry, currently standing at 155 pairs of grey herons, with little egrets present since 2000. The woodland is also famous for its colony of white-letter hairstreak butterflies, its nightingales and the display of bluebells in the spring.

Pulborough Brooks

Near: Pulborough, West Sussex
Map: 4, B2
Web: www.rspb.org
Open: visitor centre, daily, 9.30am to 5pm; nature trail, sunrise to sunset
Admission: £1/£3.50
P ♿ **WC** 🚼 **i**
🍴 🎁 🏕 ⛰ 🥾

Set in the sheltered Arun Valley in the heart of West Sussex, Pulborough Brooks is a mixed habitat of farmland and water meadows and a fantastic place for a day out for people of all ages. The River Arun floods in winter, providing a rich habitat for wading birds, ducks and geese. In autumn and winter, the reserve attracts thousands of wild ducks and other water birds. It is equally worth visiting in spring to hear and see the songbirds, while during the summer, the reserve bursts into life with wildlife of all kinds, including birds, butterflies, wildflowers and dragonflies.

> ### DID YOU KNOW?
> Female ground beetles can discharge a noxious fluid from their abdomens to deter over amorous males.

Rye Meads

Near: Hoddesdon, Hertfordshire
Map: 6, C4
Web: www.rspb.org
Open: daily, 10am to 5pm (except 25 December)
P ♿ **WC** **i**
🍴 🎁 🏕 🥾

A wildlife haven situated in the Lea Valley, one of Britain's largest wetlands, this reserve is managed by The Wildlife Trusts and the RSPB and is incredibly diverse. The Trusts' land combines ancient flood meadow, old gravel pits and willow carr, while the RSPB manages marshes and lagoons adjacent to the River Lee. Winter attracts water rail, while the breeding birdlife of summer includes several species of duck, kingfisher and common tern. Rye Meads is a good place to see snipe and green sandpiper in autumn. Meadowsweet and meadow-rue provide the pastel-coloured surroundings. Water voles, water shrews and harvest mice are abundant.

FORESTS & WOODLAND

Alice Holt Forest

Near: Farnham, Hampshire
Map: 3, E1
Web: www.forestry.gov.uk
P (££), ♿ **WC**
i 🍴 🍴 🏕 🥾

This ancient forest is famous for its oak trees, which once supplied timber for Navy ships.

More recently, Alice Holt oak has been used to build the replica of Shakespeare's Globe theatre in London. Look out for purple emperor butterflies, the forest symbol, and also for roe deer. Whether you have come to walk, cycle, clamber in the woodland climbing areas, or see the wildlife, there is something at Alice Holt for everyone who loves the countryside.

Blean Woods

Near: Canterbury, Kent
Map: 5, D1
Web: www.english-nature.org.uk
P ♿ 🍴 🏕 🥾

These splendid oak woods support a large number of woodland species, including all three types of British woodpecker, treecreepers, nuthatch, spotted flycatcher, hawfinch and nightingale. The golden oriole is a rare summer visitor. Although vast, visitors will find these woods intimate and intriguing with the mosaic of habitats, from sunny glades and heathland to ancient woodland. Up to 30 species of butterfly can be seen, including the scarce white admiral, as can the rare seven-spot ladybird, while nightjars and dormice are present on the heathland. Trees include hornbeam and sweet chestnut, while bracken – and bluebells in spring – dominate the woodland floor.

Bowdown Woods

Near: Newbury, Berkshire
Map: 2, A4
Web: www.bbowt.org.uk
P ♿ 🥾

Next to Greenham Common and overlooking the River Kennet, this ancient expanse of woodland combines mysterious hidden valleys, sunny glades and patches of heathland. For sheer variety of wildlife, Bowdown Woods is hard to beat. In spring, primrose and bluebell lie beneath the mature oak and ash, while summer brings glimpses of white admiral and purple emperor butterflies. The dry heath provides a home for reptiles and numerous dragonfly species, including the golden-ringed, which flit between ponds and fringing scrub. In autumn, around 300 species of fungus bring new interest to the woodland, while the flowering heather brings colour to the heath.

College Wood
Near: Nash, Bletchley, Buckinghamshire
Map: 2, C2
Web: www.wt-woods.org.uk
P

An ancient coppice woodland, College Wood combines semi-natural survivors and introduced species, such as Norway spruce, Scot's pine and Lawson cypress. Once part of the Whaddon Chase Hunting Forest, today the Woodland Trust is working to remove most of the conifers to allow native plants to recolonise the wood. The natural cover of ash, oak and field maple remains alongside a ground flora dominated by bluebell, while early purple orchid and wood anemone still flourish. Badgers frequent the woods and muntjak deer can be spotted, while wood white and white admiral butterflies, both requiring woodland rides as habitat, are also present.

Ebernoe Common NNR
Near: Petworth, West Sussex
Map: 4, B2
Web: www.sussexwt.org.uk
P

This reserve is a superb example of Low Weald woodland. During spring, bluebells and orchids dominate, while cowslip and betony colour the grasslands throughout the summer. The north area is clay, featuring predominantly oak and ash trees. To the south, the soil is more acidic and beech becomes the most common forest tree. Autumn brings an abundance of fungi, including stinkhorn and chanterelle. Bats, such as barbastelle and Bechstein's, make use of the cracks and hollows within the trees and hawfinch, woodpecker and nightingale breed at the reserve. Frogs and toads live in the ponds, and woodland butterflies are frequent visitors.

Ham Street Woods NNR
Near: Hamstreet and Ashford, Kent
Map: 5, C2
Web: www.english-nature.org.uk
P

Ham Street Woods form part of Orlestone Forest, a fragmented remnant of a continuous oak forest. Pedunculate oak and hornbeam are surrounded by bluebells, while tormentil is found in more acidic areas. In damper parts, ash and hazel thrive alongside dog's mercury. Many breeding birds can be seen on the reserve, including the treecreeper and sparrowhawk. A large number of rare invertebrates thrive, most notably species living on dead wood and butterflies such as the Duke of Burgundy fritillary. The site is also of archaeological interest and contains many well-preserved earthworks including a medieval ditch system and the remains of a staggered medieval dam.

Hargate Forest
Near: Tunbridge Wells, Kent
Map: 5, B1
Web: www.wt-woods.org.uk
P

Immediately south of Tunbridge Wells and traversing the Sussex border, Hargate Forest combines mixed coniferous and broad-leaved woodland to provide a number of habitats. Observing the scarcity of lowland heath in Britain, the Woodland Trust has seized the opportunity to recreate an area of heathland, which will increase the biodiversity of the forest and offer a more varied and attractive landscape. Such a project hopes to encourage greater numbers of butterflies, including the common blue and holly, while also enticing birds such as yellowhammer, nightjar and tree pipit. While small numbers of common lizard currently inhabit the heath, the Trust's regeneration hopes to support them further.

Pamber Forest
Near: Basingstoke, Hampshire
Map: 3, E1
Web: www.hwt.org.uk
P

Traditionally used to provide timber for local industries, this remnant of the Royal Forest of Windsor is now managed for conservation and visitors. Combining woodland, heathland and stream valleys, Pamber is especially good for butterflies, the purple emperor living high in the tree canopy, while the white admiral makes the most of the numerous flowering plants of the sunlit rides. Predominantly oak and birch with hazel coppice, alder carr can be found in the wetter areas by the stream. Wild daffodil and star of Bethlehem can be found here, while three species of woodpecker, woodcock and other warblers have also been recorded.

Tudeley Woods
Near: Tonbridge, Kent
Map: 5, B2
Web: www.rspb.org.uk
Open: daily, 9am to 6pm
P

Pamber Forest

The reserve is an intricate mix of woodland, heathland and pasture, supporting several rare bird species, including woodlarks, nightjars, lesser spotted woodpeckers and willow tits. Tudeley Woods supports 1,000 species of fungi, and several orchids, including greater butterfly orchids, and violet helleborines. In the spring, there are carpets of bluebells and primroses, while up on the heath the heather blooms in August.

Wendover Woods
Near: Aylesbury, Buckinghamshire
Map: 2, C2
Web: www.wt-woods.org.uk
P (££), ♿ 🚻 🍽 🎯 🔭
Situated on the northern edge of the Chiltern escarpment, Wendover Woods affords spectacular views across the Aylesbury Vale. Within 800 acres, broad-leaved woodland of oak, ash and beech is interspersed with mixed coniferous trees, such as Norway spruce and Scot's pine. In spring, large areas are covered in a carpet of bluebells, and later in the year foxgloves and willowherbs can be seen. The speckled wood and peacock butterfly have both been recorded, as has the great

spotted woodpecker. Mammals that thrive here include the fox and grey squirrel.

Wychwood NNR
Near: Witney, Oxfordshire
Map: 2, A3
Web: www.english-nature.org.uk
Wychwood is the largest continuous area of ancient broad-leaved woodland in Oxfordshire. The site also includes a series of marl lakes of special value for their invertebrate populations. The woodland habitat includes stands of oak and ash as well as beech plantation, and plants of particular interest in the ground flora include meadow saffron, herb paris, early purple orchid and adder's-tongue fern. The reserve is part of the Cornbury Park Estate. A public right of way runs through the woods but entry to other parts of the estate is by permission only. By tradition, the whole site is open to the public on Palm Sunday.

COASTS, WETLANDS & WATERWAYS

Basingstoke Canal
From: Greywell, Hampshire, to Woking, Surrey
Map: 3, E1 and 4, B1
Web: www.basingstoke-canal. co.uk
P ℹ️ 🚻 🎯
🍽 (Wednesday to Sunday)
The Basingstoke Canal was established in the eighteenth century as an agricultural waterway to connect north-east Hampshire with the London markets. The canal is unique due to the changing quality of the water, from very alkaline in its chalky springs to more acidic as it enters Surrey, resulting in more types of aquatic plant being recorded here than any other waterway in Britain. The

collapsed Greywell Tunnel also provides the largest winter hibernation site for bats in western Europe. The visitor centre, located in the village of Mytchett, is the perfect place to find out more about the canal and to start exploring this beautiful waterway.

Black Swan Lake

Near: Reading, Berkshire
Map: 2, B4
Web: www.waterscape.com/black_swan_lake

P (££), ♿ WC ♿
ℹ ◻ ♿ ◣

Black Swan Lake forms part of Dinton Pastures Country Park, more than 335 acres of rivers, meadows, lakes and wooded areas. Although primarily a recreational lake, waterfowl are recurrent, including mandarin ducks, gadwells, Egyptian geese and mute swans. Kingfishers, herons and hobbies visit, as well as the more common swifts, swallows and whitethroats. Insects abound, with records including turquoise nettle weevils, soldier beetles, lacewing larvae, dragonflies, damselflies and lots of spiders. Artificial holts and improved habitats are enticing otters back to the area, while bats have also set up home here.

Castle Water, Rye Harbour

Near: Rye, East Sussex
Map: 4, E2
Web: www.sussexwt.org.uk

P ♿ WC ♿
ℹ ◻ ♿ ◣

A large coastal reserve, Rye Harbour, which includes Castle Water, combines vegetated shingle, grassland and water features. Renowned for birdwatching at any time of year, waders such as the redshank and lapwing are common, although impressive rarities regularly appear. The lake attracts little egrets, increasingly joined to roost by the rare bittern. The saltmarsh supports such unusual plants as marsh mallow and specialised insects, including the saltmarsh bee. The rarest plant found here is the endangered least lettuce. Yellow-horned poppy and rare sea pea dot the shingle, while the fields of grazing marsh and water-filled ditches are teeming with beetles, molluscs and the rare medicinal leech.

Farlington Marshes

Near: Havant, Hampshire
Map: 3, E2
Web: www.hwt.org.uk

P ◻

Farlington, reclaimed from the sea centuries ago, is internationally important for the bird populations that

it supports. In winter, Brent geese graze the fields, while other wildfowl include wigeon and shoveler. In autumn, waders can be seen on the lake at high tide or feeding on the mudflats of Langstone Harbour in winter, while summer attracts breeding gulls and terns. Many of the birds are used to people, allowing for unusually close views without the need for hides. Uncommon species of flowering plant, such as sea barley and slender hare's-ear, have been recorded here.

Filsham Reedbed LNR

Near: Hastings, East Sussex
Map: 4, E3
Web: www.sussexwt.org.uk

P ♿ (ltd)

The largest reedbed in Sussex, Filsham LNR is tucked away in the Combe Haven Valley, an SSSI. The valley is an important migration route for birds, and during the autumn and winter the reedbed is a key stopping point for swallows, warblers and rarer species such as marsh harrier and bittern. In spring, bearded tit and water rail breed. Specialist moths, such as the wainscots, abound, as do unusual plants, including frogbit and the insectivorous bladderwort. Recent restoration has provided

Bee who you want to bee

There are more than 200 species of bee in Britain and many of them, known as solitary bees, don't live in colonies under the rule of a queen. Species of solitary bees include miner bees (Andrena), which make nests in the ground – usually in sandy soil or along paths – leaf-cutter bees, which cut neat circles out of rose leaves and petals to build their nests and saltmarsh bees, which live exclusively in saltmarsh because of the particular plants found there. The last is found at Castle Water in Rye Harbour.

much better conditions for breeding birds and other reedbed wildlife, while also improving public access.

Keyhaven and Pennington Marshes
Near: Lymington, Hampshire
Map: 3, D4
Web: www.hwt.org.uk
P WC

This large area of saltmarsh and mudflat lies either side of Lymington River and is of international importance for the bird populations that it supports. Black-headed gulls breed in large numbers, along with little and sandwich terns. The most conspicuous breeding waders are oystercatcher, ringed plover and redshank. The marshes are also important for migrating waders and waterfowl on passage. Over winter, several thousand Brent geese visit, along with waders such as dunlin and grey plover. The saltmarsh has pioneering species, including the glasswort and common cord grass, whereas the upper marshes and shingles support colourful plants, such as sea campion, thrift and little-robin.

Longmoor Lake
Near: Wokingham, Berkshire
Map: 2, C4
Web: www.waterscape.com/longmoor_lake
P (££), ♿ WC 🚻 🔖

Longmoor Lake is the central focus of California Country Park, which offers recreational facilities to visitors as well as serving as a rich habitat for local wildlife. Dug out in the nineteenth century for brick making, it was developed into one of the first holiday camps in the 1950s, and by the mid-twentieth century, locals flocked to bathe in the summer and skate in

Bird footprints in the sand of Newtown Harbour

the winter. The site around the lake consists of rare ancient bogland and lowland heath, home to interesting wildlife and plantlife, such as sphagnum mosses, springtime orchids, adders and silver-studded blue butterflies.

Newtown Harbour NNR
Near: Newport, Isle of Wight
Map: 3, D3
Web: www.english-nature.org.uk
P ♿ ⓘ 🚻
🏠 (inc ♿ access), 🔖

Newtown Harbour comprises areas of estuary and foreshore with mudflats and saltmarsh. The estuary provides a wintering ground for wildfowl and waders, with Brent geese and black-tailed godwit observable.

Lagoon sandshrimp inhabit the saline lagoon, a remnant of the old salt workings. Red squirrel and dormice inhabit adjacent woodland, a favoured location also for invertebrate communities, including butterflies such as the silver-washed fritillary. Nearby damp meadows support plants typical of unimproved grassland, such as corky-fruited water dropwort and adder's-tongue fern. The reserve is also an important geological site.

Oare Marshes
Near: Faversham, Kent
Map: 5, C1
Web: www.kentwildlife.org.uk
P (inc ♿), ♿ ⓘ
🏠 (inc ♿ access), 🔖

Internationally important for migratory, over-wintering and breeding wetland wildlife, Oare Marshes is one of the best places in north Kent for a quick birdwatch. Hides are easily accessed and roadside watching is of a good standard. Among the breeding species are avocet, redshank, snipe, bearded reedling and garganey, while migrating species include the ruff and whimbrel and over-winterers consist of dunlin, curlew and bittern. Dragonflies are abundant, and you may spot common seals on sandbanks in the estuary.

The Oxford Canal
From: Oxford to Coventry
Map: 2, B1 and 14, B4
Web: www.waterscape.com/oxford_canal
The picturesque Oxford Canal meanders slowly through 77 miles of classic scenery. It begins at Hawkesbury Junction where it connects with the Coventry Canal. At Oxford, the canal has two connections to the Thames; Dukes Cute, three miles north of the city, and through a channel called 'the sheepwash', a few hundred metres from the city centre, below Isis Lock. Briefly the principal waterway from London to the Midlands, it was superceded soon after construction by the Grand Union Canal. Consequently, the Oxford Canal has escaped large-scale development and few towns have sprung up on its banks. The southern section is particularly charming and remains largely unaltered.

Reculver Country Park
Near: Herne Bay, Kent
Map: 5, D1
Web: www.kentwildlife.org.uk
P ⓘ ⊞

A coastal site with a visitor centre providing superb displays, Reculver is excellent for combining wildlife and historical interest. Impressive twelfth-century towers and the remains of a Roman fort provide the background to a bracing clifftop walk, or head down to the beach to find fossil shells and sharks' teeth. Bishopstone woodland, a one-mile walk westwards, is a refuge for birds along an almost treeless coast. Spring and summer bring a colourful display of flowers and butterflies and a colony of sand martins nests in the cliffs in summer. Brent geese and sanderling are among the winter visitors and many migrants pass through in autumn.

River Medway
From: Maidstone to Tonbridge, Kent
Map: 5, B2
Web: www.waterscape.com/river_medway
Opened more than 250 years ago when water-borne transport was in its heyday, today the river is maintained as a public right of navigation, enabling water users to experience the delightful scenery of the Garden of England. There are opportunities to visit the locks and the parks, while several villages on or close to the river provide ample occasion for exploration and refreshment. More than 130,000 birds visit the Medway and Swale each year, as the habitat of mudflats and saltmarshes provide the rich food source required to survive migrations and winter climate.

Sandwich and Pegwell Bay LNR
Near: Ramsgate, Kent
Map: 5, E1

Web: www.kentwildlife.org.uk
P WC ⊞ & ⊞ ⊞ ⊠
This reserve is the best remaining complex of its type in south-east England, showing a complete series of seashore habitats. In winter, common waders, such as dunlin and curlew, are joined by nationally important numbers of sanderling and grey plover. In summer, redshank and oystercatcher stay to breed, joined by ringed plover and the little tern. Botanically, the saltmarsh holds sea aster and the rarer golden samphire. New dunes accommodate marram grass. On the dune pastures, southern marsh-orchids can be found, while at Stonelees, marsh helleborines and bee orchids flourish.

Stocker's Lake LNR
Near: Rickmansworth, near Watford, Hertfordshire
Map: 6, B4
Web: www.wildlifetrust.org.uk/herts
P & ⊞ ⊠
One of the oldest and largest gravel pits in the Colne Valley, Stocker's Lane is a wildlife refuge for mammals as well as birds. The 42 regular breeding species include various ducks, common terns and numerous warblers, bunting and tits. Boasting the largest heronry in Hertfordshire, in mid-May, young grey herons can be seen taking flying lessons. The lake is one of the country's foremost sites for wildfowl in the winter, including shoveler and gadwall in nationally important numbers, while the lake is also important for pochard, goldeneye, smew and goosander.

Titchfield Haven NNR
Near: Fareham, Hampshire
Map: 3, D2
Web: www.english-nature.org.uk

Wildlife Britain **75**

Open: Wednesday to Sunday and Bank Holidays, 9.30am to 4/5pm (except 25 and 26 December)
Admission: £1.90/£3.70

P (inc ♿), ♿ WC ♿
ℹ ☐ ⌂ ♿ ↘

Titchfield Haven is a low-lying and generally flat area. Formerly the estuary of the River Meon, it is a vital pre-migratory feeding place for wetland birds. The site is also home to plants and animals that have a highly restricted distribution in southern England. Recent sighting highlights include a black-throated diver offshore and a razorbill reportedly flying east. Oystercatchers are visible on the scrapes, while a firecrest has been observed along the canal path and the kingfisher makes a regular appearance. Butterfly monitoring has revealed frequent visits from the red admiral and the peacock, while damselflies and dragonflies are common.

The Tring Reservoirs

Near: Tring, Hertfordshire
Map: 6, A4
Web: www.waterscape.com/tring_reservoirs

P (inc ♿) ♿ WC ♿
☐ ⌂ ♿ ↘

Built in the early nineteenth century to feed arms of the Grand Union Canal, today the reservoirs are a designated SSSI on account of their wealth of wildlife. Throughout the year, little owl and kingfishers are observable, as are all three species of woodpecker. Winter brings an abundance of geese and duck, while red-breasted mergansers sometimes appear in cold weather and bittern over-winter in the reedbed at Marsworth Reservoir. Migrant passengers such as wheatear, redstart and whinchat are sometimes seen

in spring, while summer brings common and scarcer butterflies. The rarer winter waders can include little stint and curlew sandpiper.

Wilstone Reservoir

Near: Aston Clinton and Tring, Hertfordshire
Map: 6, A4
Web: www.wildlifetrusts.org.uk/herts

P

Wilstone is an artificial water body fed by natural springs and surrounded by ancient marshes, reedswamp and willow carr. One of the most famous birding spots in southern England, the reserve has one of the county's three regular heronries. Spring brings passage and summer migrants, while breeding duck include gadwall and shoveler. The summer moult flocks of tufted duck and pochard are nationally important and autumn passage again brings tern, gull and other vagrants. Winter water birds include nationally important levels of shoveler, teal and wigeon. Flowering plants include celery-leaved and Goldilocks buttercups.

WWT Arundel

Near: Arundel, West Sussex
Map: 4, B3
Web: www.wwt.org.uk/visit/arundel
Open: daily, 9.30am to 4.30/5pm (except 25 December)
Admission: £3.75/£6.95; free to WWT members

P ♿ WC ☐ ⌂ ♿ ↘

The new visitor centre at Arundel is surrounded by ancient woodland and overlooked by the town's

historic castle. The wetlands here are home to many rare species of wetland wildlife. Reserve regulars include kingfisher, goldcrest and woodpecker, while chiffchaffs, willow and the Cetti's warbler can still be spotted with patience. Tawny owls can be seen at dusk, while there is also the chance of seeing the occasional greenshank. New habitat piles provide refuge for hibernating grass snakes, while native shrubs include guilder rose, sloe and spindle. A November survey revealed that water vole are becoming more established and widespread.

NOT SO WILD

Ashford Community Farm

Address: North School, Essella Road, Ashford, Kent TN24 8AL
Map: 5, C2
Tel: 01233 614600
Web: www.farmgarden.org.uk
Open: term-time, 9am to 3.30pm; school holidays, 9am to noon

♿ WC ♿ ⌂ ↘

Part of the School Farm Network, Ashford Community Farm began life as a wartime garden in the 1930s. Today, it is a thriving school and community farm, with cattle, small animals and a vegetable plot incorporated into the site. Situated at North School, a state secondary school of pupils who largely come from farming backgrounds, many of whom assist with early-morning duties, grow crops on the allotment, or show animals in the Kent County Show. The farm has a healthy involvement with the local community and is open to the general public, allowing the farm to continually develop.

Birdworld

Address: Holt Pound, Farnham, Surrey GU10 4LD

Map: 4, A1
Tel: 01420 22140
Web: www.birdworld.co.uk
Open: April to October, 10am to 6pm; times vary for rest of year
Admission: £8.95/£10.95

Meerkat at Drusillas Park

View exotic birds from around the world and plan your visit to take in the penguin feeding – each day at 11.30am and 4pm. Great information available on birds ranging from ostriches and rheas to parrots and pelicans.

Chessington Zoo

Address: Chessington World of Adventures, Animal Land, Chessington, Surrey KT9 2NE
Map: 4, B1
Tel: 0870 999 0045
Web: www.chessington.co.uk
Open: varies with season
Admission: as above

Located in the Animal Land of Chessington World of Adventures, Chessington Zoo houses endearing and impressive guests. The jungle-themed experience Trail of the Kings allows for interaction with one of Europe's most successful West Lowland gorilla families, Sumatran tigers, Asiatic lions and Persian leopards. The Monkey and Bird Garden was opened in 2006, as was Creature Features – an interactive animal land with meerkats, porcupines and rheas. Sea Lion Bay and Penguin Cove provide daily shows and feedings, while the Children's Zoo is home to baby goats, sheep and rabbits. The Creepy Caves house reptiles, snakes and spiders, while otters and birds of prey can also be seen.

Cotswold Wildlife Park

Address: Burford, Oxfordshire OX18 4JP
Map: 2, A2

Tel: 01993 823006
Web: www.cotswoldwildlifepark. co.uk
Open: daily, from 10am (except 25 December)
Admission: £6.50/£9

Cotswold Wildlife Park is set in 160 acres of parkland and gardens around a listed Victorian Manor House and has been open to the public since 1970. The park is home to a fascinating and varied collection of mammals, birds, reptiles and invertebrates from all over the world. There are more than 250 different species of animals at the Cotswold Wildlife Park, many of which are endangered or threatened in the wild. Almost all the mammal and bird species at the park are captive bred, and many are part of captive breeding programmes, whereby zoological collections cooperate to increase captive populations.

Drusillas Park

Address: Alfriston, East Sussex BN26 5QS
Map: 4, D3
Tel: 01323 874100
Web: www.drusillas.co.uk
Open: daily, 10am to 4/5pm (except 24, 25 and 26 December)
Admission: varies with season

Located amid the stunning scenery of the Cuckmere Valley, Drusillas is regarded as the best small zoo in the country, and is home to a number of species, including beavers, crocodiles, lemurs, penguins and squirrel monkeys. The farmyard features pigs, cows, sheep and ponies, while visitors can see fruit bats, flamingos and also a host of insects in the Millennium Bugs exhibit. Combining naturalistic animal enclosures and low-level viewing, Drusillas enables children to come face to face with nature, while other features, such as adventure golf and the discovery centre provide for an action-packed day out.

Felicia Park Urban Community Farm

Address: Sealark Road, off Grove Road, Gosport, Hampshire PO12 4JR
Map: 3, D2
Tel: 02392 502593
Web: www.farmgarden.org.uk
Open: weekdays, 11am to 2pm; Sundays and Bank Holidays 1pm to 2pm

Felicia Park was founded 18 years ago by a Gosport family.

Using their own animals as a backbone, they began to adopt unwanted pets and other livestock. A steady increase in animals over the years was accompanied by an influx of volunteers and requests to use the animals on a teaching basis for animal husbandry. Today, the farm accommodates students of all abilities. In December 1999, a relocation allowed for a new complex, housing horses, feral and domestic cats, dogs, aviary birds, rabbits, chickens, ducks, a goat and numerous small animals, while wildlife dependent on the farm was encouraged to follow.

Howletts and Port Lympne Wild Animal Parks

Address: Howletts Wild Animal Park, Bekesbourne Road, Bekesbourne, Canterbury, Kent CT4 5EL
Map: 5, D2
Tel: 01227 721286
Address: Port Lympne Wild Animal Park, Port Lympne, near Hythe, Kent CT21 4PD
Tel: 01303 264647
Web: www.totallywild.net
Open: daily, from 10am (except 25 December)
Admission: £10.95/£13.95

Started 40 years ago by John Aspinall, Howletts and Port Lympne Wild Animal Parks conserve and breed rare and endangered animals with the intention of returning them to safe areas in their natural habitat. The largest herd of African elephants in the UK and the largest collection of breeding West Lowland gorillas in human care in the world reside at Howletts. At Port Lympne, there is the Palace of the Apes, one of the world's largest family gorilla houses, Barbary lions and the largest captive breeding

herd of black rhino outside Africa. Other animals include wolves, tapirs, red pandas and buffalo. Port Lympne also has a mansion and garden to explore.

> **DID YOU KNOW?**
>
> The male hare is called a jack and the female is a jill.

Paradise Park

Address: White Stubbs Lane, Broxbourne, Hertfordshire EN10 7QA
Map: 6, C4
Tel: 01992 470490
Web: www.pwpark.com
Open: 1 March to 31 October, 9.30am to 6pm; 1 November to 28 February, 10am to 5pm
Admission: £11/£8

As well as an outstanding collection of big cats, such as cheetahs, lions, jaguars and tigers, Paradise Wildlife Park is home to many other endangered species, including snow leopards and pied tamarins who are happily rearing their young as part of the European Endangered Species Programme. The Wonders of the Rainforest exhibition houses many types of endangered tamarin, along with the two-toed sloth and the very strange lesser hairy armadillo. At the Angkor Reptile Temple you can come face to face with snakes, turtles, hissing cockroaches from Madagascar and even a Chinese alligator. The park is renowned for its ability to offer visitors more unusual and interactive experiences.

Shepreth Wildlife Park

Address: Willersmill, Station Road, Shepreth, near Royston, Hertfordshire SG8 6PZ
Map: 6, C2
Tel: 01763 262234

Web: www.sheprethwildlifepark.co.uk
Open: daily, 10am to dusk/6pm (except 25 December)
Admission: £5.50/£7.50

Begun as a private wild animal sanctuary in 1979, Shepreth is built around three lakes, with fields and wooded areas. Residents range from the Eurasian lynx and the mountain lion to the primates, including vervet monkeys and crab-eating macaques. Shepreth is also home to wildlife from the UK, such as the red squirrel and fallow deer, and to animals such as the guanaco, hailing from South America. Bug City and Waterworld, a separate interactive attraction located in the main park building, provides a fantastic opportunity to experience giant bugs, spiders, fish, frogs, terrapins and many other insect species.

Tyland Barn Visitor Centre

Near: Maidstone, Kent
Map: 5, B2
Web: www.kentwildlife.org.uk

Tyland Barn is Kent Wildlife Trust's headquarters and its largest visitor centre. Although within walking distance of Westfield Wood, it is more of a demonstration nature park than a reserve, an ideal location for a family outing at any time of year. A restored seventeenth-century barn houses an exhibition on wildlife and conservation, with plenty of hands-on displays for children. Outside the barn, a large pond, meadow, chalkbank and scrub habitat offer a wide variety of plant species. Tadpoles can be seen in spring and summer, and visitors can try their hand at pond-dipping, while a winter visit to the feeding station will reveal which birds are feeding.

ZSL Whipsnade Zoo

Address: Dunstable, Bedfordshire LU6 2LF
Map: 6, A3
Tel: 01582 872171
Web: www.zsl.org/whipsnade
Open: daily, 10am to 4pm (except 25 December)
Admission: £9/£12

One of Europe's largest wildlife parks, Whipsnade is set in 600 acres of beautiful parkland on the Chiltern Hills, just north of London. The park is home to more than 2,500 animals, many endangered in the wild. Visitors can experience larger animals such as the Bactrian camel and Eurasian brown bear, while the pygmy hippopotamus wallows in the waters and both Arabian and scimitar-horned oryx are present. The European grey wolf and Oriental small-clawed otter are among the endangered species resident at Whipsnade, and smaller species such as the green and black poison frog and the red-kneed bird-eating spider are also observable.

Woburn Safari Park

Address: Woburn Park, Bedfordshire MK17 9QN
Map: 6, A3
Tel: 01525 290407
Web: www.woburnsafari.co.uk
Open: varies with season
Admission: £7.50/£8.50

From the comfort of your own car, take an unparalleled look at the park's animals roaming freely and behaving naturally. Visitors can drive the safari circuit as often as desired throughout the day, experiencing the white rhino and giraffes, or bears and wolves running together. Other animals include the zebra, bison, bongo antelope and patas monkey. Once you've taken in the safari reserves, park in the Wild World Leisure Area and experience more animals. To help you plan your day, there is a full timetable of animal demonstrations and keeper talks.

South West

From the rockpools in the coves of Cornwall to the tree-lined river valleys of Devon and the chalky grasslands of Wiltshire's Downs, the south-west corner of England is not only beautiful, it's abundant with wildlife.

There are marine animals spotted here that you are unlikely to see anywhere else in the country, such as turtles who feed in Cornish waters around August to October time.

Basking sharks are also summer visitors. Their large dorsal fins look pretty terrifying when seen on the sea's surface, but this huge creature only eats plankton and poses no danger to man. Some people have even been lucky enough to spot pilot whales off the coast of Devon.

On the seashore, the rockpools are a treasure trove for the wildlife explorer, revealing crabs, starfish, blennies, gobies and all manner of seaweeds and anemones.

Onland, there is a rich diversity of habitats whether you want to walk through beautiful scenery or stay put in one place.

Many of the woodlands of Devon are ancient woodlands on steep hillsides that tumble down to crystal clear rivers and brooks. Walking among the old and gnarled trees is charming at any time of the year but, come springtime, when the forest floors bloom into colour with bluebells, wood anemones and primroses, it's a veritable delight. *Tarka the Otter* was set in Devon and there are otters living in many rivers and streams in the area. However, you'll be lucky to spot this shy and silent animal. Look out for tracks and bubbles rising from the water if you think you're getting close.

The woodlands are also home to badgers, bats, dormice and owls, among others. Although these animals are nocturnal, many begin their night-time adventures around dusk.

Far easier to see wherever you are, are the birds – and the south west has a huge selection. On the open moorland of Dartmoor there are plover, red grouse and skylarks. While the estuaries fill up in the winter time with migrating waders, ducks and geese. The Exe Estuary is well known as a spot where you can see them in their thousands.

Fields and hedgerows are also alive with birds, while the numerous hay meadows in the area are filled with flowers and butterflies throughout spring and early summer.

Whenever you visit the area, and wherever you go, you'll find yourself on the doorstep of a nature reserve or bird reserve, and you won't be disappointed with what you see.

PICTURED: Dartmoor National Park

Not to be missed

● **Dartmoor National Park**
Who can resist the wild ponies who have grazed this open moorland for centuries?

● **Golitha Falls**
One of Britain's most charming nature reserves, with a winding river, waterfalls and butterflies skipping over the meadow plants.

● **Halsdon**
If you've read *Tarka the Otter*, you'll recognise this charming woodland... and you might spot one of Tarka's relations.

● **Lost Gardens of Heligan**
Discover a secret garden and follow trails into woodlands alive with badgers, owls, woodpeckers and songbirds.

● **Scilly Isles**
A unique gem of an archipelago that catches the Gulf Stream and boasts its own microcosm of plant, animal and birdlife. Also good for spotting whales and dolphins.

● **Slimbridge**
These vast wetlands attract migrating waterbirds in their thousands and are home to a large population of flamingos.

Dartmoor National Park

NATIONAL PARKS Dartmoor National Park, Devon

Map: 10, C2
Web: www.dartmoor-npa.gov.uk
Dartmoor National Park covers 368 square miles of Devon. Best known for its rugged and open moorland, the area also includes ancient woodlands and pretty tree-lined river valleys. The range of habitats and wildlife in the park is huge. High on the moor you will find mossy blanket bogs, where dunlin and golden plover nest among the cotton grass and purple moor grass. The surrounding heathland, ablaze with ling, bell and cross-leaved heather, is home to the endangered red grouse and ring ouzel, as well as meadow pipits, stonechats and skylarks. As you descend from the tors through grassland grazed by cattle, sheep and ponies, you'll be walking among turf dotted with milkwort, tormentil and heath bedstraw. Keep an eye out for pearl-bordered, small heath and high brown fritillary butterflies, as well

as wheatears and whinchats. On the sheltered sides of valleys you will come across ancient oak woodland rich in ferns, mosses and lichens and carpeted with bluebells and ramsons in spring. Squirrels, badgers and dormice forage among these ancient trees, and you might catch a glimpse of a pied flycatcher, a wood warbler or a redstart. On the fringes of the moor are the pastures and crop fields of traditional farmland, girded with drystone walls and hedgerows rich with wildflowers. Throughout the summer, the country lanes are busy with gatekeeper butterflies, song thrushes and yellow-hammers, and patrolled at night by owls and bats. Look out for rare orchids in meadows and valley mires and for herons, mink and otters along the riverbanks.

DID YOU KNOW?
The granite tors in Dartmoor are 280 million years old.

AONBs

Cranbourne Chase and West Wiltshire Downs
Near: Salisbury, Wiltshire
Map: 9, B4
Web: www.ccwwdaonb.org.uk
The chalk grassland of this area is an increasingly rare habitat and a good place to find scarce plants such as early gentian, tuberous thistle, dwarf sedge and bastard toadflax. The marsh fritillary and silver-spotted skipper butterflies also frequent this area and water voles can be found in the banks of the chalky rivers. Some of the arable land is adapting its farming practices to encourage birds, such as the skylark, corn bunting, tree sparrow, stone curlew and grey partridge, and these wide field borders are also home to red hemp nettle, dense-flowered fumitory and narrow-fruited cornsalad.

Dorset Coast
Near: Bridport, Dorset
Map: 3, A3
Web: www.dorsetaonb.org.uk
The Dorset coast is good for seabirds and wildflowers and not a bad spot from which to

see dolphins. Wildflowers on the cliffs have adapted to cope with the wind and salt spray, and include sea campion, thrift and sea lavender. On the less accessible cliff ledges, birds, such as puffins, guillemots, kittiwakes and fulmars, nest. On Chesil Beach, a great bank of shingle running from West Bay to Weymouth, there's a variety of colourful wildflowers, such as sea pea, yellow-horned poppy and sea kale. Poole Harbour supports more than 28,000 birds including over-wintering populations of avocet, shelduck and black-tailed godwit. Brownsea Island, in the harbour, is home to one of the few remaining colonies of red squirrels in England.

Mendip Hills
Near: Wells, Somerset
Map: 8, D2
Web: www.mendiphillsaonb.org.uk
The Mendip Hills rise up from the Somerset Levels providing dramatic views of the Severn Estuary and across Somerset. They comprise a mix of woodland, rough grassland, heath and even wetland, so the range of wildlife found in the diffrent habitats here is huge. In the limestone grassland you'll find orchids, dwarf mouse-ear and spring sandwort, while in the woodlands at the right time of year, there are fabulous carpets of bluebells and wild garlic. Beware of mine shafts, much of the area was formerly mined for lead.

South Devon
Near: Wembury and Totnes, Devon
Map: 10, C3
Web: www.southdevonaonb.org.uk
While South Devon's coast is a feast of saltmarshes, mudflats,

cliffs, dunes, shingle, reedbeds and freshwater lagoons, inland there are oak and wet woodlands, cereal field margins, hedges, flower-rich meadows, pastures and coastal grasslands all offering their own wildlife treasures. Many rare species are present in the AONB, including the greater horseshoe bat, strapwort, bittern and shore dock. Other species that are more plentiful in the area include the great green bush cricket, little egret, Cetti's warbler, otter, dormouse, brown hare, primrose and silver-studded blue butterfly.

DID YOU KNOW?
80 per cent of Britain's puffins are found in the South West.

Tamar Valley
Near: Plymouth, Cornwall
Map: 11, D2
Web: www.tamarvalley.org.uk
The Tamar Valley contains many important habitats for wildlife. The Tavy and Lynher estuaries attract great numbers of waterfowl in the winter months, including a large number of avocet. Several areas of semi-natural ancient woodland remain along the estuary shore and in the side valleys of the main rivers. Some of these support rare lichens, rich orchid flora and breeding butterfly populations, including the heath fritillary. Farming in the area is in small and irregular field shapes, defined by a strong network of hedgerows – these are a rich and continuous habitat for wildlife. Some fragments of meadows and pastures remain and are home to a beautiful range of orchids. There is a sizeable area of heathland where Cornish bladderseed

and eyebright grow and Dartford warblers, skylarks and linnets can be seen.

NATURE RESERVES

Black Rock
Near: Cheddar, Somerset
Map: 8, D2
Web: www.somersetwildlife.org
P
The steep slopes of this reserve are worth the climb, both for the views and for the rich flora of the limestone grassland which includes lesser meadow rue, rock stonecrop, spring cinquefoil, thyme, rockrose, violet, small scabious and sald burnet. The hill is alive with butterflies for much of the summer and the lucky might even spot a buzzard. The reserve is a stronghold for the common dormouse – but you'll be lucky to spot one of these nocturnal animals.

Catcott Reserves
Near: Bridgwater, Somerset
Map: 8, C2
Web: www.somersetwildlife.org
P
These four meadows flood every autumn providing an excellent habitat for dabbling ducks who come in their hundreds. From the hide at the car park you'll have an excellent view (the ground is too wet for walking) and you'll probably see peregrine out hunting and flocks of over-wintering lapwing. Come spring and the migrations bring whimbrel, snipe, redshank and yellow wagtail, and you're also likely to spot spoonbill and marsh harriers.

Churchtown Farm CNR
Near: Plymouth, Cornwall
Map: 11, D2
Web: www.cornwallwildlifetrust.org.uk

A comedy of puffins?

An unmistakable bird with its black and white markings, upright stance and distinctive brightly-coloured bill, the puffin's almost comical appearance is heightened by its red and black eye markings and bright orange legs. They like to breed in offshore islands and on high seacliffs, with nests in burrows, under boulders or in cracks in cliffs where predators cannot easily reach them. Best looked for at a breeding colony. Try Bempton Cliffs, South Stack, Farne Islands, the Isle of May and the Shetland and Orkney Islands.

P ⛺

Situated within the Tamar Valley AONB, the majority of this reserve is farmland consisting of haymeadows and arable fields which are great for butterflies, small mammals and flocks of birds in the summer and into autumn. In spring, however, search out the hedgerows, which you'll find are alive with wildflowers and birdsong. In winter, head to the mudflats as oystercatchers, dunlin, egrets, avocet, turnstones and greenshank fly in on their annual migration and you can barely see the ground.

Clattinger Farm
Near: Cirencester, Gloucestershire
Map: 7, D2
Web: www.wiltshirewildlife.org
⛺
This is one of the very few areas of enclosed lowland grassland in the country that has never been sprayed with artificial fertilisers. As a result, from early spring to July (when it is cut for hay), it is a stunning expanse of wildflowers teeming with butterflies and dragonflies. Flower species include snake's-head fritillary, southern marsh, green winged orchid, upright brome and the rare downy-fronted sedge.

Coombe Hill Meadows and Canal SSSI
Near: Gloucester, Gloucestershire
Map: 7, C2
Web: www.coombehillmeadows.co.uk
P ⛺ ⌂
All year round, this disused canal and its surrounding haymeadows have something for the wildlife lover to see. In winter, when the whole reserve is flooded, it's over-wintering

wildfowl including pintail, teal and wigeon. Come spring, and the water recedes, leaving muddy ditches that attract the scrapes and snipes who come out to forage for food and build nests. The harvest mouse is also an inhabitant of these ditches while, in the neighbouring haymeadows, you may even see brown hares boxing. In summer, the meadows at the northern edge of the site provide a perfect habitat for curlew and, in autumn, redwing and fieldfare are seen around the reserves hedgerows in large numbers.

> **DID YOU KNOW?**
> Aristotle wisely said: 'Nature does nothing uselessly.'

Cotswold Commons & Beechwoods NNR
Near: Sheepscombe near Stroud, Gloucestershire
Map: 7, C2
Web: www.english-nature.org.uk
P at Cranham, ⛺
Some of Britain's finest beechwoods can be found in the three woodlands which make up this reserve. Other tree species include ash, pedunculate oak, sycamore, wych elm, field maple, whitebeam, holly and yew. On the woodland floor you'll find wood anemone, sanicle, bluebell, green hellebore and bird's-nest orchid and common wintergreen. There are rarer plants, too, including fingered sedge, stinking hellebore and yellow star of Bethlehem. While your eyes are on the ground you're bound to spot spiders and snails here too and, if you're lucky, you might spot a white admiral or a white-letter hairstreak. Breeding birds include tawny owl, buzzard and wood warbler.

Draycott Sleights
Near: Cheddar, Somerset
Map: 8, D2
Web: www.somersetwildlife.org
Not only do you get fine views over the Somerset Levels, Glastonbury Tor and the Quantocks from this grassy reserve, you also get more than 200 species of flora. These include rockrose, marjoram, bird's-foot trefoil, oxeye daisy, knapweed, salad burnet and small scabious. Not surprisingly, the abundant flowers attract a good crop of butterflies – 34 species have been recorded including marbled white and chalkhill blue. In the spring and the early summer you're likely to be accompanied by the song of the skylark and able to watch peregrines teaching their young how to hunt.

Dunkery & Horner Woods NNR
Near: Minehead, Somerset
Map: 8, B2
Web: www.english-nature.org.uk
P at Horner, ♿ ⛺
This reserve near the northern boundary of Exmoor National Park, comprises two sites: Horner Woods and an upland area of heathland on Dunkery Hill. Horner Woods is an ancient oakwood that is an important site for mosses, liverworts, lichens and ferns. Local birdlife includes the pied flycatcher, wood warbler, lesser spotted woodpecker, redstart and dipper. The woods are also home to 14 of the UK's 16 known bat species, including breeding roosts of the barbastelle and Bechstein's bats. The upland area exhibits a complete range of heathland habitats showing a transition from 'true' upland down to lowland heath and has a good population of heath fritillary butterflies. Moorland birds seen here

include stonechat, whinchat, curlew, ring ouzel and merlin.

Dunsdon
Near: Holsworthy, Devon
Map: 10, B2
Web: www.devonwildlifetrust.org
P WC P

This is one of the few remaining Culm grassland sites in England and is a spectacle of colour every spring. Wildflowers and orchids fill the meadows and the delicate scent of meadow thistle hangs in the air. It's a breeding site for marsh fritillary butterflies and from mid-May to June the air is full of them. Herons nest in nearby treetops and it's a popular location for buzzards. As autumn approaches, the reserve becomes wetter and holds less appeal, apart from the possible sighting of a barn or short-eared owl.

Dunsford
Near: Exeter, Devon
Map: 10, D2
Web: www.devonwildlifetrust.org
P P

In spring, the glades of this reserve are carpeted in yellow wild daffodils which line the banks of the River Teign. Butterflies abound, including rare ones, such as the high brown and pearl-bordered fritillary. In the oak woodlands, look out for pied flycatchers, dormice and badger setts (badgers, too, if you're there at dusk or later). Down by the river, there are otters to spot while all over the heather-covered heathland there are bees busy making honey.

East Dartmoor Woods and Heath
Near: Newton Abbott, Devon
Map: 10, C3
Web: www.english-nature.org.uk
P P

There are three woodlands on this reserve, and in spring they are full of the sounds of songbirds, including chiffchaffs, willow warblers and flycatchers. Sparrowhawks also like this site for the rich pickings of baby birds that they can prey on. Come autumn, the songbirds have left and flocks of redwing and fieldfares arrive to graze on the rowan and holly berries. Over winter, the birds are fed outside a hide and you're likely to spot great tits and great spotted woodpecker.

Five Acres
Near: Truro, Cornwall
Map: 11, B2
Web: www.cornwallwildlifetrust.org.uk
P i

This was once a much-loved private garden and The Wildlife Trusts has stayed true to its heritage and converted it into an environmental awareness and wildlife garden demonstration reserve. BBC television programme *Ground Force* created the wildlife garden which comes into its own in autumn. Three species of shrew have been found here and palmate newts with their webbed feet live around the ponds. There are three small circular walks around the garden which take in the woodland, heather garden and bog garden.

Folly Farm
Near: Bristol, Somerset
Map: 8, D1
Web: www.avonwildlifetrust.org.uk
P

This peaceful and unspoilt working farm has meadows and woodland that are a haven for wildlife. In springtime, the floor of the woodland comes alive with primroses, bluebells and early purple orchids. Tawny owls nest in the trees and nuthatch, buzzard and great spotted woodpecker can be seen. The meadows are filled with beautiful wildflowers and dancing with butterflies – including the rare marsh fritillary – from springtime onwards.

Fyfield Down NNR
Near: Marlborough, Wiltshire
Map: 9, C2
Web: www.english-nature.org.uk
P near village of Broad Hinton

Situated on a high plateau of chalk grassland, Fyfield Down displays the best collection of sarsen stones in Britain. Sarsen stones are large boulders of

Spot the difference

There are many species of wild orchids in the UK but the ones you are most likely to see are the early purple orchid (pictured) and the green winged orchid. They both look very similar, with purple flowers, but the early purple orchid is more likely to be seen in woodland and the green winged orchid in meadows. Find them at Deep Dale, Winks Meadow, Pwll y Wrach, Marble Arch and along the River Forth.

Pictured: Purple orchid

Hambledon Hill

Grazed farmland and flower-rich hay meadows with the clear-watered Cotswold stream running through them ensure there's always something to see here. Perhaps it will be a resident barn owl hunting in the meadows at dusk in the summer, or a water vole scrabbling along a river bank in the autumn. Thick hedgerows are always good for songbirds who are at their most vocal in the early spring. Wildflowers throughout the summer include southern marsh orchids, ragged robin and pepper saxifrage.

siliceous sandstone that were transported to the area through glacial action during the Ice Age. Ancient peoples used these stones for building purposes and today they support rare lichen and moss communities. This special place, which is part of a World Heritage site, supports unusual wildlife, including the brown argus and marbled white butterflies, green woodpecker and roe deer.

Goss Moor NNR
Near: Roche near St Austell, Cornwall
Map: 11, C2
Web: www.english-nature.org.uk
P
Goss Moor is a unique combination of wetland habitats and more characteristic western dry heath. The site's wetland habitats – including fen meadow, bog, wet heath and open water – are a result of extensive mining operations that have been carried out in the area, which ceased in 1960. Breeding birds on the site include nightjar, reed bunting, linnet, spotted flycatcher, bullfinch and song thrush. Winter visitors include

hen harrier, great grey shrike and hobby. A number of scarce invertebrates are found at the site, including small red and variable damselflies, silver-studded blue, marsh and small pearl-bordered fritillary butterflies and narrow-bordered bee hawk and double-line moths.

Greena Moor
Near: Bude Cornwall
Map: 11, D1
Web: www.plantlife.org.uk
A rich diversity of plants thrive in the wet conditions of the culm grassland at Greena Moor including bog pimpernel, marsh violet, saw-wort and abundant meadow thistle and devil's-bit scabious. Rare species such as wavy St John's wort and whorled caraway can also be seen. Cattle graze the grassland for most of the year, but are taken off during the wet winter months.

Greystones Farm and Salmonsbury Meadows
Near: Cheltenham, Gloucestershire
Map: 7, D1
Web: www.gloucestershirewildlifetrust.co.uk
P

Hambledon Hill NNR
Near: Blandford Forum, Dorset
Map: 3, B2
Web: www.english-nature.org.uk
P near Child Okeford
Hambledon Hill NNR is an area of dramatic chalk grassland that rises steeply between the Stour and Iwerne valleys. The hilltop is encircled by an Iron Age earthwork and there are extensive and complex Neolithic features, making it a site of major archaeological importance. The grassland provides the main wildlife interest at the site but there are also areas of mixed scrub and a small yew wood. The reserve's thin infertile soils provide ideal conditions for a variety of fine grasses, sedges and flowering plants, particularly on the steep south and west-facing slopes. One of the key wildlife attractions is the local butterflies, including dingy skipper, grizzled skipper, chalkhill blue and Adonis blue.

Hardington Moor NNR
Near: Yeovil, Somerset
Map: 8, D3
Web: www.english-nature.org.uk
P

Golitha Falls

Hardington Moor NNR comprises three meadows surrounded by established hedges. The site covers partly calcareous clay-rich soils on sloping ground. The meadows are examples of species-rich unimproved neutral grassland, which is now nationally rare. The rare French oat grass is abundant on the site and the fields are home to a wide variety of plant species, most notably adder's tongue, corky-fruited water dropwort and large numbers of green winged orchid. Invertebrates found at the site include butterflies, such as gatekeeper, small tortoiseshell and common blue. Less commonly seen are large skipper, green-veined white and green hairstreak. The best time to visit the site is between early May and early July for butterflies and wildflowers.

Golitha Falls NNR

Near: Liskeard, Cornwall
Map: 11, D2
Web: www.english-nature.org.uk

Golitha NNR, on the southern edge of Bodmin Moor, is a famous local beauty spot. Oak and ash woodland covers the sides of a steep valley gorge, descending towards the River Fowey which flows along the bottom in a series of spectacular cascades. An old planted beech avenue is notable for the lichens festooning the upper branches while, elsewhere 50 liverwort species have been recorded, together with 98 moss species, some rare. Groundplants in the woodland include greater woodrush, bilberry, hard fern, wavy-hair grass and common cow-wheat as well as large patches of bluebells, and meadow areas which are home to plants, such as bugle, self-heal, white clover, common tormentil and valerian. These are best between April and July. The local area contains many abandoned mine workings and some of these are home to bats, such as the noctule, brown long-eared and lesser horseshoe. Some 30 species of breeding birds have been recorded at the site, including buzzard, dipper, nuthatch and treecreeper. The site supports 83 moth species, including the notable double-line. Local butterflies include the meadow brown, marbled white, green-veined white, gatekeeper, small skipper, ringlet, speckled wood and silver-washed fritillary.

Hartland Moor NNR

Near: Poole, Dorset
Map: 3, C3
Web: www.english-nature.org.uk
P in villages of Norden, Arne and Ridge, ♿ via Hartland Way, ⌂
Hartland Moor is adjacent to Stoborough Heath NNR and is a superb example of an extensive heathland site. The NNR covers an entire drainage basin and is unique in having a Y-shaped bog system which includes both acid and alkaline drainage systems. Heathland is a rare and threatened habitat, and many of the species of plants and animals found at Hartland are equally rare. Heathland insects include rare heath and large marsh grasshoppers and the site supports birds, such as Dartford warbler, hobby, meadow pipit, stonechat, nightjar and hen harrier.

Helman Tor

Near: Bodmin, Cornwall
Map: 11, C2
Web: www.cornwallwildlifetrust.org.uk
P ♿ (ltd), **☕**
This large wetland complex includes both dry and wet heathland, mire, sphagnum bog, wet woodland and open water. Willow tits, reed buntings, sedge and grasshopper warblers come here to breed and dragonflies, damselflies and butterflies – including the rare marsh fritillary – are found in abundance.

Hog Cliff NNR

Near: Dorchester, Dorset
Map: 3, B3
Web: www.english-nature.org.uk
☕
This is a chalk downland area comprising three seperate sites centred on Hog Cliff Hill. The reserve has downland slopes, with rich grassland communities typical of the chalk of west-central Dorset. Areas of scrub (principally on the upper slopes) and small areas of woodland add diversity to the site. The grassland supports a wide range of grasses, herbs and flowering plants. More than 100 species of fungi have also been recorded. Butterflies bring a lively splash of colour to the reserve during the summer. These include the rare Adonis blue and marsh fritillary and the more common species, such as the green hairstreak, common blue, gatekeeper, grizzled skipper and dingy skipper.

DID YOU KNOW?

The word for a young hedgehog is a hoglet.

Holt Heath NNR

Near: Ferndown, Dorset
Map: 3, C2
Web: www.english-nature.org.uk
P ☕ ⓘ
Holt Heath NNR is one of Dorset's largest remaining areas of lowland heathland. To the north west of the heath are two separate areas of semi-natural ancient woodland (Holt Forest and Holt Wood) that are also part of the reserve. Dry heath, wet heath and mire communities are all represented at the site. This is a wildlife haven. Bring your binoculars to make sure you spot Dartford warblers, stonechats and nightjars. The heath is also Dorset's only site for breeding curlew and all six of Britain's reptile species are found here. The best time to visit the site is July and August for wildflowers.

Jones's Mill,
the Vera Jeans Reserve

Near: Pewsey, Wiltshire

Map: 9, C3
Web: www.wiltshirewildlife.org
☕
The wet conditions in this fenland site make it ideal for spotting kingfisher, snipe, heron, dragonflies and the elusive water shrew. In springtime the reserve bursts into colour with pink-ragged robin, yellow flag iris and lady's-smock vying for space in the meadows. Wellies are recommended at all times of the year.

Kingcombe Meadows

Near: Beaminster, Dorset
Map: 3, A2
Web: www.wildlifetrust.org.uk/dorset
P WC ⓘ
This former low-intensity farm in the heart of Hardy country is quintessentially English, with green lanes, ancient hedgerows, mature trees and small gently flowing streams. Cows and sheep are still grazed here and every spring you can watch them tenderly care for their young. Wildflower meadows, mixed parties of tits and warblers in the hedgerows and the occasional otter are all added attractions at this wonderfully charming site.

Lancaut SSSI

Near: Chepstow, Monmouthshire
Map: 7, B2
Web: www.gloucestershirewildlifetrust.org.uk
P ☕
The dramatic cliffs at this site don't just offer fantastic views over the Wye Valley Gorge, they are also great for wildlife. Britain's fastest bird, the peregrine falcon, nests on the rock face and wildflowers such as hairy violet, lesser calamint, red valerian and shining crane's bill grow from the cracks and crevices. The ancient woodland surrounding

the cliffs is a fantastic example of its type with small-leaved lime and many rare whitebeams found here as well as beautiful old oaks and field maples.

The Lizard NNR
Near: Helston, Cornwall
Map: 11, B1
Web: www.english-nature.org.uk
This large promontory on the south coast of Cornwall contains some unique heathlands and spectacular rugged cliffs. Many uncommon plants are found here, such as orchids, harebells and dropwort, as well as the nationally rare Cornish heath heather. From the cliffs, look out for kittiwakes, peregrines and even choughs and seals surfacing down below.

Morden Bog NNR
Near: Wareham, Dorset
Map: 3, B3
Web: www.english-nature.org.uk
🅿 🛈
This valley bog carves its niche between the pine plantations of Wareham Forest. Plantlife includes carnivorous plants such as the common sundew and bladderwort, as well as the rare marsh clubmoss and brown-beak sedge. It is also home to bog asphodel. Many types of dragonfly are drawn to the damp land, together with reptiles such as the smooth snake and sand lizard. In the drier north of the reserve, the plant turns to heather and birds such as woodlark and nightjar are found.

North Meadow, Cricklade NNR
Near: Swindon, Wiltshire
Map: 9, B1
Web: www.english-nature.org.uk
🅿
North Meadow is one of the finest examples of a lowland hay meadow in Europe and

The Lizard NNR

supports Britain's largest population of the rare snake's-head fritillary with its delicate bell-like flowers appearing from April onwards. The balance of plants shifts over the year and is at its height in June, dominated by rich purple greater burnet and common knapweed, the yellows of cowslip, meadow buttercup and yellow-rattle mix with oxeye daisies, meadow rue and meadowsweet, while 20 species of grass add to the colour. The plants attract countless insects, including brightly-coloured burnet moths, dramatic blue damselflies and a host of beetles. The boundary hedges are filled with birdlife.

Pewsey Downs NNR
Near: Pewsey, Wiltshire
Map: 9, C3
Web: www.english-nature.org.uk
🅿
It is a combination of the steep slope, nutrient-poor soil and localised climate that has created the flower-rich grasslands of this reserve, where more vigorous plants cannot survive. The flowers that can are thriving and include common spotted, frog and fragrant orchids, field

fleawort, early gentian, round-headed rampion and bastard toadflax. Butterflies include marbled white, skipper, green hairstreak, wall brown and chalkhill blue.

Powerstock Common
Near: Beaminster, Dorset
Map: 3, A2
Web: www.wildlifetrust.org.uk/dorset
P

The mosaic of habitats on this site includes grasslands, wet and dry woodlands, ponds and streams and the range of wildlife you'll find is correspondingly diverse. Chiffchaffs, willow warblers, white-throats, blackcaps, marsh tits and great spotted woodpeckers are all here. The grassland flowers, including sneezewort, betony and bee orchid, are visited by a colourful range of butterflies while, if you have the patience to watch over the ponds, you might catch a glimpse of the great crested newt. Come winter, it's a popular haunt with fallow and roe deer.

Rodney Stoke NNR
Near: Wells, Somerset
Map: 8, D2
Web: www.english-nature.org.uk

Two woodlands are linked by abandoned fields that have turned to scrub, to create Rodney Stoke NNR. Small-leaved limes that were once coppiced give a dappled cover to a woodland floor that is rich with plantlife from dog's mercury, ivy and bluebells, to hart's-tongue fern, ground ivy and enchanter's nightshade. Some species seen here – such as wood anemone, nettle-leaved bellflower, meadow saffron and wood spurge – are characteristic of ancient woodland and two nationally rare plants, purple gromwell

and endemic whitebeam, are also found here. Pipistrelle and noctule bats roost in the network of branches and buzzards and spotted flycatchers come here to breed.

Ryewater Farm
Near: Beaminster, Dorset
Map: 3, A2
Web: www.plantlife.org.uk

Ryewater Farm is a truly charming nature reserve with unimproved pasture and species-rich hay meadows, enclosed by thick hedgerows and ancient woodland. In the summer, plentiful grassland flowers include dyer's greenweed, pepper saxifrage, oxeye daisy and corky-fruited water dropwort. Visit before mid-July when the hay gets cut, as do the flowers. The woodland areas are dominated by ash, oak, birch and hazel with an interesting ground flora including dog's mercury, wood anemone and moschatel. Ryewater Farm is registered as organic and is managed by a combination of hay-making and cattle grazing.

DID YOU KNOW?

The UK's largest wintering flock of avocet is found at Brownsea Island and is over 1,000 in number.

Shapwick Heath NNR
Near: Glastonbury, Somerset
Map: 8, D2
Web: www.english-nature.org.uk
(ltd),

Shapwick Heath NNR is a major wetland reserve forming a large part of the Avalon Marshes. Its wide variety of habitats includes traditionally-managed, herb-rich grassland, ferny wet

woodland, fen, scrub and ditches rich in aquatic plants and invertebrates. Otters, as well as many insects, plants and birds, populate the whole area. Small pockets of sphagnum moss, which once covered the whole valley floor, can also be found. The best time to visit the reserve for the local flora is in the spring, for birds the site can be visited all year round.

Skylark Meadows
Near: Bridgwater, Somerset
Map: 8, C2
Web: www.plantlife.org.uk

These fields are an oasis for wildlife in the middle of an intensely farmed landscape. Skylarks nest on the meadows each year and the constant sound of their wonderful song during the summer months inspired local people to name the fields Skylark Meadows. Flowers such as yellow-rattle, corky-fruited water dropwort, oxeye daisy, meadow vetchling and pepper saxifrage add colour to the hay meadows in the summer, and in the spring a good display of cowslips can be seen.

Slapton Ley NNR
Near: Kingsbridge, Devon
Map: 10, C3
Web: www.english-nature.org.uk
P WC

A large shingle bar separates a freshwater lake from the sea, providing an interesting habitat for birds and plants. Cetti's warbler, bittern and stonechat are all seen here, while rare plants include the yellow-horned poppy and strapwort. There is a hazel coppice on the reserve worth visiting in springtime, when its floor blooms with a combination of primroses, wild garlic, red campion, herb robert and bluebells.

Valley of Stones

sand lizards and smooth snakes that enjoy the dry heath, to bog orchids, cotton grass and raft spiders in the wet areas. Popular with resident UK birds and winter visitors, you can see Dartford warbler, fieldfare, meadow pipit, stonechat and redwing here. In the summer, there are butterflies, beautiful wildflowers, damselflies, orchids and beetles to attract your attention.

Stoborough Heath NNR

Near: Poole Harbour, Dorset
Map: 3, C3
Web: www.english-nature.org.uk
🌐 via Hartland Way
Stoborough Heath is a heathland reserve adjacent to Hartland Moor NNR. The habitat is made up of dry heath, mire and acid grassland. The heath is carefully maintained to provide a unique habitat for wildlife. Gorse is cut in rotation to provide habitat for nesting birds. Sand patches are rotavated to enable sand lizards to lay their eggs and to create habitat for burrowing wasps. Scrub is also cut to halt succession from heath to woodland. Invertebrates found at the site include the rare wartbiter cricket, as well as golden-ringed, ruddy darter and keeled skimmer dragonflies. Local bird species include nightjar, Dartford warbler, merlin and skylark.

Studland and Godlingston Heath NNR

Near: Swanage, Dorset
Map: 3, C3
Web: www.english-nature.org.uk
🅿 🌐 wc 📷 🚻
The Studland and Godlingston Heath NNR is on the Isle of Purbeck. The reserve

includes three miles of sandy beaches and has a wide variety of habitats: heathland, woodland, scrub, bogs, freshwater and sand dunes. The sand dune ridges have built up over the last 400 years to enclose an acidic freshwater lake – the Little Sea – in the north of the reserve. The lake attracts over-wintering wildfowl and there are four hides overlooking it. Godlingston Heath is one of the largest remaining tracts of lowland heathland. The site supports large populations of Dartford warblers, nightjars and all six British reptile species. Wintering waders feed here at low tide and many then move to the north end of Studland Beach to rest at high tide. Little egrets roost throughout the winter. The reserve also has particularly rich populations of dragonflies, grasshoppers, bees and wasps.

Tadnoll and Winfrith

Near: Dorchester, Dorset
Map: 3, B3
Web: www.wildlifetrust.org.uk/dorset
🅿 (ltd), 🌐 (ltd)
The variety of heathland habitats at this site attracts a huge range of wildlife, from

Valley of Stones NNR

Near: Dorchester, Dorset
Map: 3, B3
Web: www.english-nature.org.uk
🅿 1km east at National Trust Hardy Monument, 🚻
The Valley of Stones derives its name from the impressive train of boulders tumbling down the slope and floor of the dry chalk valley. The stones were formed at the end of the last Ice Age as the tightly cemented sandstone that capped the chalk hillsides gradually fragmented and slumped downhill, under freeze/thaw conditions. The fine chalk grassland slopes are rich in butterflies and wildflowers, such as autumn gentian, clustered bellflower and Adonis blue. The stones support many lichens, some of which are extremely rare. The grassland is managed using grazing animals, in particular cattle and sheep.

Westhay Moor NNR

Near: Glastonbury, Somerset
Map: 8, D2
Web: www.english-nature.org.uk
🅿 🚻 🏠 (inc 🌐)
Westhay Moor consists mainly of restored peat fields and water-filled compartments containing islands with areas of reeds and bulrushes. There are numerous animals to look out for on the reserve, including

eco-watch

HELIGAN WILDLIFE PROJECT

This pioneering project takes you to Horsemoor Hide where interactive technology
using live and recorded footage (eco-watch) brings you an intimate view of the
diverse wildlife found on this sensitively managed 200 acre estate.
Wildlife Trails take you on an exploration through our grassland, woodland and
wetland revealing a variety of wildlife habitats, flora and fauna.
www.eco-watch.com   01726 843744

Heligan, Pentewan, St. Austell PL26 6EN
www.heligan.com info@heligan.com 01726 845100

mammals, such as otter, water vole, water shrew and harvest mouse. Badgers and roe deer also forage across the reserve and adders and grass snakes have been recorded as well. It is the birdlife that is the most impressive, though. The reeds attract visiting bittern and bearded tit, while barn owl, marsh harrier, hen harrier, hobby, nightjar tree pipit and nightingale also make their home here. In the winter months, millions of starlings come in to roost just before dusk, creating a spectacle which attracts hundreds of visitors.

Willsbridge Valley
Near: Bristol, Avon
Map: 7, B3
Web: www.avonwildlifetrust.org.uk

This charming bluebell wood with streams and ponds is nestled in a valley surrounded by modern housing developments on the edge of Bristol. The ponds attract frogs and newts and, in the summer, dragonflies skim across the surfaces. The streams are alive with wildlife, including eel and bullhead in the water, otter and water vole on the banks and kingfisher and dipper overhead. There's also a sculpture trail here that adds to the appeal of this secret gem.

BIRD RESERVES

Arne
Near: Wareham, Dorset
Map: 3, B3
Web: www.rspb.org.uk

Arne is a fantastic example of lowland heathland, which is a rare habitat in Europe. It is home to nearly 500 types of flowering plant, and attracts Dartford warblers and nightjars. All six species of British reptile are present here as well as many species of butterflies, dragonflies, and moths.

Aylesbeare Common
Near: Exeter, Devon
Map: 10, D2
Web: www.rspb.org.uk

Like Arne in Dorset, this is another rare area of lowland heathland. During the day, you can see Dartford warblers, stonechats and yellow-hammers perching on top of the gorse and, from spring to autumn, hobbies hunt dragonflies in the air. Linger until dusk on a still summer evening and you could enjoy the sight and sound of 'churring' male nightjars as they display to females and rivals.

Exe Estuary
Near: Exeter, Devon
Map: 10, D2
Web: www.rspb.org.uk

This reserve has two separate areas of coastal grazing marsh on opposite sides of the estuary. In spring, look for breeding lapwings and redshanks. However, it is the sheer number of birds that you can see in winter that makes the Exe Estuary so spectacular. Visit during floods and at high tide to see thousands of ducks, geese and wading birds, such as curlew, lapwing, black-tailed godwit and wigeon, roosting and feeding, as well as several hundred avocets.

Garston Wood
Near: Salisbury, Wiltshire
Map: 9, B4
Web: www.rspb.org.uk

This charming site of ancient woodland is teeming with wildlife as well as birds. Dormice, bats and badgers can be spotted if you're patient and, in spring and summer, you can walk through magnificent displays of woodland flowers with butterflies flitting around. There are many different species of birds to look out for. Keep an ear out for the gentle purring of the turtle dove in spring and summer and an eye out for the flash of a male bullfinch's pink chest.

Greylake
Near: Bridgwater, Somerset
Map: 8, C2
Web: www.rspb.org.uk
Farming only stopped in these low-lying fields in Dorset's floodplains in 1999 and the RSPB has been busy putting in new ditches and digging out shallow pools to create the ideal conditions for wetland birds. Lapwings, snipe, curlews and redshanks are now regulars at the reserve along with other ground-nesting birds such as yellow wagtails – of which there were 19 pairs in 2005 – skylarks and meadow pipits. In winter, the land floods and flocks of lapwings, golden plovers and other waders arrive, as well as wintering wigeon, teal, shoveler and Bewick's swan.

Ham Wall
Near: Glastonbury, Somerset
Map: 8, D2
Web: www.rspb.org.uk

Ham Wall, a newly-created wetland of more than 490 acres, lies in the northern part of the Somerset levels and Moors about three miles west of Glastonbury. The reedbeds here come alive in spring with the explosive song of the Cetti's warbler, the squeal of the water rail, the chattering of reed warblers and sometimes even the 'boom' of the male bittern. In summer, at dawn and dusk, barn owls can be seen eagerly looking for voles and mice for their young, while broods of young ducks and grebes bob in and out of the reedbed edges.

Hayle Estuary

Near: St Ives Cornwall
Map: 11, B1
Web: www.rspb.org.uk

As Britain's warmest estuary, this is where all other birds come to when it gets too cold elsewhere. There have been as many as 18,000 birds in this reserve at one time. Migrant and over-wintering wildfowl and waders provide the main bird interest and there is a large gathering of gulls. During bad weather in winter, seaducks and divers also take refuge here, in Carnsew Pool.

Lodmoor

Near: Weymouth, Dorset
Map: 3, B3

Web: www.rspb.org.uk

When you find a range of habitats together like this – reedbed, open water, saltmarsh, wet grassland and bushes – you find a wide selection of bird species too. Bearded tit and Cetti's warbler can be seen here all year. In spring, look out for the common tern, who often fly long distances to carry fish back to their young. In autumn, a variety of migrating birds arrive, including a good selection of wading birds. In winter, bitterns, pochards and tufted ducks can be seen and, if you are lucky, water pipits

Marazion Marsh

Near: Penzance, Cornwall
Map: 11, A3
Web: www.rspb.org.uk

This large reedbed with views over St Michael's Mount, has plenty of birdlife from stonechats and linnets to sand martins and warblers. It has some quirky goings-on, too. Grey herons make their nests in the reeds here, rather than the trees, chiffchaffs sometimes stay all year rather

than migrating to north Africa and bitterns, too, are resident albeit difficult to spot among the reeds.

Radipole Lake

Near: Weymouth, Dorset
Map: 3, B3
Web: www.rspb.org.uk

This large expanse of reedbed is popular with starlings who gather here in huge roosting flocks in winter, making spectacular formations in the sky. Come spring, the reeds are full of the sound of sedge and reed warblers and flocks of swallows and martins dart over the water. There are large numbers of butterflies and dragonflies, hobbies can be seen catching the dragonflies – and small birds – in their talons and eating them mid-flight.

West Sedgemoor

Near: Taunton, Somerset
Map: 8, C3
Web: www.rspb.org.uk

This large area of wet meadow is a popular breeding area for wading birds. In the

Woodpeckers: too shy, shy

The best time of year for spotting woodpecker is springtime when they are out in force drumming on the tree trunks and the leaf cover is thin enough to see up to the tops of the trees. There are three woodpecker species in the UK, the great spotted woodpecker, the lesser spotted woodpecker and the green woodpecker. All three of them have a tendency to move around a tree to the side away from any observer which makes them frustrating to spot, but the green woodpecker does come out of the tree to feed on ants and insects in heath and grassland. Places where you might manage to creep up on them include Blean Woods, Fore Wood, Duncombe Park, Hackfall Woods and Mumbles Hill.

Pictured: Great spotted woodpecker

woodland on the edge of the reserve there is one of the UK's largest heronries that is best visited between March and June. During the winter floods the reserve attracts Bewick's swans, as well as teal, wigeon and lapwing in their thousands.

FORESTS & WOODLAND

Adcombe Wood and Woodram Copse
Near: Taunton, Somerset
Map: 8, C3
Web: www.woodlandtrust.org.uk
P
This steeply-sloped woodland is part of the Blackdown Hills which span the borders of Devon and Somerset. There are areas of coppice and scrub woodland, but it is mainly noted for its broad-leaved trees and especially the oaks in the ancient woodland area that date back to the nineteenth century. There is a grass field at the southern end of the woodland which is lovely to see, full of flowers in the springtime and butterflies throughout the summer.

Brown's Folly
Near: Bath, Avon
Map: 7, C3
Web: www.avonwildlifetrust.org.uk
P
Brown's Folly stands high above the River Avon with commanding views towards Bath. Woodland and scrub carpet the remains of old stone quarries and you'll find wild thyme, harebell and nine species of orchid growing here and woodpeckers tapping on the trunks above. The disused mine shafts are now home to greater horseshoe bats while the damp cliff faces support a variety of ferns, fungi and spiders.

Cabilla and Redrice Woods
Near: Bodmin, Cornwall
Map: 11, C2
Web: www.cornwallwildlifetrust.org.uk
P
This is one of the largest sites of ancient woodland in Cornwall and is alive with wildlife. Insects, including the rare blue ground beetle, scurry around, butterflies abound and on a calm summer's evening, you may even see one of the five species of bats that live here swooping for their prey. If you're very lucky you could even catch a glimpse of an otter around the River Fowey. Springtime brings colour to the woodland floor with wood anemones, bluebells and ramsons while in the trees, pied flycatchers, nuthatches, treecreepers and woodpeckers go about their preparations for breeding. The autumn fungi displays are fantastic.

Cardinham Woods
Near: Bodmin, Cornwall
Map: 11, C2
Web: www.forestry.gov.uk
P (££), **WC**
Cardinham is a large area of mixed woodland including oak, rowan, alder, willow and beech, and has many paths and cycle paths. There are deer, buzzard, otter and kingfisher here, as well as many other woodland birds. In the autumn the changing leaves are truly spectacular – best viewed from the Lady Vale walk – and the ground throws up a wonderful display of fungi.

Duncliffe Wood, Dorset
Near: Shaftesbury, Dorset
Map: 3, B2
Web: www.woodlandtrust.org.uk
P
This area of mixed woodland with great views over the sweeping Dorset valleys, is a reservoir of wildlife with a rich butterfly population including silver-washed fritillary, white admiral and purple hairstreak. Other resident wildlife includes roe deer, badgers, tawny owls, bats and an array of birds such as buzzard, woodpecker and treecreeper. Notable plants here include moschatel, yellow archangel, wood speedwell and early-purple orchid.

Fyne Court
Near: Taunton Somerset
Map: 8, C3
Web: www.somersetwildlife.org
P (££), **i**
This fine area of woodland also hosts an arboretum of more than 50 species of trees. Much of the woodland is oak and ash and, in summer, the early morning and evening choruses of birds are wonderful to hear. Great spotted woodpeckers nest here and you're also likely to spot treecreepers, nuthatches, chiffchaffs and blackcaps. Roe deer live in the woods but they tend to slope off when they hear humans around.

Halsdon
Near: Great Torrington, Devon
Map: 10, B1
Web: www.devonwildlifetrust.org
P (ltd),
This large woodland site with a river running through it was the setting for Henry Williamson's novel *Tarka the Otter* and there's a strong population still resident here. A stroll along the very picturesque riverbank offers the chance to see kingfisher, dipper and sand martin, while in the woodland, nesting birds include the pied flycatcher and the wood warbler. This is one of the few areas in Britain where you're likely to see the white-legged damselfly.

Hardwick Wood
Near: Plymouth, Devon
Map: 10, B3
Web: www.woodlandtrust.org.uk
Hardwick Wood is situated
on a hilltop on the outskirts
of Plymouth and Plympton
village. A mainly native broad-
leaved wood, it is criss-crossed
by a network of wide grass
rides and narrow paths. The
wood includes many of the
species you'd expect to find
in an ancient semi-native
woodland and has a superb
show of bluebell, ransom and
campion during the spring.

Highbury Wood

Highbury Wood NNR
Near: Monmouth, Gloucestershire
Map: 7, B2
Web: www.english-nature.org.uk
🏕
Highbury Wood is part of
an almost unbroken chain of
ancient woods stretching from
Chepstow to Ross-on-Wye. The
ancient woodland of Highbury
has unbroken links with the
'wildwood' which colonised the
area after the last Ice Age. Yew
trees are a particular feature
of the reserve and some may
be more than 300 years old.
Its untouched nature means it
has retained a great variety of
plant and animal species. The
dense tangle of bramble and
shrub offers protection and
food to scrub-nesting birds,
such as blackcap and garden
warbler. Another beneficiary is
the dormouse, which relies on a
wide range of nuts, berries and
– critically – honeysuckle.

Lady Park Wood NNR
Near: Monmouth, Herefordshire
Map: 7, B2
Web: www.english-nature.org.uk
Lady Park Wood NNR is part
of a large woodland complex
in the Wye Valley and one of
Britain's most important areas
for woodland conservation.
The main tree species are
beech, oak, ash, small and

large-leaved lime, wych elm
and birch. Other trees include
maple, aspen, cherry, yew,
whitebeam, alder and sallow.
The most abundant and
widespread shrub is hazel, but
dogwood, spindle, hawthorn,
privet and holly are also
present. Ground plants of
interest include wood barley,
fingered sedge, wild madder,
bird's-nest orchid, toothwort,
lily-of-the-valley and herb
paris. A rich breeding bird
community includes all
three woodpecker species,
redstart, wood warbler,
tawny owl, pied flycatcher
and treecreeper.

Langley Wood NNR
Near: Salisbury, Wiltshire
Map: 9, B4
Web: www.english-nature.org.uk
♿ (ltd), 🏕
Langley Wood NNR is an
extensive tract of ancient
(mainly oak) forest that stands
on acid clays, locally overlain
by sands and gravels. This
unique soil and drainage has
produced a rich and diverse
woodland and several species
of tree and shrub present here
are now rare or extinct in the
New Forest. Most notable
of these is small-leaved lime.
The local plantlife includes

indicators of ancient woodland
such as orpine, Solomon's seal
and southern woodrush. The
site also supports many 'old
forest' lichens. Five species of
deer are found in the wood
together with dormice and
breeding birds, such as wood
warbler, woodcock and lesser
spotted woodpecker.

Leigh Woods NNR
Near: Bristol, Avon
Map: 7, B3
Web: www.english-nature.org.uk
♿
This woodland that clads
the steep banks across the
River Avon from Bristol is
predominately mixed, broad-
leaved woodland. Rare tree
species include the Bristol
whitebeam and Wilmotts
whitebeam. More than 300
species of fungi have been
recorded in the surrounding
area and many of these are
found in the NNR itself.
Woodland birds, including
song thrush, bullfinch and
wood warbler, dine richly on
the wood's large population of
insects. The site also includes
an area of dry limestone
grassland where Bristol
rock-cress, western spiked
speedwell, hutchinsia, spring
cinquefoil and compact brome

grow. Cliff faces in the gorge are a nesting site for ravens and peregrines.

Lower Woods SSSI

Near: Chipping Sodbury, near Bristol, Gloucestershire
Map: 7, B3
Web: www.gloucestershire wildlifetrust.co.uk
P & (ltd)

Twenty-three different oak-ash woods separated by tracks and rides make up this intriguing site that also includes grassland and the Little Avon River. Kingfishers and nightingales are the most popular discoveries for visitors, and buzzards come a close third. Flowers on the woodland floor range from violet, wood anemone and early purple orchid in the spring, to autumn crocuses later in the year. The 22 species of butterflies dance over ancient woodland wildflowers and the yellow-necked mouse scuttles in the field edges.

Milltown & Lantyan Woods

Near: Lostwithiel, Cornwall
Map: 11, C2
Web: www.woodlandtrust.org.uk
P

A quiet secluded wood which rises from sea level up to an altitude of 100 metres. Many of the trees are formerly-coppiced oak, as well as beech, sycamore, sweet chestnut and ash. Ground flora varies greatly and ranges from bramble and bracken, heather under the oak, carpets of wood anemone, cow wheat, wood rush and bilberry to dense bluebells which are at their best in April and May. A row of mature hornbeam and sweet chestnut grow along the eastern boundary of Lantyan wood along the railway line.

Ravensroost Wood and Meadows

Near: Malmesbury, Wiltshire
Map: 9, A1
Web: www.wiltshirewildlife.org
P P

This site offers a choice of dappled, coppiced woodlands or wildflower-rich meadows. The woodland floor is alive with flowers, such as primrose, wood anemone and dog's mercury, and also plays host to visiting butterflies. The meadows come into their own from March through to July.

Statfold Wood

Near: Holsworthy, Devon
Map: 10, B2
Web: www.woodlandtrust.org.uk
P (ltd)

Statfold Wood is located in a shallow basin of agricultural land dominated by commercial conifer plantations. It is a small oasis within this of mixed broad-leaved woodland and culm grassland. There is also a small area of wet woodland with oak, downy birch and willow. Tracks around the wood are wide and grassy allowing good access, but parking is limited.

Otters: cute, unless you're a fish

Otter numbers are on the increase in Britain, largely due to conservation work and less intensive use of pesticides in farming that destroyed their habitats in the 1960s. The species that you see in Britain is the Eurasian otter and it is largely nocturnal, coming out at dusk to catch its diet of fish. They live in both fresh and sea water and are found all over Britain around streams at sites such as Halsdon, Howardian Hills, Snowdonia, Glencripesdale and Stanley Carrs.

Tarr Steps Woodland NNR

Near: Taunton, Somerset
Map: 8, C3
Web: www.english-nature.org.uk

🅿 🚻

Tarr Steps takes its name from the 'clapper' bridge and is constructed entirely from large stone slabs and boulders. The bridge is listed as a scheduled monument but, although it was once thought to be prehistoric, it is now widely believed to be of medieval origin. The reserve primarily consists of oak woodland, although pockets of richer soil support ash, hazel and sycamore, while drier areas have been colonised by beech. The woodland is important for its moss, liverwort and lichen populations. The river Barle runs throughout the site and is a haven for wildlife. Keep your eyes peeled for otters, deer, foxes and waterside birds.

COASTS, WETLANDS & WATERWAYS

Bridgwater and Taunton Canal

From: Bridgwater to Taunton
Map: 8, C2 to C3
Web: www.waterscape.com
As it's not part of a canal network, this isolated waterway is relatively tranquil and provides numerous options for circular walks. The population of mute swans is very strong.

Bridgwater Bay NNR

Near: Bridgwater, Somerset
Map: 8, C2
Web: www.english-nature.org.uk

🅿 ♿ 🚻

This is a large reserve on the north Somerset coast. It consists mainly of intertidal mudflats with saltmarsh, sandflats and shingle ridges, some of which

DID YOU KNOW?

There are roughly 12 times as many snails living in the otter estuary mudflats than there are people living in Britain.

are vegetated. The Bristol Channel has the second largest tidal range in the world and this exposes huge mudflats and sand banks in the area. The site has an important bird population with up to 190 species recorded on the reserve. Large numbers of wintering waders and waterfowl visit the site and some species use the area as a stop-off on migration routes. Wildfowling is permitted in some areas while the main body of the reserve is a wildlife sanctuary.

Brownsea Island

Near: Poole, Dorset
Map: 3, C3
Web: www.wildlifetrust.org.uk/dorset
Open: March to October, 10am to 5/6pm

🚾 ℹ 🏠

One of the best placed hides you'll ever come across allows fantastic viewing of nesting black-headed gulls and terns here. The lagoon setting is also popular with oystercatcher, shelduck, mallard, teal, gadwall, avocets and black-tailed godwits. Curlew sandpiper and little stint are regular visitors in autumn. By the reedbed, you might spot water voles and water rail and there are usually highly-colourful dragonflies and damselflies to be seen. The island has one of Britain's few remaining red squirrel populations. Take a ferry from Poole or Sandbanks.

The Isles of Scilly

Near: Carn Thomas (ferries from Penzance)
Map: 11, A1 (Penzance)
Web: www.ios-wildlifetrust.org.uk
ℹ at St Mary's Quay, 🏠
The Scilly Isles are a microcosm of diversity. Warmer than the rest of Britain, and the closest islands to the US, their bird-life includes puffin, fulmar, and guillemot. The sparkling clear waters around the islands are home to jewel anemones, brilliant sponges and colourful corals as well as porpoises, sun fish and occasional whales. On land, wildflowers of all descriptions can be found, exhibiting a random and continuing change of colours. Heaths, and heathers interspersed with swathes of sea pinks flourish on the exposed westerly faces of the archipelago.

Kennet and Avon Canal

From: Reading, Berkshire, to Bristol, Avon
Map: 2, B4 and 7, B3
Web: www.waterscape.com
A survey last year found that the number of water vole – better known as Ratty from *Wind in the Willows* – was on the increase along the banks of this pretty canal that joins the Thames to the Bristol Channel.

Langford Lakes

Near: Salisbury, Wiltshire
Map: 9, B4
Web: www.wiltshirewildlife.org
Open: 9am to 4/5.30pm

🅿 🚾 ♿ ℹ 🚻 🏠

These lakes buzz with birdlife throughout the year. Many species, such as waders, terns and osprey, can be seen here in the autumn as they stop over on their winter migrations. As winter proper arrives, tufted duck, pochard, gadwall and the great crested grebe

Slimbridge Wetland Centre

Near: Gloucester, Gloucestershire
Map: 7, C2
Web: www.wwt.org.uk
Open: daily, 9.30am to 5/5.30pm (except 25 December)
Admission: £3.95/£6.77

🅿 WC ♿ ❶ 🖥 🎪 🏠 🅰

Slimbridge is the headquarters of WWT, where in 1946, Sir Peter Scott's vision became a reality, when he realised how many thousands of geese depended on the shores of the Severn Estuary. Today with its award-winning visitor centre overlooking nationally and internationally protected wetlands, this world-famous site is an important wintering area for migrating water birds such as Bewick's swans. It also houses WWT's species conservation programme and is particularly renowned for its breeding programme for flamingos.

Pictured: Lesser flamingo

Grand Western Canal

From: Tiverton to Lowdwells
Map: 10, D2
Web: www.waterscape.com
🕐 (ltd)

This isolated canal is a wildlife haven and passes through some of the prettiest scenery in Devon. Moorhens, mute swans and mallards are a common sight and kingfisher are regularly seen fishing in the water. The hedgerows and bank-side vegetation provide food and shelter for the grey wagtail and long-tailed tit, as well as small mammals such as bank voles and shrews. One of the most exciting mammals to be found along the canal is the otter. The canal is a mass of colour in spring and summer, with an abundance of wild flowers growing along the water's edge. Its narrow width produces a more pronounced edge effect than a water body such as a lake or pond. Look out for the early-purple and common-spotted orchids in certain places and the elegant white water lily. The waterway is teeming with freshwater invertebrates, such as water boatmen and dragonfly larvae. They can be found living on the variety of oxygenating and emergent vegetation in the canal. The canal is also a hot spot for butterflies and dragonflies in spring, summer and early autumn, feasting on nectar and smaller insects sheltering in the vegetation. A very notable new dragonfly record for the canal in 2006 was a small population of scarce chasers being confirmed between Westcott Bridge and Ebear Bridge.

settle here and, in spring and summer, they are joined by a host of other birds, including kingfisher. Listen out for the 'plop' of a water vole as it enters the water or keep your eyes peeled for an otter that might slither through the reeds. Yellow flag iris, ragged robin, cuckoo flower and bog-bean all grow around the lake edges.

Otter Estuary
Near: Budleigh Salterton, Devon
Map: 10, D2
Web: www.devonwildlifetrust.org
🅿 (££), 🚻 🏠

It might be Devon's smallest estuary, but that doesn't stop the wigeon, teal, curlew, redshank, snipe, grey heron and little egret coming here for the winter. A visit in spring might reward you with a

sighting of black and white-striped shelduck chicks. Wild celery and divided sedge grow in the reedbed. Look out for peregrine falcons overhead.

Purbeck MWR
Near: Wareham, Dorset
Map: 3, B3
Web: www.coastlink.org/kimmeridge
🅿 (££), 🚾 ℹ

The clear waters and low tides of Kimmeridge Bay mean you don't have to get wet to observe the marine life at work here. The best low tides happen in spring, revealing enchanting rockpools with colourful seaweeds, squat lobster, brittlestar, goby and pipefish. A webcam on the seabed allows visitors to see life in the deeps from within the visitor centre.

River East Lyn
From: Malmsmead to Lynmouth, Devon
Map: 10, C1
Web: www.waterscape.com

The River East Lyn starts peacefully in northern Exmoor but ends in a dramatic rush to the Bristol Channel at Lynmouth. Its forceful beauty has been admired by everyone from the painter Thomas Gainsborough to the poet Percy Shelley. Heron, dipper and grey wagtail can be seen along the river. Trout and salmon swim up river to spawn – you might spot them as they take well-earned rests in quieter pools. In some of the more secluded parts of the river, evidence of otters has been seen.

River Exe
From: Simonsbath near Barnstaple, to Exmouth, Devon
Map: 10, C1 to 10, D2
Web: www.waterscape.com

The estuary is well known for its wildfowl and migrating birds. Further upstream, foxes, badgers, bats and deer are a common sight and otters also make their home in Baronsdown reserve.

River Fal
From: Goss Moor, near St Ives to Falmouth, Cornwall
Map: 11, B3
Web: www.waterscape.com

A boat trip along the River Fal will bring you close to a whole host of rare wildlife. Muddy creeks are home to egrets, herons, redshanks and curlews and Black Rock (en route form Falmouth to Helford) is a favourite area for grey seals. The eagle-eyed and the lucky may spot basking sharks hunting for food near the mouth of the Fal. The river runs through the Goss

Moor NNR with its various wetland habitats formed by mining activity prior to 1945. Several varieties of orchid, dragonflies, damselflies, marsh fritillary butterflies and bog bush crickets can be spotted in the area. The River Fal also boasts the Fal-Ruan Estuary nature reserve, home to the greenshank and the black-tailed godwit.

River Teign
From: Dartmoor to Teignmouth, Devon
Map: 10, C3 to D3
Web: www.waterscape.com
Dotted with tiny hamlets and winding past attractions such as Castle Drogo, the Teign Valley is a particularly

beautiful area blessed with natural formations such as Canonteign Falls, the highest waterfall in England. With herons, kingfishers, cormorants, bluebells, daffodils, the 30-mile stretch of the Teign is a haven for wildlife, even otters are making a comeback. Local shell fishermen still bring home a good catch from the mudflats around Newton Abbot and visitors gather to watch the salmon leap at Drewe's Weir. Non-native mink are present along the riverbank.

St George's Island
Near: Looe, Cornwall
Map: 11, D2

River East Lyn

Web: www.cornwallwildlifetrust. org.uk
🚫 wc
Open: boats run from Looe from Easter to late summer
A marine nature reserve with woodland, maritime grassland, cliffs, sand, shingle and rocky reef. St George's is one of only a few inhabited islands off the Cornwall coast. In the spring, the small woodland has a carpet of wild garlic and bluebells and the cool shade is a welcome resting spot on the trail around the island. The second-largest breeding colony of great black-backed gulls in Corwall can be found on the island. The cliffs are swathes of pink with thrift in the early summer and this is the time of year to see basking sharks feeding along the coast.

Wembury VMCA
Near: Plymouth, Devon
Map: 10, C3
Web: www.devonwildlifetrust. org
P (££), wc ❶ ✉
Thriving rockpools in this marine park harbour squat lobsters, porcelain crabs, sea urchins, cushion starfish, goby, shrimp, sea spiders and sea anemones. Late spring and early summer are the best times for rockpool exploring and head out to the low-tide mark to find the rarer animals. Cirl buntings and peregrines are seen here in the spring and summer months.

NOT SO WILD

Bath City Farm
Address: Twerton Hill Farm, Kelston View, Whiteway, Bath, Somerset BA2 1NW
Map: 8, E1
Tel: 01225 481269
Web: www.farmgarden.org.uk

Eden Project

Open: lower fields, all year; enclosures, phone in advance
P & (ltd), WC & ⌂

The site has many areas to explore including a farm trail, small sensory garden, wildlife pond, and small woodlands – and probably the best views of any city farm in England across open green fields to the city of Bath. Animals include a small flock of Soay sheep, pygmy goats, traditional breed chickens and ducks, golden Guernsey goats and Tamworth pigs.

Bristol Zoo Gardens
Address: Clifton, Bristol BS8 3HA
Map: 8, D1
Web: www.bristolzoo.org
Open: 9am to 5.30pm
Admission: £4.50/£10
P (££), & ⌂ WC

Get up close to swimming penguins and seals in the transparent underground viewing walkways or watch monkeys up to their antics on islands in the zoo's lakes. There are many native British species here, such as water voles, and large park areas give the zoo an open and green feel. Conservation is at the heart of the zoo's work and over the last few years it has released more than 200 animals back into the wild.

Eden Project
Address: Austell, Cornwall PL24 2SG
Map: 11, C2
Web: www.edenproject.com
Open: 9/10am to 3/6pm
Admission: £5/£13.80
P & WC & ⌂ 🚶

Famed for its inspiring design of two great

'biodomes', the Eden Project is an indoor nature reserve for the world's plants. More than 5,000 species are on display here all with information about their natural habitat and their use by man. The project is full of art installations and interactive elements to make it a fascinating day out.

Exmoor Zoo
Address: South Stowford, Bratton Fleming, Near Barnstaple, Devon EX31 4SG
Map: 10, C1
Web: www.exmoorzoo.co.uk
Open: 10am to 4/6pm
Admission: £5.50/£7.50
& WC ⌂ 🚶

Exmoor Zoo is an unusual zoo to visit, in that it specialises in smaller animals, providing living spaces for many creatures no longer seen in city zoos. A primary concern of the zoo is the conservation of animals. Many of the 200 different species in the zoo have an endangered status in the wild. The Humboldt penguins, for which the zoo is famous, are a good example of this. The careful planting of shrubs and trees provides a relaxing and natural atmosphere within the park.

Larkrise Community Farm
Address: West Ashton Road, Trowbridge, Wiltshire BA14 6DW
Map: 9, A3
Tel: 01225 751675
Web: www.farmgarden.co.uk
Open: weekdays, 10am to 3pm; weekends, by appointment
Admission: 50p/£1

This farm was developed by Larkrise Special School and although it is now open as a community farm, it is particularly geared towards the needs of students with special needs. Animals include cattle, sheep, ponies, goats, pigs, turkeys, chickens, ducks, geese, rabbits and guinea pigs.

Longleat Safari Park
Address: Warminster, Wiltshire BA12 7NW
Map: 9, A3
Web: www.longleat.co.uk
Open: weekends in March; daily, March to November
Admission: £8/£11

Longleat's drive-through Safari Park was the first of its type and allows visitors to see animals from all over the world living in an almost natural way – albeit several miles from their usual habitats. See how your car measures up to a giraffe, remember that the rhinos have right of way and beware of the meddling monkeys

– famous for their love of windscreen wipers.

The Lost Gardens of Heligan
Address: Pentewan, St Austell, Cornwall PL26 6EN
Map: 11, C2
Web: www.heligan.com
Tel: 01726 845100
Open: 10am to 5pm/6pm
Admission: £4/£7.50

The story behind these gardens is an epic tale of discovery and toil, but the wildlife resort the re-creation of the gardens has made is just as inspiring. A hide at Heligan gives views onto a bird-feeding area, a wildlife pond, a meadow and a small woodland, all specifically managed to attract a variety of species. The hide also contains plasma screens, on which visitors can watch wildlife being filmed in their nesting and roosting boxes. Badgers, bats, owls, woodpeckers, butterflies, moths and kingfishers have all been observed in this way.

Monkeyworld
Address: Longthorns, Wareham, Dorset BH20 6HH
Map: 3, B3
Tel: 01929 462537
Web: www.monkeyworld.org
Open: daily, 10am to 5/6pm
Admission: £7/£10

This centre has rescued primates from all over the world. It has more than 150 primates from 15 species, the most predominant being chimpanzees, many of which are rescued from performing for tourists in Spain.

The National Seal Sanctuary
Address: Gweek, near Helston, Cornwall TR12 6UG
Map: 11, B3

Tel: 01326 221361
Web: www.sealsanctuary.co.uk
Open: 10am, closing time depends on season
Admission: varies with season

Last season, the seal sanctuary rescued 40 seal pups that were abandoned or stranded around the Cornish coast. When possible, the seals are released back into the wild.

Newquay Zoo
Address: Trenance Gardens, Newquay, Cornwall TR7 2LZ
Map: 11, B2
Tel: 01637 873342
Web: www.newquayzoo.co.uk
Open: all year, 9.30/10am to 5/6pm
Admission: £4.15/£8.95

From its humble origins as a small pets corner in the early 1960s, Newquay Zoo has become one of the country's top zoos, with ground-breaking and innovative conservation programmes. Set in lush subtropical gardens this is the home of many of the world's endangered species.

Paignton Zoo
Address: Totnes Road, Paignton, Devon TQ4 7EU
Map: 10, D3
Tel: 01803 697500
Web: www.paigntonzoo.org.uk
Open: daily, 10am to dusk/6pm (except 25 December)
Admission: £5.65/£8.50

Paignton Zoo is home to thousands of animals and plants. You can visit the desert, cross the savannah, explore the forest and trek through the tropics – all without leaving Devon.

Paradise Park
Address: 16 Trelissick Rd, Hayle, Cornwall TR27 4HB
Map: 11, B3

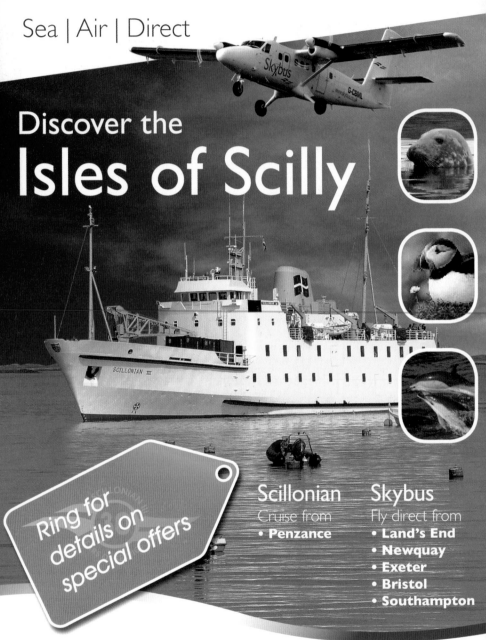

Tel: 01736 751020
Web: www.paradisepark.org.uk
Open: 10am to 3/4/5pm
Admission: £5.50/£6.50

P ♿ WC ♿ 🖼

Paradise Park was established in 1973 as a tropical bird garden. Since then, otters, red pandas, red squirrels and the rare Cornish chough have all joined the park. The park is set around a Victorian walled garden, and features tropical plants which thrive in the mild climate.

St James City Farm
Address: 23 Albany Street, Tredworth, Gloucester GL1 4NG
Map: 7, C2
Tel: 01452 305728
Web: www.farmgarden.org.uk
Open: summer, daily, 9.30am to 5pm; winter, Tuesday to Sunday, 10am to 4pm

P ♿ WC ♿ 🖼

This city farm specialises in rare breeds and nature conservation and allows visitors hands-on contact with farm animals. A piece of countryside in the city.

St Werburgh's City Farm
Address: Watercress Road, St Werburgh's, Bristol BS2 9YJ
Map: 8, D1
Tel: 0117 942 8241
Web: www.stwerburghs.org
Open: 9am to dusk/5.30pm

🖼

St Werburgh's City Farm is a green oasis in the heart of Bristol. Entry is free so anyone can experience contact with the natural world. There is a range of livestock, a community garden, an adventure playground, a café and the farm shop.

Windmill Hill City Farm
Address: Philip Street, Bedminster, Bristol BS3 4EA
Map: 8, D1
Tel: 0117 963 3252
Web: www.windmillhillcityfarm. org.uk
Open: Tuesday to Sunday, 9am to 6pm
Admission: Free except for groups of 10 or more

♿ WC ♿ 🖼

Established in 1976 as the first city farm outside London, the once derelict land on which the farm is situated has been transformed into an attractive and productive environment providing a thriving centre of community activity. Facilities include a working farm, wildlife conservation areas and community gardens run on sustainable principles.

East

The east of England is best known for its broadlands and coasts that make it one of the best places in the UK for birdwatching. Its network of internationally renowned reserves are visited by thousands of waterfowl and wildfowl each winter, including pink-footed geese, cormorants, harriers and terns. Behind the beaches, marshlands and reedbeds are abuzz with birds, such as hobbies, bearded tits, warblers and bitterns with their booming call. Further inland still, you reach the fens, home to yet more bird species, including the long-eared owl and common teal along with the marsh and spotted moths.

In the muddy valleys and winding creeks of the area you'll find nesting birds and waders that share their habitat with a community of natterjack toads. Listen out for the natterjack, which is Europe's noisiest amphibian – the male's call can be heard over a number of miles.

The wide flat countryside of the east does not have much in the way of woodland, but there is some. Seek it out and you'll find traditional woodland animals, including adders, woodpeckers and owls, and you might be able to spot hunkering muntjak deer.

The area's many nature reserves and meadows harbour bee orchid and purple heather that attract thousands of damselflies and dragonflies in summer. What is also worth finding is the bladderwort plant that catches and eats water fleas in its stomach-like sacks. The east is the only place in England where you can see the swallowtail butterfly.

Around the rivers in East Anglia you can also visit two reserves that have pools and streams that are used by otters. They share the river with warbling birds, and grass snakes live in the nearby land. Other water mammals include seals that you can see basking on the beach or swimming up to boats. Around Blakeney, there are around 500 seals in total and the colony is made up of common and grey seals. You can spot the difference between the two as the grey seals are larger and have speckles on their coats – the common seals have a more rounded face with V-shaped nostrils.

All in all, with its fens and freshwater pools, wetlands and woodlands, parks and gardens, the eastern region stands out as an area that is very rich in all kinds of wildlife.

PICTURED: Common seal at Blakeney Point, Norfolk

Not to be missed

● **Barnack Hills and Holes**
An evening visit to this old quarry is worth it for the magic of a glowing glow worm. By day, though, you can be delighted by the myriad of butterflies instead.

● **Holkham**
You don't just find huge numbers of birds at Holkham, you find a huge variety, too – all with a backdrop of a fantastic windswept coastline, dramatic dunes and a maze of little creeks.

● **Ranworth Broad**
The network of the Broads is an undoubted highlight of the area and few are better than Ranworth Broad, with its families of great crested grebes and constantly swooping damselflies.

● **Strumpshaw Fen**
If you're very, very lucky here – and very, very quiet – you might catch a glimpse of the secretive Chinese water deer with its distinctive tusks. If not, there are always the 'skydances' of the marsh harriers or the blue flashes of a kingfisher to look out for.

● **Suffolk Coast**
Listen out for the huge *ribbit* of the natterjack toad, which has been successfully reintroduced here. And keep alert for otters which thrive on the banks of reedbeds, inland from the beach.

● **Wicken Fen**
Whether it is in a mystical mist or searing sunshine, this fenland always enchants and has plenty of wildlife, too, be it owls, snails, dragonflies or birds that you are looking for.

NATIONAL PARK

The Broads
Norfolk and Suffolk
Map: 12, C1 and C2
Web: www.broads-authority.gov.uk
The best way to visit The Broads is on a boat. The national park contains 125 miles of inland waterways that weave between villages, windmills, gardens and reedbeds. There are hundreds of species of birds to see. In winter, teal and wigeon are found on the open broads, while reed, sedge and Cetti's warbler can be found in the reedbeds. The marsh harrier has made a comeback here and now breeds successfully in the fens. Bittern numbers have increased in recent years following restoration of fen habitat and improvements to water quality. More than 250 plant species grow in the fens, from the nationally protected fen orchid to the more abundant species, such as ragged robin. Invertebrates such as Britain's largest butterfly – the swallowtail – and the rare Norfolk hawker dragonfly can often be seen. Carr woodland forms a natural link between open water and dry oak or ash woodland. A largely undisturbed wilderness, Carr woodland is filled with a tangle of woody species and shade-tolerant plants. Many birds inhabit Carr woodland, including willow tits and long-tailed tits, greater and lesser spotted woodpeckers and treecreepers. Around the edges of the waterways there's much drained marshland and grazing marsh rich in plant and birdlife. Waders and wildfowl are abundant where water levels are high and the marshes are criss-crossed by dykes, often rich in water plants and invertebrates.

Sunset from near Wells, north Norfolk coast

AONB

Norfolk Coast AONB
Near: Fakenham, Norfolk
Map: 12, B1
Web: www.norfolkcoastaonb.org.uk
ⓘ
The dunes at Winterton have some of the finest dune heathland in England and support a flourishing colony of natterjack toads. Inland there is bog and heath at Dersingham, with insect-eating plants and a huge variety of insects. The farmland is loved by a number of birds, many of which are now rare in other parts of England, such as the grey partridge, corn bunting and tree sparrow. The bittern nests and feeds on fish in the freshwater reedbeds. Common seals can be found at Blakeney.

NATURE RESERVES

Barnack Hills and Holes NNR
Near: Stamford, Cambridgeshire
Map: 13, B4
Web: www.english-nature.org.uk
Ⓟ

Arising from the rubble of a medieval quarry, Barnack Hills and Holes is rich with more than 300 kinds of wildflowers, including eight species of orchids. This rich flora supports a wide variety of wildlife, especially insects, and a number of nationally scarce species are found here. Several uncommon butterflies have been recorded here, including the marbled white, chalkhill blue, brown argus and green hairstreak. Barnack Hills and Holes is one of the best places in the region to see the strange green lights of the glow worm, which occur in large numbers on warm summer nights. The grubs of this beetle feed on small snails, which are common in the limestone soils.

Barton Hills NNR
Near: Luton, Bedfordshire
Map: 6, B3
Web: www.english-nature.org.uk
The chalk grassland here is typical of the northern Chilterns and the site also includes areas of Chilterns beech woodland and ash-maple

Wildlife Britain **111**

Cley Marshes

Near: Cley next the Sea and Holt, Norfolk
Map: 12, B1
Web: www.wildlifetrust.org.uk/norfolk
P (ltd), WC 🅰 ❶ 🏠
Open: daily, 10am to 5pm (except 25 December)
Entry: free for Norfolk Wildlife Trust members and children; £3.50 for adults

Cley marshes has a well-deserved international reputation for birds – the East Bank is seen as one of the best birdwatching sites in the country. Common birds include bittern, avocet, marsh harrier, spoonbill and bearded tit, as well as large numbers of wildfowl including wigeon, teal, pintail, and Brent goose. Migrating waders like the ruff and Temminck's stint can also be seen.

woodland. The reserve has a large population of the rare pasque flower and several other rare plants are present in the downland, including greater pignut and fleawort. You'll also find chalk grassland plants, such as wild thyme, horseshoe vetch, marjoram and rockrose, and a good show of orchids in the summer. Butterflies are a feature of the site, with large numbers of chalkhill blue, marbled white and grizzled skipper.

Blakeney NNR
Near: Wells, Norfolk
Map: 12, B1
Web: www.english-nature.org.uk
🏠
The reserve at Blakeney is home to a wide range of

nationally important plant and bird communities, including shingle flora, breeding birds, waders in winter, and common seals. Birdwatchers can enjoy a visual feast from special hides, spotting little, common, sandwich, and Arctic terns, ringed plovers, oystercatchers, shelducks, Brent geese and snow buntings, although some areas may be restricted during the bird breeding season of April to July.

Castor Hanglands NNR
Near: Peterborough, Cambridgeshire
Map: 13, B4
Web: www.english-nature.org.uk
P
Castor Hanglands is made up of four habitats: woodland,

grassland, scrub and wetland, each with its own special wildlife. The woodlands are home to tawny owls, treecreepers and nuthatches. Hawthorn and blackthorn trees dominate the scrub area, which is inhabited by a number of bird species, including nightingales, whitethroat and blackcaps, while the wetland habitat supports aquatic fauna, such as the great crested newt and 18 species of dragonfly.

Cavenham Heath NNR
Near: Mildenhall, Suffolk
Map: 12, A3
Web: www.english-nature.org.uk
P
Located on the south side of the River Lark, Cavenham Heath is home to more than 280 plant species, as well as a wide variety of birds. Woodcocks, nightjars, tree pipits, green woodpeckers, little owls, kingfishers, tufted ducks and gadwalls are just some of the many birds that can be seen here. In addition, the site features sheep and rabbits, which help to maintain the heathland with their grazing.

The Chase LNR
Near: Romford, Essex
Map: 1, E1
Web: www.wildlondon.org.uk
The Chase's 120 acres of diverse habitat including wetland, grassland and scrub provide an impressive range of animals. Water voles and grass snakes are found alongside the breeding reed warblers, while grey heron and snipe can also be seen. The reserve attracts many migrating visitors, including yellow wagtail and wheatear. Grazing creates a short sward over much of the reserve, but there is a small woodland containing the rare black poplar. The open water attracts waterfowl such as teal and gadwall in the winter

and waders such as green sandpiper feed in the spring and autumn. Even if you are not especially interested in birds, it is a charming haven close to urban London.

Chippenham Fen NNR
Near: Newmarket, Cambridgeshire
Map: 13, C5
Web: www.english-nature.org.uk
P

The very rare Cambridge milk parsley is just one of more than 400 species of wildflowers growing on this reserve, which is one of the best areas of fen in the county. The reserve is also home to more than 500 species of moths, such as the silver-barred and reed leopard moth, as well as many nationally scarce and rare invertebrates, including 10 species known only in this area in the UK. The best time to visit for wildflowers is May to July.

Dersingham Bog NNR
Near: Dersingham near Kings Lynn, Norfolk
Map: 12, A1
Web: www.english-nature.org.uk
P & (ltd)

Part of the Sandringham Royal Estate, Dersingham Bog comprises three distinct habitats: mire, heath and woodland. The mire is inhabited by rare insects, including dragonflies such as the black darter, and moths such as the light knot grass. The woodland glades attract birds such as redpoll, crossbill, long-eared owl and sparrowhawk.

Fingringhoe Wick
Near: Colchester, Essex
Map: 12, B4
Web: www.essexwt.org.uk
Open: Tuesday to Sunday, 9am to 6pm
P (££), & (ltd),

An immense range of habitats can be found at Fingringhoe, including grassland, heathland, saltmarsh and inter-tidal mudflats – essential for the large number of over-wintering birds that can be seen here each winter. Nightingales can be heard at Fingringhoe Wick in the spring.

DID YOU KNOW?

Rabbits can see behind themselves without having to rotate their heads.

Grafham Water SSSI
Near: St Neots, Cambridgeshire
Map: 13, B5
Web: www.wildlifebcnp.org
P ❶

The mixture of woodland and grassland at this site provide food and shelter for the nightingale, warbler and blackcap. In winter, the reservoir attracts large numbers of diving ducks, such as gadwall and shoveler, as well as populations of coot and crested grebe. The common sandpiper, greenshank, scoter and red-throated diver can also be seen. The ponds are home to dragonflies and great crested newts.

Hatfield Forest NNR
Near: Bishop's Stortford, Essex
Map: 12, A4
Web: www.nationaltrust.org.uk
& WC ❶

This small royal forest – managed by the National Trust and comprising open grassland, coppiced woodland and marshland – dates back to medieval times. Several scarce plants, such as oxlip and stinking hellebore, grow in the woodland, while the marshland habitat contains bog pimpernel and broad blysmus. The grassland is home to

harebells, bee orchids, adder's tongue ferns and old pollarded trees supporting invertebrates, lichens and mistletoe.

Holme Fen NNR
Near: Peterborough, Cambridgeshire
Map: 13, B4
Web: www.english-nature.org.uk
P

The lowest point in Britain, Holme Fen is home to the largest pure birch woodland in the country. Around 450 species of fungi thrive here and in the reserve's scrub habitat, as well as birds such as siskin, redpoll, blackcap, woodpecker and nightingale. Plants found at the reserve include twayblade, fen woodrush, meadow rue and climbing corydalis. Areas of open water, created by commercial peat-cutting, support birds, dragonflies and marsh plants.

Langdon
Near: Basildon, Essex
Map: 12, B5
Web: www.essexwt.org.uk
Open: Tuesday to Sunday, 9am to 5pm
P (££), & (ltd), WC ❶

The reserve consists of four sections: Dunton, Lincewood, Marks Hill and Willow Park. There is plenty of wildlife to be seen, including warblers, nightingales, green winged and spotted orchids, wood anemone, purple streak and grizzled skipper butterflies, and cave spiders.

Martham Broad NNR
Near: Great Yarmouth, Norfolk
Map: 12, C2
Web: www.english-nature.org.uk
P at West Somerton

The reserve has three habitats: open water, reed and sedge fen. In summer, Martham Broad is one of the best areas to see swallowtail butterflies in Broadland. Other species

Holme Dunes NNR

Near: Hunstanton, Norfolk
Map: 12, A1
Web: www.english-nature.org.uk
P ⓘ (Easter to October),
This fantastic reserve comprises many different habitats, including sand dunes, beach, mudflats, grazing marsh, pine shelter belt, saltmarsh and freshwater pools. As a result there is always something to see here. A huge range of bird species live or pass through at different times of year. In spring and summer, ringed plovers, oystercatchers and little terns nest in the shingle ridges on the beach and the grazing marshes are the breeding ground for lapwings, redshanks, snipes and avocets. Waders, such as grey plovers, knots, bar-tailed godwits and sanderlings, can be seen on the mudflats, while large numbers of wildfowl, such as wigeon, Brent geese and teal, arrive during autumn to spend the winter feeding on the marshes. Natterjack toads breed in the dune slacks.

sighted in the area include the bearded tit, bittern and marsh harrier, as well as wildfowl and invertebrates.

Mid-Yare NNR

Near: Norwich, Norfolk
Map: 12, C2
Web: www.english-nature.org.uk
P ♿ (ltd), WC
The site shows the full range of Broadland habitats, including broads, dykes, tall fen, fen meadows and alder-willow woodland. The fen areas support a range of invertebrates, including the swallowtail butterfly and Norfolk hawker dragonfly.

Many of the UK's Cetti's warblers live in the NNR which is also a breeding site for marsh harriers and bearded tits. During the winter the lowland wet grasslands are host to wigeon, white-fronted geese and bean geese.

Monks Wood NNR

Near: Huntingdon, Cambridgeshire
Map: 13, B4
Web: www.english-nature.org.uk
P
A wide range of tree and shrub species are found in the reserve, including field maple, aspen, hawthorn, hazel, guelder rose,

wayfaring tree, spindle, privet, blackthorn and dogwood. The woodland is also a breeding site for birds such as the tawny owl, nightingale and woodcock. Monks Wood is an important site for beetles, with more than 1,000 species being recorded in the area, many of them associated with decaying wood. Monks Wood is also known for its butterflies and is home to the rare black hairstreak.

Old Sulehay

Near: Peterborough, Cambridgeshire
Map: 13, B4
Web: www.wildlifebcnp.org
P ♿ (ltd)
Old Sulehay forest sits on a variety of soil types, resulting in a very varied flora, including bluebells, nettle-leaved bellflower, wild garlic and wood anemones. The mosaic of scrub, grassland and bare earth also make for an amazing habitat for insects and wildflowers, such as bird's-foot trefoil, viper's bugloss and lesser centaury.

Orford Ness NNR

Near: Woodbridge, Suffolk
Map: 12, C3
Web: www.nationaltrust.org.uk
WC ⓘ
Orford Ness supports large lichen and moss communities. Many plant species that are nationally rare are found here in abundance. The shingle supports a number of rare and scarce invertebrates – particularly beetles and spiders – and the site is also an important breeding place for many bird species, including terns and avocets.

Redgrave and Lopham Fen NNR

Near: Diss, Suffolk
Map: 12, B2
Web: www.suffolkwildlife.co.uk
P WC ⓘ

Redgrave and Lopham Fen is the largest remaining valley fen in England. Spring, summer and autumn are the best times to visit to enjoy the fen plants, dragonflies and hobbies. In winter, starling roosts offer a dramatic spectacle. The pools are home to the fen raft spider. The reserve is grazed by Polish tarpan ponies, together with cattle and Hebridean sheep.

Roding Valley Meadows

Near: Loughton, Essex
Map: 6, C4
Web: www.essexwt.org.uk

P

Roding Valley Meadows make up the largest surviving area of traditionally managed river-valley habitat in Essex. In summer, sedge warblers, reed buntings, kingfishers and sand martins are frequently seen, along with small numbers of meadow pipits. In the winter, grey heron, little grebe, snipe, and green and common sandpiper are regular visitors.

Roydon Common NNR

Near: Roydon and Grimston, near Kings Lynn, Norfolk
Map: 12, A1
Web: www.wildlifetrust.org.uk/norfolk

P (ltd),

The common is a mosaic of dry and wet heath, valley mire, rough pasture and woodland. The pools are important breeding grounds for a variety of dragonflies, including the broad-bodied chaser and black darter. Many flowers are supported in the grassy clearings on the drier ground, and these attract butterflies such as green and purple hairstreaks and brown argus. Uncommon birds, including nightjar and curlew, breed on the site. Hen harriers, merlins and sparrowhawks use the common as a roosting site in the winter.

Thompson Common

Near: Watton, Norfolk
Map: 12, B2
Web: www.wildlifetrust.org.uk/norfolk

P

Thompson Common comprises 900 acres of wet and dry grassland and heath. It is famous for its pingos – a series of around 300 shallow pools containing a dazzling array of water plants. It is home to large numbers of water beetles and dragonflies over the summer.

DID YOU KNOW?

The smallest land mammal in Britain is the pygmy shrew, just 6cm long when fully grown.

Titchmarsh LNR

Near: Peterborough, Cambridgeshire
Map: 13, B4
Web: www.wildlifebcnp.org

P (ltd),

The main woodland at Titchmarsh contains a large heronry. In particular, goosander, wigeon and gadwall are present in large numbers. Spring sees the arrival of a colony of common tern, oystercatcher and shelduck. The grasslands provide breeding sites for skylark and redshank. The colourful flash of a darting kingfisher can often be seen along the River Nene or the Harper's Brook tributary throughout the year.

Tollesbury Wick

Near: Colchester, Essex
Map: 12, B4
Web: www.essexwt.org.uk

P

Tollesbury Wick reserve is home to small mammals such as pygmy shrews and field voles, which in turn attract birds of prey from hen harriers to short-eared owls. In the

warmer months, butterflies, bush crickets and grasshoppers thrive on the banks of the sea walls, while reed warbler, reed bunting, grey heron and little grebe can be seen or heard in the borrowdykes. Large numbers of Brent geese can also be seen in the winter.

Weeting Heath NNR

Near: Brandon, Norfolk
Map: 12, B2
Web: www.wildlifetrust.org.uk/norfolk
Open: April to September, 7am to dusk
Admission: free for Norfolk Trust members and children; adults £2

P

Weeting Heath is a wonderful piece of breck heath and is famous for its population of rare breeding stone curlew. Post-breeding flocks can be seen in late summer, before departing to over-winter in Africa in September. Little owls, woodpeckers and hobbies also frequent the reserve.

Westleton Heath NNR

Near: Reydon, Suffolk
Map: 12, C2
Web: www.english-nature.org.uk

Birds of open heath and light scrub are well represented here, and include tree pipit, Dartford warbler, stonechat and nightjar; while the woodlands support nightingale and woodcock. Of the heather species, common heather and ling predominate, and these – together with deep purple bell heather – provide an important nectar source for invertebrates such as the white admiral butterfly. Other invertebrates found here include the striped-winged grasshopper and glow worms.

Wicken Fen NNR

Near: Wicken and Upware, near Ely, Cambridgeshire
Map: 13, C4

The Wash NNR

Near: King's Lynn, Norfolk, and Sutton Bridge, Lincolnshire
Map: 13, C3
Web: www.english-nature.org.uk

The large expanses of inter-tidal sand and mud hold concentrations of invertebrate life, which make this one of Britain's most important feeding areas for waders and wildfowl. Enormous numbers of migrant birds, such as grey plover, knot, dunlin, oystercatcher and bar-tailed godwit, arrive in the autumn to feed on these areas. The best times to see large flocks of waders is on a rising tide at any time from early September to early May. At the same time of year, pink-footed geese arrive from Iceland and Greenland. The Wash is also noted for its common seals.

Woodwalton Fen is home to around 900 moth species. Species found here include marsh, lunar yellow underwing, four spotted, white-spotted pinion and silky wave. More than 1,000 beetle species have also been recorded at the site. Fly species are also well represented. A number of bird species are found at the site, including tree pipit, long-eared owl and common teal. Two scarce species seen here are great bittern and reed bunting.

BIRD RESERVES

Berney Marshes and Breydon Water
Near: Great Yarmouth, Norfolk
Map: 12, C2
Web: www.rspb.org.uk

The wet grassland section in Berney Marshes holds up to 200 pairs of breeding waders, which makes it the most important site in the Broads. During the winter, the grassland supports up to 100,000 wintering waterfowl, including golden plover, lapwing, pink-footed goose, redshank and wigeon.

Great Yarmouth
Near: Great Yarmouth, Norfolk
Map: 12, C2
Web: www.rspb.org.uk

Each year, the UK's largest colony of little terns breeds on the North Denes beach at Great Yarmouth. To protect these vulnerable birds, the RSPB operates a special wardening scheme. Visitors can watch the birds between mid-May and the end of July.

Havergate Island
Near: Framlingham, Suffolk; boats from Orford Quay
Map: 12, C3

Web: www.english-nature.org.uk

This area is attractive to a large number of birds. Species recorded living at the site include great crested grebe, cormorant, sparrowhawk, kingfisher, snipe, owls and woodcock. The reserve supports large numbers of invertebrates, including snail, spider and beetle species. Damselflies found here include the emerald, azure and common blue.

Winks Meadow SSSI
Near: Diss, Suffolk
Map: 12, B1
Web: www.plantlife.org.uk

Five species of orchid have been recorded at Winks Meadow – common-spotted, green winged, bee, pyramidal and frog orchid at its only remaining site in Suffolk. Other flowers present that are now scarce in Suffolk include spiny restharrow and sulphur clover. The meadow is enclosed by tall hedges which are mostly quite young, but the northern section is species-rich, including dogwood and field maple.

Woodwalton Fen NNR
Near: Peterborough, Cambridgeshire
Map: 13, B4
Web: www.english-nature.org.uk

Tel: 01394 450732
Web: www.rspb.org.uk
Open: April to August, Thursdays
and alternate weekends;
September to March, first
Saturday of the month
Admission: members £2/£5;
non-members £3/£7

The island consists of six
saline lagoons surrounded
by saltmarshes and mudflats.
It is famous for its breeding
avocets and terns, which
can be seen throughout the
spring and summer. In late
summer, many migrating
wading birds stop off on
Havergate Island to feed
and roost. In autumn and
winter, the island provides
a haven for large numbers
of ducks and wading birds.
Species also include the
pintail and wheatear.

Lakenheath Fen
Near: Brandon, Suffolk
Map: 12, B2
Web: www.rspb.org.uk
(ltd)

Mainly wetland consisting of
reedbeds and grazing marsh,
but there is also poplar
woodland. Marsh harriers
are common, as are hobbies,
bearded tits, reed and sedge
warblers, and golden orioles.

The Lodge
Near: Sandy, Bedfordshire
Map: 6, B2
Web: www.rspb.org.uk
(ltd),

This is the UK headquarters
of the RSPB. The offices
are surrounded by formal
gardens in an estate of forest
and heath that is managed
as a nature reserve. Visitors
can follow trails around
heathland and through
mixed woodland, where
you are likely to spot green
and spotted woodpeckers
and nuthatches. You may

see the rare breed of sheep,
Manx loghtans, which graze
the heath. The organically-
managed formal gardens are
open to visitors.

Minsmere
Near: Framlingham, Suffolk
Map: 12, C3
Web: www.rspb.org.uk
Open: 9am to dusk
(ltd)

Minsmere is the place to
visit in spring and summer to
see avocets, marsh harriers
and bitterns. In winter, the
shallow lagoons attract many
wading birds and waterfowl
including black-tailed
godwits, wigeons, teals and
Bewick's swans.

Nene Washes
Near: Whittlesey, Cambridgeshire
Map: 13, B4
Web: www.rspb.org.uk

The Nene Washes in the
Cambridgeshire Fens are
some of the best floodplain
meadows in England.
Regularly flooded by the
River Nene, they can support
thousands of waterfowl in
winter and a good variety

of breeding waterfowl in
the spring. Species include
pintails, wigeons and
shovelers. In summer, cattle
graze some fields while hay
is cut on others. The RSPB
manages 1,235 acres of the
Washes as a nature reserve
and is currently attempting to
reintroduce corncrakes.

North Warren
Near: Framlingham, Suffolk
Map: 12, C3
Web: www.rspb.org.uk

North Warren comprises
five main habitats, one
of which – wet grassland
– supports up to five
species of breeding waders,
plus nationally important
populations of wintering
wildfowl (including some of
the UK's only regular tundra
bean geese). The heathland
holds Dartford warblers and
woodlarks, while bitterns and
marsh harriers can be seen in
the reedbeds.

Ouse Washes
Near: Chatteris, Cambridgeshire
Map: 13, B4
Web: www.rspb.org.uk

Whooper swans

The Ouse Washes is a stunning example of lowland wet grassland habitat. In winter, the reserve is used by tens of thousands of ducks as well as the largest concentration of Bewick's and whooper swans anywhere in the UK. During the spring and early summer, the site fulfils an equally crucial role as a breeding habitat for hundreds of waders and ducks.

Snettisham

Near: Hunstanton, Norfolk
Map: 12, A1
Web: www.rspb.org.uk
P ☻ (ltd), 🏠

All these birds found at Snettisham include the avocet, bar-tailed godwit, knot and shelduck. Thousands of pink-footed geese assemble here from late September to March. The birds roost on The Wash but fly inland at dawn to feed on sugar beet remnants.

Stour Estuary

Near: Harwich, Essex
Map: 12, C4
Web: www.rspb.org.uk
P ☻ (ltd), 🏠

The RSPB's Stour Estuary reserve is home to the most important bird roost on the estuary. You can see all of the area's wintering bird species roosting on the saltmarsh at Deep Fleet, or feeding in the vast mudflats of Copperas Bay. Species include black-tailed godwit, Brent goose, dunlin, knot and nightingale.

Strumpshaw Fen

Near: Norwich, Norfolk
Map: 12, C2
Web: www.rspb.org.uk
Open: daily, dawn to dusk (except December 25)
Admission: 50p/£2.50; free to RSPB members
P ☻ WC 🏠 ❶ 🏠 🏠

Strumpshaw Fen, in the heart of the Norfolk Broads, is the perfect place to explore the full diversity of Broadland habitats and wildlife. A walk around the reedbeds, woodlands and orchid-rich meadows could bring some enchanting encounters with marsh harriers, bitterns and kingfishers, and perhaps a glimpse of the secretive Chinese water deer. In spring and summer, dragonflies and butterflies abound, with a chance to see the spectacular swallowtail butterfly.

DID YOU KNOW?

All these British birds get their names from their call: cuckoo, chiffchaff, hoopoe, pipit, curlew and turtle dove.

Titchwell Marsh

Near: Hunstanton, Norfolk
Map: 12, A1
Web: www.rspb.org.uk
P (££), ☻ WC 🏠
❶ 🏠 🏠 🏠 🏠

Situated on the north Norfolk coast, Titchwell Marsh is one of the RSPB's most visited reserves. Waders on the beach, terns out fishing, migrating skuas and wintering sea ducks are some of the main attractions. Hides give views over bird-filled freshwater, brackish marshes and along the edges of reedbeds.

Wolves Wood

Near: Hadleigh, Suffolk
Map: 12, B3
Web: www.rspb.org.uk
P

A wide range of birds can be seen in Wolves Wood throughout the year, but the reserve is best visited in spring. The most common birds include the garden warbler, great spotted woodpecker, marsh tit, nightingale and sparrowhawk.

FORESTS & WOODLAND

Aversley Wood

Near: Huntingdon, Cambridgeshire
Map: 13, B4
Web: www.wt-woods.org.uk
P 🏠

The wood contains 12 species of butterfly and at least 37 species of bird. Of specific interest are black hairstreak, white admiral and white letter hairstreak butterflies. The wood also harbours a population of muntjak deer.

Bedford Purlieus

Near: Peterborough, Cambridgeshire
Map: 13, B4
Web: www.english-nature.org.uk

This ancient woodland site once formed part of the Royal Forest of Rockingham. Oak and ash are dominant but small-leaved lime, hazel, wych elm, birch and pine are also found here. Muntjak and fallow deer can be seen, as well as nightingales, red kites, sparrowhawks, kestrels, little owls, tawny owls and long-eared owls. Reptiles seen on the site include adders, grass snakes, common lizards and slow worms.

Bradfield Woods

Near: Gedding, Suffolk
Map: 12, B3
Web: www.english-nature.org.uk
🏠

This working wood has been under continuous traditional management since 1252. A wander down one of its three nature trails will reveal just some of the woodland's 350 plant species and a wide range of its woodland birds and mammals. The best time to visit is April to mid-July.

Brampton Wood SSSI

Near: Huntingdon, Cambridgeshire

Not such night-owls after all

That owls are creatures of the night is a rumour hotly denied by more than one of Britain's five species of owls. The short-eared owl is often seen hunting during the day, as is the barn owl – although more frequently at dusk. The little owl doesn't get seen hunting during the day, but he's often spotted sitting on top of telegraph poles. The long-eared owl lets down the night-time myth during its breeding season in winter, when it can be spotted flying along the coasts. All this means that just the tawny owl is a true creature of the night – and it has the best *tu-whit tu-whoo* noise.

PICTURED: Short-eared owl

Map: 13, B4
Web: www.wildlifebcnp.org
🅿 ♿ (ltd)
Nationally scarce butterflies, such as the black hairstreak and white admiral, can be seen here in the summer. In spring, woodpeckers and nightingales are common. The abundance of wildflowers attracts a variety of insects and in winter the woods are inhabited by foraging animals.

Broxbourne Woods NNR
Near: Hertford, Hertfordshire
Map: 6, C3
Web: www.english-nature.org.uk
🅿 🎣
The reserve comprises four woods: Bencroft, Broxbourne, Hoddesdonpark and Wormley. The area's animal life includes badgers, weasels, grass snakes and muntjak deer, as well as woodpeckers, woodcock, treecreepers, hawfinches, buzzards and sparrowhawks. Twenty-seven species of butterfly have been recorded at the site, including grizzled skipper, white admiral and purple hairstreak.

Foxley Wood NNR
Near: Norwich, Norfolk
Map: 12, C2
Web: www.english-nature.org.uk

🅿 🚾 ⓘ
Thought to be more than 6,000 years old, Foxley Wood is the largest remaining ancient woodland in Norfolk and one of the best of its kind. The reserve is home to a range of insects, which includes several uncommon butterflies, such as the white admiral and blackcap. Tawny owls and woodcocks are also present.

Gamlingay Wood SSSI
Near: Sandy, Bedfordshire
Map: 6, B2
Web: www.wildlifebcnp.org
🅿
This ancient wood houses a rich wildlife habitat and is composed of oak, ash and maple. In summer, the glades are filled with wildflowers and insects, including butterflies such as the speckled wood. Gamlingay is also home to a good number of breeding birds. In autumn, mushrooms and toadstools of all shapes and sizes can be seen.

Hayley Wood SSSI
Near: St Neots, Cambridgeshire
Map: 13, B5
Web: www.wildlifebcnp.org
🅿 🏕
Hayley Wood is home to a good number of breeding

birds and, in summer, the rides and glades are filled with wildflowers and insects, including butterflies such as the speckled wood. In spring, the great spotted woodpecker is common, as is the nightingale, particularly in June.

Old Wood
Near: Cromer, Norfolk
Map: 12, C1
Web: www.wt-woods.org.uk
🅿 🏕
The fauna within Old Wood also supports a diverse range of species including a number represented on the long, middle and short lists of globally threatened species. There are also three species that are represented within Old Wood that are protected under the Wildlife and Countryside Act 1981: the pipistrelle bat, adder and slow worm.

Reffley Wood
Near: South Wootton and King's Lynn, Norfolk
Map: 12, A1
Web: www.wt-woods.org.uk
🅿 🏕
Reffley Wood is a 130-acre semi-natural ancient woodland site that was planted with a variety of conifers in the 1950s and 1960s. There are two types

Spot the difference: Seals

Despite its name, the common seal is less common in British waters than the Atlantic grey seal, which can also be seen all year round. To tell the difference, you need to look at the head. The common seal's head is rounder with a distinct forehead and dog-like snout, while the grey seal's head is more angular. They are often spotted off the Norfolk Coast, Anglesey, Cardigan Bay, Mourne, the Monach Isles and in the Thames Estuary.

PICTURED:
Top: Grey seal
Right: Common seal

Blakeney NNR

Near: Wells-next-the Sea, Norfolk
Map: 12, B1
Web: www.nationaltrust.org.uk
P WC ℹ ✉

Blakeney NNR extends to 2,711 acres. It includes Blakeney Point, Blakeney Freshes, Morston and Stiffkey Marshes, and supports a wide range of coastal plant communities with many nationally important species. Blakeney Point itself is a sand and shingle spit more than three miles long, noted for its colonies of breeding terns and migrant birds passing through. Both common and grey seals can also be seen.

of woodland: an oak/ash/field maple mix on the wetter clay to the south, where Scot's pine has been planted, and an oak/birch mix on the lighter sandier soils to the north, where Corsican pine has been planted.

COASTS, WETLANDS & WATERWAYS

Ant Broads and Marshes NNR
Near: Irstead, near Norwich, Norfolk
Map: 12, C3
Web: www.english-nature.org.uk
The Ant Broads and Marshes NNR is ringed by areas of reedswamp that provide a nesting habitat for wildfowl, such as gadwall, pochard, teal, shoveler and tufted duck.

There is a large population of swallowtail butterflies, and a significant number of rare and uncommon dragonflies, moths, beetles and flies.

Blackwater Estuary NNR
Near: Colchester, Essex
Map: 12, B4
Web: www.english-nature.org.uk
Blackwater Estuary is comprised of two main areas: Tollesbury Flats – a coastal strip – and Old Hall Marshes, near Salcott, managed by the RSPB. Tollesbury Flats supports a variety of invertebrates and is an important feeding place for wildfowl, including plovers, Brent geese, oystercatchers and cormorants. Old Hall Marshes is another sensitive area, which surrounds a lagoon called Pennyhole Fleet. The site

supports nationally important plant and invertebrate species. It is also home to breeding and over-wintering wildfowl and breeding bearded tits.

Bure Marshes NNR
Near: Wroxham, near Norwich
Map: 12, C1
Web: www.english-nature.org.uk
P WC ℹ 🏠

Consisting of four broads – Hoveton Great, Decoy, Ranworth and Cockshoot – Bure Marshes supports a wide range of plants and animals. The reserve is one of the main sites for the endangered swallowtail butterfly, and is also home to many other rare butterflies, aquatic insects, moths, spiders and plants, such as the crested buckler fern.

Carlton Marshes
Near: Lowestoft, Suffolk
Map: 12, C2
Web: www.suffolkwildlife.co.uk
P ℹ

Due to the profusion of wildflowers, dragonflies are abundant in the meadows at Carlton Marshes in late summer. Fifteen species have been recorded, including the Norfolk hawker. The open water at Carlton heaves with life, including the insectivorous bladderwort, which traps and digest water fleas in bladder-like sacs underwater.

Colne Estuary NNR
Near: Colchester, Essex
Map: 12, B4
Web: www.english-nature.org.uk
P

Colne Estuary is made up of three areas: Brightlingsea Marsh, East Mersea and Colne Point. Brightlingsea Marsh is an area of low-lying grazing marsh, while East Mersea is a strip of coastal land and home to a number of wintering wildfowl and waders. Colne Point is a saltmarsh with large areas of shingle banks and shell beds, which support a diverse plant and animal population.

Dunwich Heath Coastal Centre and Beach

Near: Framlingham Suffolk
Map: 12, C3
Web: www.nationaltrust.org.uk

P ☕ ⬛

Within an AONB and offering many excellent walks, the area is a remnant of the once extensive Sandlings heaths, with open tracts of heather and gorse, shady woods, sandy cliffs and beach. It is an important nature conservation area and home to scarce species like the nightjar, Dartford warbler and ant-lion.

Hamford Water NNR

Near: Walton-on-the-Naze and Harwich, Essex
Map: 12, C4
Web: www.english-nature.org.uk

P

Hamford Water is home to wintering populations of

dark-bellied Brent geese, redshank, ringed and grey plover, teal and avocet. There is also a large breeding colony of little terns. During severe winter weather, the area is an important refuge for wildfowl and waders.

Hanningfield Reservoir SSSI

Near: Billericay, Essex
Map: 12, A5
Web: www.essexwt.org.uk
Open: Tuesday to Sunday and Bank Holidays, 9am to 5pm

WC ℹ ⬛ ☕ ⬛

This reservoir is a designated SSSI due to its large numbers of wildfowl; gadwall, tufted duck and pochard all breed at Hanningfield. A raft is provided for terns to nest on in the summer. Swift, swallow and birds of prey can also be seen.

Hen Reedbeds

Near: Reydon, Suffolk
Map: 12, C2
Web: www.suffolkwildlife.co.uk

P ⬛

Hen Reedbeds was created to provide new breeding habitat for bittern and other wildlife. In summer, it is home to marsh harriers, herons, bearded tits, reed and sedge warblers and iridescent dragonfly. The pools are a good place to spot wildfowl such as gadwall, tufted duck and teal. Redshank, avocet and sandpiper are all regular feeders in the mudflats.

Hickling Broad

Near: North Walsham, Norfolk
Map: 12, C1
Web: www.english-nature.org.uk

P WC ℹ ⬛ ⬛

One of the largest areas of open water in East Anglia, Hickling Broad is made up of a variety of wetland habitats. Together they support a range of Broadland wildlife, from birds and rare insects to important aquatic plants. Visitors can get the chance to see bearded tits and wintering wildfowl, swallowtail butterflies and

Sundew

Carnivorous plants aren't unique to exotic places like the Amazon jungle, the UK has its own native species, one of which is the sundew. Sundews lure their victims by producing a sticky glue substance that glistens at the end of tentacles on its leaves, as if it were nectar. Small insects find themselves stuck to the glue and the tentacles then curl inwards, bringing the food to the centre of the leaf where digestive juices are secreted to dissolve the meal. You find these plants all over the UK, some species like bogs, others like moorland. Find them: on the Norfolk Coast and Loch Sheil.

Norfolk hawker dragonflies, and flora such as holly-leaved naiad, as well as three species of nationally rare stoneworts.

Holkham

Near: Blakeney, near Wells-next-the-Sea, Norfolk
Map: 12, B1
Web: www.english-nature.org.uk
P

Holkham is inhabited by a huge number and a variety of birds: wading birds with long beaks, such as curlews and oystercatchers; redshank, greyplover and dunlin dibble are common, as are ringed plovers, little terns and sanderlings. The Brent goose is one of Holkham's key birds, visiting in their thousands in the winter. Vast numbers of Siberian Brents over-winter here, too, grazing in the shallows. The young dune and shingle systems create important nesting areas for shore birds, such as oystercatchers.

Lackford Lakes

Near: Lackford and Bury St Edmunds, Suffolk
Map: 12, B3
Web: www.suffolkwildlife.co.uk

A superb site for wildfowl in winter and summer, Lackford attracts tufted duck, pochard, gadwall shoveler and gossander. There are large winter gull and starling roosts. This is one of the best places in Suffolk to watch kingfishers, while osprey pass through on migration. Caspian tern, spoonbill and more uncommon waders have been sighted in the autumn and spring migrations.

Leigh NNR

Near: Southend-on-Sea, Essex
Map: 12, B5
Web: www.english-nature.org.uk

Pitsford Reservoir

During autumn, thousands of Brent geese arrive on the mudflats at Leigh NNR to feed on its population of invertebrates and dense beds of eel grass, along with other waders and wildfowl. Outside the breeding season, significant numbers of waders, such as curlew, dunlin, redshank, grey plover and knot, can be seen. Winter flocks of turnstone and rare gull species are attracted by nearby cockle sheds.

Ranworth Broad NNR

Near: Norwich, Norfolk
Map: 12, C2
Web: www.wildlifetrust.org.uk/norfolk

P (ltd),

Ranworth Broad is home to a great variety of birds. In summer, common terns nest on the artificial rafts and great crested grebes can be seen diving for fish. Swallows and swifts hunt for insects over the water. In winter, large numbers of wildfowl, such as teal, wigeon, shoveler, pochard and gadwall come here to feed. Ranworth Broad is also home to one of the largest inland cormorant roosts in Britain.

River Great Ouse

From: Bedford, Bedfordshire, to The Wash, Norfolk
Map: 6, A2 and 14, A1
Web: www.waterscape.com

An abundance of wildlife is found along the Ouse's riverbanks, including birds such as moorhens, mallards, swans, grebes and herons. The Wicken Fen nature reserve near Ely is a haven for rare native insects and wildflowers. The Ouse washes, between the Bedford Rivers, are an important conservation area, where bird lovers can view many species, particularly at the Wildfowl and Wetlands Trust visitor centre at Welney and the Ouse Washes nature reserve at Welches Dam.

Scolt Head Island NNR

Near: Wells-next-the-Sea, Norfolk
Map: 12, B1
Web: www.english-nature.org.uk

During the summer breeding season, ringed plover and oystercatcher nest on the shoreline. At the ternery to the west of the island, sandwich terns, common terns, little terns and Arctic terns can be found. During the spring and autumn, additional species can be seen, such as flycatchers, warblers and chats, and, in the early summer, swifts, swallows and house martins pass from east to west as they arrive from Africa. Dark-bellied Brent and pink-footed geese are drawn to the area, and may number 50,000 by mid-winter.

Suffolk Coast NNR
Near: Reydon, Suffolk
Map: 12, C2
Web: www.english-nature.org.uk
This large nature reserve stretches down the coast along beaches, saltmarshes and saline lagoons and inland across reedbeds, hay meadows and woodlands. It contains many of Britain's breeding bitterns, as well as more than 100 species of cranefly. There are otters here and five species of deer and natterjack toads have recently been introduced to the area.

Britain's largest newt

Of all the species of newts in the UK, the great crested newt is the largest, growing up to 17cm long. They live around weedy ponds and small lakes, although some have been found in dew ponds far from any larger bodies of water. They hibernate from October to February and are nocturnal, so it's rare to see them, but they can be found at Potteric Carr, Woodhouse Washlands, Breen Oakwood and Bow Back Rivers.

The Wash NNR
Near: King's Lynn, Sutton Bridge
Web: www.english-nature.org.uk
Facilities: I, P, Picnic, Dis limited
The large expanses of intertidal sand and mud hold concentrations of invertebrate life, which make this one of Britain's most important feeding areas for waders and wildfowl. Enormous numbers of migrant birds such as grey plover, knot, dunlin, oystercatchers and bar-tailed godwit arrive in the autumn to feed on these areas. The best times to see large flocks of waders is on a rising tide at any time from early September to early May. At the same time of year, pink-footed geese arrive from Iceland and Greenland. The Wash is also noted for its common seals.

Winterton Dunes NNR
Near: Great Yarmouth, Norfolk
Map: 12, C2
Web: www.english-nature.org.uk

P wc 🚻
There are 170 species of breeding and over-wintering birds to be found at Winterton, including little tern, stonechat, nightjar, ringed plover, marsh harrier and Montagu's harrier. Natterjack toads, newts and a number of dragonfly species frequent the pools. More than 110 species of moth have been recorded here, including the rare pygmy footman.

NOT SO WILD

Africa Alive!
Address: White's Lane, Kessingland, Lowestoft, Suffolk NR33 7TF
Map: 12, C2
Tel: 01502 740291
Web: www.africa-alive.co.uk
Open: varies with season
Admission: £5.50/£6.95

P ♿ wc ♿
🚻 📷 🐾
One of the UK's largest wildlife attractions, Africa Alive! is set in 100 acres of dramatic coastal parkland. Animals include giraffes, rhinos, cheetahs, hyenas and hundreds more African animals and birds. Visitors can enjoy a bird's-eye view over the lion's enclosure.

Banham Zoo
Address: The Grove, Banham, Norfolk NR16 2HE
Map: 12, B2
Tel: 01953 887771
Web: www.banhamzoo.co.uk
Open: daily (except 25 and 26 December)
Admission: £6/£8

P ♿ wc ♿
🚻 📷 🐾
The wealth of animals residing at Banham Zoo include the Siberian tiger, snow leopard and, red kangaroo, as well as a variety of primates, such as the gibbon, tamarin and

Red panda at Banham Zoo

home for a fascinating array of beautiful creatures from around the world. Specialising in rare, endangered and unusual animals, the park has more than 100 different species. It is even possible to come into direct contact – supervised, of course – with some of the tamer and more approachable animals. These range from baby owls to giant millipedes, from African land snails to friendly snakes like the boa constrictor. Keepers' talk sessions at feeding time also allow you to find out more.

lemur. Macaws, penguins and flamingos can be seen and there are a number of reptiles and invertebrates as well. The zoo also houses farm and stable animals.

Brancaster Millennium Activity Centre
Address: Dial House, Brancaster Staithe, King's Lynn, Norfolk PE31 8BW
Map: 12, A1
Tel: 01485 210719
Web: www.nationaltrust.org.uk

The setting for the activity centre is the 4,000 acres that the National Trust cares for at Brancaster in north Norfolk, a habitat for thousands of shorebirds, as well as grey and common seals.

Colchester Zoo
Address: Maldon Road, Stanway, Colchester, Essex CO3 0SL
Map: 12, B4
Tel: 01206 331292
Web: www.colchester-zoo.co.uk
Open: daily, 9.30am to 5/6/ 6.30pm (except 25 December)
Admission: £7.50/£13.50

With more than 250 species, Colchester Zoo is well

worth a visit. Orang-utans and lar gibbons can be seen, as well as sand cats and chimpanzees. The Aquatic Zone is home to meerkats, dwarf mongoose and Humboldt penguins, while Playa Patagonia – an enclosure for the Patagonian sealions – includes a 24-metre tunnel under the water, so you can watch the sea lions swimming directly overhead. African lions can be seen at Lion Rock, and white tigers live alongside the giant anteater. Other highlights include giraffes, African elephants, cheetahs, hyenas and a falconry display, while the new Komodo dragon exhibit is home to the world's largest surviving lizard.

Hamerton Zoological Park
Address: Hamerton, near Sawtry, Cambridgeshire PE28 5RE
Map: 13, B4
Tel: 01832 293362
Web: www.hamertonzoopark.com
Open: daily, 10.30am to 4/6pm (except 25 December)
Admission: £5/£7.50

Opened as a conservation sanctuary in 1990, Hamerton Park is set in 15 acres of parkland, providing a safe

Linton Zoological Gardens
Address: Hadstock Road, Linton, Cambridgeshire CB1 6NT
Map: 13, B4
Tel: 01223 891308
Web: www.lintonzoo.com
Open: daily (except 25 and 26 December)
Admission: £4.50/£7

There is a wealth of rare and exotic creatures to see including tigers, lions, tapirs, lemurs, binturongs, owls, parrots, giant tortoises, tarantula spiders and many others. The gardens place emphasis on education and conservation.

Mole Hall Wildlife Park and Butterfly Pavilion
Address: Widdington, Saffron Walden, Essex CB11 3SS
Map: 12, A4
Tel: 01799 540400
Web: www.molehall.co.uk
Mole Hall Wildlife Park surrounds the original moated Manor House, which dates back to 1287. The park covers more than 20 acres and contains many exotic species, including otters, flamingos, sarus cranes, primates (including chimpanzees), owls, birds, guanacos and wallabies.

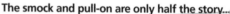

There is also a beautiful tropical Butterfly Pavilion, and much more to enjoy.

New Ark Adventure Playground and City Farm
Address: Hill Close, Reeves Way, Eastfield, Peterborough PE1 5LZ
Map: 13, B4
Tel: 01733 340605
Web: www.farmgarden.org.uk
Open: varies with season
Admission: free
WC

New Ark Adventure Playground has been on its present site for 20 years and the City Farm is 17 years old. There is a well-established wildlife pond and a herb and butterfly garden and the farm includes sheep, goats, ducks, chickens, a pot-bellied pig, rabbits and guinea pigs.

Norfolk Wildlife Centre
Address: Fakenham Road, Great Witchingham, Norfolk NR9 5QS
Map: 12, C2
Tel: 01603 872274
Web: www.norfolkwildlife.co.uk
WC

The Wildlife Centre was originally opened in 1963 and was the first green-field country park wildlife collection in the United Kingdom. Animals include wolves, meerkats, prairie dogs, llamas, emus, storks and black swans, and there are separate houses for reptiles, animals and birds of prey.

Pensthorpe
Address: Pensthorpe, Fakenham, Norfolk NR21 0LN
Map: 12, B1
Tel: 01328 851465
Web: www.pensthorpe.com

Open: daily; April to December, 10am to 5pm (except 25 and 26 December); January to March, 10am to 4pm
Admission: £7/£3.50
P WC

Pensthorpe is a multi award-winning experience for all those who love nature, wildlife and the outdoors. It combines stunning gardens from award-winning designers with the opportunity to get really close to some of Britain's most endangered species. Habitats include a patchwork of lakes and ponds, water meadows, mixed woodland and heath and scrub, which are all easy to explore along the numerous nature trails. The conservation centre provides a special home for a regionally important collection of bird species and incorporates a cranery, which houses eight of the world's 15 species of cranes. More than half of these species are endangered or threatened.

Thrigby Hall Wildlife Gardens
Address: Filby, Great Yarmouth, Norfolk NR29 3DR
Map: 12, C2
Tel: 01493 369477
Web: www.thrigby.plus.com
Open: daily, from 10am
Admission: £6.50/£8.50
P WC (summer only),

Animals at the gardens include primates, such as lemurs and gibbon. Red pandas can be seen, as can small mammals and birds, such as the peacock, Bali starling and hill mynah. Cats include the Sumatran

tiger, clouded leopard and the Asian golden cat. The swamp house holds Burmese pythons, Tokay geckos and the mangrove snake.

Tropical Wings World of Wildlife
Address: Wickford Road, South Woodham Ferrers, Essex CM3 5QZ
Map: 12, B5
Tel: 01245 425394
Web: www.tropicalwings.co.uk
Open: daily, 9.30/10.30am to 4.30/5.30pm
Admission: £4/£6.25
P (££), WC

Tropical Wings is set in acres of attractive gardens and features one of the largest butterfly houses in the country. There are many different species of birds, insects and animals, and many interactive elements to the displays. A daily programme of animal encounter sessions will entertain, educate, and introduce you to wildlife face to face. Livestock includes butterflies, a large collection of exotic parrots, marmoset monkeys, skunks, pets' corner and farmyard area.

Wellgate Community Farm
Address: Collier Row Road, Romford, Essex RM5 2BX
Map: 1, E1
Tel: 01708 747850
Web: www.farmsforschools.org.uk
Open: daily, 9am to 3.30pm; Bank Holidays, 9am to noon
Admission: free

Animals to see at Wellgate Community Farm include sheep, cattle, pigs, goats, horses, chickens and mice.

East Midlands

T he East Midlands is not an easily defined region, which makes it all the more fun to explore. To the north-west there is the Peak District National Park – parts of it are wild, others are farmed. Further south there is Rutland Water, an artificially constructed reservoir built to include wildlife sanctuaries, while over to the east there are the flatlands of Lincolnshire. The variety of habitats that you'll find here is huge.

Open moorlands are rife with orchids and cowslips each spring, there's bogland, there's woodlands with songbirds, and there's pretty valleys with dragonflies darting across the streams in summertime – and that's before you have even left the Peak District.

Around Rutland Water you'll be treated to the spectacle of large numbers of gathering wildfowl in the winter-time, while in the summer it is a haven for butterflies and dragonflies. Other waterways host their own populations of waterbirds. Lincoln is well known for its large swan population, which dates back at least to the twelfth century when Saint Hugh of Avalon was Bishop of Lincoln. It is said he was always accompanied by a white swan, and they are now an integral part of the town's heritage.

Across towards the coast from Lincoln is the stunning area of the Lincolnshire Wolds. This Area of Outstanding Natural Beauty (AONB) has woodlands and valleys and large open fields that gently roll across the countryside. As well as many nature reserves within the AONB, there are also several signposted walks that take in all sorts of habitats as well as fantastic scenery.

Once you arrive at the coast there are some great dune systems, such as Donna Nook, that are visited by numerous wildfowl over the winter, but are rich in invertebrate life in summer.

The East Midlands is also where you will find one of Britain's most ambitious wildlife projects: the National Forest. This is a 200-mile area crossing three counties, where new forest is being created to complement existing woodlands and open spaces. The aim is to create a large, inter-connected area that benefits local communities and Britain's wildlife. Woodlands are a great haven for badgers and other woodland wildlife. Dusk is the best time for sightings.

Not to be missed

● **Attenborough SSSI**
An intricate network of flooded gravel pits and islands. Best known for its impressive birdwatching opportunities, including migrant birds, waders and breeding birds.

● **Derbyshire Dales**
The five dales of Lathkill, Cressbrook, Monk's, Long and Hay represent some of the best examples of wildlife and geology in the White Peak region.

● **Everdon Stubbs SSSI**
An ancient woodland comprising of four different types of woodland community. Home to locally rare plants and woodland wildlife.

● **National Forest**
Covering 200 square miles, the National Forest is a series of woodlands, providing a wonderful habitat for a variety of wildlife.

● **Peak District National Park**
Britain's first national park, with its famous limestone cliffs, woodlands and purple heather moors. Home to a diverse range of wildlife, particularly rare birds.

● **Rutland Water**
One of the most important inland sites in the UK for passage waders – up to 19 species have been recorded in a single day.

PICTURED:
Left: Shining Tor in the Peak District
Above: A fallow deer from the National Forest

Peak District

NATIONAL PARK

Peak District National Park
Near: Bakewell, Derbyshire
Map: 14, A2
Web: www.peakdistrict.org

P WC ♿ ❶ ⛲

The Peak District was Britain's first national park, established in April 1951. The park covers 555 square miles and is famous for its magnificent contrasting landscape of limestone cliffs, hay meadows, moorland and wooded river valleys. Limestone, shale and gritstone form the foundations upon which this 'living landscape' has evolved. Each of these rock types supports their own distinctive habitat – a perfect relationship between rock, soil, plants and animals. There is an abundance of flora and fauna to be found in these varied habitats, from the rare lichen and insects clinging to the scree slopes of the steep cliffs, to the water voles and white-clawed crayfish living in and along the rivers. The park is also home to an impressive range of birds, including the curlew, lapwing and twite, which have been protected by the Peak Birds Project for endangered species since 2001. A birdwatching course is also available.

AONB

Lincolnshire Wolds AONB
Near: Louth and Market Rasen, Lincolnshire
Map: 13, B1
Web: www.lincswolds.org.uk

❶

The Lincolnshire Wolds offer fantastic walking country – from open hilltops to sheltered valleys with hidden villages. As well as traditional farm animals and freshwater wildlife, a range of farmland birds inhabit the Wolds, including the grey partridge, lapwing and tree sparrow.

Photographers
on Safari

Fantastic Wildlife Photography Days Out

Photographers On Safari are the experts at getting you behind the scenes and providing privileged access to photograph wildlife in Britain. We endeavour to get you extremely close to species that are difficult to approach in the wild. We have arrangements in place with zoos and parks, that will enable you to get right up to, or even inside some animal enclosures. All the surrounding photos were taken on our photographic workshops in the UK last year. You can take pictures like these yourself.

Locations in England, Scotland & Wales

We use locations in England from Kent to Northumberland, Bass Rock & the Cairngorms in Scotland, plus Skomer & Skokholm in Wales. Most of our courses are for one day, but they can be up to a week long. Tips & tuition sessions are always included, both in a group format, and also on a one to one basis through the day. Enjoy your day's photography while you are learning to perfect techniques like aperture priotity, fill-in flash & exposure. Master the interpretation of histograms at the same time.

Locations & Subjects

- Badgers, Foxes, Wolves, Pine Marten in natural surroundings in Kent.
- Puffins, Oystercatchers, Guillemots, Razorbills, Fulmars. Residential stay on Skokholm or Skomer. Photograph birds from sunrise until sunset.
- 50,000 pairs of Gannets on Bass Rock. Close-up & in-flight photography.
- Foxes, Otters, Scottish Wildcat, Buzzards, Owls, Deer, Snakes in Surrey.
- Golden Eagle experience. Leicestershire countryside & woodland.
- 3 Gorilla sessions, Colubus Monkeys, Red Panda, Off-road Safari, Kent.
- Lions, Tigers, Wolves, Bears, Rhinos, Zebra etc. Off-road Safari, Woburn
- Puffins, Shags, Arctic Terns, Kittiwakes, Razorbills etc. Farne Islands.
- Lions, Tigers, Leopards, Snow Leopards, Cheetahs, Ocelot. WHF Kent.
- Snow Leopards, Lynx, Bobcats, Caracals, Jaguar, Ocelot, Puma. Herts.
- Red Deer Rut, Wolves, Woodpecker, Red Squirrel, Eagles. Scotland.
- Birds of Prey. Both in-flight, & static shots in natural surroundings. Beds.
- Snow, Asian, Clouded & African Leopard. Puma & Panther, Herts.
- Photograph Bats in flight and learn Fill-in Flash techniques, Oxfordshire.
- Cheetahs & Corsac Foxes. Practical wildlife photography tuition. Cambs.

Tel: John Wright on 01664 474040 or 07779 648850   Email: info@photographersonsafari.com

www.photographersonsafari.com

NATURE RESERVES

Besthorpe

Near: Besthorpe and Newark-on-Trent, Nottinghamshire
Map: 14, C2
Web: www.wildlifetrust.org.uk/nottinghamshire
🅿 🏠

Besthorpe Nature Reserve covers around 168 acres and lies in the Trent floodplain. The landscape includes willow scrub, reedbeds and orchid areas. The reserve also comprises two SSSI wildflower meadows, to the south of which lies Mons Pool, containing a colony of nesting cormorants and a heronry. As well as these, many species of water bird can be found, including, in the winter, a variety of ducks, such as the tufted duck, pochard and goosander.

Biggin Dale NNR

Near: Ashbourne, Derbyshire
Map: 14, A1
Web: www.english-nature.org.uk
♿ (ltd), 🚻

This National Trust reserve is situated in the northernmost reaches of Dove Dale in the Peak District National Park. The grassland is species-rich and, in May and June, visitors can see early purple orchids, cowslips, harebells and salad burnet. Birdlife found on the reserve includes redstart, yellow-hammer, wheatear, skylark, linnet, raven, buzzard and partridge; while butterflies include northern brown argus and white-letter hairstreak.

Burbage Common and Woods

Near: Hinckley, Leicestershire
Map: 14, B4
Web: www.lros.org.uk/burbage
ℹ

Burbage Common and Woods is 204 acres of ancient woodlands and open countryside, with free and

Dove Dale and Biggin Dale SSSI, Derbyshire

open access at all times. Most common birds can be found in the woods – owls, thrushes, sparrows and kestrels – and there are a number of butterfly species and water voles in addition. An exhibition includes displays on local wildlife, history, recreation and conservation, all housed in a log cabin visitor centre.

Calke Park NNR

Near: Ticknall, Derbyshire, and Ashby de la Zouch, Leicestershire
Map: 14, A3
Web: www.english-nature.org.uk
🅿 ♿ (ltd), 🍽 at Calke Abbey

Calke Park NNR encompasses the ancient deer park of the Calke Abbey estate. The reserve includes rich wood pasture and has concentrations of very large, old, stag-headed oak trees, as well as lime and beeches. A good diversity of woodland birds can be seen, holes in trees proving valuable nesting sites. Calke Park is also an important habitat for bats. At least eight species have been recorded, including the serotine bat, which is not recorded anywhere else in the county.

Carr Vale Flash

Near: Bolsover, Derbyshire
Map: 14, B1

Web: www.derbyshirewildlifetrust.org.uk
🅿 at Stockley Trail, ♿ (ltd)

Carr Vale Flash provides a mixture of open water, marsh, grassland and scrub that provides habitat for wintering wildfowl and raptors, migrating waders, breeding ducks and passerines such as reed bunting. The nature reserve also attracts wintering flocks of finches and buntings, which feed along the field boundaries, and considerable roosts of swallows in September. In early summer, the marsh and scrub are home to a range of breeding birds, including reed and sedge warblers, white-throat, yellow-hammer, moorhen and gadwall.

Cribbs Meadow SSSI

Near: Melton Mowbray, Leicestershire
Map: 14, C3
Web: www.english-nature.org.uk
🅿

The reserve, which covers 12 acres, is an SSSI. Habitats include herb-rich grassland, two ponds, scrub and mature trees. The fields support a number of notable species: adder's-tongue, cowslip, green winged orchid, common-spotted orchid and water avens in spring and early summer; agrimony, great burnet and yellow-rattle later in the year. All areas are good for butterflies such as grizzled skipper and green hairstreak.

Crowle Moor
Near: Scunthorpe Lincolnshire
Map: 13, A1
Web: www.lincstrust.org.uk
P

The extensive tract of Hatfield, Thorne, Goole and Crowle Moors is a complex of moor, bog and fen. The reserve is one of the richest lowland peat vegetation areas in the north of England – its higher, drier areas carrying heather, bracken and birch scrub. These varied habitats support a rich bird, mammal and insect fauna. The large heath butterfly occurs here at the south-eastern limit of its range in Britain. More than 30 breeding birds have been recorded, including long-eared owl, woodcock, nightjar and tree pipit.

Deep Dale SSSI
Near: Bakewell, Derbyshire
Map: 14, A2
Web: www.plantlife.org.uk

Located in the heart of the Peak District National Park, Deep Dale's sides are steeply sloping and rich in wildflowers. In spring, swathes of early-purple orchids and cowslips dominate the grassland, while in early summer species such as meadow saxifrage, common rock-rose and kidney vetch can be seen. The reserve is also home to a large number of butterfly species, including green hairstreak, dingy skipper and dark green fritillary. The grassland at Deep Dale is lightly grazed by cattle.

Derbyshire Dales NNR
Near: Bakewell, Derbyshire
Map: 14, A2
Web: www.english-nature.org.uk
P **&** (ltd)

The five limestone valleys of Lathkill, Cressbrook, Monk's, Long and Hay make up the Derbyshire Dales NNR. These five dales represent some of the best examples of wildlife and geology in the White Peak. Lathkill Dale offers spectacular views, fine woods and a great display of blue-flowered Jacob's ladder in June, as well as a river with many dippers swooping over it. Cressbrook Dale, broken by rocky outcrops and screes, is alive with butterflies and moths. Hay and Long Dales are small and make a great trip for naturalists looking for limestone flowers and insects.

Epworth Turbary
Near: Scunthorpe, Lincolnshire
Map: 13, A1
Web: www.english-nature.org.uk
P **🏠**

Breeding birds in the area include teal, snipe, woodcock, long-eared owl, tree pipit, green and great spotted woodpeckers. Various bird species new to the reserve have also been attracted to these areas, including greenshank,

Watch that toad

Like most amphibians, toads are creatures of habit. Every spring, they will return to the pond where they started life as a tadpole to breed. In many cases this means crossing roads and because – unlike frogs – toads are slow lumbering creatures, many of them are killed each year by cars. In 1994, the Department of Transport created a roadsign to warn drivers of toads crossing.

green sandpiper and little grebe. Among moths, the wood tiger is well established. The ponds also attract 11 species of breeding dragonflies and damselflies.

Far Ings

Near: Barton upon Humber, Lincolnshire
Map: 13, B1
Web: www.english-nature.org.uk
P WC ⓘ ✉

Far Ings comprises a series of former clay pits that have been flooded to create reedbeds. As well as reedbeds, the reserve contains a mosaic of rough grassland and scrub, open water and wetland habitats. The reserve is the most important site for breeding bitterns in the UK, outside of the Norfolk Broads. Marsh harrier, bearded tit and grey partridge also breed at the site. Wetland birds seen here include redshank, ringed plover, shelduck and dunlin.

Gibraltar Point NNR

Near: Skegness, Lincolnshire
Map: 13, C2
Web: www.english-nature.org.uk
P ♿ (ltd), WC ⓘ ✉ ⌂

Large numbers of migrant and over-wintering birds visit Gibraltar Point. Brent geese, shoelark and snow bunting are common, as are thrushes, finches and the odd harrier. In autumn, huge whirling flocks of waders can be seen at close range during the monthly high tides. In summer, the little tern, skylark and meadow pipit are in full song. Natterjack toads are vocal during April and May.

Hilton Gravel Pits SSSI

Near: Derby, Derbyshire, and Burton-on-Trent, Staffordshire
Map: 14, B2
Web: www.derbyshirewildlifetrust.org.uk
P ♿ (ltd)

Humberhead Peatlands

The combination of lakes and ponds, woodland and sheltered sunny areas make the former gravel pits at Hilton a haven for wildlife. The reserve supports species that are fast declining in this country, including the great crested newt and black poplar. Hilton is also well known for its dragonflies and damselflies, among them the emperor and ruddy darter dragonflies and the emerald and red-eyed damselflies. The ponds and lakes attract many species of waterfowl – including the coot, great crested grebe and tufted duck. In spring, frogs, toads, newts and kingfishers are all common.

Humberhead Peatlands NNR

Near: Thorne, South Yorkshire, and Scunthorpe, Lincolnshire
Map: 13, A1
Web: www.english-nature.org.uk
WC ⌷

The moors form the largest complex of lowland raised bog in Britain. As well as bog, the reserve also contains areas of fen, wet and dry heath and scrub, woodland and nutrient-poor grassland. The wide range of habitats supports a huge variety of plants and animals:

over 4,500 invertebrate species have been recorded on the reserve. Birds recorded at the site include little grebe, teal, coot, mute swan, kingfisher, swift, marsh harrier, hobby, long and short-eared owl, wren, whinchat, nightjar and willow warbler.

Lea Meadows SSSI

Near: Newtown Linford, near Leicester, Leicestershire
Map: 14, B3
Web: www.lrwt.org.uk

The profusion of wildflowers in early summer remains the main sight to behold at Lea Meadows, while later in the summer, the mixture of betony, harebell and devil's-bit scabious spread a mauve quilt among the sedges and rushes. The stream provides a suitable habitat for the white-clawed crayfish and the brook lamprey. Other fish, such as bullhead, minnow, three-spined stickleback and brown trout, have also been recorded. Seventy-six species of birds live on the reserve. Kingfishers have occasionally been seen along the stream and the alders alongside are home to wintering flocks of siskin and redpoll.

Messingham Quarry

Near: Scunthorpe, Lincolnshire
Map: 13, A1
Web: www.lincstrust.co.uk
P ♿ (ltd), 🏠
A series of lagoons of differing depths, fringed by reed, reedmace and rushes, share the landscape with remnants of the heathland, woodland and marsh. This environment is inhabited by 370 species of plant; more than 180 species of bird (73 of which breed here); 20 species of butterfly; 16 species of dragonfly; and more than 285 species of moth and many other invertebrates.

Mill Hill Quarry

Near: Alford, Lincolnshire
Map: 13, C2
Web: www.lincstrust.org.uk
P
Near to the eastern edge of the Wolds on a steep valley slope, the reserve consists of a disused chalk pit and a spinney as well as a cliff face of middle and lower chalk with an intervening band of grey marl. Breeding birds include spotted flycatcher, pied wagtail, tawny owl, four species of warblers and five species of finches. The area is also home to sun-loving butterflies, such as wall, common blue and small copper, and many bumblebees frequent the warm and sunny south-facing slope.

Muston Meadows

Near: Grantham Leicestershire
Map: 14, C2
Web: www.english-nature.org.uk
This reserve is arguably one of the finest lowland meadows in England. It is notable for its colony of more than 10,000 green winged orchids. The meadows are also rich in wildlife: several ponds are now home to various species of dragonflies and frogs, as well as the rare great crested newt. Skylarks and meadow pipits

build their nests in the long grass, while yellow-hammers, linnets and white-throats nest in hedgerows. There are large numbers of bank and field voles, and on summer evenings, bats can be seen hunting for insects over the site.

DID YOU KNOW?

The daisy gets its name from being the 'day's eye', as its yellow flower looks like a tiny sun, and it opens in the early morning and closes in the evening.

Narborough Bog SSSI

Near: Leicester, Leicestershire
Map: 14, B3
Web: www.lrwt.org.uk
Narborough Bog has a number of habitats: wet woodland with willow and alder predominating, a reedbed, areas of dense scrub and two dump meadows. The large number of habitats on the reserve make it especially rich in many forms of wildlife. More than 130 species of birds have been recorded, including all three species of woodpeckers, six species of tits, tawny owl, sparrowhawk and kingfisher. A good variety of butterflies occur, including common blue, meadow brown, and large and small skippers.

Oakerthorpe Nature Reserve

Near: Ripley, Derbyshire
Map: 14, B2
Web: www.derbyshirewildlifetrust.org.uk
P at Oakerthorpe Village
The pond platform at Oakerthorpe Nature Reserve is an ideal location to spot frogs, toads and common newt. Among the other visitors to the pond are numerous damselflies and the occasional dragonfly. The water vole may be seen on the reserve,

while flowers such as common spotted orchid and ragged robin thrive in the marshy margins. Willow, alder and birch grow in the woodland areas and provide shelter for the many flowers that grow there, including wood avens, bluebell and yellow archangel.

Rainworth Heath SSSI

Near: Rainworth and Mansfield, Nottinghamshire
Map: 14, B2
Web: www.wildlifetrust.org.uk/nottinghamshire
This heathland at Rainworth includes areas of both wet and dry heath. The drier heathland includes species such as heather, bell heather, bracken, wavy-hair grass sheep's sorrel and mat grass. Higher ground to the east of the site holds stands of broom and gorse, and the western edge of the reserve has developing birch woodland. Birds recorded include green woodpecker, tree pipit and turtle dove.

Seaton Meadows

Near: Oakham, Rutland, near Corby, Northamptonshire
Map: 14, C4
Web: www.plantlife.org.uk
Large areas of the reserve are prone to flooding during the winter, and these areas are characterised by species such as great burnet, meadowsweet, meadow vetchling and greater bird's-foot trefoil. Some areas of the reserve are on higher ground, so escape regular flooding and these areas support a different suite of species, including pignut, lady's bedstraw and oxeye daisy. The reserve is also home to a number of bird species, including meadow pipit, snipe and skylark.

Snipe Dales

Near: Winceby and Spilsby, near Horncastle, Lincolnshire

Map: 13, B2
Web: www.lincstrust.org.uk

P ♿ (ltd), WC ♿
ℹ️ 🚻 🚂 🏠

Snipe Dales offers a variety of attractive walks through two valleys fretted with streams – half with grassland maintained by cattle grazing and half with mainly coniferous wood. The wide range of habitats support a variety of birds, from owls and woodpeckers in the woodland to snipe and wagtails on the wet grassland. The reserve is also rich in insects and is a good place to see butterflies and dragonflies.

Summer Leys

Near: Wellingborough, Northamptonshire
Map: 14, C4
Web: www.wildlifebcnp.org

P (££), 🏠

Summer Leys is one of the best birding sites in the Nene Valley. During the summer, the reserve supports one of the largest breeding colonies of tree sparrows in Northamptonshire. Skylarks, common tern and hobby are common and, in the winter, lapwing and golden plover are in abundance.

Treswell Wood SSSI

Near: Treswell and Nottingham, Nottinghamshire
Map: 14, B2
Web: www.wildlifetrust.org.uk/nottinghamshire

P for keyholders

The wood is one of the best examples of an ash/oak/maple wood in Nottinghamshire. The ponds add interest, supporting marsh marigold, yellow iris, water crowfoot and animals such as great crested newt, smooth newt and more than 12 species of water beetle. Stoats and foxes are regularly seen in the woodland and large molehills are evident. The woodland

birds include woodcock, jay, great spotted and lesser spotted woodpecker and nuthatch and, in summer, blackcap, garden warbler and spotted flycatcher.

Whisby Nature Park

Near: Lincoln, Lincolnshire
Map: 13, A2
Web: www.lincstrust.org.uk

♿ (ltd), WC ℹ️ 🚻 🏠

The reserve of flooded disused gravel pits, scrub woodland and grassland is home to nightingales, sand martins and common terns in the spring. During early summer, more than 7,000 southern marsh orchids bloom in one small area, and many of the 15 breeding species of dragonfly and damselfly can be seen. Autumn brings birds such as the goldcrest, redpoll and the grey wagtail. In winter, wildfowl can be numerous and varied.

Wilwell Farm Cutting

Near: Ruddington, near Nottingham, Nottinghamshire
Map: 14, B2
Web: www.wildlifetrust.org.uk/nottinghamshire

P (££), 🚻

Twenty species of butterfly have been recorded in this tranquil wildlife haven. Most common are gatekeeper,

meadow brown, ringlet, small skipper, peacock and speckled wood. In one evening, a moth survey recorded more than 80 species. Foxes are frequently seen, as are rabbits and squirrels. A range of birds pass through the site during the year, including owls, sparrowhawk and green woodpecker. Various tits and wagtails, as well as common garden birds such as thrush, blackbirds and wrens, make up the local population.

Wye Valley Reserves

Near: Buxton, Derbyshire
Map: 14, A1
Web: www.wyevalleyaonb.org.uk

P WC 🚻

The National Trust's three reserves, Miller's Dale, Chee Dale and Priestcliffe Lees, stretch along the Wye Valley. These reserves are wonderful places to see insects, including butterflies such as dark green fritillary and brown argus, as well as the day-flying cistus forester moth. All year, the river gives the chance of seeing dipper, grey wagtail and water vole. In the summer, cliff-nesting birds, such as the kestrel, take advantage of the long-disused limestone quarry faces.

Dor beetle: worth its weight in... cow pat

It wouldn't take long rustling in the humus of a forest floor to uncover some of the beetles living there. These hardy creatures have been around since before the dinosaurs and there are around 4,000 species in the UK. Ground beetles are the ones you're most likely to find on the woodland floor, but they also find shelter under loose bark. Soldier beetles, however, wait around on flowers for other unsuspecting insects to come along, which they then eat. And the dor beetle is a particular type of dung beetle with a fondness for cow pats. It eats its own weight in dung every day.

BIRD RESERVES

Frampton Marsh
Near: Boston, Lincolnshire
Map: 13, B3
Web: www.rspb.org.uk
ⓘ
Birds can be seen here all year round, but high tides from autumn to spring are best for roosting wading birds: the bigger the tide the better the spectacle. In winter there are Brent geese, birds of prey, twites, corn buntings, rock pipits and, with luck, Lapland buntings. In summer, large numbers of redshanks breed at an exceptionally high density. Other breeding species include oystercatchers, skylarks and reed buntings. Marsh harriers can frequently be seen hunting over the reserve.

Freiston Shore
Near: Boston, Lincolnshire
Map: 13, B3
Web: www.rspb.org.uk
P ♿ (ltd), 🚻
Freiston Shore is a developing nature reserve with an

expanding range of wetland habitats. The reserve is situated on The Wash – the most important site in the UK for wintering birds, with over a third of a million wildfowl and wading birds present during the winter. An individually designed and created lagoon, dotted with islands and overlooked by an observation hide, provides great views of some of the birds of The Wash – avocets and shelducks in summer, Brent geese and huge flocks of roosting waders in winter.

FORESTS & WOODLAND

Bardney Limewoods NNR
Near: Bardney and Wragby, near Horncastle, Lincolnshire
Map: 13, B2
Web: www.english-nature.org.uk
P WC ⓘ 🚻 🅿
Bardney Limewoods is a group of small woods, the largest of which is Chambers Farm Wood. The woods are the most important

examples of small-leaved lime woodland in Britain. Spring and summer are the best time to visit for butterflies and wildflowers. There is a designated butterfly garden in Chambers Farm Wood.

Burrs Wood
Near: Dronfield, Derbyshire
Map: 14, A1
Web: www.wt-woods.org.uk
P (nearby)
Burrs Wood is a secluded and largely unspoilt wood. A survey of beetles in April 2000 turned up 50 species. This survey is a good indicator of the high level of invertebrate diversity. The wood is home to the usual range of woodland mammals, from mice to roe deer.

Centenary and Royal Tigers Wood
Near: Hinckley, Leicestershire
Map: 14, B4
Web: www.wt-woods.org.uk
P 🅿
Centenary and Royal Tigers Wood occupies a prominent

Badgers: hygiene kings of the natural world?

Badgers are very clean animals. Not only do they refresh their bedding of moss, grass and leaves every couple of days, they also dig latrines a short distance away from their sett entrance. Badgers are found all over Britain, but exist in their largest numbers in the South and South West. Usually they live in woodland that's near pastureland and they like to make their setts on a slope in well-drained soil. Up to 15 badgers will live together in one sett, which is a maze of chambers and tunnels with passing places dug into the tunnel design. Young are born between January and March in litters of two or three. Classed as Britain's largest carnivore (they can grow up to a metre in length) the badger's diet is very varied, including acorns, bulbs, roots, earthworms, snails, mice, voles, frogs and even baby rabbits. The best time to see them is at dusk when they emerge for their nightly forage for food. Woodlands you can visit for badgers include: Ashford Hangers, Cannock Forest, Skipton Woods, Drumlamph Wood, Kew Gardens and Gight Wood.

hillside position. Hedgerows, a stream and several mature trees add to the diversity of the site, which was in arable crop production prior to tree planting. Open areas of grassland have been retained and are mown for hay in July to encourage a rich mixture of wild grasses and flowers.

Coton Wood

Near: Coton in the Elms, near Tamworth, Derbyshire
Map: 14, A3
Web: www.wt-woods.org.uk
P 🌳

There is an interesting community of invertebrates and plants thriving in these grassland/scrub edge conditions: Timothy grass, gorse, small copper butterfly, brown hawker dragonfly, meadow brown butterfly, marbled white butterfly and Roselle's bush cricket to name just a few. Conditions are also good for common farm and garden birds, such as yellow-hammer and dunnock. There is evidence of badger activity over much of the wood.

Duke's Wood

Near: Kirklington, near Mansfield, Nottinghamshire
Map: 14, B2
Web: www.wildlifetrust.org.uk/nottinghamshire
P

Duke's Wood is situated on a ridge of high ground. The usual woodland birds can be seen, including blackcap, garden warbler and spotted flycatcher in summer. Greater spotted woodpecker and jay are regularly seen and hawfinch are a possibility. Butterflies attracted to the varied ground flora include common blue, comma, peacock, brimstone, gatekeeper and wall brown. Red deer, fox, stoat and

badger do occur, but are rarely seen.

> **DID YOU KNOW?**
> Queen ants can live for up to 15 years.

Everdon Stubbs SSSI

Near: Everdon, near Northampton, Northamptonshire
Map: 14, C4
Web: www.wt-woods.org.uk
P 🌳

Everdon Stubbs comprises four different types of woodland community. Ecological features within the wood that are of significance, include the number of old trees – sweet chestnut, rowan, field maple and wild cherry; an area of hornbeam; large semi-permanent gaps and glades; small pond and wet flush; and locally rare plants such as moschatel, broom, gorse and wild raspberry.

Felicity's Wood

Near: Loughborough, Leicestershire
Map: 14, B3
Web: www.wt-woods.org.uk
P ℹ️

The exceptionally clean waters of the wood brook provide a habitat for grey wagtails, stone loach and white-clawed crayfish – the only species of crayfish native to the UK. Like its marine cousin the lobster, it has been caught and eaten for centuries by humans, as well as otters and other animals.

Great Merrible Wood SSSI

Near: Oakham, Leicestershire
Map: 14, C3
Web: www.lrwt.org.uk
P

The wood is a breeding place for various common woodland birds and a refuge and feeding place for badgers, foxes, deer and many small

mammals. A number of first county records of invertebrate species have been made in the wood, which has a wonderful show of bluebells in the spring.

Harrison's Plantation

Near: Nottingham, Nottinghamshire
Map: 14, B2
Web: www.nottinghamcity.gov.uk

This wildlife reservoir is linked to Martin's Pond. The woodland is dominated by sycamore, ash, wild cherry and oak. Birds widespread in the area include the grey spotted woodpecker, kingfisher, nuthatch, blackcap, redpoll and spotted flycatcher. A meadow and fishing pond (known as Raleigh Pond) have been recently created to the eastern end of the plantation.

Launde Big Wood SSSI

Near: Launde near Oakham, Leicestershire
Map: 14, C3
Web: www.lrwt.org.uk

Launde Big Wood is one of the largest and most important semi-natural ancient woodlands in the East Midlands. It is home to a number of mammals, including the badger, stoat and weasel and, among the birds, the nightingale and nuthatch. The purple and white-letter hairstreak butterflies can be found here, as well as an array of ground flora that provide lovely displays in the spring.

Mapperley Wood

Near: Ilkeston, Derbyshire
Map: 14, B2
Web: www.derbyshirewildlifetrust.org.uk
Admission: permit needed for hide; £4/£8 for WT members
♿ 🏠

Paths running through the reserve allow permit holders to see birds such as coot, moorhen, mallard, kingfisher

The National Forest

Young female fallow deer

Map: 14, A3
Web: www.nationalforest.org

The National Forest is an area of 200 square miles across Staffordshire, Derbyshire and Leicestershire, where new woodlands are being created to complement ancient woodland, meadows, lakes and rivers to create a new forest for the benefit of all – including wildlife.

Bignall's Wood
Near: Lount, Leicestershire
P & (ltd), WC ⓘ

Fallow deer and badgers are known to use Bignall's Wood as part of their territory as they come out from the neighbouring woodland of Rough Heath. As well as kestrels and buzzards, which regularly patrol the skies above Bignall's Wood, the old barn has been used as a roosting site for bats and potentially even a nesting site for barn owls.

Burroughs Wood
Near: Ratby, Leicestershire
P 🚻

Burroughs Wood is a wood of two halves, both of them large sites and linked via a public right of way. The northern section is a broad-leaved woodland with ancient origins, proving a draw in the spring when the woodland floor is awash with bluebells. South of this is a newly planted woodland, created in 1996 and 1997, with native broadleaf species such as silver birch, with its distinctive white bark and pale-green leaves, and hawthorn, whose heavily scented flowers appear in May and early June.

Jaguar Lount Wood
Near: Lount, Leicestershire

Jaguar Lount Wood is frequented by badgers, as well as fallow and muntjak deer from neighbouring existing woodlands. Brown hares have also been seen within the wood. Skylarks are common, and buzzards and kestrels can be seen hunting over the wood or resting in the hedgerows and adjacent woodland.

Seale Wood
Near: Overseale, Derbyshire
⛺

Badgers are well known to use Seale Wood, and foxes and weasels have been sighted. Rabbits are present in large numbers. A wide variety of bird species visit Seale Wood, including tits, warblers, chiffchaffs, skylarks and goldfinches. Buzzards, sparrowhawks and kestrels can also be seen hunting over the grassy areas of the wood. The brook, riverside and pond are the best areas to see butterflies, dragonflies, bees and other insect species in the summer.

Sence Valley
Near: Ibstock, Leicestershire
P & (ltd), WC ⓘ

Long grassy areas have become home for many wild mammals, including field voles, shrews, stoats, rabbits, bats and foxes. It has recently become evident that otters too are once again using the River Sence. The forest park attracts a wide variety of bird species: the lakes provide habitat for species such as heron, coots, tufted duck, pochard, wigeon and great crested grebe.

Willesley Wood
Near: Ashby de la Zouch and Oakthorpe, Leicestershire
P

The site has 62 acres of new tree planting with 15 acres of original woodland. The lake – stocked with carp, pike and tench – is surrounded by marginal wetland fringes important to amphibians and waterfowl: it is popular with swans and coots which breed here. The marsh is a good place to find unusual insects and butterflies are common in the open parkland area.

and other woodland species. In spring, the woodland is inhabited by chiffchaff, willow warbler and blackcap, as well as the more familiar calls of robin and chaffinch. Great spotted woodpecker and nuthatch also make their homes among the trees. In winter, small numbers of waterfowl visit the ponds and water rail can be found in the marshy areas, its presence only given away by its distinctive squealing call.

Martin's Wood
Near: Loughborough, Leicestershire
Map: 24, B3
Web: www.wt-woods.org.uk
P
Martin's Wood is situated in Charnwood Forest with spectacular views over the River Soar and Trent Valley. The wood's mature shelterbelts are dominated by oak, with some beech, holly, sycamore and rowan; while flowers include bluebell and foxglove. Drystone boundary and enclosure walls of ancient volcanic rock add to the attractiveness of both woods.

Martinshaw Wood
Near: Ratby and Groby, near Leicester, Leicestershire
Map: 14, B3
Web: www.wt-woods.org.uk
P P
This ancient woodland has been managed since the thirteenth century variously as a timber source, as wood pasture and also as pheasant cover. It consists of many native and exotic broad-leaved trees and there has been some conifer planting in the past. The most interesting areas are the woodland margins and the areas around the marl pits in the north. Plants include lily-of-the-valley and wood anemone, and broad-leaved

helleborine have also been identified in the past.

Mill Field Wood
Near: Wigston, Leicestershire
Map: 14, B3
Web: www.wt-woods.org.uk
P
The site lies adjacent to the Grand Union Canal and is bounded by mature hedgerows containing a few mature ash and oak trees. In the past, floristically diverse species, such as wild thyme, spiny restharrow and ragged robin, have been prevalent.

Nor Wood, Cook Spring and Owler Car
Near: Dronfield, Derbyshire
Map: 14, B1
Web: www.wt-woods.org.uk
P
Although mining, felling and replanting have all been carried out in these woods over the last two centuries, maps show that the woods have been here since 1600 and that they are best categorised as ancient semi-natural woodland, with fine examples of oak and ash. At least 25 species of birds have been recorded in the woods, including the occasional turtle dove.

Old Wood
Near: Skellingthorpe and Lincoln, Lincolnshire
Map: 13, A2
Web: www.wt-woods.org.uk

P
Old Wood is renowned for its butterfly populations: more than 20 species of butterfly and eight species of dragonfly have been recorded in recent years, among them white admiral and a healthy population of purple hairstreak. A wide range of birds also make use of the wood throughout the year, including buzzard, goshawk, lesser spotted woodpecker, song thrush, siskin and bullfinch. All the usual woodland mammals are present and deer species are particularly well represented, with muntjak, roe and even red deer being spotted.

Oldmoor Wood
Near: Ilkeston, Nottinghamshire
Map: 14, B2
Web: www.wt-woods.org.uk
This charming woodland has many paths, making for pleasant circular walks, and a large pond with an island planted with yew trees. Other smaller ponds are dotted around the woodland.

Owlet
Near: Laughton and Gainsborough, Lincolnshire
Map: 13, A1
Web: www.wt-woods.org.uk
P ♿ (ltd)
Birds species of note at Owlet include green and great spotted woodpecker, nuthatch, treecreeper and woodcock. Along with the

Wood anemone

This pretty woodland flower is an indicator of an ancient woodland. It flowers in the early spring, but if it's dull and grey the flowers don't open. It's sometimes called the windflower as Pliny wrote that the flowers didn't open until the wind blew.

The elevated walkway at Salcey Forest

common woodland birds, hen harrier and buzzard are sometimes seen hunting over the area. The open areas of the site are of considerable interest for their invertebrate fauna. Large red, common blue and azure damselfly have been recorded, as have a total of 16 types of butterfly. Spiders are common throughout.

Prior's Coppice SSSI
Near: Oakham and Uppingham, Rutland
Map: 14, C3
Web: www.lrwt.org.uk
P (££)
The ancient woods of east Leicestershire and west Rutland are extremely rich in plantlife, and Prior's Coppice is no exception. So far, 230 species of flowering plants and ferns have been recorded, as have – in animal life – badger, fox, stout, muntjak and grass snake. There are good numbers of nuthatch, blackcap, garden warbler and many other birds, too. Orange-tip and brimstone butterflies are common in spring, and both purple and white-letter hairstreaks are present.

Rockingham Forest
Near: Stamford, Lincolnshire, and Kettering, Northamptonshire
Map: 14, C4
Web: www.forestry.gov.uk
P **&** (ltd), **WC** **i**
Rockingham Forest has a rich and varied landscape, with farmland, open pasture, pockets of woodland and villages built from local stone. It is rich in wildlife, from three species of deer to dormice and badgers. Nightingales can be heard in some of these woods in summertime, as can many warblers, and you may also see various birds of prey, including the red kite. Adder, grass snake and common lizard can be found in parts of the forest.

Salcey Forest
Near: Northampton, Northamptonshire
Map: 14, C4
Web: www.forestry.gov.uk
P **&** (ltd), **WC** **i** **☐** **⛲**
The Royal Forest of Salcey is an ancient woodland offering walking and opportunities to view an amazing range of wildlife. Fallow and muntjak deer are common, as are

dormice and several species of bat (including noctule, pipistrelle and brown long-eared). All three woodpecker species live here and flocks of warblers visit in the summer. The ponds in Salcey are inhabited by newts, common lizards, grass snakes and slow worms. Thirty species of butterfly and more than 300 species of moth make their home here.

Sherwood Forest NNR
Near: Nottingham, Nottinghamshire
Map: 14, B2
Web: www.english-nature.org.uk
WC **&** **i** **☐**
Once part of the 10,000-acre Royal Forest of Sherwood, the Sherwood Forest NNR comprises Birklands Forest which is thought to be more than 1,000 years old. The forest is home to approximately 1,000 beetle and spider species – many of which are rare – and more than 200 species of fungi have been recorded here. Local birdlife includes the great spotted woodpecker, green woodpecker, tawny owl, redstart and nightjar. The area also supports a number of bat species, including the noctule.

Stoke Wood
Near: Corby, Northamptonshire
Map: 14, C4
Web: www.wt-woods.org.uk
P (nearby), **☐**
Stoke Wood is a wet ash/field maple wood. It has a very rich assortment of plants associated with true woodland and more open ride habitats, including herb paris, wood anemone, wood sorrel, yellow archangel, early purple orchid, bird's-nest orchid, wood speedwell, greater butterfly orchid, nettle-leaved bellflower and broad-leaved helleborine, as

well as a good assemblage of grasses, sedges and rush.

Tattershall Carrs

Near: Sleaford, Lincolnshire
Map: 13, B3
Web: www.wt-woods.org.uk

P

The invertebrate fauna of the woodland at Tattershall Carrs is of considerable interest, with two nationally scarce and 12 local species of beetle recorded in recent years. Notable bird species include garden warbler, woodcock, great spotted woodpecker, green woodpecker, turtle dove, bullfinch and a good population of song thrushes. There is evidence that both muntjak and roe deer are increasing in the woodlands.

COASTS, WETLANDS & WATERWAYS

Ashby Canal

Near: Ashby de la Zouch, Leicestershire
Map: 14, B3
Web: www.waterscape.com
The 22-mile long canal supports many species of plantlife and wildlife, including heron, kingfisher, moorhen and varied aquatic plantlife, as well as a number of coarse fish, including bream, roach, chub and pike.

Attenborough SSSI

Near: Beeston, Nottinghamshire
Map: 14, B2
Web: www.wildlifetrust.org.uk/nottinghamshire

P **i** **□** **⌂**

This complex of flooded gravel pits and islands covers 358 acres and supports a wide range of habitats. The reserve has a wide range of fish, amphibians and invertebrates, but the area is best known for its birds. These include a high proportion of the

county's shoveler and diving ducks, with larger numbers of mallard, teal, and occasionally wigeon. At different times during the year, the reserve also attracts migrant birds, waders, breeding birds and sedge warblers, as well as some rarer species such as grasshopper warbler, sawbills and sea ducks. The reserve is a venue for guided walks, Wildlife Watch activities and research.

DID YOU KNOW?

A fully-grown oak in the UK grows – and sheds – 250,000 leaves every year and produces around 2,000 acorns in a good year.

Carsington Water

Near: Ashbourne, Derbyshire
Map: 14, A2
Web: www.stwater.co.uk

P **♿** **(ltd)**, **WC**
i **□** **☂** **⌂**

The open water provides year-round habitat for fish such as rudd and brown trout, and birds such as gulls, kingfishers and great crested grebes, as well as a winter feeding ground for wildfowl species, including wigeon, teal, pochard and gadwall. Snipe and water rail inhabit the fringes of the reservoir, while shingle areas provide ideal nesting conditions for little ringed plovers and other waders. Swallows, swifts, sand and house martins all hunt over the water in spring catching mayflies. Other species found in and around the reservoir include large numbers of toads, frogs and newts and many bat species.

Chesterfield Canal

From: Chesterfield, Derbyshire, to Retford, Nottinghamshire
Map: 14, B1

Website: www.chesterfield-canal-trust.org.uk
i **□** at Tapton Lock Visitor Centre, Chesterfield
Known locally as Cuckoo Dyke, the canal runs from Chesterfield to the River Trent at West Stockwith. An abundance of wildlife incorporates an aquatic plant community of rarities, such as Linton's pondweed and brackish water crowfoot. Mallard and teal can be found in the reedbeds, while regular waders include lapwing and redshank. The green woodpecker is frequently observed, joined by swifts and swallows in the summer. The male bullfinch has been spotted, alongside the yellow-hammer and kingfisher. Raptors include the kestrel and buzzard, while red kite and osprey have been seen on rare occasions.

Cromford Canal

Near: Whatstandwell, near Ripley Derbyshire
Map: 14, B2
Web: www.derbyshirewildlifetrust.org.uk

WC **i**

This important wetland area is home to a variety of bird life, from ducks, moorhens and other waterfowl along the canal itself, to woodland birds such as blackbirds, robins and wrens. In spring and summer, the canal attracts many insects, especially dragonflies and damselflies, and it is a regular haunt for grass snakes and water voles.

Derwent Reservoir

Near: Upper Derwent Valley, Peak District National Park
Map: 14, B1
Web: www.waterscape.com

P **WC** **☂**

Derwent Reservoir is a prime location for catching wild rainbow and wild

Fossdyke Navigation

From: Torksey to Lincoln, Lincolnshire
Map: 13, A2
Web: www.waterscape.com

Constructed by the Romans around 12AD, the Fossdyke Navigation has a strong claim as Britain's oldest canal. It flows through almost entirely rural scenery for 11 miles, from the River Trent at Torksey to the River Witham at Lincoln. Although the Fossdyke's surroundings are plain and flat, they offer an undoubted charm, including spectacular sunsets. The fenland environments of the navigation create an ecosystem all of their own. Hedgerows are scarce, but the banks provide wildlife refuges. In the water, you might spot the white-clawed crayfish or several varieties of mussel.

Grand Union Canal

From: Central London to Birmingham, West Midlands
Map: 1 and 14, A4
Web: www.waterscape.com

The Grand Union Canal is home to a great variety of wildlife, from feeding herons and hunting owls to water voles. Butterflies abound in the hedgerows and canal banks, in the form of meadow brown, cabbage white, tortoiseshell and peacocks. Waterfowl include the common coots, moorhens, and mallards, but also swans, herons and kingfishers.

Grantham Canal

From: Nottingham, Nottinghamshire, to Grantham, Lincolnshire
Map: 14, B2 to C2
Web: www.granthamcanal.com

From the market town of Grantham to the River Trent, the Grantham Canal runs for 33 miles passing through the beautiful Vale of Belvoir.

Geese lining the banks of the Grand Union Canel

and stocked brown trout. Recent conservation has involved projects such as pond creations, heathland restoration, tree-planting, habitat creation and grassland management.

Donna Nook

Near: Saltfleet, Lincolnshire, near Mablethorpe
Map: 13, C2
Web: www.english-nature.org.uk

Birdlife is rich in this reserve of dunes, slacks, saltmarsh and inter-tidal areas. In summer, breeding dune birds include red-legged partridge, dunnock, white-throat, linnet, skylark, yellow-hammer and tree sparrow; while the mudflats provide a winter home for numbers of Brent geese, shelduck, twite, Lapland bunting, shore lark, knot and dunlin, as well as a wide variety of other wading birds. In addition, Donna Nook has one of the largest and most accessible breeding colonies of grey seals in the UK.

Erewash Canal

Near: Ripley, Nottinghamshire
Map: 14, B2
Web: www.waterscape.com

Woodlands by Erewash Canal and its nearby valleys contain a mixture of beech, ash, field maple and elm, and a wide range of flora, including carpets of bluebells and other woodland flowers. Grassland meadows display a richness of wildflowers like the bluebell, yellow archangel and lesser celandine frequented by damselflies, dragonflies and butterflies. The waterway and local ponds are home to ducks and moorhens, as well as frogs, great crested newts, and the water vole.

Foremark Reservoir

Near: Derby, Derbyshire, and Burton-on-Trent, Staffordshire
Map: 14, A3 and B2
Web: www.waterscape.com

Foremark Reservoir covers 230 acres in the heart of the National Forest between Derby and Burton-on-Trent. The reservoir is a good place to see waders.

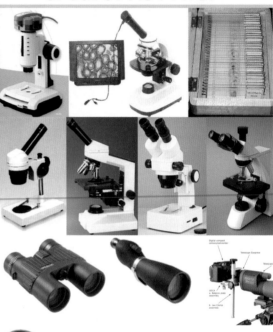

Closed to boating many years ago, much of the line is a designated SSSI. During the years of dereliction, the Grantham Canal has become a valuable wetland habitat for local wildlife.

Ladybower Reservoir
Near: Sheffield Derbyshire
Map: 14, A1
Web: www.waterscape.com
P **&** (ltd), **i**
As the reservoir holds very acid water, it supports little wildlife except for some wildfowl such as red-breasted mergansers. Trout are put into the reservoirs for anglers. Common sandpipers nest on the shores but are easily disturbed. Nearby streams often have grey wagtails and dippers.

Lincolnshire Coast and Marshes
Near: Saltfleetby, Lincolnshire
Map: 13, C1
Web: www.english-nature.org.uk
The Lincolnshire Coast and Marshes natural area is a generally flat coastal plain that is largely under arable cultivation. Wet grasslands near the coast support large numbers of wildfowl and coastal birds, such as lapwing, snipe and redshank. Freshwater habitats include streams, drainage ditches, blow wells and a disused sea bank clay pit. All support a diversity of wildlife: the last two contain reedbeds that support nationally rare birds, such as the bearded tit.

Makin Fisheries
Near: Wolvey and Hinckley, Leicestershire
Map: 14, B4
Web: www.waterscape.com
P **wc**
In the heart of the Warwickshire countryside,

this fishery has been created for the angler's enjoyment, with 18 clean and landscaped pools and more than 500 well maintained and reed fringed permanent swims. The lakes are stocked with 14 different species of fish, including chub, barbel, vast stocks of common, ghost, mirror and koi carp.

DID YOU KNOW?
A pipistrelle bat weighs only 5g – no more than a 2p coin.

Melton Mowbray Navigation
Near: Melton Mowbray, Leicestershire
Map: 14, C3
Web: www.waterscape.com
The Melton Mowbray Navigation follows the course of the River Wreake, winding through the Leicestershire countryside. The river has a good population of endangered white-clawed crayfish, and otters are believed to be breeding in the area. Several abandoned loops of the navigation, which were shortened when the new railway was opened, have since returned to nature and provide valuable habitats.

Moulton Marsh
Near: Holbeach, Lincolnshire
Map: 13, B3
Web: www.english-nature.org.uk
P
The marsh is made up of a man-made long narrow stretch of land planted with trees, several saline lagoons and a small area of saltmarsh. Inhabiting the marsh are 120 recorded species of bird, including winter waders, wildfowl, short-eared owl, warblers, finch, bunting. Also notable are strawberry clover, sea milkwort and two species of grasshopper.

Pitsford Reservoir
Near: Northampton, Northamptonshire
Map: 14, C4
Web: www.wildlifebcnp.org
P **wc** **⌂**
Wildfowl numbers at Pitsford Reservoir can exceed 10,000 in winter with 14 species of duck present alongside grebes, geese, coot and swans. In spring, breeding populations comprise 55 different species of bird. In July and August, common blue and emerald damselflies and ruddy darter dragonflies, among others, total hundreds or thousands on the reserve. Twenty-three species of butterfly have been recorded.

River Ancholme
From: South Ferriby to Snitterby, Lincolnshire
Map: 13, A1
Web: www.waterscape.com
Running straight as an arrow from Snitterby in rural Lincolnshire to the mighty Humber Estuary at Ferriby Bridge, the Ancholme is a veritable wildlife haven. Most notable are otters and voles, while spined loach, migrating waterfowl and invertebrates are more common. The barn owl is also present, feeding on the voles. The diverse birdlife includes kingfishers, herons, warblers, reed bunting and sand martins, while a variety of beetles, dragonflies and damselflies also thrive. The white-clawed crayfish is resident, as are various molluscs. Inhabitant mammals include bats and water shrews, while all sorts of plants abound, from pondweed to water plantain.

River Dove
From: Axe Edge Moor to River Trent
Map: 14, A2
Web: www.peakdistrict-nationalpark.info

The River Dove follows the boundary between limestone and shale. This affects the vegetation and wildlife, so that different species can be found on each side of the river. Herons often feed in the quiet, northern stretches of the river. Trout, dippers, grey wagtails, moorhens and water voles can be seen in, on and by the river.

River Nene
From: Northamptonshire to The Wash, Norfolk
Map: 14, C4 and 12, A1
Web: www.waterscape.com
Birds, such as moorhens, mallards, swans, grebes and herons, can be found on the Nene's riverbanks. The river at Wellingborough is a haven for swans. Near Titchmarsh is a nature reserve famous for its heronry and other birds which flock to it each year. There is a National Dragonfly Museum at Ashton. Along the River Nene is Nene Park, which contains a number of woods, lakes and fields which are home to all kinds of wildlife and particularly notable for birds and badgers.

River Soar
Flows through: Leicestershire
Map: 14, B3 and C3
Web: www.waterscape.com
The River Soar is rich in wildlife: swans, moorhen and drakes are joined by Canadian geese in the summer. The waters hold many coarse fish, including perch, pike and bream. The river also boasts healthy populations of the endangered white-clawed crayfish.

River Witham
Flows through: Lincolnshire
Map: 13
Web: www.waterscape.com
The area around Beckingham has wet grassland areas that provide ideal conditions for wildflowers, insects and birds. The river itself supports a large swan population. Ostlers Plantation has been replanted with trees and attracts a wide variety of wildlife.

Rutland Water SSSI
Near: Egleton, Oakham, Rutland
Map: 14, C3
Web: www.rutlandwater.org.uk
P (at Egleton and Lyndon), (ltd), WC 🖼 ℹ 🏠
Rutland Water is recognised as one of the most important inland sites in the UK for passage waders and up to 19 species have been recorded in a single day. It also boasts up to 20 species of wildfowl in winter (probably the most important inland wildfowl sanctuary in the UK) and 24 species of butterfly, damselfly and dragonfly.

Saltfleetby-Theddlethorpe Dunes NNR
Near: Saltfleet and Mablethorpe, Lincolnshire
Map: 13, C1 and C2
Web: www.english-nature.org.uk
P (ltd), WC 🖼
Saltfleetby-Theddlethorpe Dunes are a five-mile stretch of dunes and foreshore on the Lincolnshire coast. In winter the fruit of dense scrub, which covers most of the fore-dune, provides an food source for many birds, especially fieldfare and blackbirds.

Staunton Harold Reservoir
Near: Derby, Derbyshire
Map: 14, B3
Web: www.waterscape.com
The Dimminsdale Nature Reserve, beside the Staunton Harold Reservoir, is an SSSI. The range of habitats within the reserve means there are plenty of different species to spot. In particular, in the large field to the south you may see hares and green woodpeckers.

Around the entrance to the site is plenty of hawthorn, and the mix of habitat types brings a rich array of insects.

Trent and Mersey Canal
Flows through: Derby and Stoke-on-Trent
Map: 14, B2 and 15, C1
Web: www.waterscape.com
Otters have recently been spotted in the Trent and Mersey Canal and local councils have begun to provide stop-off otter holts to encourage them. Water voles have also been seen.

Willington Gravel Pits
Near: Derby, Derbyshire
Map: 14, B2
Web: www.derbyshireos.org.uk
This is a typical Trent Valley ex-gravel pit site close to the river and village of Willington. In 2000, a survey reported that 119 species of bird were recorded here with highlights including bar-tailed godwit, honey buzzard, little stint, purple sandpiper, red-necked phalarope and spotted crake.

NOT SO WILD

Bryers Heritage Farm
Address: Markeaton, Derby DE22 4NH
Map: 14, B2
Tel: 01332 204597
Web: www.farmgarden.org.uk
Open: weekends, Bank Holidays and school holidays, 11am to 4pm
(ltd), ℹ 📧
The educational centre provides the opportunity to learn about British breeds of farm animals, including geese, Tamworth pigs and lambs.

Clumber Park
Address: Worksop, Nottinghamshire S80 3AZ
Map: 14, B1
Tel: 01909 476592
Web: www.nationaltrust.org.uk

Open: daily, dawn to dusk (except 25 December)
Admission: free; £2 for walled kitchen garden

🅿 ♿ WC ⬛ ⬛ ⬛

The park is more than 3,800 acres, including peaceful woods, open heath and rolling farmland, with a superb serpentine lake at its heart. Although the house was demolished in 1938, many fascinating features of the estate remain, including a walled kitchen garden, with spectacular glass houses, where vegetables are grown.

Gorse Hill City Farm
Address: Anstey Lane, Leicester, Leicestershire LE4 0FJ
Map: 14, B3
Tel: 0116 2537582
Web: www.aboutbritain.com/GorseHillCityFarm
Open: daily, 10am to 4.30pm
Admission: donation

🅿 WC ⬛ 🎪 ⬛

Gorse Hill City Farm was started in 1985 by The Friends of Leicester City Farm. A whole host of farm animals can be seen here, including pigs, cattle, sheep and goats.

Haddon Hall
Address: Bakewell, Derbyshire DE45 1LA
Map: 14, A2
Tel: 01629 812855
Web: www.haddonhall.co.uk
Admission: £4.50/£8.50

⬛

Haddon Hall is a fortified medieval manor house dating from the twelfth century. It is surrounded by terraced Elizabethan gardens.

Hodsock Priory
Address: Blyth, near Worksop, Nottinghamshire S81 0TY
Map: 14, B1
Tel: 01909 591204

Web: www.hodsockpriory.com
Open: daily, February/March for four weeks, 10am to 4pm
Admission: £4

The Hodsock Priory garden has a terrace, herbaceous borders, a lake, a bog garden and an old moat.

Stonebridge City Farm
Address: Stonebridge Road, St Ann's, Nottingham NG3 2FR
Map: 14, B2
Tel: 0115 950 5113
Web: www.farmgarden.org
Open: Saturday to Thursday, 10am to 3/4pm

♿ (ltd), WC ⬛

Stonebridge City Farm works mainly with people with learning disabilities or high support needs. There are seven paddocks and a barn for cows, pigs, goats, sheep, chickens and rabbits.

West Midlands

The West Midlands is more often associated with industrial development and traffic jams than wildlife, but you don't have to travel far from the concrete sprawl to escape into nature's grasp.

The canal network in this part of England is one of the most developed, but whereas its banks were once teeming with labourers and the water full of barges laden with coal, they are now home to water voles, shrews, wildflowers, kingfishers and heron. Reservoirs that were created to supply the canals with water are now wonderful wetland habitats with large bird populations, especially in the wintertime.

The canals often connect rivers which are their own reward for the wildlife lover. The River Wye meanders its way through dramatic limestone cliffs around Chepstow to the gentler rolling hills of Herefordshire.

Conservation work is slowly undoing the damage caused by previous heavy industrialisation of the area and the very rare polecat has now repopulated the lower reaches of the Wye Valley, where otter numbers are also increasing. Before mining took over this area of Britain, much of the land was covered in forest and pockets of ancient woodland still remain today. The dark and damp conditions are perfect for fungi and an autumntime visit can reveal many, many different species including some of the rarer, more poisonous, ones.

To the south of the Black Country, farming took the place of mining as the area's main breadwinner and Herefordshire is often described as England's most rural county, with a rich mosaic landscape of small fields, ancient hedgerows and wooded hills. From the Black Mountains in the west to the Malvern Hills in the east and down to the sweeping Wye Valley, the county embodies the finer characteristics of a rapidly vanishing traditional landscape.

The hedges, a haven for songbirds and dormice, often enclose examples of unimproved hay meadows – a habitat found less and less frequently in Britain – with great examples of colourful wildflowers such as knapwort, green winged orchid and St John's wort.

Staffordshire, to the north of the Black Country, is a heavily wooded area again with many fine examples of ancient woodland, old oaks and beeches. The sandy soils are popular with many reptiles and amphibians, such as grass snakes and lizards, as well as badgers, hedgehogs, stoats, weasels and hares.

West Midlands residents are proud of the rich diversity of wildlife that can be found here, and visitors can't fail to be delighted with the secret gems of wildlife reserves here.

PICTURED: Wye Valley AONB

Not to be missed

● **Cannock Forest**
This extensive forest is a haven for wildlife including a large number of reptiles and amphibians.

● **Rhos Fiddle**
A wonderful upland reserve and a great place for birdwatching, botanising or chasing insects.

● **Wood Lane**
One of the premier birdwatching sites in Shropshire. Winter or summer, there is always something to see.

● **Wye Valley**
If you're hoping to see polecats, then this dramatic river valley of limestone cliffs and narrow floodplains is your best bet in the area.

● **Wyre Forest**
Ancient woodland is always a delight for man and beast and the coppiced oaks here give shelter to many mammals, birds and invertebrates.

● **Wyrley and Essington Canal**
This charming, part-rural waterway is home to rich and varied flora and fauna, including kingfishers, white-clawed crayfish, dragonflies and herons, and even the odd otter and water vole.

Shropshire Hills AONB

Near: Shropshire
Map: 15, B2 and B3
Web: www.shropshirehills
aonb.co.uk
ⓘ (in Church Stretton,
Shrewsbury and Ludlow)
The most mountainous
part of the English West
Midlands, where the
pastoral English lowlands
meet the remote Welsh
uplands, the Shropshire
Hills AONB extends
from the Wrekin to the
Clun Forest and from
the Stiperstones across
to the Clee Hills. It is a
landscape of contrasts
with meandering rivers
and fertile valleys, rolling
pastoral fields and patches
of woodland, picturesque
villages and historic
buildings, hillforts and
ancient monuments. There
are many celebrated sites,
and much geological and

wildlife interest, including
limestone rocks and
400-year-old hedgerows.
The area is surrounded
by historic market-towns
and dotted with attractive
villages. A wealth of
wildlife is found within
the Shropshire Hills.
On the hilltops, heather,
grasses and bracken
flourish. Look out for the
sparkling yellow flowers
of bog asphodel, and the
delicate cotton grass and
marsh violets that nestle
alongside them. These
upland areas are home to a
variety of birds, including
red grouse, curlew,
skylark and meadow pipit.
Buzzard, raven and the
occasional red kite can
be seen soaring above
the hills. The valleys and
hillsides are a patchwork
of small fields where you

can still find wildflower
meadows. Wood warbler,
pied flycatcher and redstart
may be seen in the summer.
Careful management
ensures healthy habitats for
a multitude of flowering
plants, mosses, fungi,
lichens, innumerable
butterflies, moths and
other insects. Trees are
another important feature
of the Shropshire Hills.
The area is a stronghold
of the black poplar, one
of our rarest native trees.
A large number of veteran
trees have been recorded
in the area, providing ideal
habitats for many rare and
specialised invertebrates.
Many of the rivers and
streams are lined with alder
and willow, which was
traditionally coppiced for
timber clog soles, firewood
and charcoal gunpowder.

AONBs

Wye Valley AONB

Near: Hereford, Herefordshire, and Chepstow, Gloucestershire
Map: 16, B2 and 7, B2
Web: www.wyevalleyaonb.org.uk

Wye Valley AONB surrounds a 72-mile stretch of the River Wye from the rocky outcrop of Chepstow Castle to just south of the city of Hereford, straddling the borders between England and Wales, Gloucestershire, Herefordshire and Monmouthshire in the process. The Wye Valley AONB is made up of a collection of different landscapes which can be divided broadly into two halves: the Lower Wye Gorge between Chepstow and Symonds Yat, with its dramatic limestone cliffs and narrow floodplain, and the gentler Herefordshire Lowlands north of Ross on Wye, where the river meanders across the red sandstone. The Wye Valley is particularly important for its rich wildlife habitats, and has a high concentration of designated sites, covering approximately 10 per cent of the area. These include three sites of international importance, designated as candidate Special Areas of Conservation (cSACs) under the European Union's Habitats Directive. The three cSACs are the River Wye itself, more than 1,975 acres of ancient semi-natural woodland in the heart of the Wye Gorge and a collection of sites in the Lower Wye Valley used as roosts by Greater and Lesser Horseshoe bats. It is also home to the nationally rare polecat, which has now re-colonised the Lower Wye Valley after an absence of more than a century. Otter numbers are also on the increase.

NATURE RESERVES

Aqualate Mere NNR

Near: Newport, Staffordshire
Map: 15, C2
Web: www.english-nature.org.uk
🏞️ 🏠

Aqualate Mere NNR is a large lowland reserve situated in the grounds of Aqualate Hall. Aqualate Mere is the largest natural lake in the West Midlands – the reserve also includes reedbeds, woodland and low-lying wet grassland. The mere supports a diverse fish population and large numbers of wintering and breeding wildfowl. The reserve also has a significant ornithological interest – including breeding curlew and snipe – and is important for its botanical and invertebrate communities. Mammals found here include polecat, water vole and harvest mouse, together with bats such as pipistrelle, Daubenton's, Natterer's, Brandt's and whiskered.

> **DID YOU KNOW?**
>
> In the breeding season, the male smooth newt grows a wavy crest down the length of his back.

Bateswood

Near: Newcastle-under-Lyme, Staffordshire
Map: 15, C1
Web: www.staffs-wildlife.org.uk
🏞️

The 61 acres of Bateswood are best known for their population of skylarks. Visit from mid-March onwards and you'll hear their continuous song as they soar above you. The reserve consists of a large range of habitats including scrub, mature woodland, plantation, wet grassland, meadows and open water.

Look out for lapwing, linnet and grey partridge along with summer-flowering plants such as oxeye daisy, meadow vetchling and bird's-foot trefoil. On warm sunny days, there's an abundance of dragonflies and damselflies flitting across the network of ponds and scrapes.

Brandon Marsh SSSI

Near: Coventry, Warwickshire
Map: 14, B4
Web: www.warwickshire-wildlife-trust.org.uk
🅿️ 🚻 ℹ️ 🍴 🏠 ♿

This reserve is one of the best birdwatching sites in the Midlands, and includes open water, marsh, reedbeds, woodland and grassland alongside the River Avon. It has been designated an SSSI for its ornithological interest. Breeding birds include Cetti's and grasshopper warblers, with substantial numbers of reed and sedge warblers in the reeds. In the autumn, large flocks of lapwing gather. During autumn and spring, a wide range of passage migrants pass through including waders and the occasional osprey. Winter attracts a wide range of ducks, and long-eared owls often visit for long periods.

Bredon Hill NNR

Near: Evesham, Worcestershire
Map: 16, E2
Web: www.english-nature.org.uk
🏞️

The site ranks as one of the top five places in Britain to see invertebrates. More than 230 invertebrate species have been recorded here and the site is home to seven rare and notable beetles – including the very rare violet click beetle – and six rare and notable species of fly. Glow worms are frequently seen at the site and butterflies found in

Shropshire Hills AONB

the grassland areas include marbled white, brown argus and dingy skipper. The scrub areas – characterised by hawthorn and ivy, with elder and blackthorn – provide important breeding sites for many bird species including white-throat, linnet and yellow-hammer.

Brown End Quarry

Near: Leek, Staffordshire
Map: 15, D1
Web: www.staffs-wildlife.org.uk
🅿 🚻

The country's first geological nature reserve, these 3.5 acres were quarried for limestone from the mid-eighteenth century until the mid-1960s. The site is important for its exposed rocks and fossils of the lower carboniferous period. The old spoil heaps and quarry floor have vegetated over, developing a typical limestone flora. Most notable are the numerous cowslips, which flower in spring. Later in the year, knapweed, scabious and oxeye daisies provide a nectar source for butterflies and other invertebrates. The fringing scrub provides good cover for small nesting birds such as warblers and tits.

Cotton Dell

Near: Cheadle, Staffordshire
Map: 15, D1
Web: www.staffs-wildlife.org.uk
🅿 🚻

This is an incredibly diverse area of unimproved grassland, broad-leaved and planted conifer woodland, geological exposures and a range of riverside habitats. The Cotton Brook winds its way through the centre of the reserve from Cotton to the village of Oakamoor, where it joins the River Churnet. In summer, the grasslands are buzzing with life as bees,

Cotton Dell

butterflies and other insects feed on the variety of plants, while dippers fly up and down stream collecting food for their young. In autumn, it will be the superb colours of the trees, particularly the beech, which will grab your attention.

Davies Meadows

Near: Norton Canon, near Hereford, Herefordshire
Map: 16, B2
Web: www.plantlife.org.uk
🅿

This tranquil 20-acre nature reserve in west Herefordshire is bordered by thick hedgerows, which enclose three unimproved hay meadows, a perry pear orchard and a pond. Colourful old hay meadows, such as those found at this nature reserve, are now extremely uncommon in the British countryside – more than 98 per cent of unimproved meadows have been lost over the last 60 years. The mixed hedgerows, pond and old meadows also provide excellent habitat for other wildlife. Frogs and toads

are regularly seen and grass snakes have been recorded in the past.

The Devil's Spittleful and Rifle Range

Near: Bewdley, Worcestershire
Map: 16, D1
Web: www.worcswildlifetrust. co.uk
🅿 🚻 🏞

This reserve contains a diverse range of habitats (heathland, grassland and woodland), making it an important home for an unusual set of plants and animals. In spring, green tiger beetles can be seen running and flying among the heather and on sandy paths, together with holly blue and orange-tip butterflies. Birds around this time of year are woodcock, skylark, chiffchaff and willow warbler. In summer, grass snakes can be spotted, as can toads and common lizards. Birds such as redstart, cuckoo, turtledove and lesser white-throat can also be seen.

The Doward Reserves

Near: Ross-on-Wye, Herefordshire
Map: 16, C3

Web: www.wildlifetrust.org.uk/
hereford

P T

The Doward Reserves include
King Arthur's Cave, White
Rocks, Leeping Stocks,
Miners Rest, Woodside Lords
and Wood Quarry. All of
the reserves are within easy
walking distance of each
other. They are predominantly
woodland, but with patches
of unimproved and restored
grassland. There are fine
displays of spring and summer
woodland flowers, including
columbine, several species of
orchid and meadow saffron.
White Rocks, Woodside and
Miners Rest are noted for
their summer butterflies, and
peregrines have been seen.
During the autumn, this is
the place to be for fungi. More
than 100 species have been
recorded including the rare
devil's-bolete.

Doxey Marshes

Near: Stafford, Staffordshire
Map: 15, D2
Web: www.staffs-wildlife.org.uk

P WC T A

Doxey Marshes is regionally
important for breeding and
wintering birds. The reserve
contains a wonderful mosaic of
habitats, including reedbeds,
pools, hedgerows and the
largest area of reed sweetgrass
in the Midlands. It is best
known for its impressive
diversity of birds, with more
than 80 species recorded. Most
significant are the populations
of breeding waders, such as
snipe, lapwing, redshank and
little ringed plover, which can
all be seen in the spring and
summer. Large flocks of
waders, including golden
plover, are regular winter
visitors, while in spring and
autumn, look out for
oystercatcher, green and
common sandpiper, greenshank
and black-tailed godwit.

Earl's Hill

Near: Shrewsbury, Shropshire
Map: 15, B2
Web: www.shropshirewildlifetrust.
org.uk

P

Earl's Hill is renowned for
its variety of habitats and
offers excellent views of
Shropshire from its Iron
Age hillfort summit. Pied
flycatchers, redstarts and
tree pipits nest in the wood,
while buzzards and ravens
wheel overhead. A colony of
grayling butterflies flitter over
the rocky scree where yellow
rock stonecrop flourishes. In
spring, bluebells, wood gorge
anemones and primroses
carpet the woodland floor
and moschatel, ramsons and
the rare upland enchanter's
nightshade clothe the banks
of the brook. There are a
variety of different walks to
choose from.

Fenn's Whixall and Bettisfield Mosses NNR

Near: Ross-on-Wye Shropshire
Map: 16, C3
Web: www.english-nature.org.uk

P

This is a site of international
importance for its wildlife.
The Mosses are one of the
most southerly lowland
raised bogs in Britain and,
at 2,340 acres, are the third
largest. Around 1,900 species
of invertebrates thrive; large
heath butterflies, white-faced
darter dragonflies, bog bush-
crickets and raft spiders. In
spring, calls of breeding teal,
mallard, curlew, skylark and
meadow pipit fill the air. In
summer, acrobatic hobby
catch myriad dragonflies and
nightjar enjoy dusk's clouds
of moths. Keep an eye out
for adders.

Hulme Quarry NNR

Near: Stoke-on-Trent,
Staffordshire

Map: 15, C1
Web: www.english-nature.org.uk

P WC A 0 T E

Hulme Quarry NNR is part
of the Park Hall Country
Park, an area that features
heathland, woodland,
grassland and scrub, as well
as a number of small pools
and geological features. The
reserve comprises a series of
sandstone canyons. These
were formed as a result of
extensive quarrying which
has exposed red sandstones
and conglomerates formed
in the Triassic period. Apart
from their geological interest,
the sandstone canyons are
also nesting sites for kestrels,
little owls and sand martins.

Ipsley Alders Marsh

Near: Redditch, Worcestershire
Map: 16, E1
Web: www.worcswildlifetrust.
co.uk

T

Ipsley Alders, a fen marsh, is
a wildlife oasis in an urban
area. At least 170 species of
plant have been recorded on
the reserve and dragonflies
and other invertebrates are
numerous. Birds breeding on
the site include reed bunting
and cuckoo. Snipe and
woodcock often feed on the
marsh and in the wood, and
all three species of woodpecker
breed here. Mallard, coot, teal,
moorhen and Canada goose
are frequently seen on the
pools. The alder trees attract
flocks of redpoll and siskin
during the winter.

Joan's Hill Farm

Near: Hereford, Herefordshire
Map: 16, B2
Web: www.plantlife.org.uk

P

This 46-acre nature reserve
enjoys views across hillsides
at the northern edge of the
Wye Valley AONB. The
reserve is a microcosm

A day in the life of Widget

SAVE £5!

£5 voucher for Burns Real Food for Dogs, and Guide to Natural Health Care, call 0800 018 18 90 (quote Wildlife Britain)

www.burns-pet-nutrition.co.uk

Last year Widget was diagnosed with chronic heart disease, but no-one seems to have told her - try telling a Spaniel to slow down!

Twice a day it's down the country park doing what Widget does best - chasing balls, squirrels, in fact anything that moves.

Diet is important, particularly as Widget can't tolerate chicken, so a fish based food suits nicely.

And the food of choice? Burns Real Food naturally!

of the characteristic old Herefordshire landscape, comprising hay meadows and orchards enclosed by thick hedgerows. Some of the fields at Joan's Hill Farm have escaped agricultural 'improvement' and are home to some of the classic flowers of old English hay meadows, including dyer's greenweed, knapweed, lady's bedstraw, green winged orchid and perforate St John's wort.

The Knapp and Papermill
Near: Worcester, Worcestershire
Map: 16, D2
Web: www.worcswildlifetrust.co.uk
P ⊞
This reserve has a diverse range of habitats in a relatively small area – orchards, meadows, ancient woodland and a brook – making it a haven for wildlife. In summer, keep an eye out for kingfisher feeding their young on the Leigh Brook. Other interesting birds include the three species of woodpecker, pied and spotted flycatcher, grey wagtail and breeding buzzard. More than 30 species of butterfly have also been spotted, including common and holly blue, white-letter and purple hairstreak, white admiral and brown argus.

Lugg Meadows
Near: Hereford, Herefordshire
Map: 16, B2
Web: www.wildlifetrust.org.uk/hereford
P ⊞
Also partly owned by Plantlife UK, Lugg Meadow and Lower House Farm consist of traditionally managed, unimproved flood plain meadow, stream ditches and a fragment of ancient woodland. The reserves are noted for their spectacular displays of

snake's head fritillary, which can be seen in late spring, along with a wide range of typical summer meadow flowers. Otters, kingfishers and sand martins frequent the river and curlew and lapwings can be seen during the winter. The river is particularly rich in invertebrates and is a good place to look for damselflies and dragonflies. Lower House Farm, a superb early Jacobean timber-framed building, is The Wildlife Trusts' headquarters.

Monkwood
Near: Worcester, Worcestershire
Map: 16, D2
Web: www.worcswildlifetrust.co.uk
P ⊞
Jointly owned by Butterfly Conservation, Monkwood is an actively managed coppice and a very important reserve in the county for moths and butterflies. Thirty-six species of butterfly have been recorded and more than 500 species of moth.

It is one of the few places you can see wood white butterflies in Worcestershire. Migrants such as blackcaps, garden and willow warblers and white-throats also return. Dragonflies can be seen around the pools in the summer, including the emperor dragonfly. In summer, the woodland rides are in flower with knapweed, meadowsweet, meliot and betony. In autumn, there is an impressive display of fungi, including many poisonous species.

Moseley Bog
Near: Moseley and Birmingham, West Midlands
Map: 15, D3
Web: www.birmingham.gov.uk
P at Sarehole Mill
A magical mosaic of habitats, including wet woodlands, wet meadows, a small bog and woodland plantation, this site also has an amazing history, from Bronze Age burnt mounds to mill pools and was the playground of JRR Tolkien for part of

Fungi

Britain has more than 2,000 species of fungi, most of which are poisonous to a greater or lesser degree and only about 200 of which can be eaten. They are an essential element of the ecosystem, recyling leaf litter into nutrients and forming symbiotic relationships with plants. It is also estimated that more than 1,000 species of insects rely on fungi for food and shelter. Fungi range in colour from white to brown, red and yellow and are at their best in woodlands in autumn, although some species grow in grasslands and others in the spring and summer.

PICTURED: Fly agaric

his childhood. Spring is the best time of year to see and hear abundant birdlife, such as woodpeckers, willow warblers, and nuthatches. In the summer the site is alive with insects. Butterflies abound and, after nightfall, moths take their place and frequently fall prey to the foraging bats.

Mottey Meadows NNR

Near: Wheaton Aston, near Telford, Staffordshire
Map: 15, C2
Web: www.english-nature.org.uk
📮

Mottey Meadows NNR is a series of flood meadows which have been managed as hay meadows for many centuries. The site supports a number of invertebrate species, including the rare horsetail weevil, while snipe, curlew and lapwing all breed here. The reserve's grassland supports more than 240 species of flowering plants, including the rare snake's head fritillary, while ditches on the site are home to plants such as common meadow rue, yellow flag and water mint. The best time to visit the reserve is in June to early July for meadow flowers, a permit is needed for access.

Piper's Hill and Dodderhill Common SSSI

Near: Bromsgrove, Worcestershire
Map: 16, D1
Web: www.worcswildlifetrust.co.uk
📮📮

Also known as Hanbury Woods, this woodland SSSI contains some of the oldest and largest trees in Worcestershire, including ancient beech, sweet chestnut pollards and big oaks believed to be 300-400 years old. Autumn is the time of year when the woods truly come to life, as more than 200

Rhos Fiddle

species of fungi have been found, such as chanterelles and beefsteak fungus. This is a great place to look out for woodland creatures and small invertebrates. You can also catch a glimpse of all three species of woodpecker, tits and the common nuthatch.

Rhos Fiddle

Near: Ludlow, Shropshire
Map: 15, B3
Web: www.shropshirewildlifetrust.org.uk
📮📮📮

A wonderful upland reserve on the border between England and Wales, this is an extensive area of heathland habitat that was once widespread on the surrounding hilltops. This is a great place for birdwatching, botanising, or chasing insects and has something of interest for everyone. In spring and summer, listen out for the calling of curlews and the song of the ascending skylark. In autumn, the heather and cotton grass are at their best, while in winter, you can appreciate the colours and textures of the mosses and lichens. Don't miss the yellow mountain pansies growing in the improved grassland areas on the south-western slopes of the reserve which flower from May to July.

Side Farm Meadows

Near: Stoke-on-Trent, Staffordshire
Map: 15, C1
Web: www.plantlife.org.uk

Side Farm is situated in the secluded valley of Cotton Dell in north-east Staffordshire. Perhaps because of the steep and difficult terrain, much of the valley has escaped agricultural 'improvement' and provides important habitat for a range of wildlife. As well as being an important area for fauna, the sheltered valley also provides an ideal habitat for invertebrates and large numbers of butterflies can be found on the reserve during the summer, including meadow brown, small heath and large skipper. The reserve also includes two ponds, which support five species of dragonfly.

Stiperstones NNR

Near: Church Stretton, West Midlands
Map: 15, B3
Web: www.english-nature.org.uk
📮

Stiperstones NNR includes the major part of the Stiperstones ridge in south Shropshire, near the Welsh border. In the lower areas of the reserve, heather and gorse heath is dominant, while ling and bilberry predominate on the uplands. The site supports a variety of wildlife, including common lizard, brown hare and common frog; and birdlife, such as curlew, red grouse, skylark, meadow pipit, buzzard, pied flycatcher and wood warbler. Invertebrates found here include grayling and green hairstreak butterflies, fox and emperor moths. The best time to visit the site is in late summer, when the heather and gorse is in bloom.

Stockwood Meadows

Near: Inkberrow, Worcestershire
Map: 16, D2
Web: www.plantlife.org.uk
Designated an SSSI for its wildlife, Stockwood Meadows was once part of the ancient Forest of Feckenham. The reserve is comprised of two hay meadows enclosed by tall hedges of hazel, hawthorn, guelder rose and dogwood. More than 103 species of grasses and herbs have been recorded in the meadows including green

winged orchid, common spotted orchid, adder's tongue, pepper saxifrage, yellow-rattle and saw-wort. On a warm summer's day, a number of butterfly species can be seen on the reserve including common blue, green-veined white and meadow brown.

The Sturts SSSI

Near: Eardisley, Herefordshire
Map: 16, A2
Web: www.wildlifetrust.org.uk/hereford

P 🚻

The Sturts SSSI is one of the largest expanses of species-rich unimproved neutral grassland in Herefordshire. The reserve is a complex mosaic of grassland types, bounded by mature hedgerows, and veteran trees, drainage ditches and streams. Visit the site between spring and autumn and see a wide range of typical meadow and wetland plants, including great burnet, common knapweed, dyer's greenweed, skullcap, ragged robin and devil's-bit scabious. The site

floods in the winter, when the nearby River Wye bursts its banks, but this attracts a variety of waterfowl.

Sutton Park NNR

Near: Birmingham, West Midlands
Map: 15, D3
Web: www.english-nature.org.uk

P 🚻 (ltd), 🚻 🍴 ℹ️ 🚻 🚌

Sutton Park is Birmingham's largest park, covering 2,400 acres consisting of woodlands, heathlands and wetlands. It is the home for a wide variety of wildlife, many species of which are uncommon elsewhere in the West Midlands region. Visitors benefit from a true countryside experience, remarkably within six miles of the very heart of the city. The visitor centre contains displays and information related to the park. The park is a remnant of an extensive forest that used to cover much of the Midlands. Sutton Park has retained many ancient features including prehistoric mounds and ruins as well as a Roman road making it of great interest to historical enthusiasts.

Titley Pool SSSI

Near: Kington, Herefordshire
Map: 16, A2
Web: www.wildlifetrust.org.uk/hereford

P 🚻 🏠

This is one of the largest areas of open water in Herefordshire and one of a number of naturally formed lakes around Kington and Mortimer's Cross. The mixture of habitats on the reserve attracts a wide range of birds. In winter, the pool is home to a wide variety of waterfowl, including teal, wigeon, tufted duck and pochard. At other times of the year, the

Rabbits and hares – know the difference

Seen from a distance, hares are much larger than rabbits and tend to move more quickly across the ground with a loping gait. If you see them more closely, their ears which are about the same length as their heads – proportionately much bigger than rabbits – are black at the tips. Usually seen in grassland and fields, they hide out and rest in hedgerows and woodland throughout the UK, except north-western Scotland. Mad March hares are actually unreceptive females fending off males during the mating season. Places to spot them include: Cannock Forest, Coombe Hill Meadow and the Clwydian Range.

Wood Lane

Near: Ellesmere, Shropshire
Map: 15, B1
Web: www.shropshirewildlifetrust.org.uk
P WC at Colemere Country Park,

Wood Lane demonstrates what can be done to give wildlife a chance. This former wasteland has been restored into one of the premier birdwatching sites in North Shropshire. Winter or summer, there is always something to see and the hides provide all-weather viewing opportunities. In spring, passage waders, such as greenshank, redshank, whimbrel, dunlin and green sandpiper pass through. At the same time lapwing, little ringed plover, shelduck and mallard move in to breed. The old faces of the gravel pits provide a home for a large colony of sand martins and tree sparrows occupy nest boxes. Buzzards are also regular visitors, as are kestrel. In the summer, hobbies occasionally harass the sand martins and ospreys pass through on migration. Gulls are always present, using the site for roosting, and in autumn and winter, thousands pass through the site to the main roosts of Ellesmere and Colemere.

reserve is an ideal breeding ground for great crested grebe, mute swan and little grebe. The reserve is particularly good for dragonflies, including common and ruddy darters and southern hawkers.

Upton Ham SSSI
Near: Upton upon Severn, near Tewkesbury, Worcestershire
Map: 16, D3
Web: www.plantlife.org.uk

The importance of the meadows at Upton Ham is reflected in their official designation as an SSSI. Species found in the meadows include great burnet, meadow foxtail, red fescue, meadow saffron, narrow-leaved water dropwort, mousetail, and the unusual small-flowered winter-cress on the banks of the Severn. The meadows are also important for breeding waders including redshank and curlew.

Wem Moss NNR
Near: Ellesmere, Shropshire
Map: 15, B1
Web: www.shropshirewildlife trust.org.uk

Wem Moss is an outstanding example of a lowland raised bog, a wildlife habitat that exists in Britain today in just tiny remnant fragments. If you like big spiders, then this is the place for you. The peat bog is home to the great raft spider, a six-inch monster that walks across the water and catches small fish. Some of the plants here are monsters too, all three British species of sundew grow here, catching unsuspecting insects in their sticky, hairy leaves. Look too, in late summer, for the starry golden spikes of bog asphodel, bog myrtle and bog rosemary.

Wren's Nest NNR
Near: Dudley, West Midlands
Map: 15, C3
Web: www.english-nature.org.uk
P WC

Wren's Nest is known for its spectacular outcrops of Silurian limestone and well-preserved fossils, especially trilobites. More than 650 types of fossil have been found here and 86 are unique to the site. In addition to its geological interest, the reserve supports many wildflowers that are otherwise rare or absent in the West Midlands, such as autumn gentian, common gromwell and bee orchid. The caverns offer important roost sites for several bat species and areas of ash-elm woodland on the site are home to birds such as sparrowhawk, stock dove, tawny owl, nuthatch and both green and great spotted woodpecker.

BIRD RESERVES

Black Brook SAC
Near: Leek, Staffordshire
Map: 15, D1
Web: www.staffs-wildlife.org.uk

Most of the moorland and woodland of Black Brook is situated within Leek Moors SSSI. This reserve is recognised as an SAC for its upland breeding birds. Key species include curlew, whose arrival in March is one of the first signs to herald the end of the harsh moorland winters, while lapwing and snipe like the rough, tussocky, damp fields. Dippers frequent the brook from which the reserve takes it name, while other moorland birds include whinchat and twite.

Coombes and Churnet Valley RSPB Reserve
Near: Leek, Staffordshire
Map: 15, D1
Web: www.rspb.org.uk

On this reserve you'll find scenic, steep-sided valleys with oak woodland and a rocky stream. A wide range of fascinating birds can be enjoyed, from dippers and grey wagtails along the stream to migrant redstarts, pied flycatchers and a variety of warblers. It's also great in spring and summer for flowers and insects. Buzzards and sparrowhawks can be seen regularly 'floating' over the valley thoughout the year. With patience, dippers and grey wagtails can also be seen along the Coombes brook. Woodcocks are often seen displaying (known as 'roding') at dusk and dawn during the spring and summer.

Holywell Dingle
Near: Eardisley, Herefordshire
Map: 16, A2
Web: www.wildlifetrust.org.uk/hereford

This is a great reserve to see all sorts of woodland birds. Situated in a steep-sided valley, through which meanders a stream that has numerous waterfalls and rapids. Look out for great spotted woodpeckers, nuthatches, treecreepers, pied flycatchers and a variety of warblers. The unpolluted stream supports many species of invertebrate and fish, which in turn attract the occasional kingfisher and dipper.

Sandwell Valley RSPB Reserve
Near: West Bromwich, West Midlands
Map: 15, D3
Web: www.rspb.org.uk

Sandwell Valley is an oasis for wildlife on the outskirts of Birmingham, next to the Sandwell Valley Country Park. From the visitor centre, there are excellent views over the site and you can watch a variety of garden birds on the feeders. In the hedgerows around the centre, you will find finches and thrushes in winter and warblers in summer, including white-throats and lesser white-throats. Flowers and butterflies fill the grassy areas in summer.

FORESTS & WOODLAND

Chaddesley Woods NNR
Near: Bromsgrove, Worcestershire
Map: 16, D1
Web: www.english-nature.org.uk

Chaddesley is the largest block of woodland in the county outside the Wyre Forest and is The Wildlife Trusts' largest

Hedgehogs: for fully organic slug control

What everybody wants to know is: how do hedgehogs mate? Apart from very carefully, the answer is that the female completely flattens her back so that her 5,000 or so spines no longer stick upwards and then the male can mount her in safety. It normally takes him an hour or so of very loud grunting and snuffling to persuade her to mate and as one of their favourite habitats is gardens, it's a ritual that many Brits have overheard. Hedgehogs are usually a popular garden visitor as they eat slugs, snails and caterpillars and have a healthy appetite, eating around 200g of food each night – one fifth of their bodyweight. They also live in hedgerows and grassland where they dig out dens for shelter. They are nocturnal animals and hibernate between October and April, so the chances of seeing one on a country walk are limited.

reserve. All the common woodland birds are found in the wood, plus tree pipits, woodcock and sometimes crossbills, which breed in the coniferous parts following a late summer invasion from northern Europe. Invertebrate life is rich with many moths, and also the land or terrestrial caddis, an unusual insect which lives in leaf litter (most caddis are aquatic). It has a strange and unexplained national distribution in woods of north-west Worcestershire and south Shropshire. Although common here, it is a national rarity.

Credenhill Park Wood

Near: Hereford, Herefordshire
Map: 16, B2
Web: www.wt-woods.org.uk/credenhillparkwood

P ⛺

Credenhill Park Wood is a 225-acre ancient woodland located within the Hereford

Hills major ancient woodland concentration. It occupies steep slopes and a prominent place in the landscape. A scheduled ancient monument crowns the top of the site with oval shaped ramparts. Despite the loss of much of the broad-leaved woodland, Park Wood supports a very valuable habitat. Many of the most interesting components of the habitat are associated with the ancient woodland origins. Trees, such as small-leaved lime, and plants, such as herb paris, are of particular interest as they are strongly indicative of ancient woodland sites.

Ercall Woods

Near: Teflord, Shropshire
Map: 15, C2
Web: www.shropshirewildlifetrust.org.uk

P ⛺

Ancient woodland, spectacular views and more than 500

million years of geological history can be enjoyed here. This reserve is internationally famous for its geology. It visibly marks the boundary between a time of very little life, the Precambrian, and an explosion in the variety of life during the Cambrian. Aside from the amazing geology, the flora and fauna is equally interesting. In spring the woods are full of bluebells and singing with birds just returned from Africa. In summer it is a favourite spot for butterflies, including the dingy skipper.

Ryton and Wappenbury Woods

Near: Coventry, Warwickshire
Map: 14, B4
Web: www.warwickshire-wildlife-trust.org.uk

P WC ✉

These two adjacent blocks of semi-natural ancient woodland form a substantial part of the largest group of woodlands in Warwickshire. It is a great place to spot small birds, especially in the winter, when you will hear the distinctive call of the long-tailed tits. In summer, butterflies can be spectacular on the many open rides, including good numbers of white admiral and more occasional glimpses of small pearl-bordered fritillary.

Snitterfield Bushes

Near: Stratford-upon-Avon, Warwickshire
Map: 14, A5
Web: www.warwickshire-wildlife-trust.org.uk

P

A 121-acre remnant of a once much larger ancient woodland, home to many plants that are uncommon in Warwickshire. Herb Paris, greater butterfly orchid and broad-leaved helleborine can all be found, as can butterflies, such as white admiral and purple

Cannock Forest

Near: Rugeley, Staffordshire
Map: 15, D2
Web: www.forestry.gov.uk

P ♿ WC ⓘ
⛺ ✉

The forest covers a wide area and conditions vary from flat through to rolling hills. The wide variety of habitats found in Cannock Forest support an equally diverse number of animals, birds and plants. Cannock Forest has a rich variety of mammals including three types of deer. The wide range of habitats provide rich food sources for many of England's mammals including badger, fox, hare, stoat, weasel, hedgehog and more. There are also numerous birds to see, including crossbill,

siskin, goshawk, goldcrest, long-tailed tit and many more. The broad-leaved areas provide homes for woodpeckers, nuthatches, white-throats and jays. The nationally rare heathland areas are ideal for the elusive nightjar, woodlarks, buzzards and a whole variety of others. Cannock Forest is a haven for reptiles and amphibians including grass snakes, adders, newts and lizards. The purpose-built lagoon pools and basking areas provide the ideal habitats for many ground-dwelling species.

DID YOU KNOW?
When it comes to digging, the badger is the fastest mammal on the planet – without a JCB.

Wyre Forest NNR

Near: Bewdley, Worcestershire
Map: 16, D1
Web: www.english-nature.gov.uk
🕒 (ltd), 🚾 ❶ 🖃
The Wyre Forest NNR is managed by Natural England and the Forestry Commission. It is part of one of the largest ancient lowland coppice oak woodlands in England. The reserve overlies a plateau containing shales and sandstones of the Upper Carboniferous Coal Measures. The area is heavily faulted, giving rise to steep valleys. The site supports an important invertebrate population that includes England's largest colony of pearl-bordered fritillary butterflies. Breeding birds in the area include redstart, pied flycatcher, wood warbler, buzzard and raven, while dipper, grey wagtail and kingfisher are found on the larger streams. Mammals found in the reserve include fallow, roe and muntjak deer, polecats, otters and mink. Yellow-neck mice, dormice, voles and water shrews are also found here. Several bat species live in the area, including pipistrelle and Daubenton's.

hairstreak. Coppicing has been reintroduced to maintain woodland diversity.

Sot's Hole
Near: West Bromwich, West Midlands
Map: 16, D1
Web: www.bbcwildlife.org.uk
Sot's Hole is a fragment of ancient woodland that has miraculously survived in an urban area. It is home to a range of plant and insect life and is also a great place to look out for some rare birds. Keep your eyes peeled for the greater spotted woodpecker, blue tit and also sparrowhawk. It also attracts a number of migrant birds.

COASTS, WETLANDS & WATERWAYS

Alvecote Pools and Meadow SSSI
Near: Polesworth and Tamworth, Warwickshire
Map: 15, E2
Web: www.warwickshire-wildlife-trust.org.uk

❶
Alvecote Pool is Warwickshire's largest SSSI, totalling 318 acres. These wetlands, which have developed as a result of mining subsidence, have been designated an SSSI because of their importance for breeding, passage and wintering wetland birds. Look out for occasional oystercatcher, common tern, or little ringed plover among the more common birds such as great crested grebe, tufted duck and snipe. In summer, the area is awash with dragonfly, ruddy darter and common hawker. Large numbers of mute swans moult at the site each autumn.

Birmingham and Fazeley Canal
Near: Birmingham, West Midlands
Map: 15, D3
Web: www.waterscape.com
The Birmingham and Fazeley Canal soon leaves urban Birmingham behind for the green, peaceful and rural Midlands. Acting as a link between the inner city and the countryside, the canal provides a watery pathway

for wildlife to migrate into the city. Birds, fish, insects and mammals use the waterway to reach the doorsteps and back gardens of thousands of city dwellers. Canal managers British Waterways are working to protect and enhance the different species and habitats – such as the rare water voles who make their home along the canal's banks.

Birmingham Canal Old Main Line
From: Birmingham to Wolverhampton, West Midlands
Map: 15, D3
Web: www.waterscape.com
This quiet canal sees few boats since the opening of the shorter straighter New Main Line. Water voles live on its banks which are rich with a sense of history.

Blithfield Reservoir
Near: Rugeley, Staffordshire
Map: 15, D2
Web: www.waterscape.com
🅿 ♨
Opened in 1953, Blithfield Reservoir is 790 acres

of surface water, and is surrounded by a large woodland that is home to a variety of wildlife, particularly birds. Resident birds to the area include great crested grebe, cormorant, shoveler, tufted duck, sparrowhawk, little owl, tawny owl and kingfisher and many others visit on their migrations.

Caldon Canal
From: Stoke-on-Trent to Froghall, near Cheadle, Staffordshire
Map: 15, C1 to D1
Web: www.waterscape.com
🅿 ♿ (ltd)
Most of Caldon Canal's 20-mile length is rural, and is home to all manner of flora and fauna. The canal passes through the industrial heartland of the Potteries and then out into the wonderful rural scenery, where herons and kingfishers are regularly seen.

Cannock Extension Canal
Near: Walsall, West Midlands
Map: 15, D2
Web: www.waterscape.com
Although a lesser-used canal, the Cannock Extension – situated at the very north of the Birmingham system – offers an intriguing short diversion off the Wyrley and Essington, through heathland with colliery workings along the way and boatyards at its

terminus. Today's canal extends for almost two miles from Pelsall Common to the A5 road. The waterway plays host to one of the country's largest populations of the protected floating water plantain, a rare plant found chiefly in lesser-used canals and numerous water-side animals can be found along the banks.

Chasewater
Near: Cannock, Staffordshire
Map: 15, D2
Web: www.waterscape.com
Chasewater was originally created as a canal feeder reservoir in the eighteenth century and remains the largest in use in the region today. It is a designated country park, with 890 acres of water and open space, ideally suited to lovers of leisure activities. The varying habitats here support many species of flora and fauna. Heather is in abundance, particularly ling, bell and cross-leaved varieties. The grasslands are home to beautiful wildflowers and butterflies, and the songbirds love the hawthorn and willow carr. In terms of birdlife near or on the water, the less common wagtails and great crested grebes can be seen, as well as Canada geese, mute swans and plenty of mallards. Animals to be found in the park include

foxes, red deer, rabbits and perhaps even a common lizard.

Coventry Canal
Near: Coventry, Warwickshire
Map: 14, A4
Web: www.waterscape.com
The Coventry Canal is a haven for rich and varied wildlife. Some very rare species can also be found among the more common dwellers and visitors to the canal. Pondlife loves the tranquility of the canal's waters: you may find hornworts, floating water lilies and branched bur-reeds. Looking along the banks and in the hedges, you may find kingfishers, white-clawed crayfish, dragonflies and herons – and even the odd otter. Bats love the seclusion of bridges and tunnels, and all sorts of amphibians and reptiles – frogs, toads, newts and grass snakes – will dip in and out of the waters.

Hatherton Canal
Near: Birmingham, West Midlands
Map: 14, A4
Web: www.waterscape.com
The Hatherton Canal was opened as a branch of the Staffordshire and Worcestershire Canal, providing a rural route into the Black Country. The 6.5-mile canal was closed after World War II. The line has lain derelict for years, but is undergoing restoration that includes plans to create a wildlife corridor along the canal. The Lichfield and Hatherton Canals Restoration Trust is planting hawthorn, sycamore and other plants and trees, to encourage wildlife.

Lichfield Canal
Near: Birmingham, West Midlands
Map: 15, D3
Web: www.waterscape.com
The restored canal will be a corridor for wildlife, with

How to find dormice

Dormouse nests are a woven ball about four inches across, close to the ground in bramble bushes or thick undergrowth beneath trees such as sweet chestnut or hazels. Clues that they're there include discarded nibbled nuts with teeth marks on the outside.

hawthorn, holly, rowan, sycamore, silver birch, lime, oak and chestnut being planted along the banks to encourage the return of birds.

Llangollen Canal
Near: Ellesmere, Shropshire
Map: 15, B2
Web: www.waterscape.com
One of the most popular waterways in Europe, the Llangollen Canal boasts scenic beauty and breathtaking engineering in equal measure. The magnificent Pontcysyllte Aqueduct across the River Dee is worth the journey alone and is simply a must-see. This 46-mile canal is beautiful throughout and is understandably very busy in the high season. Understated rural countryside, including the market towns of Whitchurch and Ellesmere, gives way to the majesty of the Chirk and Pontcysyllte Aqueducts – two of Britain's greatest waterway landmarks. The final few miles of canal hug the side of the River Dee valley on their approach to Llangollen. The canal beyond the moorings at Llangollen, continuing to the water feeder at Horseshoe Falls, is an attractive spot for a walk. The Llangollen Canal contains some important marine plantlife, as well as dragonflies, butterflies and wildflowers at the water's edge.

Llangollen Canal

River Trent
From: Stoke-on-Trent, Staffordshire, to Scunthorpe, Lincolnshire
Map: 15, C1 and 13, A1
Website: www.waterscape.com
Flowing for 171 miles, the Trent is one of England's major rivers. Recent deindustrialisation and improvements in water quality have given wildlife a chance to recover from centuries of industrial development. Otters have begun to return, and the Trent Otters and Rivers Project is working to restore otter populations through training of volunteers and construction of artificial holts. The Trent Valley also incorporates the Attenborough Nature Reserve, an SSSI with an endless list of flora and fauna. Migrant visitors reside alongside waders, pintails and mute swans, while butterflies and dragonflies are also present.

Rudyard Lake
Near: Rudyard, Leek, Staffordshire
Map: 15, D1
Web: www.waterscape.com
P & (ltd), WC ⓘ ✉
The lake that gave its name to the famous author is home to several bird varieties including ducks, herons, seagulls, swans and Canada geese. Other temporary residents include a wide variety of wading birds, such as greenshanks and sandpipers, skylarks and meadow pipits, willow warblers and other songbirds. Tree branches are alive with coaltits, goldcrests and finches. The woods shelter badgers, foxes, squirrels, voles, mice and other small rodents.

Staffordshire and Worcestershire Canal
From: Worcestershire to Staffordshire
Map: 15 and 16
Web: www.waterscape.com
Staffordshire and Worcestershire Canal runs for 46 miles through almost entirely rural surroundings. The canal is a haven for rich and varied wildlife. The southern reaches of the canal run close to the River Stour, which is an important wetland habitat. The canal near Kidderminster and Kinver has unusual sandstone 'cliffs' with their own ecology.

Wildlife Britain **167**

Shropshire Union Canal

Near: Wolverhampton, Warwickshire
Map: 15, C2
Web: www.waterscape.com
Arrow-straight for much of its length, this charming rural waterway strides across the landscape. North of Nantwich, the canal – built originally as the Chester Canal – is a wide waterway following the gentle rolling landscape of western Cheshire to Ellesmere Port. But the southern half of the canal – built in the twilight of the canal age – is an astonishing feat of engineering. Its long embankments, deep cuttings and grandiose bridges frequently dominate the scenery. The deep cuttings of the Shropshire Union are particularly attractive to wildlife and you will often see herons and kingfishers along the canal. The 180-acre reservoir at Belvide, near Brewood, was constructed to supply the canal with water – but is now a major attraction for birdwatchers. Wading birds and wildfowl of all varieties are seen here.

Stourbridge Canal

From: Stourton Junction, Staffordshire/Worcestershire to the Dudley No 1 Canal, West Midlands
Map: 15, C3
Web: www.waterscape.com
The canal provides a haven for wildlife in an industrial landscape. Swans glide along its surface and canal edges are an important refuge and breeding ground for water voles.

Tame Valley Canal

Near: Birmingham, West Midlands
Map: 15, D3
Web: www.waterscape.com
Compared with earlier canals, the Tame Valley is relatively sophisticated – with bold engineering, brick-lined banks and twin towpaths. The towpath is open to cyclists, anglers and walkers and has plenty of pubs en route. The nearby Sandwell Valley, an oasis of green in the centre of an industrialised area provides woods, parkland, marsh and fields rich in wildlife.

Trent and Mersey Canal

Near: Stoke-on-Trent, Staffordshire
Map: 15, C1
Web: www.waterscape.com
This cross-country canal through the North Midlands offers excellent views over the Cheshire Plain and impressive engineering feats – including Harecastle Tunnel, the first of its kind. Otters have recently been spotted in the canal and local councils have begun to provide stop-off otter holts (dens) to encourage them. Water voles have also been seen and it is hoped that they will return in numbers. 'Flashes' – where the canal suddenly widens into a miniature lake – are a common sight along the canal through Cheshire. The heavy salt mining in the area caused the ground to subside, so that former agricultural land was submerged under the canal water level. These flashes are not navigated by boats and so encourage a different ecosystem to thrive.

Wednesbury Old Canal

Near: Birmingham, West Midlands
Map: 15, D3
Web: www.waterscape.com
From the quaintly named Pudding Green Junction to Swan Bridge, the 1.5 miles of Brindley's Wednesbury Old Canal is an underused gateway to the northern waters of the Birmingham Canal Network The area is industrialised, yet the towpath can be peppered with wildflowers in a juxtaposition that harks back to when the surroundings were heathland.

Worcester and Birmingham Canal

From: Birmingham, West Midlands to Worcester, Worcestershire
Map: 15, D3 and 16, D2
Web: www.waterscape.com
This canal has the most locks of any in the country. The Tardebigge Flight has 30 locks in just over two miles, making it one of Britain's steepest. Though largely rural, the line is steeped in history and its five tunnels contribute an aura of mystique. A wide variety of plants and wildlife from the surrounding countryside have adapted to the canal environment, creating a continuous corridor for species to move along. The canal is designated a county wildlife site throughout Worcestershire. Deep cuttings around King's Norton provide a sheltered refuge, while the less developed lengths around Hanbury offer valuable reed habitats. There is believed to be a thriving water vole population on the canal.

Wyrley and Essington Canal

From: Wolverhampton to Brownhills, West Midlands
Map: 15, C2 and D2
Web: www.waterscape.com
The Wyrley and Essington Canal is aptly nicknamed

the Curley Wyrley, due to its twisting course. The canal is a haven for rich and varied wildlife. Much pondlife, which loves the tranquility of the canal's waters and its particularly good water quality, can be found here, including marsh pennywort, floating water lilies, branched bur-reed, sponges and molluscs. Rare plants, such as floating water plantain and grass wrack pondweed, are protected by law. All sorts of amphibians and reptiles, such as frogs, toads, newts and grass snakes, will dip in and out of the waters, loving the wetland habitat. Moorhens, ducks and mute swans glide along the waters here.

NOT SO WILD

Balsall Heath City Farm
Address: Clifton Road, Balsall Heath, Birmingham, West Midlands B12 8NJ
Map: 15, D3
Tel: 0121 464 1888
Web: www.farmgarden.org.uk
Open: daily, 9am to 3.30pm
Admission: free

Part of St Paul's community project, the farm was started in 1981 on land leased from Birmingham City Council. Animals at the farm include sheep, goats, chickens, ducks, geese, turkeys, rabbits, guinea pigs and fish.

Birmingham Ecopark
Address: 258a Hob Moor Road, Small Heath, Birmingham B10 9HH
Map: 15, D3
Tel: 0121 7850553
Web: www.bbcwildlife.org.uk
Open: Wednesdays, 10am to 4pm
Admission: free

This is a great place to go to find out how to create a sustainable garden. In spring, early displays of bulbs are the first highlights, followed by the first flowers and spring flush. Summer is an excellent time of year for insects and birds as well as the best flowers. Autumn is a great time to see birds, including woodpeckers. The park is designed to provide a stimulating and educational environment. There is a path to take the visitor beside ponds, through woodland, flowering meadows and heathland.

Blackbrook Zoological Park
Address: Winkhill, near Leek, Staffordshire
Map: 15, D1
Tel: 01538 308293 or 01565 873282
Open: April to September, 10.30am to 5.30pm.
Admission: £5/£7.50

Set amid the Staffordshire Moorlands, Blackbrook Zoological Park has developed into a large and varied collection of some of the most rare and endangered species to be found in the world. There is a wide variety of birds, animals, reptiles and fish on view. Many unusual species of birds are now at home here, including the largest collection of wildfowl to be seen in the British Isles – the swans and geese are of particular interest and do well in the moorland climate. Around the grounds are various aviaries housing a rapidly growing collection of pheasants and softbills. The centre also holds the largest collection of cranes and storks

in the British Isles along with ibis, owls and kookaburras.

Coventry City Farm
Address: 1 Clarence Street, Hillfields, Coventry, West Midlands CV1 5SS
Map: 14, B4
Tel: 024 7622 5323
Web: www.coventrycityfarm.org.uk
Open: daily, 10am to 4pm
Admission: free

This city farm offers a small area of rural life in a densely populated inner city area. It has a diverse selection of animals and educational facilities. The farm opened in 1983 and has been going strong ever since.

Drayton Manor Park's Zoo
Address: near Tamworth, Staffordshire B78 3TW
Map: 15, D2
Tel: 08708 725252
Web: www.draytonmanor.co.uk
Open: daily, from 10am (except 23 December to 3 January)

Drayton Manor Park Zoo is home to more than 100 species from all over the world. Animals include big cats, reptiles, monkeys, eagles, owls and parrots as well as an exotic creature reserve.

Dudley Zoological Gardens-
Address: 2 The Broadway, Dudley, West Midlands DY1 4QB
Map: 15, D3
Tel: 01384 215313
Web: www.dudleyzoo.org.uk
Open: daily, from 10am (except 25 December)
Admission: £6.75/£9.95

Dudley Zoological Gardens has long been home to some of the world's biggest, rarest and most exotic animals. Among the many endangered species the zoo is helping to save are Asiatic lions and Sumatran tigers.

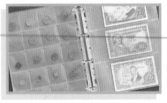

National Sea Life Centre

Address: The Waters Edge,
Brindley Place, Birmingham,
West Midlands B1 2HL
Map: 15, D3
Tel: 0121 643 6777
Web: www.sealifeeurope.com
Open: all year
Admission: prices vary with
season

P ⊟

The National Sea Life
Centre takes visitors on a
spectacular undersea voyage
with more than 60 displays
of freshwater and marine
life, creating a wonderland
for visitors of all ages. The
attraction boasts an enormous
one-million-litre ocean tank
housing giant green sea
turtles, black tip reef sharks
and tropical reef fish. All
this in addition to dozens
of other displays featuring
otters, seahorses, crabs and
lobsters, sharks and stingrays,
guarantees a memorable and
enjoyable experience.

Twycross Zoo

Address: Atherstone, near
Hinckley, Warwickshire CV9 3PX
Map: 14, B4
Tel: 01827 880250/880440
Web: www.twycrosszoo.com
Open: daily, 10am to 4/5.30pm
(except 25 December)
Admissin: £4.55/£8.50

P ☺ (ltd), wc ☒
☒ ☒ ⊟

Twycross Zoo opened in 1963
on a site in Leicestershire
and has grown into one of
the major British zoos. It
is famous for its collection
of primates, including
spider monkeys, gibbons,
chimpanzees and orang-utans,
as well as deer, goat, a variety
of birds, as well as tortoises
and crocodiles.

West Midland Safari Park

Address: Spring Grove,
Bewdley, Worcestershire
DY12 1LF

Emporer tamarin
at Twycross Zoo

Map: 16, D2
Tel: 01299 402114
Web: www.wmsp.co.uk
Open: March to October, daily,
from 10am
Admission: £9.50

P ☺ wc ☒ ⊟

The four-mile drive-through
West Midland Safari Park,
takes you past a variety of
exotic and unusual animals.
New in 2006 was the Buffalo
Boma exhibit, forming part
of the African Big Five. There
are also elephants, rhinos,
giraffes, lions, wallabies,
tigers, emus, camels, zebras,
gnus, elands, ankole cattle,
yaks, Przewalski's horses,
Asian buffalos, wolves, llamas
and antelope.

Woodgate Valley Urban Farm

Address: Clapgate Lane/Watery
Lane, Bartley Green, Birmingham,
West Midlands
Map: 15, D3
Tel: 0121 426 1871
Web: www.farmgarden.org.uk
Open: daily, 10.30am to 4/6pm
Admission: free

☺ wc ⊟

There are currently 12 species
of livestock here. Part of the
farm is a traditional orchard,
demonstration garden and
wildlife area. Animals include
Limousin cattle, Kune Kune
pigs, pygmy goats, soay,
Swaledale and Jacob sheep,
poultry, rabbits, guinea pigs,
ferrets and bees.

Wildlife Britain **171**

Yorkshire and Humberside

A fascinating combination of urban urgency and tranquil, uninterrupted natural beauty, the Yorkshire and Humberside region provides something for everyone, from the most intrepid wildlife explorer to those content to marvel at whatever they may stumble upon, this northern pocket will not disappoint.

The landscape is dominated by rolling hills incorporating the famous Three Peaks and stunning views are abundant. The industrialisation of the early twentieth century introduced a network of waterways that today – less commercialised – house rare and unusual species.

The Atlantic white-clawed crayfish nestles deep in abandoned tunnels of reservoirs and canals, while aquatic beetles run free and dragonflies traverse the winding waterways. Committed to restoration of both the waterways and wildlife, organisations are working to entice the otter back to its natural habitat.

The water banks are littered with aquatic plants, willows and orchids, while waterside wildlife includes water voles, grass snakes and the occasional deer.

Adopting a primary location en-route to warmer climates, this area is superb to watch birds and their migration. Passage times bring curlew, dunlin, knot and turnstone to reside alongside more common wildfowl, such as mallard and shelduck, while other arrivals can include flycatchers, redwing and whinchat, while the tern is not adverse to a stopover.

Woodland areas of the hills and valleys are dotted with bluebells and celandine, attracting badgers, foxes, roe deer and – in some regions – at least five species of bat, including the rare brown long-eared, alongside the pipistrelle, barbastrelle and Bechstein's. Fungi is a key feature of these woodland glades, most notably the puffball and cup, which can be spotted in the breathtaking Nidd Gorge, a splendid example of this area's landscape. Butterflies, including common blue and peacock, flutter through the corridors, while woodcock, woodpecker and goldcrest frequent the shaded areas.

The seashore never fails to disappoint, playing home to animals that will enthral and excite. Spot a seal, common or grey, or await the arrival of a rare puffin. Wait patiently, and you may even see a harbour porpoise frolicking in the waves.

Dedication to conservation is strong in this area, evident in the otter rejuvenation programme, specific heather tending to ensure red grouse protection, and the reintroduction of red kite. Look closely, stay alert, and you will see them all, against a backdrop of incomparable scenery.

PICTURED: A drystone wall in Swaledale, Yorkshire Dales National Park

Not to be missed

● **Hone Wood**
Take a walk through this ancient woodland with its twisted oak trees and spot the variety of ferns and mosses along the banks of its trickling streams.

● **Malham Tarn**
The craggy limestone rocks are a favourite with climbers, but are also a beautiful windswept wild area.

● **Nidderdale AONB**
Surreal rock formations, a beautiful limestone gorge and lush green pastures, rightly give Nidderdale its AONB status.

● **Spurn NNR**
The mudflats and saltmarshes of this sandy peninsula attract migrating birds in their thousands.

● **Tropical Butterfly House, Sheffield**
Explore the rainforest as colourful butterflies and tropical birds fly free around you and leaf-cutter ants march across the jungle floor.

● **Yorkshire Dales National Park**
One of Britain's greenest areas, this easily accessible national park spans the Pennines and is a haven for rare butterflies and plants.

Merlin falcon

NATIONAL PARKS

North York Moors National Park
Yorkshire
Map: 17, C1 to D1
Web: www.moors.uk.net
MOORS CENTRE
Near: Danby
🅿 (inc ♿), ♿ 🆆🅲 🖼 🖵 ⛺
SUTTON BANK CENTRE
Near: Thirsk
🅿 (inc ♿), ♿ 🆆🅲 🖼 🖵
OLD COASTGUARD STATION
Near: Robin Hood's Bay
🅿 (inc ♿), ♿ 🆆🅲 🖼 🍴

One of the most stunning landscapes in the country, North York Moors National Park incorporates vast open spaces of moorland, woodland and coastlines of sandy beaches. The heather-dominated moorland explodes with colour in the summer, while bilberry, crowberry and wavy hair grass abound in the drier areas. Bog plants can also be found, including sphagnum moss and the nodding cottonwool, while the bracken-edged slopes provide a refuge for plants vulnerable to grazing, such as chickweed wintergreen. Some of the less common plantlife found on the Moors are relics of the Ice Age. Unable to survive in lowland Britain as the climate warmed, species such as dwarf cornel, cloudberry and bog rosemary can still be found in the uplands of the Moors. The moorland is internationally important for its breeding population of merlin, while also attracting the golden plover, red grouse, curlew and ring ouzel. Adders are also frequently spotted. The woodland landscape combines natives such as oak and rowan with new plantations in the larger forests of Dalby, Cropton and Boltby. Moving to the coastal habitats, the variety and sheer number of animal and plantlife is staggering, one square metre of rock may support more than 30,000 barnacles, while the warm and salty rockpools provide a home for creatures that normally live entirely submerged by the sea.

Yorkshire Dales National Park

North Yorkshire and Cumbria
Map: 17, B1 and B2
Web: www.yorkshiredales.org.uk
Established in 1954, the Yorkshire Dales National Park spans 1,095 miles across the central Pennines in North Yorkshire and Cumbria. Habitats range from wildflower-rich hay meadows to open heather moorland, while limestone pavements are home to a rich and diverse wildlife. Woodland is scarce, yet an important component in the mosaic of habitats. Nationally important populations of breeding waders, black grouse, yellow wagtail and skylark thrive, while rare lime-loving plants such as bird's-eye primrose, rigid buckler fern and globeflower are also present. Scarce invertebrates are attracted to the park, such as the northern brown argus butterfly and the Atlantic white-clawed crayfish.

AONBS

Howardian Hills AONB
Near: Pickering, North Yorkshire and York, East Riding of Yorkshire
Map: 17, D1
Web: www.howardianhills.org.uk
Rising between the flat agricultural plains of Pickering and York, the Howardian Hills form a distinct area of well-wooded countryside, incorporating pastures, valleys and rolling farmland. Devoid of towns and with a simple scattering of attractive stone-built villages, the hills are home to a number of key species. Lapwing and redshank flourish, while plantlife, such as baneberry and rare knapweed broomrape thrive. The river Derwent provides refuge for otter and water vole, while the white-clawed crayfish and great crested newt are also important to the area. Bumblebees abound and the brown hare is frequently spotted, while priority species include the skylark and the linnet.

Nidderdale AONB
Near: Harrogate, North Yorkshire
Map: 17, C2
Web: www.nidderdaleaonb.org.uk
Designated in 1994, this AONB is located on the eastern flanks of the Yorkshire Pennines. Nidderdale has some of the finest heather moorland in Britain, yet although it looks natural, it is the result of management to maintain populations of red grouse who feed on the shoots of young heather. Combined with dwarf shrubs, such as bilberry and crowberry, the moorland provides a habitat for many species of birds. Nidderdale grassland supports plants, such as mountain pansy and moonwort, while the heavy metal concentration in these soils permits a high diversity of species. Curlew and snipe are also frequently attracted to the waterlogged areas of grassland.

NATURE RESERVES

Blacka Moor SSSI
Near: Sheffield, South Yorkshire
Map: 17, C3
Web: www.wildsheffield.com
P ♿ (ltd)
Covering 445 acres of breathtaking scenery just inside the Peak District, Blacka Moor is the largest of Sheffield Wildlife Trust's reserves. Numerous upland birds live and breed here, from sparrowhawk and green woodpecker to wren, robin, blackcap and willow warbler. Bilberry and birch give the reserve a truly wild feel, while adders emerging from hibernation may be glimpsed in the spring. In summer, the reserve is streaked with purple heather, while the landscape softens at the onset of autumn before bleakening into a classic bare, open heathland in winter.

Blackburn Meadows
Near: Rotherham, South Yorkshire
Map: 17, C3

Web: www.wildsheffield.com

🅿 🏕 🏠

In the midst of the industrial area between Sheffield and Rotherham, Blackburn Meadows provides a welcome respite from the surrounding environment. Consisting of two artificial lakes, reedbed, marginal vegetation and shingle beach surrounded by areas of grassland and shrub, there are also pockets of young woodland, willow carr and a dipping pond. Twenty-three species of butterfly have been observed here, including the Camberwell beauty. Blackburn Meadows is the best birdwatching site inside Sheffield's city boundary, and over-wintering wildfowl such as wigeon and teal are observable, while the spring influx of passenger wading birds and warblers includes common white-throat. Summer sees the resident swans and moorhens joined by kingfishers and herons.

Catcliffe Flash

Near: Rotherham, South Yorkshire
Map: 17, C3
Web: www.rotherham.gov.uk
Covering an area of 30 acres, Catcliffe Flash is an open stretch of water surrounded by marshland and willow carr, beyond which carr grassland extends to the river. This shallow subsidence flash is washland for the River Rother and, as the water level can rise very quickly with rainfall, it provides relatively undisturbed areas for water birds to roost. Herons frequent the flash, while great crested and little grebes breed. Surrounding willow scrub attracts blackcap, while spring and summer bring hirundine and kingfisher. Catcliffe Flash also holds a magpie roost throughout the autumn and winter, while less common

ROCKPOOLS

There is all sorts of life in British rockpools and some of it is quite surprising. The cushion starfish, for example, is sludgy green or browny orange in colour with five stubby legs and is a rare thing in nature in that it changes its sex. All young cushion starfish are born male and they become female after about four years. The shore crab can also be found in rockpools and also changes sex, but not of its own accord. A type of orange barnacle sometimes attaches itself to the crab's abdomen and this barnacle causes the male crabs to turn female. Potter in rockpools: in the Menai Strait and in Portrush.

species include the marsh harrier and osprey.

Duncombe Park NNR

Near: Malton, North Yorkshire
Map: 17, D2
Web: www.english-nature.org.uk
Open: Sunday to Thursday, 11am to 4.30pm
Admission: £1/£3.50
🅿 ♿ (ltd), 🆆🅲 ✉

Covering 450 acres of the parkland of Duncombe Park, a country house built in 1713, this NNR is home to many ancient trees. The trees themselves are home to rare invertebrates and fungi, while rot holes provide nest and roost sites for birds and bats. Birds present all year include woodpecker, nuthatch and hawfinch, joined in summer by pied flycatcher and redstart. In spring, bluebells, primroses and wild garlic dominate the woodland floor. The River Rye, flowing through the reserve, accommodates many rare insects, trout, otter and birds, such as dipper, grey wagtail, kingfisher, grey heron and sand martin.

Lower Derwent Valley NNR

Near: Sutton upon Derwent, East near Selby, Riding of Yorkshire
Map: 17, C2
Web: www.english-nature.org.uk
🅿 ♿ 🏠

This wetland area supports outstanding populations of breeding and wintering birds, resulting in its declaration as a special protection area. Breeding wildfowl are particularly important, with 13 species found, including the pintail and gadwall. Resident breeding waders include snipe and redshank, while, in the winter, the grasslands support Bewick's swan and pochard. A diverse plantlife includes reed sweetgrass and bladder sedge in the wetter areas while sneezewort and the rare marsh pea nestle amidst the rich herb flora. Noctule, pipistrelle and Daubenton's bats frequent the reserve, occasionally accompanied by the brown long-eared bat. The brown hare is very common here.

Malham Tarn

Near: Skipton, North Yorkshire
Map: 17, B2

Ingleborough NNR

Near: Skipton, North Yorkshire
Map: 17, B2
Web: www.english-nature.org.uk
P

A wonderful but demanding reserve, and one of the famous Three Peaks, the range of rock types, soils and altitudes of Ingleborough Hill have developed to produce intriguing and varied communities of plants, birds and other wildlife. Some of the best limestone pavements in Britain, characterised by complex systems of clints and grikes, support specialist plants, such as the very rare Yorkshire sandwort and baneberry. Garden spiders spin vast webs across the grikes, while lizards dart and curlews cry. The blanket bog of the higher areas supports cranberry and sundews, while bilberry grows on the heathland. A few fragile areas of ancient woodland combine ash, hazel and guelder rose with other plants, such as giant bellflower and alpine cinquefoil, providing support for redstarts and woodcocks.

Web: www.nationaltrust.org.uk
P (££), (ltd),
i

This outstanding area of high moorland landscape consists of a large tarn surrounded by six farms on upland limestone, some with flower-rich hay meadows. Residing amid stunning scenery of rolling hills, cliffs and limestone pavements, England's highest freshwater lake is protected by the National Trust. The Malham Tarn House houses the Field Studies Council, while Townhead Barn in nearby Malham village provides an excellent exhibition. The Tarn provides a unique wildlife habitat for rare insects, such as the caddis fly, and freshwater molluscs at the highest-known altitude in Britain. This exceptional natural lake has also attracted the great crested grebe.

New House Farm NNR
Near: Malham and Threshfield, near Skipton, North Yorkshire
Map: 17, B2
Web: www.nationaltrust.org.uk

Owned and managed by the National Trust, New House is a small working farm in the Yorkshire Dales. The unimproved hay meadows of the reserve have affinities with some Scandinavian grasslands and are characterised by abundant sweet vernal grass with wood crane's bill, lady's-mantle, pignut and melancholy thistle. Limestone outcrops harbour alpine cinquefoil, hoary whitlowgrass and orpine. The farm is traditionally managed without resort to artificial fertilisers or herbicides, while livestock is restricted to 10 sucker cows and 35 sheep.

Potteric Carr Nature Reserve
Near: Doncaster, South Yorkshire
Map: 17, C3
Web: www.potteric-carr.org.uk
Open: daily, 9am to 5pm
Admission: £1.50/£2.50
P wc
i (inc)

Incorporating a wide range of habitats, from open water to marsh and woodland, Potteric Carr supports a rich diversity of wildlife. An abundance of nestling wildfowl, including shoveler, water rail and colonies of reed and sedge warblers, are the primary attraction, hence the numerous hides. Passenger birds are equally interesting and visitors have included the great crested grebe, bittern and wryneck. Soils of acidic peat and limestone encourage a varied plantlife, while hedgehogs, badgers and long-eared bats have all made a home at Potteric Carr. Look closely near the pools and you might spot a smooth, palmate or great crested newt.

Woodhouse Washlands

Near: Rotherham, South Yorkshire
Map: 17, C3
Web: www.yorkshire-wildlife-trust.org.uk

Located on the Sheffield-Rotherham border, Woodhouse Washlands traverses the River Rother to provide a mixture of grassland, marsh and pond habitats. Breeding birds, such as snipe, lapwing and reed bunting, feature regularly and the reserve is considered a regionally important bird migration route in the Rother Valley. Grazing by rare cattle breeds, combined with pond excavations, have provided additional water sources, resulting in a rise in breeding amphibians, including the great crested newt. Other species found at Woodhouse include harvest mouse, water voles and various dragonflies.

Wyming Brook/Fox Hagg

Near: Sheffield, South Yorkshire
Map: 17, C3
Web: www.wildsheffield.com

P 🐾 (ltd), 🚻 🅿

Nestled between post-industrial Sheffield and the Peak District, these combined reserves offer magnificent views of the Rivelin Valley. The Wyming Brook, a fast flowing stream that descends quickly into the valley through deciduous and coniferous woodland, is home to an astonishingly varied birdlife. Alongside the woodland birds, birds of prey visit the moorland area. Fox Hagg offers a similarly stunning mix of habitats. A heathland dominated by heather and bilberry attracts the viviparous lizard and the tree pipit, while woodland areas support sparrowhawk, green woodpecker and linnet. It is quite astonishing to think that such diverse wildlife is present so close to the city.

BIRD RESERVES

Bempton Cliffs

Near: Bempton, near Bridlington, East Riding of Yorkshire
Map: 17, E2
Web: www.rspb.org.uk

P (££, inc 🐾), 🐾 🚾 🅿
ℹ 🅿 🚻 🅿 🅿

Boasting five viewing points along a three-mile stretch of sheer chalk cliff, this RSPB reserve offers excellent views of a fantastically diverse wildlife. Home to almost a quarter of a million seabirds, star species include gannets, guillemots and kittiwakes,

while colourful puffins may also be spotted. For the keen birdwatcher, rarer migrants such as Lapland buntings and warblers from eastern Europe and Siberia can be found in the fields and hedgerows along the cliff tops. On occasion, it is possible to see harbour porpoises and seals, while short-eared owls may also be spotted.

Blacktoft Sands

Near: Goole, near Selby, East Riding of Yorkshire
Map: 17, C2
Web: www.rspb.org.uk

P 🐾 🚾 🅿 ℹ
🅿 🚻 🅿 🅿

This reserve has a tidal reedbed that is the largest in England and has breeding populations of bearded tits, marsh harriers and bitterns. It is also home to large numbers of reed warblers and reed buntings as well as hundreds of species of rare and specialist insects. There are also saline lagoons where you'll find breeding and migrant waders, including avocets. Grazing marsh attracts wintering ducks and breeding waders. More than 270 species of bird have been recorded on the reserve and 60 of these have bred. All six observation hides offer great close-up views of the birds and there are guided walks throughout the year.

Brown long-eared bats

Although the brown long-eared bat does have very long ears – about 5cm, the same length as its body – you can't always see them. The ears get tucked away under wings or rolled up like rams' horns leaving just little pointy inner lobes visible. When they are up and in use, they are incredibly sensitive and the brown long-eared bat will often use hearing to locate its insect prey, rather than echolocation. Good-sized colonies are found: in the Lower Derwent Forest, in Skipton Woods and in Kew Gardens.

Eccup Reservoir SSSI

Near: Leeds, West Yorkshire
Map: 17, C2
Web: www.yorkshirewater.com

P (ltd), ♿ ⛾

A private reservoir with a public footpath that borders part of the bank, Eccup attracts a variety of wildlife, resulting in a SSSI designation. Winter attracts a mix of wildfowl, while woodland and hedgerow birds are present throughout the year and roosting gulls may also be observed. Eccup is most significant as a prime location for viewing the red kite, reintroduced to the area as part of a national programme. The Yorkshire project introduced 69 kites to the area between 1999 and 2003, a population that has thrived and an observation point has consequently been established at the eastern end of the reservoir.

Fairburn Ings

Near: Castleford, West Yorkshire
Map: 17, C3
Web: www.rspb.org.uk

P ♿ **WC** 🔧 ❶
🪑 🚻 ⛾ 🅰 ⛏

Fairburn Ings is the ideal place to see wetland birds at close quarters throughout the year. In winter, the large numbers of wildfowl include smews, goldeneyes and goosanders. In summer, breeding wading birds include redshanks, snipe and lapwings.

Old Moor

Near: Barnsley, South Yorkshire
Map: 17, C3
Web: www.rspb.org.uk
Open: daily, 9.30am to 4.30/5.15pm (except 25 and 26 December)
Admission: RSPB members free, £1.25/£2.50 others

P ♿ **WC** 🔧 ❶
🛒 🪑 🚻 🅰 ⛏

Old Moor is one of the RSPB's Dearne Valley reserves, playing a central role in the RSPB's commitment to transforming the valley into a nationally important wildlife area. Combining landscapes of open water, marsh, reedbed and grassland, Old Moor is a haven for birds in the midst of an old mining centre. Star species include kingfisher, little owl, lapwing and tree sparrow. In winter, more than 8,000 golden plovers join other wading birds and waterfowl, while summer attracts swallows and martins over the open water. Other sites in the area include Wombwell Ings and Gypsy Marsh, to which Old Moor staff will be happy to guide you.

FORESTS & WOODLAND

Bilton Beck and Rudding Bottoms

Near: Harrogate, North Yorkshire
Map: 17, C2
Web: www.wt-woods.org.uk

P

Nestling in the wooded valley of the Nidd Gorge, this wood provides a rich mixture of vegetation communities and wildlife habitats. Forty-two species of bird have been recorded here, including the dipper, grey wagtail and kingfisher. Roe deer, water vole, mink and foxes have all been spotted but sadly, no otters currently live in the Bilton Beck area of the gorge. The woodland contains both broad-leaved and coniferous species, including larch, pine, wild cherry and willow. The conifers provide refuge for the coal tit and goldcrest, while the alders lining the River Nidd can reveal siskin and the occasional redpoll.

Bitholmes Wood

Near: Sheffield, South Yorkshire
Map: 17, C3
Web: www.wt-woods.org.uk

Separated from the larger Wharncliffe Woods by the River Don, Bitholmes consists of predominantly ancient semi-natural woodland. Several significant crags of sandstone and gritstone remain as a result of past quarrying, rendering the soils acidic and the hanging sessile oak dominant. The lower wood is predominantly sycamore, yet retains an ancient woodland character in its ground flora, which includes wood mellick and bluebells. Several significant areas of bracken and three small, restocked areas further add to site diversity. Bitholmes supports a variety of woodland birds, including woodpeckers and pied flycatchers. The usual woodland animals reside, yet red or roe deer activity is minimal.

Boggle Top

Near: Pickering, North Yorkshire
Map: 17, D1
Web: www.wt-woods.org.uk

⛾

Planted in April 2001 as part of The Woodland Trust's Woods on Your Doorstep project, Boggle Top sits amid ancient semi-natural woodland and improved pasture land, within the North York Moors National Park. The site has two permanent springs, thus seasonally is very wet, with areas of rush traversing the entire slope on which the woodland is located. Tree species include oak, field maple, hawthorn and dog rose. Seating is provided to the south of the site, affording magnificent views north to Robin Hood's Bay.

Yorkshire and Humberside

Briscoe Wood
Near: Harrogate, North Yorkshire
Map: 17, C2
Web: www.wt-woods.org.uk

P 🚻

Superbly located for excellent views, Briscoe Wood holds a prominent position in the landscape along Briscoe Rigg, a gentle ridge of higher land. Purchased in 1999 as part of The Woodland Trust's Woods on Your Doorstep project, the northern boundary of the land is separated from the highway by a valuable wildlife corridor of mixed scrub including hawthorn, oak and willow. Designed as a fundamentally recreational facility and landscape feature, planting since 2000 has introduced cherry, rowan and ash, while shrubs include dog rose and hazel. The ground layer is mainly mixed grass.

Brow Wood
Near: Pickering, North Yorkshire
Map: 17, D1
Web: www.wt-woods.org.uk
Located within the North York Moors National Park, Brow Wood forms part of a larger woodland included within the Newtondale SSSI. The upper slopes are composed mainly of birch, with remnant oak, rowan and lime apparent alongside an understorey of hazel and holly. A scrub edge to the west represents blackthorn, birch and gorse, while the lower slopes consist of mixed broad-leaves such as alder and ash. Large areas of open ground and low growing scrub create an open wooded feel that opens up into a wet meadow/marsh area which is seasonally waterlogged.

Chalk Pit
Near: Bainton, near Driffield, East Riding of Yorkshire
Map: 17, D2

Mixed woodland in Forge Valley Woods NNR

Web: www.wt-woods.org.uk

P

A small woodland on the sloping Yorkshire Wolds, Chalk Pit has three distinct areas, combining a mixture of ash, beech, crab and cherry in one domain, a former chalk pit which is now a site of mature trees and a grass field with mixed broad-leaves.

Forge Valley Woods NNR
Near: Scarborough, North Yorkshire
Map: 17, D1
Web: www.english-nature.org.uk

P ♿ 🚻 🔥

A fantastic example of mixed deciduous woodland, Forge Valley flanks the east and west facing slopes of the Derwent river valley. The woodland types that transcend the valley sides range from alder and willow in the wet valley bottom, accompanied by a ground flora of yellow flay and pendulous sedge, to a canopy of ash and wych elm on the middle slopes. Here, a diverse flora, dominated by dog's mercury, also incorporates sanicle and toothwort, while the top slopes support pedunculate oak. A rich population of breeding birds includes the treecreeper and blackcap, while the river is home to trout and crayfish.

Hackfall Woods SSSI
Near: Grewelthorpe, near Ripon, North Yorkshire
Map: 17, C2
Web: www.wt-woods.org.uk
Forming part of the Nidderdale AONB, Hackfall Wood covers the north and east-facing slopes above the Ure Gorge, and its individual national importance has been recognised as a designated SSSI. A fine example of ancient semi natural woodland, Hackfall supports a wide range of bird species. All three woodpeckers are present and other woodland birds include woodcock, spotted and pied flycatcher, nuthatch and treecreeper. The River Ure, meandering through the lower woodland, attracts kingfisher, dipper and common sandpiper, while the wood warbler and redstart have also been recorded. A range of wild plants includes a stunning display of bluebells.

Harry's Folly
Near: Whitby, North Yorkshire
Map: 17, D1
Web: www.wt-woods.org.uk

Covering 15 acres of ancient woodland, Harry's Folly forms an important part of a larger wooded valley complex. Only nearly two miles from Robin Hood's Bay, wholly native woodland, planted in 1999, includes oak, blackthorn hazel and field maple, while grazing land acquired in 2006 comprises three semi-improved fields containing a mixture of mature trees. The ground flora is extremely rich and varied, dominated by snowdrops, primroses and daffodils in late winter and early spring, then bluebells in the late spring.

Hone Wood
Near: Pickering, North Yorkshire
Map: 17, D1
Web: www.wt-woods.org.uk
Situated on a moderate slope and prominent in the immediate local landscape, Hone Woods forms a central part of a larger wooded complex of semi natural and part-coniferised ancient woodland. Hone is bound to the south by the broad-leaved Boggle Top woodland, while Harry's Folly to the west and Ox Pasture to the north consist in ancient semi-natural woodland. Dominated by sessile oak, very occasional semi-mature sycamores have regenerated, while the shrub layer is especially rich, combining hazel coppice with spindle and dog rose. Variant ground conditions allow for an undisturbed ground flora including acidic areas of bluebell and a range of ferns and mosses. Although there is no formal access, Hone Wood is well-linked and reachable through neighbouring woods.

Little Wold Plantation
Near: South Cave, near Hull, East Riding of Yorkshire

Map: 17, D2
Web: www.wt-woods.org.uk
P
Adopting an elevated position on the southern edge of a ridge, this prominent landscape feature is an attractive mature woodland of mainly beech and ash, with a small representation of sycamore. Shrub species are minimal, however, and the ground flora is poor, consisting mainly of ivy covering much of the ground in the shaded areas dominated by beech. Large colonies of deadly nightshade also grow within the woodland. Little Wold is reported to have a rich birdlife.

Lower Grass Wood
Near: Grassington, near Skipton, North Yorkshire
Map: 17, B2
Web: www.wt-woods.org.uk
P
A narrow woodland holding along the north-east bank of the River Wharf, Lower Grass Wood forms an important part of the larger Grass and Bastow Wood, a semi-natural and coniferised ancient woodland. Lower Grass comprises planted sycamore, sessile and pedunculate oak, ash and birch with occasional planted larch and beech. A rabbit fence has been installed, which has led to a good level of regrowth within the woodland. The ground flora is representative of both ancient woodland and calcareous grassland, including bluebell, orchids and a variety of wild herbs, such as thyme, marjoram and basil.

New Covert and Park Woods
Near: Melbourne, North Yorkshire
Map: 17, C2
Web: www.wt-woods.org.uk
P **⚑**
A combination of woodland, scrub and open glades provide a wealth of wildlife habitats. There is a large central clearing, which is a popular haunt of barn owls. While the wet woodland of New Covert contains typical birch, willow and alder,

Nidd Gorge
Near: Knaresborough, near Harrogate, North Yorkshire
Map: 17, C2
Web: www.wt-woods.org.uk
P **⚑**
Since glacial action diverted the River Nidd from its original course some 15,000 years ago, Nidd Gorge has emerged and deepened to today exist as a steep sided, well-wooded valley, with impressive views obtainable from the upper slopes. Diverse soil, resulting from a variant geology of limestone and carboniferous rocks, produces a rich bryophyte flora, dependent on continuous tree cover. Bracken abounds in light areas, while bluebells and celandine feature heavily in the oak areas. Ninety-one species of fungi have been identified in the Gorge, including puffballs and cup fungi. Butterflies include the common blue and peacock, while the woodland areas attract birds, such as the goldcrest and woodcock, and the river is home to kingfishers and siskins. Roe deer, stoats, badgers and foxes inhabit the woodland, but sadly otter are no longer present.

Foxes: talkative loners

If you've ever wondered whether animals can talk, then listening to foxes could convince you. Every fox has a distinctive voice which can span five octaves. They make different sounds for differing occasions: a monosyllabic bark is usually used to warn cubs of danger; a stuttering, throaty noise called gekkering is used in aggressive encounters; a howly *woah-woah-woah* sound is used for 'conversation' between animals. The further apart the animals are, the louder the sound they make. Although they are clearly talkative, foxes are solitary animals and only rarely form together into a pack. They are found all over Britain in woodland, scrubland and mountains as well as suburban gardens.

which may once have been coppiced, most probably for firewood. Great thickets of willow and alder make a glade that links New Covert and Park Wood, and are ideal for spotting willow tits. Just a little bit further, and the ancient woodland of Park Wood emerges. Comprising mainly birch and scattered oak trees, the associated flora is especially rich.

Nut Wood and Wauldby Scrogs
Near: Beverley, Humberside
Map: 17, D2
Web: www.wt-woods.org.uk
P

Nut Wood, Wauldby Scrogs and Constantine Wood occupy a gentle slope of a small dry valley in the Yorkshire Wolds. A planting programme in 1999 saw the reintroduction

of native species such as oak, small-leaved lime and cherry with shrubs, including dog rose and hazel. Additional grasses and wildflowers thrive and provide a haven for many interesting insects as well as a great spectacle for visitors. This is a popular recreational woodland, and many rarer mammals stay away, but you might spot rabbit, deer and fox. More than 36 species of birds have been spotted, along with 20 species of insects and anthropods. Known locally as Bluebell Wood, a rich ground flora includes dog's mercury, wood anemone, wild garlic and bluebells.

Preston Spring Wood
Near: Preston-under-Scar, near Richmond, North Yorkshire
Map: 17, B1
Web: www.wt-woods.org.uk

Located just outside the Yorkshire Dales National Park (excluded due to local quarrying activity and MOD firing ranges), Preston Spring is made up of unimproved pasture grassland and semi-natural ancient woodland. The pasture supports bluebell and primrose, while the unimproved area contains a small wet flush, dominated by rush with frequent marsh marigold. The woodland has sessile oak, elm and planted mature sycamore evident on the lowers slopes, while hazel coppice prevails in the understorey. A spectacular ground flora can be found here due to the variety of habitats in such a small area, including grassland, continuous and scattered bracken and dry modified bogs, and the number of species found in each one.

Raincliffe Meadows

Near: Scarborough,
North Yorkshire
Map: 17, D1
Web: www.wt-woods.org.uk
P

Created in January 1998, Raincliffe Meadows forms part of the larger mixed woodland of Raincliffe Woods. An area of formerly improved grassland, dominated by improved ryegrass, the meadows were planted with native woodland species including oak, rowan birch and holly. Surrounding areas combine planted woodland scattered with areas of ancient semi-natural woodland, while wet flushes and occasional native natural regeneration are also evident.

Roffe Wood

Near: Sinnington, near Pickering,
North Yorkshire
Map: 17, D1
Web: www.wt-woods.org.uk
P

This newly planted woodland, sitting amid arable and pasture land, lies just outside the boundary of the North York Moors National Park. As former grazing land, the site has been improved and is composed of predominantly ryegrass. Wholly native woodland plantations include oak, field maple, rowan and ash.

Scar and Castlebeck Woods

Near: Harwood Dale, near
Scarborough, North Yorkshire
Map: 17, D1
Web: www.wt-woods.org.uk
As one of the largest ancient semi-natural woodlands within the Scarborough district, Scar and Castlebeck is characterised by a multitude of ancient woodland indicator species. Particularly notable for its rich ground flora, the site

also boasts records of 21 nationally scarce invertebrates and 35 locally rare species. The huge importance of this woodland is reflected in additional designations, including recognition as an Important Bird Area in Europe in 2000 and in the north-western area as a SAC. Oak and ash dominate, with an understorey of holly, hazel and honeysuckle. A variety of habitats abound throughout the woodland, including wet flushes, open heathland and moorland dominated by heather and bilberry.

Scoska Wood

Near: Arncliffe, near Skipton,
North Yorkshire
Map: 17, B2
Web: www.english-nature.org.uk
Located on the slopes of Littondale, the valley of the River Skirfare, Scoska Wood is a strip of ash woodland and pasture. The woodland clings to the limestone scars of the upper slopes, then merges into herb-rich neutral or calcareous pasture below. At the boundary, a number of springs emerge. Ash dominates, with an understorey of hazel and hawthorn, while downy birch and bird cherry also occur. A rich ground flora includes dog's mercury, ramsons, sanicle and herb paris, while there is a tall-herb community at the wood's end, comprising wood crane's bill, melancholy thistle and meadowsweet.

Skipton Woods

Near: Skipton, North Yorkshire
Map: 17, B2
Web: www.wt-woods.org.uk
P **P**
The majority of Skipton is broad-leaved, oak and ash, yet beech, sycamore and a scattering of other non-native species, such as hornbeam and sweet chestnut, are also

present. Scot's pine and Norway spruce have also been introduced. The ground flora is typical of ancient semi-natural woodland, with dense carpets of wild garlic, bluebells and dog's mercury throughout. Recent resurfacing provides excellent access, yet despite the high visitor numbers, Skipton supports a rich diversity of wildlife, notably badgers, roe deer and at least five species of bat, including the brown long-eared, Daubenton's and noctule. The woods also support kingfishers, spotted and green woodpeckers and sparrowhawks.

COASTS, WETLANDS & WATERWAYS

Aire and Calder Navigation

From: Leeds to Goole, with
Wakefield to Castleford branch
Map: 17, C3
Web: www.waterscape.com
Covering 33 miles between Leeds and Goole, with an additional Wakefield to Castleford branch, the Aire and Calder is an active freight waterway. An essential link between the Yorkshire waterways and the canals of the Pennines, this navigation is attractive and increasingly used for recreational boating. The waterway walls support freshwater sponges, while inhabitants include water vole and white-clawed (native) crayfish. A number of reserves are situated along the canal, including the Fairburn Ings RSPB reserve where wildfowl can be spotted, including smews and goldeneyes. The areas around Woodlesford (where a bird hide has been installed) and Methley are also popular for birdwatching.

Calder and Hebble Navigation

From: Wakefield to Sowerby Bridge, near Halifax, West Yorkshire
Map: 17, B3 to C3
Web: www.waterscape.com

Traversing 21 mostly rural miles between Wakefield and Sowerby Bridge, Calder and Hebble is both a charming waterway and a vital connection between the Yorkshire waterways and Pennine canals of Huddersfield and Rochdale. Although the waterway once served a busy industrial area, its route is surprisingly untroubled by modern life and a cruise or walk is a relaxing experience. Moorhens, ducks and some aggressively territorial mute swans glide along the water, while swallows, tits and thrushes nest in the trees along the verges. Aquatic plants, such as lilies and varied species of moss, abound along the fertile ground of the canal's water and banks.

Dearne and Dove Canal

From: Sheffield and South Yorkshire Navigation at Swinton to Barnsley, South Yorkshire
Map: 17, C3
Web: www.waterscape.com

Once a busy, deep canal, the Dearne and Dove connected the River Don and Sheffield waterways to Barnsley and the Yorkshire coalfield, with additional branches to Worsborough and Elsecar. Closed in the 1960s following problems of mining subsidence, it is now derelict yet still easily traceable, while the end of the Elsecar branch has already been restored. The Barnsley Dearne and Dove Canals Trust is campaigning for further restoration.

Driffield Navigation

From: Driffield to Struncheon Hill Lock, East Riding of Yorkshire
Map: 17, D2
Web: www.waterscape.com

Derelict for many years, this seven-mile stretch between Driffield and Struncheon Hill is now undergoing restoration. The navigation entices plenty of wildfowl and birds, as well as some summer migrants. As part of the nationwide Wildlife Trusts' Water for Wildlife project, the Yorkshire branch is working with the Environment Agency and other organisations to implement the national Otter Biodiversity Action Plan, aimed at encouraging breeding otters back to all Yorkshire's rivers and waterways by 2010. The same project is also involved in organising conservation efforts in the local community, with the intention to protect a wide range of important species, including damselflies, kingfishers and water voles.

Elsecar Reservoir NNR

Near: Barnsley, South Yorkshire
Map: 17, C3
Web: www.waterscape.com
P **&**

Originally built to service the Dearne and Dove Canal, the reservoir combines a large area of mature willow carr, grassland containing acid grass, a large water area and associated water fringe habitats to create a site of considerable natural value. For the keen angler, the main fish species are bream, carp, perch, pike and roach. The regular bird population includes great crested and little grebes, and is also capable of the odd surprise. Red-throated diver, black-necked grebe and great grey shrike have all been recorded, while every species of tern on the Sheffield list has been observed, including the area's first recording of the white-winged black tern.

Huddersfield Broad Canal

From: Huddersfield to Mirfield
Map: 17, B3
Web: www.waterscape.com

A surprisingly pleasant urban waterway, the three-mile Huddersfield Broad Canal connects the Huddersfield Narrow Canal to the Calder and Hebble, thus also incorporating the Yorkshire Rivers. Once known as Sir John Ramsden's Canal, after the one-time Lord of the Manor, it later became the Broad Canal to distinguish it from the Narrow Canal. Although previously cruised by a few boaters, weed growth and abandonment mean that today the canal is almost exclusively the preserve of anglers and cyclists. However, since the reopening of the Narrow Canal in 2001, boats are beginning to cruise the Broad Canal once again on their way across the Pennines.

Huddersfield Narrow Canal

From: Huddersfield, West Yorkshire to Ashton under Lyne, Greater Manchester
Map: 17, B3
Web: www.waterscape.com

Spanning 20 miles between Huddersfield and Ashton under Lyne, the Huddersfield Narrow Canal was reopened in May 2001, after 50 years of abandonment. Boasting Britain's longest canal tunnel, the Standedge, and with a summit confirming it as the highest navigable waterway, the HNC combines stretches of tranquil, well-wooded countryside with dramatic mills and historic industry. Once dubbed impossible, the restoration has confounded doubters. Special habitat sites were established for the endangered white-clawed crayfish. In addition, sensitive planting on top of the walls softened the canal edges and

Huddersfield Narrow Canal

created habitats for birds, while small nesting platforms, shielded by ivy, were welded into the wall recesses.

Leeds and Liverpool Canal
From: Leeds, North Yorkshire, to Liverpool, Merseyside
Map: 17, C2 to A3
Web: www.waterscape.com
At 127 miles, the Leeds and Liverpool canal is the longest in Britain and, via its connection with the Aire and Calder at Leeds, offers a coast-to-coast route across Northern England. Kirkstall Valley Nature Reserve, an SSSI near Leeds, incorporates a five-mile stretch of the canal and the nearby River Aire. Birds, such as the kingfisher, sedge warbler and reed bunting, are all present, as are 16 species of butterfly, while purified water is pumped to man-made ponds to support various insects, frogs, beetles and pondlife such as water lilies. The Kirkstall woodland also accommodates warblers, tits, thrushes and songbirds.

New Junction Canal
From: Stainforth and Keadby Cana, near Doncaster and Pontefract
Map: 17, C3
Web: www.waterscape.com
The New Junction Canal meanders a short, perfectly straight course between the Stainforth and Keadby Canal and the Aire and Calder Navigation. The canal is incorporated into the Humberhead Peatlands NNR, which is made up of Thorne, Hatfield and Crowle Moors. Comprising lowland raised bog, such a vast wilderness is home to a wealth of wildlife. The rare European nightjar has been spotted, alongside the merlin and short-eared owl. Mammals include deer and water vole, while adders prevail among the reptile population. More than 3,000 species of invertebrates have also been recorded, including the largeheath butterfly. Plantlife includes bog-rosemary and cranberry, while bird's-foot trefoil can also be seen.

Pocklington Canal
From: River Derwent near Thorganby to Canal Head near York, North Yorkshire,
Map: 17, C2
Web: www.waterscape.com
Flowing through the Vale of York from a junction with the River Derwent to Canal Head near Pocklington, the canal almost became a permanent dumping ground for industrial waste, yet a passionate campaign has resulted in partial restoration. Today, Pocklington is one of Britain's most significant canals for wildlife. Plants such as fan-leaved water crowfoot reflect the canal's limestone origins in the Yorkshire Wolds. Diverse vegetation provides ideal conditions for a wide range of aquatic invertebrates. Breeding birds of open water and their margins are attracted to the canal, while it also provides additional habitat for breeding and wintering wildfowl.

Ripon Canal
From: Ripon to Oxclose Lock, North Yorkshire

Leeds and Liverpool Canal

Map: 17, C2
Web: www.waterscape.com
🛈 at Ripon Racecourse Marina,
🆆🅲 ▣ in Ripon, ♿
Covering just 2.5 miles
between Ripon town centre
and the Oxclose Lock
junction with the River Ure,
Ripon Canal is one of the
most northerly in England.
With an impressive record of
76 bird species spotted, two
hides on the canal's towpath
provide views over a
washlands area.

River Aire

From: Bank Dole Lock to the
River Ouse, near Pontefract
Map: 17, C3
Web: www.waterscape.com
This 22.5-mile link between
the Aire and Calder and
River Ouse, beginning at
the Bank Dole Lock, was
once the main route from
Leeds to the Humber.
The Aire's twisting route
incorporates a wealth of
wildlife. Meandering through
a wildlife park at Shipley,
recent improvements to
the water quality attract
kingfishers, ducks and other
river wildlife. A portion of
the Kirkstall Valley Reserve
makes up an island in the
Aire, the sands providing an
ideal habitat for oak trees
and the clearings are happily
strewn with bluebells in
the spring. Prohibited
pedestrian access to the
island secures it as a refuge
for roe deer, heron and
numerous waterfowl.

River Don

From: The Pennines, South
Yorkshire, to the River Ouse,
Selby, East Riding of Yorkshire
Map: 17, B2 to C3
Web: www.waterscape.com
Rising in the Pennines of
South Yorkshire, in the midst
of the beautiful Peak District
National Park, the River
Don flows through Sheffield,
Rotherham and Doncaster to
join the River Ouse at Goole.
Flowing through breathtaking
countryside, the river has
traditionally been rich in all
manner of wildlife. Fig trees
flourish along its banks,
and although at one time
industry pollution threatened
the fish population, today
salmon and trout once again
thrive. Families of ducks are
resident, while a project is
now underway to encourage
barn owls along the length of
the river.

Sheffield and South
Yorkshire Navigation
Between: Sheffield, South
Yorkshire, and River Trent,
Lincolnshire
Map: 17, C3 to D3
Web: www.waterscape.com
Running for 40 miles
between Sheffield and the
River Trent, this Navigation
comprises the Sheffield
and Tinsley Canal, Don
Navigation and Stainforth
and Keadby Canal, along
with the New Junction
Canal. Although capable
of commercial traffic, the
waterway is predominantly
used by pleasure boats, and
is also popular with walkers
and cyclists. A new Hawk

and Owl Trust project aims to encourage barn owls along the length of the waterway, while Sheffield City Council is working to improve water quality in the Don section, encouraging more wildlife to the canal.

Spurn NNR

Near: Kilnsea, near Kingston upon Hull, East Riding of Yorkshire
Map: 17, E2
Web: www.yorkshire-wildlife-trust.org.uk

Stretching 3.5 miles to the mouth of the Humber Estuary, Spurn NNR combines a narrow sandy peninsula with areas of saltmarsh and extensive mudflats. Breezy and invigorating, as a place to watch birds and their migration, Spurn is incomparable. While wildfowl, such as mallard and shelduck, may shelter here in winter, during passage times, curlew, dunlin, knot and turnstone arrive. Other arrivals can include flycatchers, redwing and whinchat, while terns also pass through. Among the hundreds of plant species recorded, lyme grass, marram and sea holly are all prevalent. A unique coastal reserve, this wildlife haven also offers the chance of spotting seals.

Tophill Low Nature Reserve

Near: Driffield, East Riding of Yorkshire
Map: 17, D2
Web: www.yorkshirewater.com

(inc access),

Featuring two reservoirs and marsh and mud lagoons, Tophill Low is one of Yorkshire's best nature reserves. An extensive bird population combines

residents with migrants who use the coast and River Humber as flight ways to and from Europe, and beyond. Regular residents of the reserve include kingfishers, herons, roe deer, foxes, bats and butterflies, while recent sightings have included rarer species such as bittern, spotted crake and wood sandpiper. Notable is the site's recent accolade, the national award from the British Trust of Ornithology for best example of a large wetland site in 2004.

DID YOU KNOW?

Kingfishers don't have blue pigment. Their colour comes from light reflected and refracted within their feathers.

Wheldrake Ings

Near: York, East Riding of Yorkshire
Map: 17, C2
Web: www.yorkshire-wildlife-trust.org.uk

(ltd),

A great seasonal wetland, Wheldrake Ings transforms from wetland in the winter to meadow in the warmer months. The winter floods have enriched the silt, which when combined with traditional management staying free from artificial fertilisation brings forth a rich display of wildflowers. Typical flowers, such as the tall great burnet, are present, while rarities include the narrow-leaved water dropwort. Bewick's swan, geese and other wildfowl are attracted by the winter wetlands, while the breeding birds of summer include snipe and redshank, with mallard and moorhen often busy on the pond. You may also see a short-eared owl in the daylight, or a barn owl at

NOT SO WILD

Bradford City Farm

Address: Illingworth Fields, Walker Drive, Girlington, Bradford, West Yorkshire BD8 9EZ
Map: 17, B2
Tel: 01274 543500
Web: www.farmgarden.org.uk
Open: weekdays, 3pm to 4pm; school holidays, by arrangement
Admission: free

Since 1984, Bradford City Farm has offered recreational facilities and educational opportunities to a variety of individuals, groups and organisations. With available activities ranging from the practice of organic horticulture to good animal husbandry, the farm offers a hands-on experience to all who visit. Combined environments of coppice, orchard, reedbed and a pond attract a variety of wildlife, while animals, including the white-faced woodland sheep, Anglo-nubian goat, Shetland pony and Dexter cattle, are resident on the farm. Other inhabitants include donkeys, maran and white Sussex chickens, while various fruit and vegetables are homegrown.

Burton Agnes

Address: Driffield, Yorkshire YO25 0ND
Map: 17, D2
Tel: 01262 490324
Web: www.burton-agnes.co.uk
Open: daily, April to October, 11am to 5pm
Admission: £2.60/£5.20

Burton Agnes is a grand Elizabethan house, full of treasures both old and modern, with legends and stories wrapped in its walls, gardens full of interest and surprises, and a history going back to Norman

Animal tracks

By its very nature, much of the wildlife we'd most like to see has a habit of keeping out of our way. But if you know the signs to look for, your chances of tracking down a glimpse of an otter or a fox are that much more likely. The best place to look is soft bare ground, such as the mud at the edge of a stream or pond, or on sandy paths.

Fox: tear-shaped with four digits, the two lower outer ones curling in towards the higher inner ones.

Badger: broad with five digits and a large kidney-shaped pad.

Squirrel: Small, with four digits on the front foot and five on the rear.

Otter: five digits on an almost round pad. You can sometimes see webbing between the digits.

Deer: hoof tracks in two parts, often seen near streams and puddles where they go to drink.

Rabbit: the hind legs leave longer imprints than the front, tracks are rarely clearly defined because of their furry feet.

Dog: broad ovals with four digits, usually with visible claws.

Cat: four digits on a round pad, very rarely with claws.

Rats or mice: Similar to squirrel with wider spread digits.

times. Situated on the north east coast of Yorkshire, the bracing climate has never been tamed within spectacular walled gardens. Along with herbaceous borders, the scented garden and jungle garden, there are giant outdoor board games to be found between the plants.

The Deep
Address: Hull, Humberside HU1 4DP
Map: 17, D2
Tel: 01482 381000
Web: www.thedeep.co.uk
Open: daily, 10am to 6pm (except 24 and 25 December)
Admission: £6/£8
P (inc &), &
WC
Opened in 2002, The Deep is a charitable public aquarium dedicated to increasing enjoyment and understanding of the world's oceans. Using

a combination of hands-on interactive exhibits and audiovisual presentations, visitors will be taken from the beginning of time through to the present-day oceans. The central living exhibit, a tank containing 2.5 million litres of water and 87 tonnes of salt, is home to 14 species of shark, as well as moray eels, rays and hundreds of other stunning sea creatures. You can experience the depths from the world's only underwater lift and Europe's deepest viewing tunnel, all part of a truly one in a million experience.

East Hull Community Farm
Address: Barham Road, Bilton Grange Estate, Hull, Humberside HU9 4EE
Map: 17, D2
Tel: 01482 783990
Web: www.farmgarden.org.uk
Open: weekdays, 8.30am to 4pm

Admission: free
& WC &
Having developed from its school farm routes at Andrew Marvel School, East Hull Community Farm is well on the way to achieving its potential by serving the local community as well as the students. Although adjacent to the school, the county council has granted a seven-year lease to the farm company, at a peppercorn rent. Livestock include cattle, sheep, goats and pigs. Facilities, such as the community building and the training room, ensure this farm educates and inspires.

Flamingo Land Zoo and Theme Park
Address: The Rectory, Kirby Misperton, near Malton, North Yorkshire YO17 6UX

Map: 17, D2
Tel: 01653 68287
Web: www.flamingoland.co.uk
Open: daily, 1 April to 29 October,
10am to 5/6pm
Admission: £19

P ♿ WC 🅿 🖴 📷 🐾

Home to more than 1,000
animals and boasting many
white-knuckle thrill rides,
Flamingo Land Zoo and
Theme Park offers something
for everyone. Animals
resident at the zoo include
African lions, giraffes,
Siberian tigers and Grant
zebras. Bactrian camels, sea
lions and Humboldt penguins
are also present and, of
course, there's the famous
pink flamingos, the largest
flock in the country. The
Bird Walk houses birds of
all shapes and sizes, from
the ostrich to the finch,
while the new Muddy Duck
Farm allows youngsters to
drive their very own tractor
around to meet their favourite
farmland animals.

Harewood Bird Garden

Address: Harewood, Leeds,
North Yorkshire LS17 9LG
Map: 17, C2
Tel: 0113 218 1010
Web: www.harewood.org
Open: varies with season
Admission: weekdays ,£6.50/
£9.75; weekends and Bank
Holidays £8/£12

P (inc ♿), ♿
WC 🅿 🖴 🐾

Situated in the grounds of
Harewood House, home of
the Queen's cousin, the Earl
of Harewood, Harewood Bird
Garden is one of the country's
premier avian collections.
More than 100 species of
threatened and exotic birds
from all over the world
are housed in sympathetic
environments with the aim
of promoting conservation
and education. Featuring
birds such as the omei

shan liocichla – a vulnerable
species only known to exist
on one mountain in China
– the Princess of Wales
parakeet from Australasia
and the white stork of
the African grasslands,
Harewood truly represents
the extraordinary diversity of
the natural world.

DID YOU KNOW?

The UK's fastest mammal
is the hare which can reach
speeds of up to 45mph.

Heeley City Farm

Address: Richards Road, Sheffield,
South Yorkshire S2 3DT
Map: 17, C3
Tel: 0114 258 0482
Web: www.heeleyfarm.org.uk
Open: 9.30am to 4.30/5pm
Admission: free

P ♿ WC ℹ 🖴 🐾

Started in 1981, this
community-based project
in inner-city Sheffield aims
to teach, train and employ.
Combining an environmental
visitor centre with other
exceptional facilities, Heeley
City Farm is also home to
a range of rare and unusual
domestic animals. Exmoor
ponies, Irish moiled
cows, Soay sheep and a
variety of goats, including
the saanene and pypony,
are all present, along with
large black pigs, rabbits
and guinea pigs. The farm
is also rich in plantlife,
boasting a herb garden and
wildflower areas, while the
one-acre market garden and
additional demonstration
plots provide Asian and more
common vegetables.

Meanwood Valley Urban Farm

Address: Sugarwell Road,
Meanwood, Leeds, North Yorkshire
LS7 2QG

Map: 17, C2
Tel: 0113 262 9759
Web: www.farmgarden.org.uk
Open: 9am to 4pm
Admission: 50p/£1

P (inc ♿), ♿
🖴 📷 🐾

Located only one and a half
miles from the centre of Leeds,
the 14 acres of Meanwood
Valley Urban Farm offer rare
breed animals, an organic
market garden and wonderful
facilities. A haven for children,
its established links with
inner-city schools ensure full
access to farm animals and
a rural environment that
children might not otherwise
experience. Rare breeds
resident at Meanwood include
the white-faced woodland,
Suffolk and Hebridean
sheep, Dexter cattle and the
Gloucester old spot pig.

Renishaw Hall

Address: Sheffield S21 3WB
Map: 17, C3
Web: www.sitwell.co.uk
Open: April to September,
Thursday to Sunday, 10.30am
to 4.30pm
Admission: £4.20/£5

Renishaw Hall and its
impressive gardens have been
the home of the Sitwell family
for more than 350 years. The
beautiful Italianate garden,
park and lake were the
creation of the eccentric Sir
George Sitwell, grandfather
of the present owner. The
hall is not open to the public,
however, private guided
group and connoisseur tours
of 25 persons or more of
the downstairs only may be
arranged by prior agreement.

Scarborough Sea-Life Centre

Address: Scalby Mills,
Scarborough, North Yorkshire
YO12 6RP
Map: 17, D1
Tel: 01723 373414
Web: www.sealifeeurope.com

Open: 10am to 4/5/6pm
Admission: £8.95/£10.95
P (inc ☺), ☺ (ltd),
WC ♿ ▢ ▥

Housing thousands of fascinating sea creatures, Scarborough Sea-Life Centre is situated to the east of the town centre, on the edge of the North Sea. The newly opened Turtle Reef, with colourful Caribbean-style coral reef and hundreds of dazzling reef fish sharing quarters with turtles and tropical sharks, is just one of a whole range of breathtaking exhibits. A successful marine sanctuary for orphaned, sickly and injured seal pups, as well as a sea turtles' convalescence facility demonstrate the centre's commitment to creatures of the deep.

The Tropical Butterfly House, Wildlife and Falconry Centre
Address: Hungerhill Farm, Woodsetts Road, North Anston, Sheffield S25 4EQ
Map: 17, C3
Tel: 01909 569416

Web: www.butterflyhouse.co.uk
Open: daily, 10/11am to 4.30/5.30pm (except 25 and 31 December and 1 January)
Admission: £4.99/£5.99
P WC ▢

Having evolved since 1994 to accommodate a wide range of animals, the centre is today home to the Tropical House and Bird of Prey Centre, as well as a baby animal nursery and pets' corner. These areas house an amazing array of exotic plants and animals, from Philippine butterflies and African falcon to South American marmoset monkeys and Australian bearded dragons, while a mature nature trail provides a sanctuary for a variety of native species. The Tropical House contains caiman and leaf-cutter ants, and the nocturnal room is home to sticky-footed geckos, luminous tree frogs and slithering snakes. The nature trail offers sightings of honeybees, kestrels, woodpeckers and stoats, as well as stickleback fish and newts in the pond.

Yorkshire Dales Falconry and Conservation Centre
Address: Crows Nest, near Giggleswick, Settle, North Yorkshire LA2 8AS
Map: 17, B2
Tel: 01729 822832
Web: www.falconryandwildlife.com
Open: daily, 10am to 4.30pm (except 25 and 26 December and 1 January)
Admission: £3.50/£5.50
P WC ⓘ ▢

Since its creation in 1991, the centre has provided a glimpse into the sport of falconry as well as an invaluable insight to various birds of prey. However, as part of a worldwide breeding and conservation programme that hopes, one day, to return all species safely to their natural habitats, the primary goal is to assist with the re-population of birds of prey. Residents include snowy owls and Bateleur eagles, while the centre is designed to take up minimal land, thus allowing sufficient space for the birds' exercise and training.

North West

By far the most dominant landscape of the North West is the Lake District, with its towering purple hills and sparkling blue lakes. The mountains' height cuts the area off from the rest of England and, as a result, some areas are a veritable wildlife sanctuary, harbouring species that are endangered elsewhere in the UK, such as red squirrels and white-clawed crayfish.

Up in the hills, the exposed nature of the terrain limits fauna to the hardy, such as peregrine falcons, golden eagles, ospreys and some red deer, while the lakes are home to Arctic char fish and vendace fish, and the surrounding areas are popular with many species of owls as well as natterjack toads.

But the area isn't all about the Lake District. When it comes to wildlife spotting, there are many other places the enthusiast should head to. For example, large numbers of wildfowl over-winter on the flats and marshes along the Cumbrian coast that lead down to the wide expanse of Morecambe Bay – also a popular spot for moths and butterflies. You'll see avocets, water rail, geese, godwits and even bitterns if you're lucky. Further south still, Ribble Estuary is one of Britain's most important sites for over-wintering wildfowl with more than 150,000 arriving each year.

Inland in Lancashire, the Forest of Bowland is an area of upland fells and heather-clad moors that descend into steep-sided wooded valleys. One of Britain's most endangered birds of prey, the hen harrier, nests in the uplands here in greater numbers than elsewhere in the country. It offers one of nature's most fantastic aerial shows as it impresses a mate in the spring with rollercoaster moves and tumbling acrobatics. Many other upland birds also nest here – it's the sort of place where you want to double-check you have your binoculars on you, as there will always be something for you to see.

PICTURED:
Left: Langdale Valley in the Lake District, at sunset
Right: Sand lizard

Not to be missed

● **Ainsdale Sand Dunes**
See if you can spot a sand lizard as it moves stealthily among the many great examples of dune plants found in this wild and alluring nature reserve.

● **Cuerden Valley Park**
This lovely park includes woodlands, meadows, lakes and farmland, offering all sorts of walks that take in many different plants, trees, birds and mammals – if you're lucky, you might see a water vole.

● **Finglandrigg Woods**
One of Cumbria's delightful woodlands where you're likely to see red squirrels in their natural habitat.

● **Lake District**
The best bit of England. Don't miss the stunning views of purple mountains and twinkling blue lakes. Wildlife is truly wild, with many birds of prey circling the exposed mountain slopes.

● **Ribble Estuary**
In winter the estuary is an amazing sight with thousands upon thousands of ducks, geese and waders arriving to dine on the river mouth's worms and snails.

● **Smardale Gill**
An old disused railway line makes an appealing glade where you will find delicate butterflies searching for pollen among the wildflowers.

NATIONAL PARK
Lake District

Cumbria
Map: 19
Web: www.lake-district.gov.uk

The Lake District is the largest of England's national parks, containing eight NNRs. There are more than 14 lakes and tarns – although officially Bassenthwaite Lake is the only titled 'lake', the rest are 'meres' or 'waters'. The rocks forming the Lake District provide a dramatic record of nearly 500 million years. Colliding continents, deep oceans, tropical seas, and 0.5-mile-thick ice sheets helped shape the landscape we see today. The red squirrel is still found here, as well as the Arctic char fish, red deer, peregrine falcons and Britain's only nesting pairs of golden eagles and ospreys. The lakes, tarns and rivers are well known for their range of habitats and species, such as the natterjack toad and water vole, as well as fish, such as crayfish, vendace, charr and schelly. The wildflowers and orchids found in the meadows attract butterflies such as the fritillary, large heath and Scotch argus.

PICTURED: Ullswater

DID YOU KNOW?
It was while walking by Ullswater in 1802 that Wordsworth gazed upon the 'host of golden daffodils' that inspired his poem.

AONBs

Arnside and Silverdale
Near: Morecambe, Lancashire
Map: 18, B1
Web: www.arnsidesilverdaleaonb.
org.uk
♿ (ltd), ❶
The landscape of Arnside and
Silverdale AONB is made up
of hills, woodlands, valleys
and farms. There are also
wide views over the Kent
Estuary to the Lake District.
The reed and willow
swamps of Leighton Moss
are a major breeding site for
marshland birds, including
bearded tit, marsh harrier
and the rare bittern. The
sands and saltmarshes of
Morecambe Bay are home to
wading birds and wildfowl,
sheep graze on the higher
rough pastures.

Forest of Bowland
Near: Clitheroe, Lancashire,
and Settle, North Yorkshire
Map: 18, B2
Web: www.forestofbowland.com
❶

Birds such as hen harriers,
ring ouzels and winchats
are found on the hills and
valleys of the fells and the
area is known as a 'hot spot'
for merlins and wading birds
such as lapwings, curlews and
redshanks (who feed on the
insects in the farmland by the
moors). Upland songbirds
include stonechats, wheatears
and reed buntings.

Solway Coast
Near: Cumbria
Map: 19
Web: www.solwaycoastaonb.
org.uk
Open: daily, 10am to 4.30pm
❶
Stretching along the
Cumbrian shore of the
Solway Firth, this is a low,
open and windswept AONB.
The Upper Solway's flats
and marshes are an over-
wintering site for huge
numbers of wildfowl, and
seals, dolphins and porpoises
have been seen offshore.
Inshore fishing includes
shrimping and cockles.

NATURE RESERVES

Blelham Bog NNR
Near: Windermere, Cumbria
Map: 19, C3
Web: www.english-nature.org.uk
🚾 ▭
Blelham Bog is notable for
its invertebrate population,
particularly caddis fly, of
which around 50 species
have been recorded, some of
them rare. Also found at the
site are the scarce raft spider,
flat valve snail and downy
emerald dragonfly.

Bowness on Solway
Near: Carlisle, Cumbria
Map: 19, C2
Web: www.wildlifetrust.org.uk/
cumbria
🅿 ♿ ▭
From summer to autumn, the
reserve comes alive with up
to 11 species of dragonflies
and damselflies. Butterflies
are attracted to the various
orchids (northern marsh,
common spotted and hybrid
varieties) that are found next
to the footpaths. In winter,

fieldfare, redwing and thrushes can be seen feeding on berries.

Cliburn Moss NNR
Near: Penrith, Cumbria
Map: 19, C2
Web: www.english-nature.org.uk
P WC ✉
Plantlife on the reserve includes cotton grass, heather, cross-leaved heath, bog bilberry, dyer's green weed, crowberry and cowberry. Northern marsh and lesser butterfly orchid are also seen. The site is home to large numbers of birds, including breeding populations of sparrowhawk, buzzard, treecreeper and great spotted woodpecker. Red squirrels, stoats and weasels are some of the local mammals.

Cuerden Valley Park WT
Near: Preston, Lancashire
Map: 18, B2
Web: www.cuerdenvalleypark.org.uk
Open: daily, 9am to 5pm
P (££), ♿ (ltd), WC ℹ ✉
Cuerdan Valley covers 600 acres of farmland, open space meadows, woodland and water. In spring, many of the woods attract woodpecker, treecreeper and nuthatch and the ground is carpeted in bluebells. The ponds and the river are home to kingfishers, dippers and water voles, while in summer, damselflies and dragonflies (including the banded demoiselle) patrol the lake. Autumn and winter are good times to see fieldfare and redwing on the pastures, and wildfowl on the lake.

Drumburgh Moss NNR
Near: Carlisle, Cumbria
Map: 19, C2
Web: www.english-nature.org.uk
WC ✉
Red grouse, curlew, redshank and grasshopper warbler all breed on the site at Drumburgh

Spot the difference: Common dolphin and harbour porpoise

At least 29 different types of whales, dolphins and porpoises have been seen in UK waters, but the ones you're most likely to spot from land are the harbour porpoise and the bottlenose dolphin. The harbour porpoise has a rounded head and no beak, while the bottlenose dolphin has a pronounced beak, a curved dorsal fin, and is far more likely to be appearing above the waves than the shy harbour porpoise. Neither animal sleeps in the way that we do, instead each side of their brain takes it in turn to switch off while the other half stays vigilant and keeps the animal breathing. They are seen all round the coast, try spotting them from the cliffs above the Giant's Causeway, Cardigan Bay, and the Bempton Cliffs in Yorkshire.

PICTURED:
Left: Harbour porpoise
Right: Bottlenose dolphin

Moss, and short-eared owls can sometimes be seen hunting here. In winter, the reserve often hosts small numbers of geese from the huge flocks on the Solway. The summer brings out lizards and adders, while mammals include roe deer, hare and occasionally fox.

Gait Barrows NNR
Near: Morecambe Bay, Lancashire
Map: 18, B1
Web: www.english-nature.org.uk
WC 🏕 ✉
Around 800 species of moth have been recorded on the reserve, including the rare silky

wainscot. Dragonflies and damselflies are also common, as are butterflies such as the Duke of Burgundy, high brown and pearl-bordered fritillary. Wood ants are common at the site and the rare narrow-mouthed whorl snail is also found here. Local birdlife includes green woodpecker, reed warbler, blackcap, bittern and marsh harrier.

Gowk Bank NNR
Near: Hexham, Cumbria
Map: 19, C2
Web: www.english-nature.org.uk
WC ✉

In addition to the grassland communities of the meadows, Gowk Bank is made up of alder and willow scrub and an area of acidic, boggy grassland. The vegetation of the uncut banks is dominated by herbaceous plants, particularly wood crane's bill, but also includes a variety of other species, such as pignut, meadow vetchling, wood anemone, zigzag clover and great burnet. Rare species found here include globe-flower and melancholy thistle.

Gowy Meadows
Near: Chester, Cheshire
Map: 18, A4
Web: www.wildlifetrust.org.uk/cheshire
P

It is thought that the Gowy Meadows were drained during the late Middle Ages. Apart from providing habitat for numerous plants and animals, the reserve is acting as part of a major flood alleviation scheme for the Stanlow Complex. During the winter months, localised sluices will be inserted to enable specific parts of the site to flood to provide feeding areas for waders and wildfowl. The site is important for its water vole population as well as ditch flora and a number of scarce invertebrates including lesser silver diving beetle. As the site develops bird numbers will increase. Snipe and teal numbers have already soared. Buzzards are a common sight and peregrine falcon can often be observed.

Great Asby Scar NNR
Near: Great Asby, Cumbria
Map: 19, C3
Web: www.english-nature.org.uk
WC

Great Asby Scar contains some of the best examples of limestone pavement in the

Limestone pavement in Gait Barrows NNR

country. The grasslands are dominated by blue moor grass, rock-rose, thyme and fairy flax and the shaded areas are dominated by wood anemone, dog's mercury and scarce rigid buckler fern. The summer months are best times to view the limestone pavement flora.

High Leys NNR
Near: Rowrah and Whitehaven, Cumbria
Map: 19, B3
Web: www.english-nature.org.uk
P WC

High Leys is home to breeding populations of willow warbler, curlew, lapwing and meadow pipit as well as butterflies, such as common blue, green-veined white, painted lady and meadow brown. The wildflowers include marsh marigold, black knapweed, cuckoo flower, tormentil, oxeye daisy, marsh willowherb, yellow-rattle, smooth

hawksbeard and lousewort. There are several orchid species including common spotted, greater and lesser butterfly, early-purple, northern marsh and heath spotted.

Hutton Roof Crags WT
Near: Kendal, Cumbria
Map: 19, C3
Web: www.wildlifetrust.org.uk/cumbria
P

All year round, there are excellent views from the Roof Crags across to the Pennines, the Lakeland fells and Morecambe Bay. In spring, the first butterflies (brimstone and speckled wood) appear, followed by high brown, dark green and small pearl-bordered fritillary varieties in the summer. On the limestone pavement, look for wild plants such as rigid buckler and dark red helleborine, and grayling butterflies basking in the sun.

Smardale Gill NNR

Smardale Gill NNR

Near: Brough, Cumbria
Map: 19, C3
Web: www.wildlifetrust.org.uk/cumbria

P ♿ (ltd), ⊞ ⊟ ◥

Smardale Gill is a hidden valley home to woodland birds such as the great spotted woodpecker, treecreeper and long-tailed tit. Red squirrels can be seen in autumn as well as the bright red leaves of bloody crane's-bill. In summer, the railway line is alive with butterflies – Scotch argus, northern brown argus and dark green fritillary – that are attracted by the fragrant orchid and bird's-eye primrose.

BIRD RESERVES

Leighton Moss

Near: Silverdale, Lancashire
Map: 18, B1
Web: www.rspb.org.uk
Open: daily, 9am to dusk (except 25 December)
Admission: £1/£4.50, free to members and anyone arriving by public transport or bike

P ♿ WC ⌓ ❶
⊟ ⛺ 🚻 ⌂ ◥

Leighton Moss is the largest remaining reedbed in north-west England. The reserve is well-known for its special birds, including breeding bitterns, bearded tits, marsh harriers and avocets. With the arrival of summer, visiting birds fill the reedbed with their rattling calls, birdsong can be enjoyed in the woodland and buzzards can be seen daily flying over the reserve.

FORESTS & WOODLAND

Alkincoates Woodland

Near: Colne, Lancashire
Map: 18, C2
Web: www.lifescapes.org.uk

P ♿ (ltd), ⊞ ◥

Oak, hawthorn, alder, hazel and field maple are among the trees now established on this site and there is a wide range of grasses, wildflowers and plants. Bird varieties observed include blue tits, jays and starlings, and visitors may be lucky enough to spot deer, rabbits, shrews, hares or foxes. The wetland areas are home to frogs, newts and water voles.

Beckmickle Ing

Near: Kendal, Cumbria
Map: 19, C3
Web: www.wt-woods.org.uk

P ⊞

Beckmickle Ing has many diverse wildflowers including bluebells, pignut, lords-and-ladies, moschatel and Solomon's seal. Roe deer frequent the wood, and the red squirrel, now an endangered species, is still seen. A great spotted woodpecker is resident, and the river and bank are habitat to otters, dipper and the common sandpiper.

Beech Hill Wood

Near: Windermere, Cumbria
Map: 19, C3
Web: www.wt-woods.org.uk

P ⊞

The canopy is dominated largely by sessile oak and a mixture of ash, beech and birch with alder dominant in the wet flushes. Mature trees of approximately 100 years old are present with a small number of much older beech and yew. Throughout the woodland there is standing and fallen deadwood at varying stages of decay.

Dobshall Wood

Near: Silverdale, Lancashire
Map: 18, B1
Web: www.wt-woods.org.uk

P ⊞

The ground flora under the trees includes abundant primrose, bramble and frequent cowslip. Other species include common dog-violet, wood avens, dog's mercury and wild strawberry. Less frequent are lords-and-ladies, bluebells and male fern. Frequent yarrow, self-heal and harebell can be seen and occasional early purple orchid, common spotted orchid and bird's-foot trefoil.

Dufton Ghyll Wood

Near: Brough, Cumbria
Map: 19, C3
Web: www.wt-woods.org.uk

P ⊞

The woodland lies within the broad fertile river valley of the River Eden, a rural area, with a mix of farm and woodland. Public access can be gained via six entrances to the woodland.

Deer frequent the wood and the red squirrel is still occasionally seen.

Fell Foot Park
Near: Ulverston, Cumbria
Map: 19, B3
Web: www.nationaltrust.org.uk
Open: daily, 9am to 5pm

Fell Foot Park offers substantial access to the lakeshore of Windermere. Spring and early summer bring impressive displays of daffodils, followed by rhododendrons, and there are magnificent views of the Lakeland fells.

Finglandrigg Woods NNR
Near: Carlisle, Cumbria
Map: 19, C2
Web: www.english-nature.org.uk

Red squirrels, roe deer, brown hares and woodmice can be seen here, as well as the more elusive badger and otter. The site has more than 40 species of breeding birds, including buzzard, tawny owl, willow tit, grasshopper warbler, reed bunting, garden warbler and long-tailed tit. Insect life is plentiful, with small pearl-bordered fritillary, purple hairstreak and ringlet butterflies.

Great Knott Wood
Near: Windermere, Cumbria
Map: 19, C3
Web: www.wt-woods.org.uk

Great Knott Wood is located on the south-west shore of Lake Windermere, within the Lake District National Park. This location has one of the highest densities of woodland cover anywhere in northern England, much of which is ancient woodland.

Green Wood
Near: Runcorn, Cheshire
Map: 18, B4
Web: www.wt-woods.org.uk

One of Green Wood's key features is a fairly large pond in the south-west corner of the site, which is popular with anglers. The main nature interest at Green Wood is the presence of 14 to 15 pairs of grey heron that nest on site.

Grizedale Forest Park
Near: Lake District National Park
Map: 19, B1 and C1
Web: www.forestry.gov.uk

Grizedale Forest Park offers good views of Coniston Water, Windermere and the Grizedale Valley. The forest is good for wildlife-spotting with owls, squirrels and deer to be seen. The highest point at Carron Crag provides a panorama of the Lake District fells.

Mere Sands Wood
Near: Ormskirk Lancashire
Map: 18, A3
Web: www.lancswt.org.uk

Snipe, green sandpiper, greenshank and other waders frequent the wetland of Mere Sands in autumn, while in winter teal and gadwall visit in significant numbers. At the feeding stations, great spotted woodpeckers, bullfinches, tree

Going, going, gone

Within the last millennia, several carnivorous mammals have become extinct in the UK. Beavers were wiped out in the 1100s, prized for their musk glands and their fur. Brown bears fell victim to the Romans who exported them for shows back home. The last wild wolves were found in Scotland and Ireland in the eighteenth century and wild boar were hunted to extinction in the sixteenth century. These latter two are now making successful comebacks, wolves under the control of man, and boar where they have escaped from captivity and are breeding successfully in the wild.

Pictured: Grey wolf with blue eyes. Wolf eyes, though blue when young, normally change to gold or orange as they grow up. It is highly unusual for an adult wolf to retain its blue eyes.

sparrows and reed buntings are common. During spring, grebes feed their young on the lake and the reedbeds are filled with warblers. Summer brings the butterflies and dragonflies.

Miltonrigg Wood

Near: Carlisle, Cumbria
Map: 19, C2
Web: www.wt-woods.org.uk

Breeding birds previously recorded at Miltonrigg include willow tit, great spotted woodpecker, woodcock, sparrowhawk and wood warbler. Tawny owl, kestrel, redstart and coal tit may also be seen. The wood is populated by red squirrel, roe deer, and the regionally notable ash black slug.

Pope Lane and Boilton Wood

Near: Preston, Lancashire
Map: 18, B2
Web: www.english-nature.org.uk
The site mainly consists of areas of woodland (Boilton Wood) and semi-improved grassland (Pope Lane Field): all of the woodland contained in the site forms part of the Red Scar and Tun Brook SSSI. Bluebells are abundant throughout the woodland ground flora. Badgers, roe deer and tawny owls have all been seen on site.

Sea Wood

Near: Ulverston, Cumbria
Map: 19, C3
Web: www.wt-woods.org.uk

Invertebrates are plentiful at Sea Wood, particularly on the brambles. Many small mammals inhabit the ground vegetation and small birds, blackbirds and thrushes are abundant. There is a small seasonal pond in quite dense vegetation in the north-east corner of the upper wood and much of the wood is enclosed

by drystone walls. More than 28 species of lichen have been identified.

Shank Wood

Near: Hethersgill and Longtown, near Brampton, Cumbria
Map: 19, C2
Web: www.wt-woods.org.uk

The ground flora at Shank Wood is particularly rich in the areas adjacent to the river, and in the steep gullies and wet flushes. Elsewhere, the flora has been reduced by grazing pigs and sheep, as well as by the invasion of bracken. This is an important habitat for woodland birds.

Sunnyhurst Woods

Near: Darwen, Lancashire
Map: 18, B3
Web: www.english-nature.og.uk

This site is a Biological Heritage Site selected for its woodland and scrub habitats, breeding birds, flowering plants and ferns. Birds include kingfisher and heron. Around 702 species of plants, birds, invertebrates and mammals have been recorded on site.

DID YOU KNOW?

Haymeadows are being lost at a rate of 10 per cent each year.

Whinlatter Forest Park

Near: Keswick, Cumbria
Map: 19, B3
Web: www.forestry.gov.uk

Autumn and winter are the best times to see red squirrels in the forest. From late spring to late summer is the best time to see the osprey raise their young near Bassenthwaite Lake.

Worsley Woods

Near: Salford, Lancashire
Map: 18, C3
Web: www.english-nature.org.uk
Today Worsley Woods' 72-acre site is home to mature plantation woodland through which Kempnough Brook meanders until it reaches Old Warke Dam. With carpets of bluebells and wild garlic in the summer, Worsley Woods is an ideal location for walking and observing wildlife.

COASTS, WETLANDS & WATERWAYS

Ainsdale Sand Dunes NNR

Near: Ainsdale and Formby, Merseyside
Map: 18, A3
Web: www.english-nature.org.uk

The dunes are home to more than 450 plant species, including 33 that are locally or regionally rare, such as petalwort, seaside centaury, yellow bartsia, round-leaved wintergreen, dune helleborine and pendulous-flowered helleborine. Sand lizards and great crested newts are found here, together with a large population of natterjack toads. Inland, areas of pine woodland are home to red squirrels.

Ashton Canal

From: Manchester to Ashton-under-Lyne, Lancashire
Map: 18, C3
Web: www.waterscape.com
Local wildlife is limited along Ashton Canal, as it closely borders the city of Manchester. However, a number of varieties of birds can be seen, and the likes of ducks and moorhens cruise the waters.

Bassenthwaite Lake

Near: Keswick, Cumbria
Map: 19, B2
Web: www.waterscape.com

P **ⓘ**

In Dodd Wood, overlooking Bassenthwaite Lake, park environmentalists bred twin osprey chicks in 2002 – the first successful breeding in the UK for 150 years. The lake contains brown trout, roach, large pike and vendace.

Belmont Reservoir
Near: Chorley, Lancashire
Map: 18, B3
Web: www.waterscape.com
Belmont Reservoir is home to breeding waders, such as the oystercatcher, snipe and lapwing. Its woodlands and plantations attract breeding woodcock, redstart and pied flycatcher.

Buttermere
Near: Keswick, Cumbria
Map: 19, B3
Web: www.nationaltrust.org.uk
P **🍴**
As well as providing a base for some lovely walks up into the mountains, Buttermere is also a good lake to circumnavigate. It is one and a half miles long and three-quarters of a mile wide, and takes about three hours to get round. Much of the way you will be on lakeside paths with views over the water and whatever wildfowl might be visiting, but you'll also pass through woodland which has nature trails to follow.

Cabin Hill NNR
Near: Formby, Merseyside
Map: 18, A3
Web: www.english-nature.org.uk
P **wc** **🍴** **🚌**
The shore provides feeding and roosting grounds for many migrating and over-wintering birds including knot, grey plover and bar-tailed godwit. Also seen on the site are song thrush, reed bunting, linnet and skylark. A number of invertebrates, such as the

View of Buttermere from Fleetwith Pike

northern dune tiger beetle, dark-green fritillary, grayling and various moths, inhabit the sandy margins. Reptiles and amphibians include the common lizard, sand lizard and natterjack toad.

Coniston Water
Near: Coniston, Cumbria
Map: 19, B3
Web: www.waterscape.com
P **ⓘ**
Coniston Water has lots of wild red deer and red squirrels, among a whole host of birds, waterfowl and insects.

Elterwater
Near: Windermere, Cumbria
Map: 19, B3
Web: www.waterscape.com
Elterwater's name is from the Norse word 'elter', which means swan, as the lake is a popular migration spot for whooper swans over the winter. They are only one of a large variety of wildlife that visit the reeds along the lakeshore. There are also woodlands of larch, birch and oak nearby, that provide a home to many birds and insects.

Ennerdale Water
Near: Keswick, Cumbria
Map: 19, B3

Web: www.waterscape.com
P **ⓘ**
Ennerdale Water is the most westerly of all the lakes in the Lake District. The fish population includes the rare Arctic charr. The stony margin of the lake has plant species including water lobelia and quillwort, which are frequent in Cumbria but uncommon elsewhere in England. This woodland is important not just for the native oak and birch but for the many varieties of ferns, mosses and lichens that grow on the rocks and scree.

Esthwaite Water
Near: Windermere, Cumbria
Map: 19, B3
Web: www.waterscape.com
Esthwaite Water is the most nutrient-rich of all the lakes in the Lake District and consequently holds many fish: it is excellent for rainbow and wild brown trout, pike, roach, rudd, perch, tench and even the occasional eel. The lake is a haven for wildlife, and in summer months the surface is carpeted with waterlilies.

Grasmere
Near: Windermere, Cumbria
Map: 19, C3
Web: www.waterscape.com

North West

P **ℹ**

As Wordsworth described it, 'the most loveliest spot that man hath found'. A small lake with good displays of daffodils and bluebells in the spring. Bats are very common here.

Haweswater
Near: Penrith, Cumbria
Map: 19, C2
Web: www.rspb.org.uk
P

The reserve is most famous for holding England's only golden eagle territory. In spring, ring ousels, wheatears, warblers and other migrant birds return to breed in the grassland. Red deer and red squirrels are common on the reserve. Buzzards and ravens soar over the grassland, and peregrines and the occasional merlin can be seen hunting. Dippers can be seen at the lake's edge and by the becks. In winter and early spring, the reservoir provides protection to more than 20,000 common roosting gulls.

Huddersfield Narrow Canal
From: Manchester, Lancashire, to Huddersfield, West Yorkshire
Map: 18, C3 and 17, B3
Web: www.waterscape.com
P **ℹ**

White-clawed crayfish live below water in gaps in drystone wash walls in this beautifully restored canal.

Lancaster Canal
From: Preston to Tewitfield, near Lancaster, Lancashire
Map: 18, B1 and B2
Web: www.waterscape.com
ℹ

Gulls are present at all times, including Mediterranean and yellow-legged gulls. Whooper and Berwick swans can sometimes be seen, together with over-wintering pink-footed geese. Bats, water voles and kingfishers are also common.

Leeds and Liverpool Canal
From: Liverpool, Merseyside, to Leeds, West Yorkshire
Map: 18, A4 and 17, C2
Web: www.waterscape.com

The Leeds and Liverpool Canal is visited by a range of birds including waterfowl such as swans, mallards, grebes, and also herons and kingfishers. The Kirkstall Valley Nature Reserve, an SSSI near Leeds, is bounded by a five-mile stretch of the Leeds and Liverpool Canal and is a nesting site for sedge warbler and reed bunting, and currently for 16 species of butterfly. Purified water is pumped to man-made ponds to give life to various insects, frogs, beetles, snails and pondlife such as water lilies. Warblers, tits, thrushes and songbirds live in the woodlands.

Loweswater
Near: Keswick, Cumbria
Map: 19, B3
Web: www.waterscape.com
ℹ

Loweswater is one of the smallest lakes in the Lake District, located in the Vale of Lorton, and remains very peaceful. The woodland valley surrounding the lake is popular with red squirrels.

DID YOU KNOW?

Britain has 4,000 miles of rivers, lakes and canals.

Macclesfield Canal
From: Crewe, Cheshire, to Stockport, Lancashire
Map: 18, B5 to C4
Web: www.waterscape.com
ℹ

The canal is a haven for rare wildlife. Water voles have been spotted at several locations, and even the very rare osprey has been sighted over the canal. Macclesfield Forest is

a combination of coniferous forest, lakes and moorland, with wildlife including herons.

Martin Mere
Near: Ormskirk and Southport, Lancashire
Map: 18, A3
Web: www.wwt.org.uk
P **♿** (ltd), **WC** **♿**
ℹ ☐ 🏠 ◣

On the west side of the Martin Mere there are a number of pens providing habitats for birds from Africa, Australasia, North and South America, Siberia and Asia. The pens are populated by 100 species of rare and endangered ducks, Hawaiian geese, swans and flamingos. The area is also excellent for wintering birds of prey, such as hen harrier, peregrine and merlin.

Morecambe Bay
Near: Morecambe, Lancashire
Map: 18, B1
Web: www.morecambebay.com
🏠

Morecambe Bay is the second largest bay in Britain after The Wash. It contains a range of habitats from saltmarshes and huge areas of sand to the dense beds of mussels that cover boulders and cobbles. The sands are filled with worms, tiny crustaceans and shellfish that attract thousands of gulls to the area as well as waterfowl, wildfowl and waders. There are large numbers of pink-footed goose, knot, curlew, oystercatcher, godwil, turnstone, shelduck and redshank.

Ribble Estuary NNR
Near: Preston, Lancashire
Map: 18, B2
Web: www.english-nature.org.uk
WC 🚹 ☐

The estuary the Ribble creates between Blackpool and Southport is a major UK river estuary for wintering

birds such as whooper and Bewick's swans, pink-footed geese, wigeons, knots, dunlins, sanderlings and bar-tailed and black-tailed godwits. An incredible 250,000 birds make the estuary their winter home every year. In the summer, the saltmarshes support large numbers of breeding birds including black-headed gull, herring gull, lesser black-backed gull, common tern and redshank. Skylark, meadow pipit and linnet nest on the grazing marsh.

Ribble Link
From: Lancaster Canal to River Ribble, Lancashire
Map: 18, B2
Web: www.waterscape.com
The four-mile stretch of Ribble Link is Britain's newest inland waterway. Savick Brook, which runs off the River Ribble, supports breeding colonies of sand martins that nest in the cliffs along the waterway. At the bottom end of the Ribble Link the reedbed and mature trees provide a habitat for Daubenton's bats.

Rochdale Canal
From: Manchester, Lancashire, to Halifax, West Yorkshire
Map: 17, B3
Web: www.waterscape.com
The canal has the best population of floating water plantain in Britain, estimated to be in excess of 20,000 individual plants. The towpath, cuttings, canalside buildings and embankments are home for many mammal species: wood mice, bank voles, water voles, bats, badgers and foxes. Also in the area are grass snakes, frogs, toads and newts. Birds include sparrows, finches, wrens, thrushes, warblers, herons, kingfishers, mute swans, moorhens and coots. White-clawed crayfish can be found in the canal. Flying among the flowers of the towpath you can see mayflies, caddis flies, alderflies, damselflies and dragonflies.

Rostherne Mere NNR
Near: Knutsford, Cheshire
Map: 18, B4
Web: www.english-nature.org.uk
Being exceptionally deep for a natural lowland lake, the mere's water rarely freezes over and, in hard winters, can support large numbers of wintering wildfowl, particularly pochard. Mallard, teal, pintail and shoveler are also regular visitors and, in cold weather, ruddy duck, gadwall and goosander are often spotted on the site. Woodland on the reserve supports all three native woodpecker species together with sparrowhawk and kestrel.

South Walney
Near: Walney Island and Barrow-in-Furness, Cumbria

Map: 19, B3
Web: www.wildlifetrust.org.uk/
cumbria
🅿 (££), ♿ (ltd),
♿ 🚻 ♿

In summer, South Walney is a breeding ground for 28,000 pairs of gulls. After their departure, greenshank, redshank, oystercatcher and curlew inhabit the central pools in winter, together with teal, wigeon and goldeneye. Henbane, viper's bugloss, hound's-tongue and yellow-horned poppy make up the shingle flora. Good views of snow-covered Lakeland fells can be seen on clear days.

Ulverston Canal
From: Ulverston to Canal Lock, Morecambe Bay, Lancashire
Map: 19, B3 and C3
Web: www.waterscape.com
🅿 ♿ ▭

The Ulverston Canal is – at 1.5 miles long – the shortest, widest and deepest canal in Britain. It has been closed since 1945 but there are current proposals to bring it back to life as part of a town regeneration scheme. Despite its short length, the canal boasts populations of tench, roach, carp, rudd, eel and bream.

NOT SO WILD

Acorn Venture Urban Farm
Address: Depot Road, Kirkby, Knowsley, Merseyside L33 3AR
Map: 18, A3
Tel: 0151 548 1524
Web: www.acornfarm.co.uk
Open: daily, 10am to 4/5pm
Admission: 50p/£1
♿ (ltd), ♿ ♿

The Acorn Venture Urban Farm was created in 1985 and is widely used in a range of activities by all sectors of the local community. Barnyard animals that can be seen here include goats (saanen, toggenburg, alpine and anglo-nubian), sheep, mules, pigs, saddle-back cattle, horses, rabbits, hens, ducks, fancy poultry, bantams and guinea pigs.

Appleby Castle Conservation Centre
Address: Appleby Castle, Appleby-in-Westmoreland, near Brough, Cumbria
Map: 19, C3
Tel: 01768 351402
Web: www.lakesnet.co.uk
As well as the white park cattle, the Rare Breeds Trust Survival Centre at Appleby is home to the bagot goat and the Vietnamese pot-bellied pig.

Aquarium of the Lakes
Address: Lakeside, Newby Bridge, Cumbria LA12 8AS
Map: 19, B3
Tel: 01539 530153
Web: www.aquariumofthelakes.co.uk
Open: daily, 9am to 4/5pm
Admission: £4.50/£7
🅿 ♿ ♿ ♿ ❶ ♿

The aquarium's stunning displays bring you face to face with an array of life found in and around the lakes. You can see Lakeland pike, char, otters and giant carp, diving ducks, sharks and rays from around the Cumbrian coast. In the rockpools there are crabs, sea anemone, prawns and flatfish.

Blackpool Sea Life Centre
Address: The Promenade, Blackpool, Lancashire FY1 5AA
Map: 18, A2
Tel: 01253 622445
Web: www.sealifeeurope.com
Open: daily, from 10am
Admission: £6.95/£9.50
🅿 ♿ ♿ ♿ ❶ ♿ ♿

Blackpool Sea Life Centre is home to one of the largest collections of tropical sharks in Europe. It houses 50 displays of marine and freshwater creatures including sharks, rays, seahorses and piranhas. There is also a

Crayfish war

Britain has traditionally had a strong population of crayfish. These lobster-like animals hide under rocks or in holes in the bank and use their large pincers to catch prey. However, since the American signal crayfish was introduced to Britain for the catering trade in the 1970s, our native species, the white-clawed crayfish has been all but wiped out. A few strongholds remain in Cumbria and the north, where the native species are identifiable by their creamy white claws.

PICTURED: White-clawed crayfish

recently created jellyfish display, including a collection of UV-enhanced moon, lagoon and upside-down jellyfish.

Blackpool Zoo
Address: East Park Drive, Blackpool, Lancashire FY3 8PP
Map: 18, A2
Tel: 01253 830830
Web: www.blackpoolzoo.org.uk
Open: daily, 10am to 3/6pm (except 25 December)
P 🐾 **wc** 🖼 **i** 🔖

This 32-acre animal kingdom is home to scores of species from lions, tigers, gorillas and orang-utans to peacocks, gorillas, elephants, tree squirrels and reptiles. There is a waterworld section, home to sea lions, terrapins and penguins, and you can also see woodland animals such as the muntjak deer and great grey owl.

Brantwood
Address: Brantwood, Coniston, Cumbria LA21 8AD
Map: 19, B3
Tel: 01539 441396
Web: www.gbd.org.uk/garden.html
Open: mid-November to mid-March, 11am to 5pm
P 🐾 (ltd), **wc** 🖼 **i**

Brantwood is made up of 250 acres of gardens, pastures, ancient woods and high moors. In spring, the Lower Garden is full of a combination of wild daffodils and apple blossom. In summer, scented azaleas and bluebells carpet the landscape.

Cannon Aquarium and Vivarium
Address: University of Manchester, Oxford Road, Manchester, Lancashire M13 9PL
Map: 18, C3
Tel: 0161 275 2634
Web: www.museum.man.ac.uk
Open: Tuesday to Saturday, 10am to 5pm; Mondays, Sundays and Bank Holidays, 11am to 4pm

Admission: free
P **i**

The vivarium is the only collection of living animals in the Manchester area with a zoo licence. Key displays include a rocky desert exhibit with monitor lizards and a variety of unusual reptiles and amphibians, including a colourful panther chameleon and some endangered tomato frogs from Madagascar. Behind the scenes, the vivarium is particularly notable for its large collection of tree frogs, which is probably the largest in the world.

DID YOU KNOW?
The slow worm is not a snake but a legless lizard.

Lake District Coast Aquarium
Address: South Quay, Maryport, Cumbria CA15 8AB
Map: 19, B2
Tel: 01900 817760
Web: www.lakedistrict-coastaquarium.co.uk
Open: daily, 10am to 5pm
Admission: £3.25/£5
P **wc** **i** 🍴

There are freshwater displays at the aquarium, where you can see trout and perch in a large rockpool with cascading waterfalls. The display for the Solway Estuary contains grey mullet and flounder. There are more than 2,000 specimens, with approximately 150 different species of local aquatic life, in more than 35 display tanks. In the rockpool, you are allowed to make contact with some of the inhabitants and, in the ray pool, gentle stroking of the rays is allowed.

Marbury Country Park
Address: Comberbach, Northwich, Cheshire CW9 6AT

Map: 18, B4
Tel: 01606 77741
Web: www.cheshire.gov.uk/countryside
Open: daily (except 25 December and 1 January)
Admission: free
P (££), 🐾 **wc** 🖼 🍴 🔖

The hall of this former grand estate has been demolished, leaving woodlands, carpeted with bluebells in the springtime and avenues of limes. There is a mere within the grounds with a hide overlooking the plentiful birdlife, as well as an arboretum and community orchard.

Muncaster
Address: Ravenglass, Cumbria CA18 1RQ
Map: 19, B3
Tel: 01229 717614
Web: www.muncaster.co.uk
Open: daily, 10.30am to 6pm
Admission: £4.50/£6.50
P **wc** **i**

On the Muncaster site you can find the World Owl Centre which is the headquarters of the World Owl Trust. The centre is home to a diverse range of these birds, from bizarre fish owls to pygmy owls. There are also buzzards, kestrels, red kites and herons in the area.

Rice Lane City Farm
Address: No 2 Lodge, Walton Park Cemetery, off Rawcliffe Road, Liverpool, Merseyside L9 1AW
Map: 18, A4
Tel: 0151 530 1066
Web: www.visitliverpool.com
Open: daily, 9am to 4.30pm
i **P** **wc** 🍴

Rice Lane City Farm covers 224 acres of countryside, 11 of which are managed woodland. A variety of rare breed farm animals are kept here, including pigs, red poll cattle and Ryeland sheep, as well as various

Rhinos and giraffes at South Lakes Wild Animal Park

goats and poultry. Donkey, rabbits and geese can also be seen on the farm.

South Lakes Wild Animal Park

Address: Crossgates, Dalton-in-Furness, near Ulverston, Cumbria LA15 8JR
Map: 19, B3
Tel: 01229 466086.
Web: www.wildanimalpark.co.uk
Open: all year
Admission: £7/£10.50

P (££), WC ⓘ ▣ ⌖

Dalton-in-Furness is the Lake District's only zoological park and is recognised as one of Europe's leading conservation zoos. This is the only zoo in Britain to hold both amur and sumatran tigers, the biggest and smallest tigers left in the world. In the Australian Bush area, many animals have complete freedom to wander at will, such as lemur monkeys, exotic deer, emus, wallabies and kangaroos. Parrots fly freely in the trees.

Tam O'Shanter Urban Farm

Address: Boundary Road, Bidston, Wirral, Merseyside CH43 7PD
Map: 18, A4
Tel: 0151 653 9332
Web: www.tamoshanterfarm. org.uk
Open: daily, 9.30am to 4.30pm
Admission: free

P ▣ ⌖

Tam O'Shanter Urban Farm is situated alongside 100 acres of heathland and woodland – a public open space known as Bidston Hill. Poultry, pigs, sheep and goats can all be seen on the farm, alongside rabbits, bees, a pony and a donkey.

Three Owls Bird Sanctuary and Reserve

Address: Wolstenholme Fold, Norden, Rochdale OL11 5UD
Map: 18, C3
Tel: 01706 642162
Web: www.threeowls.co.uk
Open: Monday to Friday, 1pm to 3pm; Sundays, noon to 4pm

& WC ⌖ ⓘ ▸

The sanctuary is open to visitors every Sunday when there are guided tours around the 4.5-acre reserve. Depending on the time of year, you may see between 200 and 1,000 birds undergoing various stages of rehabilitation. The sanctuary is not only for owls, in the past other birds have also been treated here.

Williamson Park and Butterfly House

Address: Lancaster LA1 1UX
Map: 18, B1
Tel: 01524 33318
Web: www.williamsonpark.com
Open: daily, 10am to 4/5pm (except 25 December)
Admission: £2.75/£4.25

P & WC ⌖ ▣ ▸

As well as enjoying woodland walks through the 54-acre grounds of this park, visitors can also watch butterflies flying free among tropical plants in the former hothouse. Pupae are placed in a special display case and you may even get to watch a butterfly emerge from its chrysalis.

North East

From the wide, open and sandy beaches of Durham's coast to the bleak, wind-ravaged heathland of Northumberland National Park, the scenery in England's north-east corner is nothing if not spectacular. Rivers wind their way through wooded valleys, old quarries dot the landscape and acres and acres of fields broken by hedgerows and meadows provide sanctuary for many a weary bird as it arrives in the North East after crossing northern Europe.

Birds regularly seen in the area include the curlew – the emblem of Northumberland National Park – the ring ouzel, sedge warblers, wigeons, lapwings and skylarks, as well as any number of migrant birds.

Many wildlife spotters come to the park with the hope of spotting a red squirrel, as this is one of the few places left in England where they can be found. Unlike their grey relation, they tend to spend most of their time up in the tops of the trees, so can be difficult to see. But if you notice pine cones gnawed into an apple core shape, keep your eyes peeled as that's good evidence that they're around somewhere.

The many rivers in the area such as the Wear, the Tyne and the Tees attract water voles, butterflies and dragonflies and wildfowl in large numbers, while at Kielder Water – the largest man-made reservoir in Europe – visitors can again spot red squirrel, deer and a number of rare birds.

The great estates of noble gentry in the area – both past and present – are often more interesting for the legacies of their gardens than for their lineage and the choice of places to visit

Not to be missed

● **Castle Eden Dene**
This large reserve has woodland, grassland and spectacular limestone cliffs and gorges. If you're there at the right time, you might see roe deer, foxes and badgers, as well as a multitude of songbirds.

● **Durham Coast**
Striking limestone cliffs harbour common and rare wild plants and are a great place for spotting butterflies and moths.

● **Farne Islands**
Rocky cliffs make ideal breeding sites for seabirds, which is why a trip here is always such a delight. Look out for seals in the water.

● **Kielder Water and Forest Park**
Beautiful Kielder Water is the largest man-made lake in Europe and, with the surrounding forest, it's one of Britain's biggest nature resorts and home to red squirrels, deer and rare birds.

● **Nunsborough Wood**
A winding river, steep valley slopes and a charming woodland put this reserve at the top of the local woodlands list.

● **Teesmouth**
As well as having large numbers of birds throughout the year, this reserve is also an interesting visit for the number of rare plants found on the dunes.

is large. Kitchen gardens with wonderful varieties of native vegetables, lakeside walks, bog gardens, conifer collections... and all of them come with an attending array of birds and wildlife who seem to recognise a fine home when they see one.

PICTURED
Main: Autumn in the Cheviots, Northumberland National Park **Above:** A curlew, the emblem of Northumberland National Park

NATIONAL PARK Northumberland National Park

Near: Hexham, Northumberland
Map: 19, C2
Web: www.northumberland-national-park.org.uk

Spread over the hills and valleys at the very top of England, Northumberland National Park has a wide range of habitats within its boundaries and is home to many species, including some that are rarely seen in other parts of the UK. Much of the park is heather moorland that comes into a purple bloom in late summer. The mountain bumblebee and emperor moth make their home here, as well as a small bird of prey, the merlin. On the moorland edges you will often hear the haunting cry of the curlew, which is the park's emblem, and in summer you may be lucky enough to spot mountain blackbird, ring ouzel. Bogland within the park

contains carpets of sphagnum moss and plants such as bog rosemary, as well as Britain's largest population of the large heath butterfly. Ancient woodlands that remain along river valleys or in upland gullies contain aspen and juniper trees and are home to one of England's rare populations of red squirrels, while the rivers contain salmon, sea trout and otters, and plants, such as water-crowfoot. Hay meadows are dotted around the park and are a feast of colour in the summer with plants, such as eyebright and lady's mantle, growing here. The rare plant Jacob's ladder is found on rocky ledges at two sites within the park. The park is keen on conservation and a wonderful place to watch wildlife at any time of the year.

PICTURED: Hadrian's Wall

AONBs

North Pennines
Co Durham
Map: 19
Web: www.northpennines.org.uk

This AONB is rich in wildlife and includes herb-rich hay meadows, juniper, alpine limestone flora and a diversity of moorland and wading birds. Parts are protected NNRs and SSSIs.

NATURE RESERVES

Bishop Middleham Quarry SSSI
Near: Bishop Middleham Village, near Durham, Co Durham
Map: 19, D2
Web: www.durhamwildlifetrust.org.uk

Notable for its rich flora, this reserve is a large magnesian quarry, providing the keen botanist with the opportunity to get excellent close-up views of a large variety of uncommon plants confined to these grasslands. This internationally rare habitat type is particularly rich in orchid species including the pyramidal, common spotted, fragrant, bee orchid and large numbers of dark red helleborines. The site is one of the best in the region for butterflies, including the dingy skipper, common blue, small heath, ringlet and small and large skippers, which can all be seen throughout the year. Extensive areas of common rock rose in the quarry support one of the country's largest colonies of northern brown argus butterfly, which can be seen from June to July.

Cassop Vale NNR
Near: Durham Co Durham
Map: 19, D2
Web: www.english-nature.org.uk
Cassop Vale NNR is the most diverse site on County Durham's magnesian limestone. The grassland supports blue moor grass, globeflower and bird's-eye primrose, along with several insects such as the northern brown argus butterfly. Hawthorn, gorse and rose scrub thrive on the grassland margins and, in places, grades into true woodland, characterised by ash and hazel. The scrub and woodland support many breeding birds including yellow-hammer, white-throat and green woodpecker. In the valley bottom, fen and swamp vegetation surround a small pond where there are breeding snipe, moorhen and coot. The best time to experience the flora and fauna of Cassop Vale is between April and August.

Castle Eden Dene NNR
Near: Peterlee, Co Durham
Map: 19, D2

Northumberland Coast AONB

Northumberland
Map: 19, D1 and D2
Web: www.northumberland-coast.co.uk
This bright, wild, lonely coast sweeps along some of Britain's finest beaches and is internationally noted for its wildlife. The AONB, a narrow coastal strip, stretches from Berwick-upon-Tweed to Amble. Soft sandstone and limestone rocks, dipping gently as a plain to the sea, make this essentially a low-lying coast with long views. Open miles of beach are backed in places by extensive sand dunes and the AONB takes in the island of Lindisfarne and its treacherous intertidal flats, as well as the numerous small islands and rocks of the Farne Islands further out from the coast. The dunes, marshes and mudflats of the Lindisfarne NNR are one of the best sites in Europe for waders and waterfowl and offshore, the Farne Islands are a protected seabird sanctuary.

PICTURED: The Holy Island of Lindisfarne

Web: www.english-nature.org.uk

P

Castle Eden Dene is the largest area of semi-natural woodland in north-east England. Renowned for yew trees, it boasts 545 acres of woodland, lowland grassland, spectacular limestone cliffs and gorges. The reserve is home to roe deer, foxes and badgers, although the latter usually stay hidden in the undergrowth. Living and dying trees are home to fungi and insects that feed many woodland birds. In autumn, berries provide a feast for thousands of exhausted birds arriving from northern Europe.

Bloody crane's-bill on the Durham Coast

Druridge Pools

Near: Ashington, Northumberland
Map: 19, D2
Web: www.nwt.org.uk

P

The site at Druridge Pools consists of a deep lake and two wet fields. Large flocks of wintering wildfowl visit the lake, mostly wigeon and teal but also goldeneye. A group of whooper swans which spend the winter at Druridge Bay are often seen here. In summer, great crested grebes breed here and wading birds feed along the shores. The two adjacent wet fields are very good feeding sites, especially for snipe, redshank and teal. Ruff are regularly seen, along with occasional rarities such as pectoral sandpiper and black-winged stilt.

Durham Coast NNR

Near: Durham
Map: 19, D2
Web: www.english-nature.org.uk
The Durham coastline comprises striking limestone cliffs, headlands and beaches. The magnesian limestone grasslands support plants

including bloody crane's-bill, primrose and quaking grass, the rare bird's-eye and primrose. The grasslands are noted for their insect life. It is home to two national rarities, the Durham argus butterfly and the day-flying least minor moth. Other moth species seen here include the northern brown argus, cistus forrester, purple barred, and chalk carpet. There is a site for breeding little tern at Crimdon and large numbers of wintering purple sandpiper feed on the foreshore. Sanderling, turnstone and knot also use the site for feeding and roosting in winter.

Hannah's Meadow SSSI

Near: Barnard Castle, Co Durham
Map: 19, D3
Web: www.durhamwildlifetrust.org.uk

WC 🚻 📷

The meadows and pasture at Hannah's Meadow have evolved as a result of traditional farming practices over several centuries, including sheep and lamb grazing, and are considered some of the least improved and species-rich in upland

Durham. Meadow fox-tail, sweet vernal grass and crested dog's-tail with wildflowers, including ragged robin, wood crane's-bill, marsh marigold, yellow-rattle, adder's tongue fern and globeflower all dominate the grass sward. The pasture has a more acidic character, with rushes and sedges dominating, and supports breeding birds, such as lapwing, skylark, redshank, curlew and meadowpit.

Hawthorn Dene

Near: Sunderland, Co Durham
Map: 19, D2
Web: www.wildlifetrust.org.uk

WC 🚻 📷

Hawthorne Dene is the second largest coastal dene in County Durham, comprising a steep-sided ravine woodland cutting through magnesian limestone. The eastern end of the reserve contains an area of species-rich calcareous grassland attracting large numbers of butterflies, best seen in July and August. The reserve provides suitable conditions for a wide range of woodland birds, including jay, treecreeper, green and great spotted woodpeckers and summer passerines. The reserve is home to mammals such as roe deer, fox and badger.

Kielder Mires NNR

Near: Hexham, Northumberland
Map: 19, C2
Web: www.english-nature.org.uk
Comprising two separate sites, this reserve is an extensive tract of moorland that supports a wide range of upland habitats, including blanket bog, dry heath, rocky outcrops, mire systems and wooded cleughs (ravines or small valleys). The reserve is an important area for upland breeding birds, such as golden plover, dunlin, dipper, common sandpiper, ring ouzel, wheatear and whinchat. Waders, such as lapwing, curlew and oystercatcher, are seen on the lower slopes and grassland.

Kielder Water and Forest Park

Near: Bellingham, near New Castle, Northumberland
Map: 19, D2
Web: www.kielder.org

Tucked away at the top of Northumberland, close to the Scottish border and Hadrian's Wall, beautiful Kielder Water is the largest man-made lake in Europe. Kielder Forest, one of Britain's biggest nature resorts, is home to red squirrels, deer and rare birds. The lake fringes and forest glades can best be explored by walking, cycling or riding on horseback and there are many self-guided trails. Activities for all the family, a variety of accommodation, easy accessibility and closeness to villages and Northumberland National Park are among the many attractions, making Kielder ideal for holidays or leisure pursuits, including fishing, boating and riding.

Kielder Water

Kielderhead NNR

Near: Hexham Northumberland
Map: 19, C2
Web: www.english-nature.org.uk
Keilderhead NNR is a large expanse of moorland that exhibits a wide range of upland ecosystems including rock outcrops, mire systems and wooded cleughs (ravines or small valleys). It is home to breeding birds, including golden plover, dunlin, lapwing, oystercatcher, curlew, dipper, common sandpiper, ring ouzel, wheatear and whinchat.

Low Barns SSSI

Near: Witton-le-Wear and Bishop Auckland, Co Durham
Map: 19, D2
Web: www.durhamwildlifetrust.org.uk

This reserve comprises a series of inter-connected lakes along with extensive alder woodland and species-rich grasslands. Mammals, such as stoat, fox and roe deer, are frequently seen at the site and the lakes are visited by otters. In spring and summer,

the resident bird populations are swollen by numbers of migrants, including redstart, pied flycatcher and several warbler species. In winter, large numbers of wildfowl, such as tufted duck, mallard, golden eye and goosander, can be seen. The small ponds are also home to dragonflies and the grasslands support various butterfly species.

Maze Park

Near: Stockton-on-Tees, Co Durham
Map: 19, D3
Web: www.durhamwildlifetrust.org.uk

Maze Park is a grassland reserve on the southern bank of the River Tees. In winter, many birds can bee seen on the site and riverside, with species including stonechat, lapwing, redshank and finches. Spring exhibits the different vegetation communities on the mounds at their best. The great variety of butterflies and the grayling can be found in the summer and the annual run of the River Tees salmon at the Tees

Barrage and the common seals that follow them occurs in autumn.

Moor House – Upper Teesdale NNR
Near: Upper Teesdale, near Bishop Auckland, Co Durham
Map: 19, D2
Web: www.english-nature.org.uk
Moor House – Upper Teesdale is one of England's largest NNRs and boasts a diversity of rare habitats. It is home to rare rock formations, such as outcropping sugar limestone and the Great Whin Sill. The reserve encompasses an almost complete range of upland habitats typical of the North Pennines, from lower lying hay meadows, rough grazing and juniper wood to limestone grassland, blanket bogs and the summit heaths of the high fells. The reserve has a number of walks, allowing visitors to see and experience the geology, birds and plants that the reserve has to offer.

Rainton Meadows
Near: Houghton-le-Spring, near Durham, Tyne and Wear
Map: 19, D2
Web: www.durhamwildlifetrust.org.uk
The reserve, which lies in the heart of the former Durham coalfield, provides an oasis of wildlife, attracting large numbers of wildfowl and waders. During spring and summer, the grasslands provide an ideal breeding habitat for skylark, meadow pipit and lapwing. In late summer and autumn, Rainton Meadows attracts passage waders such as redshank, little ringed plover and oystercatcher, with large numbers of mute swan visiting each winter. All five species of owl have been recorded on the reserve, with long-eared and short-eared owls hunting over the grasslands during the winter. Water vole and brown hare are also frequently seen.

Thrislington NNR
Near: Bishop Auckland, Durham
Map: 19, D2
Web: www.english-nature.org.uk
Thrislington Plantation NNR is the most valuable wildlife site on County Durham's magnesian limestone. The limestone grassland at the site supports scarce plant species, including blue moor grass, small scabious, rock-rose, and dark red helleborine. Insects abound with many unusual species present. Notable examples are northern brown argus butterfly and glow worm.

Teesmouth NNR
Near: Hartlepool, Co Durham
Map: 19, D2
Web: www.english-nature.org.uk
Apart from typical sand dune and saltmarsh plant communities, Teesmouth NNR is home to four species of marsh orchid, adder's tongue fern and three rare plant species: rush-leaved fescue, stiff-leaved saltmarsh grass and brackish water crow's-foot. Common blue butterflies, burnet moths and lyme grass moth are all found here, while birds include knot, redshank, sandwich tern, cormorant and ringed plover, as well as large populations of wader and wildfowl in the winter. There is a colony of common seals living here and grey seals are also frequent visitors to the area.

Whitelee Moor NNR
Near: Carter Bar and Redesdale, Northumberland
Map: 19, C1
Web: www.nwt.org.uk
Whitelee Moor is one of England's largest and most important NNRs. It has an active blanket bog, mires, flushes and heather heaths and is thus a site of European conservation importance. Otters often hunt along the River Rede. Birds, such as merlin and stonechat breed at the reserve, while visiting birds include black grouse, sky lark, curlew, golden plover and ring ouzel.

The wonderful world of orchids
The flowers of orchids may all look extremely different, but the form is always the same, three petals and three sepals. Different varieties grow in woodland, in meadows, in heathland and even in bogs, but they're always a pleasure to come across in the wild. See them at Lewes Down, East Sussex; Winks Meadow, Suffolk; Pentwyn Farm, Wales; Causeway Caost, Northern Ireland; or Smardale Gill, Cumbria.

BIRD RESERVES

Big Waters, Seaton Burn
Near: Newcastle,
Northumberland
Map: 19, D2
Web: www.newcastle.gov.uk

Big Waters is one of the
largest subsidence ponds in
south-east Northumberland.
Surrounded by fen and
carr, the land around the
lake is generally flat, rising
to the north-east. Big Waters
covers an area of almost
124 acres, which includes
the lake, stream, ponds,
marshland, grassland and
woodland. There are facilities
for walking, picnicking,
fishing, birdwatching and
nature studies. Big Waters
is a good place for observing
wildfowl and autumn
waders and has an excellent
passerine feeding station.
There is also a public hide
at the east end.

St Mary's Freshwater Wetland Pond
Near: Whitley Bay,
Northumberland
Map: 19, D2
Web: www.northtyneside.gov.uk

The site is situated on the
coast at Whitley Bay and
forms part of the much
larger Northumberland
Coast SSSI. St Mary's
Freshwater Wetland Pond
comprises clifftop grassland,
wetland, tidal and sub-tidal
habitats, the small semi-
tidal island and a freshwater
pond. The area holds major
geological, ornithological and
marine interest. The wetland
is particularly important as
a high-tide roost for golden
plover, oystercatcher, curlew
and redshank, and as an
important landfall for
passing migrants in spring
and autumn.

FOREST & WOODLAND

Black Plantation
Near: Durham, Co Durham
Map: 19, D2
Web: www.wt-woods.org.uk
Covering an area of nearly
35 acres, Black Plantation is
dominated by semi-mature
birch growing on brown clay
earth, wet in places, along
with a scattering of oak and
other broad-leaves and the
odd Scot's pine.

DID YOU KNOW?

The bird on the RSPB's logo
is an avocet.

Borough Woods LNR
Near: Morpeth, Northumberland
Map: 19, D2
Web: www.castlemorpeth.gov.uk

Borough Woods is
predominantly oak, ash and
elm with a shrub layer of holly,
hazel, hawthorn, elder and
guelder rose in places. The
quiet visitor may well see red
squirrels, badgers, roe deer and
otters in this wood. There are
various birds to be spotted here
too, including great spotted
woodpecker, treecreeper,
nuthatch, wren, chiffchaff,
blackcap, white-throat,
tawny owl, sparrowhawk and
kingfisher. A wide variety of
woodland plants and fungi
can be seen, some of which
are only found in ancient
woodlands. Watch out for
the beds of wood anemone
in March and April and the
common twayblade in June.

Briarwood Banks SSSI
Near: Haydon Bridge, near
Hexham, Northumberland
Map: 19, C2
Web: www.nwt.org.uk

Briarwood Banks is one of
the richest areas of ancient
semi-natural woodland in
the county, boasting a mixed
deciduous wood with a diverse
field layer. Typical bird fauna,
such as flycatcher and the great
spotted woodpecker, as well as
native fauna and a wide range
of mammals, including red
squirrels, roe deer, dormice,
all make this an ideal place for
woodland walks.

Faith Wood
Near: Middlesborough, Durham
Map: 19, D3
Web: www.woodland-trust.org.uk

Faith Wood, acquired by the
Woodland Trust in December
1993, is a part of the much
larger Cowpen Bewley
Woodland Park situated
on low lying land on the
north-east edge of Billingham
in Teesside. The site contains
a mix of semi-natural habitats
and has wide rides and paths
that provide good access
and incorporate a sculpture
trail. Trees include oak, ash,
rowan, birch, cherry, crack
willow, alder, hawthorn,
blackthorn, hazel, guelder
rose and dog rose.

Hartburn Glebe
Near: Morpeth, Northumberland
Map: 19, D2
Web: www.woodland-trust.org.uk
Hartburn Glebe is an area of
rural woodland occupying
the steep sides of the valley
of artburn, near Morpeth,
Northumberland. The
woodland lies over millstone
grit, which outcrops as
precipitous cliffs in parts,
curving along the side of the
river Hart Burn. At the curve
of the river is a deep pool
known as the Baker's Chest,
reputed to have been used
to hide silver and valuables
during Viking Raids. The
wood plays host to a rich and
varied wildlife, including red
squirrels and otters.

Hartburn Glebe

Irthing Gorge Woodland

Near: Hexham Northumberland
Map: 19, C2
Web: www.woodland-trust.org.uk
P

The gorge lies at an altitude of 150-210 metres and is cut through gently undulating moorland. Both sides of the gorge support an excellent example of upland gorge woodland. The Woodland Trust property lies to the east of the river which is fast-flowing and rocky. The cliffs are up to 10 metres high with many smaller crags and ledges with rich and varied bryophyte communities, lichens in the drier areas and several species of ferns.

Letah Wood

Near: Hexham, Northumberland
Map: 19, C2
Web: www.woodland-trust.org.uk
P **i**

A rural woodland, set within farmland, Letah Wood

is a mixed broad-leaved woodland with abundant ash and beech, frequent sessile oak and occasional to rare downy birch, sycamore, Douglas fir, wych elm, wild cherry, rowan, Scot's pine, horse chestnut and yew. The understorey includes hazel, holly, elder and hawthorn. On the south-facing slopes, north of the Burn that runs through the woodland, are abundant native wild daffodils, as well as wild garlic, great woodrush, dog's mercury, lesser celendine and wood sorrel. A rich variety of birds have been recorded within the wood and at the southern end there is a large rabbit warren. There are several sizeable colonies of wood ant.

Nunsborough Wood

Near: Ordley and Hexham, Northumberland
Map: 19, C2
Web: www.wt-woods.org.uk

The river winds dramatically through the valley giving much character to this wood, which lines the steep slopes directly above the river. The woodland is well used by local people and visitors. There is an extensive network of public footpaths linking the woodland to adjacent land. Nunsborough Woodland borders the Devil's Water to the east and north and beyond this is mixed woodland.

Pontburn Woods

Near: Hamsterley Mill, near Newcastle, Co Durham
Map: 19, D2
Web: www.woodland-trust.org.uk
P

Pontburn Woods consists of a number of adjoining woodlands situated approximately 3.4 miles north-west of Consett in Co Durham. The site has a mosaic of broad-leaved and

Chiffchaff

conifer high forest stretching southwards from the River Derwent down the west side of Hamsterley Mill. Several public rights of way cross the site, providing access to the woodland from most directions.

Railway Wood
Near: Fence Houses, near Chester-le-Street, Co Durham
Map: 19, D2
Web: www.woodland-trust.org.uk
Railway Wood is one of two woods that make up Fence Houses. It is made up of 12 acres of new native woodland planted in 2000 on ex-agricultural land put down to grass. It was created under The Woodland Trust's millennium project, Woods on Your Doorstep.

Saltburn Gill SSSI
Near: Middlesbrough, Cleveland
Map: 19, D3
Web: www.wildlifetrust.org.uk/teesvalley
P WC ♿

The Saltburn Gill is a brilliant reserve for the complete woodland experience. It is a 52-acre woodland, with a public footpath running the entire length, providing opportunities to see all the reserve has to offer. Spring and summer showcase the reserve's wildflowers, including the woodruff, bugle, moschatel and wood avens. Summer welcomes the arrival of the migrant birds, such as chiffchaffs. Autumn heralds the mixed tit flocks and the blooming of many fungi and toadstools. The reserve is also home to mammals, such as the roe deer and weasel.

Scotch Hill Wood LNR
Near: Morpeth, Northumberland
Map: 19, D2
Web: www.english-nature.org.uk
Ancient wild woodland nature reserve with a short round walk including footways along the steep slopes of the River Wansbeck valley.

Westlaw Wood
Near: Consett, Durham
Map: 19, D2
Web: www.woodland-trust.org.uk
This woodland runs along a gentle slope down to the River Derwent. The outer fringe is mature broad-leaved trees, consisting mainly of oak and sycamore, while the centre of the site was clear felled in the early 1980s and regenerated naturally, mostly by birch. The Woodland Trust has carried out work to thin the birch and recreate as much of a broad-leaved woodland area as possible.

Whittle Dene
Near: Newcastle, Northumberland
Map: 19, D2
Web: www.wt-woods.org.uk
Whittle Dene Wood lies on the edge of Northumberland National Park. It is formed in the steep sided valley of the Whittle, the name given to the small 'burn' (river) which runs through the valley, north to south. The

wood extends along both sides of the valley, but that in the Trust's ownership is mainly on the west-facing slope. The wood is rural with information boards at the entrances north and south. The wood supports a diverse birdlife including kingfisher, dipper, heron and great spotted woodpecker. Deer are frequent visitors.

COAST, WETLANDS & WATERWAYS

Balderhead Reservoir
Near: Barnard Castle, Durham
Map: 19, D3
Web: www.waterscape.com
Small pockets of native trees, including oak, wych elm, Scot's pine and ash have been planted in sheltered locations on the northern and southern sides of the reservoir. Mallard regularly visit Balderhead in the winter, as do wigeon, tufted duck, goldeneye, teal, cormorant and goosander. Whooper swans and white-fronted geese are also sometimes recorded here in winter months. The surrounding grassland forms important feeding areas for waders, such as curlew, redshank, golden plover and snipe, that breed on the surrounding moorland. Populations of these species have suffered declines in recent years, due to destruction of their habitat. Common sandpiper and oystercatcher breed along the reservoir margins.

Coatham Marsh
Near: Middlesborough
Map: 19, D3
Web: www.wildlifetrust.org.uk
This 134-acre reserve with wetland features, including

two large lakes, attracts a diverse number of birds. Spring is often heralded by the return of the shelduck that come to the Tees Estuary to breed, while summer sees the return of sedge warblers and grasshopper warblers. Species to look out for in autumn include odd-ruff, black-tailed godwit, and curlew sandpiper. Winter is the time for wildfowl with large numbers of wigeon and teal over-wintering on the flooded grasslands, as well as shovler, gadwall, tuffeted duck and pochard. The reserve is a great place for migrant birds and is also home to a number of mammals, such as fox and stoat.

Cow Green Reservoir
Near: Durham, Co Durham
Map: 19, D2
Web: www.waterscape.com
Cow Green lies in a shallow basin on the upper reaches of the River Tees and is encircled by the Pennine

Moors. Cow Green, at the head of Teesdale, is in wonderful and dramatic walking country. The area supports rare alpine flora and the lake is a wild brown fishery. Its high altitude means that the conditions are too extreme for many species of wildfowl and wader, as the water regularly freezes over in the winter. However, a number of species of duck and goose can be seen here. Regular visitors include teal, mallard and goosander.

Derwent Reservoir
Near: Consett, Co Durham
Map: 19, D2
Web: www.waterscape.com
This 1,000-acre, three-mile long reservoir lies in an AONB in the North Pennines. The boundary between Northumberland and Durham runs right through the middle of the lake. There are riverside paths and routes along disused railway lines and the reservoir is a good spot for birdwatching.

Blackton Reservoir
Near: Hury South, near Barnard Castle, Co Durham
Map: 19, D3
Web: www.waterscape.com
Blackton offers great fishing and sights for nature lovers that make it well worth a visit. Due to the variety of wildlife habitats, there are quite a number of birds associated with the site, including mistle thrush, song thrush, blackbird and great tit. Wheatear, meadow pipit and skylark, whose populations have declined dramatically, are found in the grassland. Coot, moorhen, sedge warbler and reed bunting nest at the western end of the reservoir. Herons and a variety of waders, including oystercatcher, snipe, redshank and curlew, visit the site to feed, especially when the reservoir has been drawn down, exposing the muddy margins at the western end. Wildfowl also visit the reservoir during the winter months in small numbers. During bad winters, black grouse come down to feed on the birch on the south western end of the reservoir.

Seagulls and shags on the Farne Islands

of the gulls gathered are from other areas of England such as the North East and East Anglia, some have been recorded from as far afield as Denmark. Ducks are also common visitors to the reservoir, including the widgeon and teal. Other wildfowl, such as tufted duck, coot and moorhen, also breed here. This grassland is used as breeding grounds by a host of waders. Species that can be seen include snipe, oystercatcher and lapwing.

Greenlee Lough NNR

Near: Bardon Mill, near Hexham, Northumberland
Map: 19, C2
Web: www.english-natue.org.uk

P ♿ WC

Greenlee Lough NNR is a shallow lake fringed with water plants. Most of the reserve is open water. The lake's edge has reedbed, herb fen and blanket bog. It is used extensively by wildfowl and waders that feed in the shallow waters and wetlands. The best times to visit are during spring and summer.

Hauxley

Near: Ashington, Northumberland
Map: 19, D1
Web: www.nwt.org.uk

P ♿ WC 🔧 🏠 🔦

The body of water, islands, reedbeds and trees at this reserve attracts a large number of birds, including waders and many migrants, Bewick's swan, shoveler, lapwing and purple sandpiper. The site is home to butterflies and dragonflies, as well as great crested newts. Hauxley also boasts diverse flora, including kidney vetch, yellow-wort, ragged robin and bloody crane's-bill, which

Farne Islands NNR

Near: Alnwick, Northumberland
Map: 19, D1
Web: www.english-nature.org.uk
Farne Islands NNR is home to a large grey seal colony and is a renowned seabird site, with 18 to 21 species breeding here regularly. Shags, sandwich terns, roseate terns and Arctic terns are present in huge numbers and the islands are also an important stopover site for migrant birds. Farne Islands also boasts cliffs and sloping rocky sandy beaches, which can be enjoyed throughout the year, especially between April and August.

Grassholme Reservoir

Near: Barnard Castle, Durham
Map: 19, D3
Web: www.waterscape.com
P WC 🔧 ℹ️ ✉️ (all available in the summer), ♿ 🔦
Huge flocks of up to 2,000 black-headed gulls can be seen on the wetlands near the main inflow between March and June at Grassholme. Although many

make the site particularly attractive in the summer.

Hury Reservoir
Near: Barnard Castle, Co Durham
Map: 19. D3
Web: www.waterscape.com
P

Hury Reservoir, built in 1894, is the oldest of the five reservoirs in the Tees Valley and is heavily stocked with rainbow trout, making it a popular place for fishing. It is also an important site for wildlife, particularly during the winter, when wildfowl such as black-backed gulls and waders can be seen creating what is often a noisy spectacle. Hury is the most important of the Teesdale reservoirs for Canada geese. Also keep an eye out for oystercatchers, lapwings and curlews.

Lindisfarne
Near: Berwick-upon-Tweed, Northumberland

Map: 19, D1
Web: www.waterscape.com

Sitting on the top of the easterly section of the Whin Sill, this small island – also known as Holy Island – is separated from the mainland by a narrow causeway which is covered by water at high tide. Golden beaches, blue seas and a vast array of wildlife are some of the highlights of a trip to this natural treasure trove. Lindisfarne boasts one of the most stunning beaches in Britain, a brilliant spot for birdwatching and rock-pooling. Rock pools provide protection for marine creatures from the action of the waves, and also protection from drying out for a wide range of creatures. These creatures include rock crabs, sponges, anemones, starfish and pipe fish. You will need to be prepared to get your hands dirty and start turning over the seaweed that gets washed up on the shore

if you want to see the marine life at its best. Also look out for crabs' shell cases trapped in the seaweed.

Portrack Marsh
Near: Stockton-on-Tees, Cleveland
Map: 19, D3
Web: www.wildlifetrust.org.uk/teesvalley
P **WC** 🅿 ▭

Portrack Marsh is the last remaining wetland area on the lower River Tees. With its large water bodies, different birds can be seen throughout the year, but it is especially a magnet for local and migrating birds during winter and spring, when the vegetation is low and they can be seen feeding in the hawthorn scrub. In the summer, the ditches are home to water vole and kingfisher, while in the autumn, visitors can witness the annual salmon run along the River Tees and nests of harvest mice can be found in reedbeds.

Spot the difference: dragonflies and damselflies

There are several clear indicators to tell the difference between dragonflies and damselflies. While damselflies' wings are all more or less equal in size, dragonflies have back wings that are shorter and broader than their front ones. Dragonflies are also stronger fliers and can be seen further from water than damselflies which stay close to banks and water surfaces. When at rest, a dragonfly leaves its wings out perpendicular to its body, while damselflies fold theirs in along their body. Neither species bite or sting humans. Look out for both around water.

PICTURED
Right: Dragonfly. Notice the smaller rear wings, left perpendicular to its body.
Below: Damselfly. Notice the separated eyes and wings folded along its body.

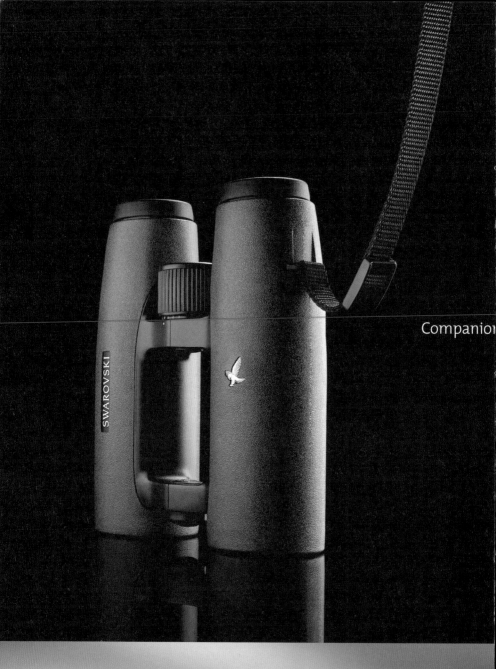

Companion

A Lifelong Friend

The EL binoculars combine maximum functionality with innovation and design. The unique wrap-around grip allows comfortable one-handed operation. Their lightness and perfectly balanced weight makes the EL feel so good you won't want to be separated from them, and the quality of the EL will ensure a lifetime of enjoyment.

SWAROVSK
OPTIK

Swarovski U.K. LTD., Perrywood Business Park, Salfords, Surrey RH1 5JQ, Tel. 01737-856812, Fax 01737-856885

www.swarovskioptik.com

Calm waters are kingfisher territory

Britain has one native species of kingfisher that can be seen throughout the UK, especially in central and southern England. Look out for its distinctive blue flash at still or slow-flowing water such as lakes or canals. Good places to spot them include: Shropshire Union Canal, West Midlands; Blackburn Meadows, Sheffield; Wicken Fen, East Anglia; Titchfield Haven, Hampshire, and Portrack Marsh, County Durham.

River Tees

From: Tees Valley to the Pennines
Map: 19, C2 and D2
Web: www.waterscape.com
This medieval trading river was, until recently, a major commercial navigation. Now that the river no longer reflects the glow from steel works and ship yards, it is becoming more accessible to the people of Teesside and beyond. Visitors can stroll over the 70-metre-wide Tees Barrage to see its navigation lock and enjoy the impressive panoramic views.

River Tweed

From: Berwick-upon-Tweed, Northumberland, to Scottish Borders
Map: 19, D1 and 21, E2
Web: www.waterscape.com
Scotland's border counties provide an evocative backdrop for the River Tweed, which is one of the world's greatest salmon fisheries. It catches more Atlantic salmon than any river in the European Union, and has been a haven for anglers since the seventeenth century. The ruins of watchtowers and fortresses from England and Scotland's many disputes add a hint of romance to the pretty borderland scenery.

River Tyne

From: Hedwin Streams at Ryton, Tyne and Wear, to Tynemouth, Northumberland
Map: 19, D2
Web: www.waterscape.com
P (££), ♿ (ltd)
Navigable by larger craft for 16 miles, the River Tyne's full 62 miles are appreciated by anglers, rowers, canoeists and wildlife spotters.

River Wansbeck

From: Borough of Castle Morpeth to North Sea at Sandy Bay
Map: 19, D2
Web: www.waterscape.com
This Northumbrian river is navigable through one lock from the coast to Ashington. Upstream, it continues through Morpeth, where Telford bridged the river. Water voles have been spotted on the River Wansbeck.

River Wear

From: Chester-le-Street
to Sunderland,
Co Durham
Map: 19, D2
Web: www.waterscape.com

A walk along the banks of
the River Wear will give
you countless opportunities
to observe birds, insects,
plants and animals. At
Washington, for example,
it passes through the
Wildfowl and Wetlands
Trust wetland centre
– full of numerous species
of birds and well worth a
visit. It meanders through
oak and ash woodlands to
Claxheugh Rock – a fossil-
rich limestone and sandstone
cliff formed in the days
before the dinosaurs ruled
the Earth.

Washington Wetland Centre

Near: Sunderland,
Co Durham
Map: 19, D2
Web: www.wwt.org.uk
Admission: £3.95/£5.95

P (££), **&** **WC** **&**
i **&** **&** **&** **&**

Set in 100 acres of stunning
wetland and woodland
on the River Wear, the
Washington Wetland Centre
is one of the North East's
biggest conservation success
stories. Its wild reserve is
home to a nesting colony
of nearly 50 grey herons,
while Hawthorn Wood Hide
offers spectacular views of
woodland birds, including
great spotted woodpecker
and bullfinch. See hundreds
of rare and endangered
ducks, geese and swans,
plus a colourful breeding
colony of Chilean flamingos.
And don't miss the insects
and plants that thrive in
the ponds, streams and
grasslands of Spring
Gill Wood.

NOT SO WILD

Bide-A-Wee Cottage Gardens

Address: Stanton, Morpeth,
Northumberland NE65 8PR
Map: 19, D2
Tel: 01670 772238
Web: www.bideawee.co.uk
Open: May to August, Saturdays
and Wednesdays, 1.30pm to 5pm

P **WC** **&**

The Bide-A-Wee Cottage
Gardens were built out of a
former quarry over the last 25
years and are host to numerous
different flora species, including
ferns, shrubs, perennials,
grasses and the national
collection of centaurea. The
gardens were also described by
Gardeners' World magazine
as a 'very special garden' and
as a 'highlight of many visitors
itinerary in Northumberland'.

DID YOU KNOW?

Frogs can't swallow. They use
their large eyes to push food
into their stomachs which
is why they close their eyes
to eat.

Bill Quay Community Farm

Address: Hainingwood Terrace,
Bill Quay, Gateshead, Tyne and
Wear NE10 0UE
Map: 19, D2
Tel: 0191 433 5780
Web: www.farmgarden.org.uk
Open: daily, 9am to 5pm
Admission: free

P **&** **WC** **&** **&** **&**

Bill Quay Community Farm
is truly unique. The project
is a partnership between
Gateshead Council and a
voluntary group of local
people – Bill Quay Community
Farm Association. The council
own and largely fund the
farm which is managed by
the farm association. Open
since 1986, the project has an
excellent collection of pedigree
and rare breed livestock and

---

an abundance of artworks.
It is also a green retreat for
wildlife. The farm site offers
panoramic views of the River
Tyne, and has developed into
a rare breeds centre with
animals including cows,
goats, pigs, sheep, chickens
and rabbits.

Clarences Community Farm

Address: Off Holly Terrace, Port
Clarence Road, Port Clarence,
Middlesbrough TS2 1SZ
Map: 19, D3
Tel: 01642 391975
Web: www.farmgarden.org.uk
Open: summer, Tuesday to Friday,
9am to 5pm; winter, weekends,
9am to 4pm
Admission: free

P **&** **WC** **&** **&** **&**

Port Clarence was once
included as a category-D
village (known as 'death
villages', due for demolition).
It has now been resurrected
with renovated homes
bringing together High and
Low Port Clarence. Clarences
Community Farm offers you
the chance to experience
authentic rural life and see
the day-to-day working of a
real animal farm. The farm,
which borders the Teesmouth
International Nature Reserve
and the regenerated Clarences
Estate, was built to give town
children the great experience
of country life, allowing
them to see rare breeds of
pigs, as well as cattle-belted
galloways, sheep, goats and
free-range poultry.

Cragside

Address: Rothbury, Morpeth,
Northumberland NE65 7PX
Map: 19, D2
Tel: 01669 620333
Web: www.nationaltrust.org.uk
Open: 17 March to 4 November,
Tuesday to Sunday, 10.30am
to 5.30pm; 7 November to 16
December, Wednesday to Sunday,
11am to 4pm

Red squirrels

Even when you konw where to go to spot red squirrels, they are still difficult to see as they tend to spend their time up in the treetops gnawing pine cones. Instead, look out for evidence of them such as scratch marks on the bark of trees and large nests – or dreys – at the forks in trees. Look out also for the remnants of pine cones gnawed into the shape of an apple core. And red squirrels don't hibernate, they store up fungi to see them through, so look out for them all year in places in Cumbria, Scotland, the Isle of Wight and some areas of East Anglia.

Admission: varies with season

[P] [WC] [symbols]

Cragside, creation of Victorian inventor and landscape genius Lord Armstrong, is a garden of breathtaking drama whatever the season. Surrounding the house is one of the largest rock gardens in Europe. Beyond is a vast woodland garden where rhododendrons and azaleas reach full bloom during late May and June. Soaring high above are the magnificent spires of Armstrong's transatlantic conifer collection, which provide shelter to the estate's red squirrel population. Across the valley, in the terraced garden, the Orchard House still produces fresh fruit of all varieties. Summer features splendid carpet bedding, and autumn, the colourful dahlia walk. The lakeside walks, adventure play area and labyrinth are all good reasons for children to visit Cragside.

Crook Hall and Gardens

Address: Frankland Lane, Sidegate, near Durham DH1 5SZ
Map: 19, D2
Tel: 0191 384 8028
Web: www.crookhallgardens.co.uk
Open: varies with season
Admission: £4/£4.50

[P] (££), [symbol] (ltd),
[WC] [symbols]

Crook Hall is a beautiful Grade I-listed medieval manor house surrounded by abundant cottage gardens. In the Shakespeare Garden, plants, such as lovage, borage and meadowsweet, date back to the days of the Bard.

Hall Hill Farm

Address: Lanchester, near Durham, Co Durham DH7 0TA
Map: 19, D2
Tel: 01388 731333
Web: www.hallhillfarm.co.uk

Open: daily, 17 March to 9 September, 10.30am to 5pm; weekends, 10 September to December, 10.30am to 5.30pm
Admission: £3.50/£4.75

[P] [symbol] [WC] [symbols]

Hall Hill Farm is a mixed farm of 715 acres that includes a woodland and crop area. The farm was first opened to the public in 1981 and has been in the same family for three generations. There are a number of friendly animals to meet including chicks, lambs, pigs, donkeys, ponies and rabbits. There are other more unusual animals such as llamas, wallabies and Highland cattle.

DID YOU KNOW?

Thirty per cent of the world's population of bluebells is found in the UK.

Highland Cattle Centre

Address: Dere Street Farm, Dere Street, Stocksfield, Northumberland NE43 7SB
Map: 19, D2
Tel: 07968 865591
Web: www.thehighlandcattle centre.co.uk
Open: Tuesday to Sunday, 10am to 5pm (except 25 December and 1 January)
Admission: £3/£3.50

[P] [symbol] [WC] [symbols]
[symbols]

Not just Highland cattle, but Gloucester old spot pigs and rare breed hens reside at this friendly working farm with lovely views over Northumberland. The pets' corner is popular with kids.

Kielder Water Birds of Prey Centre

Address: Leaplish Waterside Park, Falstone, Hexham, Northumberland NE48 1AX
Map: 19, C2
Tel: 01434 250400

Web: www.discoverit.co.uk/ falconry
Open: daily, from 10.30am (except 25 December and 1 January)
Admission: £2.50/£4.50

[WC] [symbol]

The Kielder Water Birds of Prey Centre has one of the largest and most fascinating collections of birds of prey in the north of England, located within the magnificent forest lakeside surrounding Kielder Water at Leaplish Waterside Park. Visitors are given the opportunity to enjoy a direct hands-on experience during which they will meet all northern region's indigenous owls as well as birds of prey and other owls from around the world – all within a supervised environment.

The Sanctuary Wildlife Care Centre

Address: Crowden Hill Farm, Ulgham, Morpeth, Northumberland NE61 3NH
Map: 19, D2
Tel: 01670 791778
Web: www.wildlife-sanctuary.co.uk
Open: Friday to Monday, 11am to 5pm
Admission: £4/£5

[P] [symbol] [WC] [symbols] [symbol]
[symbols]

Unique in the North East, The Sanctuary Wildlife Care Centre offers visitors of all ages and abilities the opportunity to see most species of British wildlife, including foxes, badgers, deer, owls and hedgehogs, viewed from purpose-built wildlife hides.

Tyne Riverside Country Park

Address: Station Road, Prudhoe, near New Castle, Northumberland NE42 6UP
Map: 19, D2
Tel: 01661 834135
Web: www.northumberlandlife. org/tyneriversidecountrypark

Open: Closed at Christmas and New Year
Admission: free
P **&** (ltd), **WC** **&** **N**

Tyne Riverside Country Park follows the River Tyne for four miles through 200 acres of meadows, chalk grassland, woodland and riverbank all within a short distance of Newcastle and Gateshead. The park is a very popular place for walking, cycling, horse-riding or just having a lazy day by the river. The park has a wide range of wildlife habitats and is an ideal place to watch birds and butterflies.

Tynemouth Blue Reef Aquarium
Address: Grand Parade, Tynemouth, near Whitely Bay, Northumberland NE30 4JF
Map: 19, D2
Tel: 0191 258 1031

Web: www.bluereefaquarium.co.uk
Open: daily from 10am
Admission: £3.99/£5.99
P **&** **WC** **&** **N**

Blue Reef Aquarium is part of an exciting new generation of wildlife attractions designed to inspire deeper understanding and appreciation of the natural world. Open-top tanks allow close encounters with friendly rays, while hands-on tide pools and crashing surf displays recreate the sea's many different aspects. At the heart of the aquarium giant ocean tanks with spectacular underwater walk-through tunnels offer unforgettable journeys through exotic coral reefs – home to sharks and colourful fish.

Wallington
Address: Cambo, Morpeth, Northumberland NE61 4AR

Map: 19, D2
Tel: 01670 773600
Web: www.nationaltrust.org.uk
Open: daily, dawn to dusk
Admission: £2.75/£5.50
P (££), **&** **WC** **&**
i **&** **&** **N**

Wallington's beautiful 100-acre grounds consist of lawns, lakes, gardens (famous for their scented roses) and woodland, with a particularly attractive walled garden and conservatory. The grounds bear the distinctive hallmark of landscape architect Capability Brown, who was born in Cambo. There are fine walks along the River Wansbeck. The woods attract a variety of interesting birdlife including both green and great spotted woodpeckers. The gardens include scented plants and a Braille guide is available.

Scotland

Scotland offers a raw beauty unrivalled by other parts of Britain. It is a land of dramatic contrasts – from the rolling hills of the Southern Uplands to the splendour of the Highlands, breaking up in the north and west into a succession of headlands, sea lochs, islands and stacks. Its rugged charm is similar to that found in Wales and the Lake District, but on a much grander scale. The scenery is simply breathtaking and can change before your eyes as the weather suddenly turns and the light plays across the landscape.

It is easy to get distracted by the sheer beauty of the terrain, but equally fascinating are the diverse range of species that have made their home here. Scotland is a haven for more than 90,000 species, from the bottlenose dolphins of the Moray Firth to the capercaillie grouse of the Central Highlands and the thousands of seals and puffins inhabiting the coastline.

The high mountains attract only the hardiest of species, such as the ptarmigan and mountain hare, who both don their white winter coats to aid camouflage in these gruelling habitats. Meanwhile, the coast attracts thousands of migratory species every winter. Two fantastic locations are Loch of Strathbeg, near Crimond, Aberdeenshire, and Montrose Basin, Angus: both excellent for pink-footed geese and whooper swans among other species. Further south Caerlaverock, in Dumfries and Galloway, is excellent for barnacle geese.

An iconic species to look out for are red deer. Their numbers have increased dramatically in recent years and their current population stands at roughly 300,000. They can mainly be found in the Highlands and islands, although large numbers can be found in the Galloway Hills.

One of the hardest Scottish mammals to spot in the wild (primarily due to its nocturnal habits), is the pine marten. This sleek woodland predator is slowly expanding its range again throughout Scotland. Once persecuted for its highly prized fur, it is now becoming an ever-more regular visitor to gardens across the Highland mainland and Eastern Lowlands.

The spectacular coastlines also offer some great marine life. Grey seals are widespread on Scotland's rockier west coast. The Scottish population is estimated at up to 120,000. Summer is a great time to see them, when they can be found basking on the rocks, soaking up the sun. Bottlenose dolphins can be seen all around the coastline, although Moray Firth is the most renowned place for spotting them.

With such a diverse range of landscapes and habitats on offer, there are endless places to explore in Scotland and once you've had a taste for it, you'll want to go back for more.

PICTURED: Red deer stag on Glen Garry moorland in the west Highlands

Not to be missed

● **Beinn Eighe**
With its wonderful mountain scenery and ancient pinewood fragments, it's easy to see why this was the first place in Britain to be made an NNR. Red deer, golden eagle and the elusive pine marten all live here and there's a spectacular range of mosses and liverworts in the woods.

● **The Cairngorm Mountains**
The snowy high-tops, heather-clad moors and lochs of this stunning mountain range are home to rare native birds – including the ptarmigan and capercaillie.

● **Glen Nant**
Not much of the native forests which once covered the Scottish Highlands remains, but here is a true flavour of ancient times. The sheltered environment is popular with many birds and mammals.

● **Loch Garten, Abernethy**
This is the ancestral home of the osprey in Scotland and it's brilliantly set up with binoculars, telescopes and CCTV so you can watch every antic of this fish-eating bird of prey at close quarters.

NATIONAL PARKS

Cairngorms National Park

Near: Grantown on Spey, East Highlands
Map: 20, D2
Web: www.cairngorms.co.uk

Cairngorms National Park is Britain's largest and newest national park. It contains within it a unique range of landscapes, wildlife, habitats and people and is home to 25 per cent of the UK's threatened bird, animal and plant species. At its heart is a wild mountain range, but all around are moorlands, forests, rivers, lochs and glens. Cairngorms is one of the few places in Britain where you can see the Scottish crossbill, the only bird unique to Britain. Golden eagle, osprey, dotterel, capercaillie and crested tit are just a few other bird species found here. The national park is home to a wide variety of animals, too, including pine martens, red squirrels, badgers, wildcats, water vole and otters. The rivers are home to a rising population of the globally endangered freshwater pearl mussel, as well as salmon, trout and rare lampreys.

PICTURED: Lairig Ghru, Cairngorms, Scottish Highlands

Loch Lomond and The Trossachs National Park
Near: Balloch, Argyll and Stirling
Map: 21, C1
Web: www.lochlomond-trossachs.org

The woods, mountains, lochs and coasts of Loch Lomond and The Trossachs National Park are rich in wildlife. In summer, Loch Lomond's ancient oakwoods ring with birdsong – look out for redstarts, pied flycatchers and wood warblers. Ospreys are summer visitors to the loch and nearby Lake of Menteith, while golden eagles may be seen soaring over mountain slopes. Ben Lui is known for plants, such as saxifrage and mountain avens. Porpoises and seals swim in the sheltered waters of Loch Long and Loch Goil, while crabs and sea anemones can be found in rock pools and flocks of wading birds feed

at the mouth of the River Eachaig at Kilmun. Winter is also often a good time to spot wildlife. Whooper swans and goldeneye find refuge on quiet Trossachs lochs, while Greenland white-fronted geese graze by the River Endrick. Red deer, which frequent the high mountain areas, move down the slopes to find food, and when the trees are bare you can often glimpse Loch Lomond's herd of fallow deer bounding through the woods.

NSAs

Assynt-Coigach
Near: Ullapool, Northern Highlands
Map: 20, C1
Web: www.opsi.gov.uk

This is a wild and beautiful stretch of Scotland, dominated by a handful of imposing mountains thrusting out alone from the cragged landscape.

The Cairngorm Mountains
Near: Grantown on Spey, East Highlands
Map: 20, D2
Web: www.cairngorms.co.uk

Take time to explore this incredible area and look out for some special wildlife. The ancient pine forests of Abernethy and Rothiemurchus, the alpine plateau of the Cairngorms, the snowy high-tops, the heather-clad moors and the lochs are home to some of our rarest native birds, including osprey, crested tit, ptarmigan, capercaillie, Scottish crossbill and golden eagle. There are red squirrels, hares, and even reindeer, which you can visit in their mountain home.

The Cuillin Hills
Near: Isle of Skye, Western Isles
Map: 20, B2
Web: www.snh.org.uk

The Cuillin Hills are counted among the most spectacular peaks in Scotland. Whether you come to Skye to climb the Cuillins or just to admire them from a safe distance, you cannot escape their presence.

Deeside and Lochnagar
Near: Banchory, Aberdeen and Grampian
Map: 20, E2
Web: www.snh.org.uk
Discovering Royal Deeside and Lochnagar provides visitors with an opportunity to explore and appreciate the spectacularly scenic Cairngorms National Park, as well as tours to Loch Ness, Edinburgh and Pitlochry. There are royal and historic castles, whisky distilleries, archaeological features and interesting villages. You may see red deer, highland cattle, eagles and salmon. In August, the hillsides are stunning, covered in purple heather, while in the autumn, the trees are vibrant with colour.

Dornoch Firth
Near: Cromarty, East Highlands
Map: 20, D2
Web: www.snh.org.uk
This is the northernmost firth on the east coast of Scotland. The mudflats found here are of great importance to wintering waders and wildfowl. During autumn and winter, you may see large numbers of wigeon, oyster-catcher, knot and dunlin. Common and grey seals are often visible hauled out on the sandbanks at low tide and the common seals give birth to their pups here in June and July. The dunes at Dornoch are rich in flowers, including purple milk-vetch and a variety of orchids.

Eildon and Leaderfoot
Near: Galashiels, Borders
Map: 21, D2

Web: www.snh.org.uk
The Eildon and Leaderfoot NSA covers 8,895 acres in the Central Borders and includes the confluence of the River Tweed and the Leader Water. Shapely uniform hills enclose the valley, as the river winds its way through steep wooded hillsides, arable land and moorland.

Glen Strathfarrar
Near: Inverness, East Highlands
Map: 20, D2
Web: www.snh.org.uk
Glen Strathfarrar boasts stunning scenery, classic Highland vistas and ancient Caledonian pinewoods. This peaceful haven is home to a range of wildlife, including otters, red deer, pine marten and golden eagles. The glen is also a great place for outdoor activities.

Hoy and West Mainland
Near: Orkney, Northern Isles
Web: www.outwestcharters.co.uk

Loch Lomond

Ben Nevis and Glen Coe

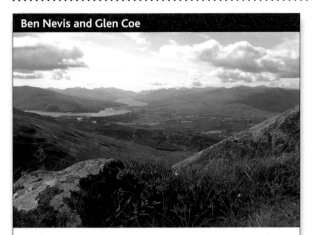

Near: Fort William, West Highlands
Map: 20, C3
Web: www.jmt.org

At 1,344 metres, Ben Nevis is the highest mountain in the British Isles. Glen Nevis boasts stunning natural woodlands of native pinewood, oak and birch, as well as alder and ash closer to the streams. The lower slopes are heather moorland, grass slopes and peaty bogs. Look out for blaeberry (bilberry), heather, mat grass, mosses, thyme and milkwort. Bracken is abundant. Plants include deer grass, common butterwort, sundews and bog asphodel. Beside the Red Burn, starry saxifrage may be seen. On the summit plateau there are few flowers and vegetation is limited to mainly mosses and lichens, many of which are Arctic-alpine species. They include woolly fringe moss, forming a dense covering on boulders and ground. Patient observers are likely to find numerous invertebrates, including some rarities such as the mountain ringlet butterfly. The wide variety of habitats makes the whole Ben Nevis area a fabulous home for birds. The snow bunting and ptarmigan prefer the higher areas while golden eagles, ravens, kestrels and buzzards can also be seen. Smaller birds of the hillside include meadow pipits, stonechats, whinchats, wheatears and ring ouzels. Chaffinches, tits, thrushes, siskins, blackbirds, wrens, warblers, flycatchers and owls can be found in the wooded areas, while dippers, common sandpipers, herons, mallards and goosanders live along the streams.

PICTURED
Main: View from Ben Nevis
Below: Golden Eagle

While exploring the Hoy and West Mainland, you may be able to see common and grey seals and a large variety of seabirds, including puffins, razorbills, guillemots, black guillemots, fulmars, shags, great skuas and many gull species. Gannets, Arctic skuas and commorants are also around, but in lesser numbers. On certain trips and explorations of the coastline, you may also be able to spot dolphins and whales.

Jura
Near: Islay, Western Isles
Map: 21, B1 and B2
Web: www.theisleofjura.co.uk
The Island of Jura is a place of wild natural beauty. Many unique plants, insects, birds and animal species thrive in the diverse range of habitats, from the scree-covered Paps to the heather and blaeberry hillsides. There is the rugged coastline with its famous raised beaches, historic caves, crumbling cliffs and long stretches of sand to the blue-green sea. These surroundings provide a fascinating range of plantlife, which gives shelter and food for the many insects and birds, as well as the mammals. Wildlife you may see includes stoats, adders, seals and red deer.

Kintail
Near: Isle of Skye, Western Isles
Map: 20, B2
Web: www.visitkintail.co.uk
Kintail is an area of mountains in the north-west Highlands of Scotland. The area is rich in wildlife and, with some patience and determination, you will be able to see sea otters playing on the shore of Loch Duich and golden eagles soaring around the mountain peaks. There are

also deer, pine martens, badgers, and wild goats to be seen here.

Knapdale
Near: Lochgilphead, Argyll and Stirling
Map: 21, C1
Web: www.swt.org.uk
ℹ️
The woodlands at Knapdale support many bird species, as well as red squirrels and notable plants. You may also hear the great spotted woodpecker drumming. Visit any time of year for birds, sea plants and attractive scenery, or from May to July for woodland plants. Marine life at the cliff base ranges from anemones and starfish to spider crabs and carpets of seaweed. Herons and cormorants frequently fish from the rocky promontories, while other coastal birds include oystercatchers, redshank and curlew.

Knoydart
Near: Inverie, Knoydart, West Highlands
Map: 20, C2
Web: www.knoydart-foundation. com
The Knoydart peninsula is accessible by boat from Mallaig or alternatively by a 20-mile hike on foot. The surrounding waters are popular with seals, several species of dolphin, minke whales, northern bottlenose whales and even killer whales. While on land there are otters and red deer, as well as all manner of insects and small mammals in the area's woodland. Eagles, puffins and guillemots are some of the more eagerly spotted birdlife.

Kyle of Tongue
Near: Tongue, Sutherland, North Highlands
Map: 20, C1

Web: www.undiscoveredscotland. co.uk
🅿️
Kyle of Tongue boasts beautiful panoramic views of Ben Hope and Ben Loyal, the two highest peaks in northern Scotland as well as walks along untouched sandy beaches. At low tides, seals, waders and seabirds can be seen from the causeway car parks. Oystercatcher, dunlin, redshank and heron are commonly seen species.

Kyles of Bute
Near: Islay and Bute, Western Isles
Map: 21, B2
Web: www.visitscotland.co.uk
ℹ️
An AONB, this narrow stretch of water separates Bute from Argyll. Feral goats and a variety of birds may be seen on the coast around here.

Loch of the Lowes
Near: Perth, Perthshire
Map: 20, D3
Web: www.swt.org.uk
ℹ️ 🏠 ⛺
The star attraction at Loch of the Lowes from early April to late August is a pair of osprey. Otters are present, but sightings are unpredictable. Fallow and roe deer are seen regularly from the hide, while red squirrels are present in the woodland. You may also see pied flycatcher and kingfisher. Wildfowl, including coots, mallards and mute swans, can be observed all year round.

Loch Rannoch and Glen Lyon
Near: Pitlochry, Perthshire
Map: 20, D3
Web: www.visitscotland.com
Glen Lyon is the longest enclosed glen in Scotland. Loch Lyon and Loch an Daimh lie in the wild upper reaches of the glen and the hauntingly beautiful remnants of the ancient Caledonian forest are also visible. Visitors may also be interested by a lovely packhorse bridge and abundant wildlife. A wild devil cat is said to inhabit this glen – luckily it only makes an appearance at Hallowe'en.

Loch Tummel
Near: Blair Atholl, Perthshire
Map: 20, D3
Web: www.visitscotland.co.uk
On the hillside just west of the Queens View there are a number of Forestry Commission waymarked walking and cycling routes through Allean Forest. The trails offer magnificent views of Loch Tummel and surrounding countryside, with plenty of historical and wildlife interest along the way. Seed-eating birds like siskin, goldcrest and crossbill can often be seen on the lower slopes of the forest among the conifer trees. Wildcats and badgers also make their home here but a sighting is largely a matter of luck as these animals are mainly nocturnal. Keep your eyes and ears peeled for red squirrel and the elegant roe deer – these

---

Britain's oldest tree

There is a yew tree in the small village of Fortingall in Perthshire that is believed to be the oldest tree in Britain, somewhere between 3,000 and 5,000 years old. That means it has been standing since well before Julius Caesar invaded Britain in 55BC. Yew trees are notoriously long lived and often start to grow again at 500 years old.

Scotland

attractive mammals are more easily spotted in the daytime as they forage for food in the forest.

Morar, Moidart and Ardnamurchan
Near: Acharacle, West Highlands
Map: 20, B3
Web: www.visitscotland.com
There is abundant wildlife across these peninsulas, including otters, seals and pine martens. The otter is an elusive animal, whose presence is often revealed only by the remains of its prey, while smaller creatures, such as the pine marten, come right on to people's lawns to munch. There are many bird species, including eagles, harriers, buzzards and ravens. Plantlife abounds, with particularly interesting species of mosses, lichens and orchids.

North Arran
Near: Brodick and Lamlash, Strathclyde and Ayrshire
Map: 21, B2
Web: www.forestry.gov.uk
P (££), WC ℹ 🚻 🚆
Giants' graves, waterfalls, birds of prey, red squirrels and much more await the visitor to the woods of Arran. Varied levels of walks provide the perfect background to enjoy the scenery, wildlife and history of Scotland in miniature.

North-West Sutherland
Near: Northern Highlands
Map: 20, C1
Web: www.visitscotland.co.uk
North-West Sutherland is one of the last great scenic secrets of Europe. It is a vast wilderness of extraordinary mountains, the highest sea cliffs, the highest waterfalls, and many other extremes of the natural world. Durness has superb beaches, while Smoo Cave is nearby, as is Faraid Head, where you can

Loch na Keal, Isle of Mull

Near: Western Isles
Map: 21, B1
Web: www.mullbirds.com
Loch na Keal is one of the largest sea lochs and offers many opportunities to see Mull's finest bird species. In winter through to early spring, you'll find the Slavonion grebe, great northern and red-throated diver and occasional black-throated diver. Winter ducks include wigeon, teal and goldeneye, plus there are the year-round birds, such as red-breasted merganser, mallard, eider and shelduck. There is always the chance, after the winter storms, of picking up a vagrant or rare bird from North America. Seabirds include gannet, fulmar, kittewake, guillemot and black guillemot. Regular waders include (in autumn and winter) greenshank, redshank, dunlin and turnstone. In spring and summer months, common sandpiper and ringed plover can be spotted, with rock pipet on the shore. In the open areas around the loch, meadow pipit, tree pipit and skylark can be found. The scrub areas hold stonechat, whinchat, white-throat, willow and many other warblers in the summer months. A scan of the hills can regularly include white-tailed sea eagles and golden eagles (often flying together), as well as ravens, kestrels, sparrowhawks and buzzards. Peregrine falcons are occasionally seen near the sea cliffs at Griburn, hunting rock dove and feral pigeon, and there is always the chance of picking up a merlin as it flashes past. In summer months, a very rewarding walk along the shore of Loch Ba can produce sightings of red-throated diver, common sandpiper, pied and grey wagtail, dipper, redstart, wood and willow warbler, spotted flycatcher and treecreeper. Keep an eye on the horizon and hills for raptors.

PICTURED: Oystercatcher

Scotland

Loch Shiel

Near: Acharacle, West Highlands
Map: 20, C4
Web: www.lochshielfestival.com

Loch Shiel boasts outstanding scenic value, cultural and historical interest, and is one of the finest parts of the Highlands for wildlife and natural history. A variety of water birds feed and breed here, including black-throated divers with their extraordinarily patterned plumage and mournful cries. Another loch inhabitant is the otter. The area is rich in wetland insect fauna, including 10 species of dragonflies and damselflies, such as the Highland darter. Specialised plants grow on the bog surface, including three types of insect-eating sundews. As well as dragonflies, these bogs are also haunts for birds such as hen harrier and white-fronted geese, but beware – the bog surface can be treacherous.

Loch Shiel is hemmed in on all sides by the dramatic peaks of Moidart, Ardgour and Sunart – home to golden eagles and ravens. You may see the large herds of red deer that inhabit the loch. Lochaber is famous for its woodlands, particularly of oak and birch, which some of the most important examples in Europe occur on the north shore of Loch Shiel, between Glenfinnan and Langal. These woods are especially rich in mosses, liverworts, ferns and lichens, which grow luxuriantly on the trunks and branches of the trees, as well as over rocks and the ground beneath. There are some very fine woodlands of this type around Loch Moidart and Loch Sunart too. The fauna of these woodlands includes rare insects, such as the chequered skipper butterfly, and mammals, such as pine marten, wildcat and red squirrel.

see puffins and other seabirds. Reach Cape Wrath – the most north-westerly point in Britain – via ferry service and minibus. At more than 900 feet, the Clo Mor seacliffs at Cape Wrath are the highest in Britain and home to a huge colony of seabirds.

St Kilda

Near: Mallaig, West Highlands
Map: 20, B2
Web: www.kilda.org.uk

One of the most remote reserves in Britain, St Kilda's landscapes, birdlife and human history are truly outstanding. The islands support the largest gannet colony in the world and over a million seabirds in total. St Kilda also has its own subspecies of wren and

fieldmouse, as well as a wild flock of Soay sheep.

Shetland

Near: Lerwick, Northern Isles
Web: www.visitshetland.co.uk
ⓘ

Shetland is notorious as a world-class location for birdwatching, as well as seal, otter and porpoise spotting. The several wildlife reserves located in Shetland are testament to the islands' pristine environment. Shetland is even home to unique species which have adapted to the islands, such as the wonderful miniature Shetland ponies. Shetland also boasts a wide variety of wildflowers, including sea campion, red campion, ragged robin and

Loch Shiel

The Trossachs

Near: Loch Lomond, near Dumbarton, Argyll and Stirling
Map: 21, C2
Web: www.lochlomond-trossachs.org
ⓘ

The woods, mountains, lochs and coasts of Loch Lomond and The Trossachs National Park are rich in wildlife. What you find depends on where and when you look. In summer Loch Lomond's ancient oakwoods ring with birdsong. Look out for redstarts, pied flycatchers and wood warblers. Ospreys are summer visitors to the loch and nearby Lake of Menteith. In the high country of Breadalbane, golden eagles may be seen soaring over mountain slopes. Ben Lui is known for plants, such as saxifrage and mountain avens. Porpoises and seals swim in the sheltered waters of Loch Long and Loch Goil, while crabs and sea anemones can be found in rock pools. Flocks of wading birds feed at the mouth of the River Eachaig at Kilmun. Winter is often a good time to spot wildlife. Whooper swans and goldeneye find refuge on quiet Trossachs lochs, while Greenland white-fronted geese graze by the River Endrick. Red deer, which frequent the high mountain areas, move down the slopes to find food. When the trees are bare you can often glimpse Loch Lomond's herd of fallow deer as they bound through the woods.

PICTURED: Loch Achray, The Trossachs

in Europe. Lewis and Harris form the northernmost island in the Hebrides – though actually part of the same land mass, they are thought of as different islands and each has its own distinctive culture, traditions and heritage. Lewis in the north is the largest island in the group, and its main town of Stornoway is a busy centre of island life. Its natural harbour is a thriving fishing port.

South Uist
Near: Lochboisdale
Map: 20 A2 and B2
Web: www.visitscotland.com

South Uist is a relatively large island lying between Barra and Benbecula in the Outer Hebrides. The east side of South Uist is mountainous, the highest point being 2,034-foot Beinn Mhor. The west is characterised by some of the best beaches anywhere – a long line of sandy stretches backed by dunes and flower-filled machair. The island's main settlement, and port, is at Lochboisdale on the east coast.

NATURE RESERVES

Beinn Eighe
Near: Inverness, East Highlands
Map: 20, D2
Web: www.snh.org.uk
P WC ⓘ 🏛

Beinn Eighe, Britain's first NNR, features wonderful mountain scenery and ancient pinewood fragments overlooking Loch Maree. The reserve is home to typical Highland wildlife, including red deer, golden eagle and the elusive pine marten. The woodland is rich in moisture-loving mosses and liverworts, and the bogs support an outstanding variety of dragonflies.

marsh marigold. With more than 930 miles of coastline, spectacular scenery is around every corner.

South Lewis, Harris and North Uist
Near: Loch Maddy, Western Isles
Map: 20, A2 and B1
Web: www.visitscotland.co.uk

Wildlife abounds among the North Uist's unusual landscape of tidal strands, lochan, bog and flowery machair. You may be able to see otters, and the male corncrake – one of Britain's rarest birds. They are easy to hear, yet notoriously difficult to see. Every year around 9,000 grey seal pups are born on the Monach Islands off the west coast of North Uist – the largest breeding colony

Ben Lawers
Near: Killin, Argyll and Stirling
Map: 20, C3
Web: www.snh.org.uk
ⓘ (May to late September)
Few places in Britain can rival the unique range of mountain plants you find at Ben Lawers in Breadalbane above Loch Tay. The soils are unusually rich at high altitude and support a superb collection of Arctic-alpine plants and mountain scrub amid fine upland scenery. Visit in June to August for alpine plants.

Ben Lui
Near: Tyndrum, West Highlands
Map: 20, C3
Web: www.snh.org.uk
The four high peaks of this reserve attract both walkers and naturalists. Moist cliffs and rocky outcrops support an unusually lush growth of mountain plants, thriving on soils that are less acid than elsewhere. Look out especially for beautiful saxifrages in the rich carpets of mosses and lichens.

Ben Wyvis
Near: Inverness, East Highlands
Map: 20, D2
Web: www.snh.org.uk
The great whaleback ridge of Ben Wyvis, covered in a carpet of woolly hair-moss, is one of the highest mountains in Easter Ross. The reserve is home to many interesting plants and animals. Red and roe deer, pine marten and golden eagle are all found here. The lower slopes support dwarf shrub heath and boglands with plants, such as dwarf birch, cloudberry and dwarf cornel.

Blawhorn Moss
Near: Blackridge Village, near Airdrie, Forth and Borders
Map: 21, D2
Web: www.snh.org.uk
🅿 (ltd)
Peatland was once common in central Scotland, but there's not much left today. Most bogs have been cut for peat, drained for farming or planted for forestry. Blawhorn Moss is one of the few in this area that's still relatively undamaged. The best times to visit are between April and July.

Cairnsmore of Fleet
Near: Newton Stewart, Dumfries and Galloway
Map: 21, C3
Web: www.snh.org.uk
🅿 ⓘ
Rising from heather moorland and peatlands, the granite mass of Cairnsmore and dramatic Clints of Dromore are both popular with walkers. The reserve is important for its upland animals and plants, supporting species such as peregrine falcons, red and black grouse, red deer and feral goats.

Claish Moss
Near: Acharacle, West Highlands
Map: 20, B3
Web: www.snh.org.uk
🚻
This is one of the best examples in Britain of a raised bog that has evolved over the last 8,000 years. The dome-shaped surface holds water up within the peat and a network of pools speckles the bog surface. Pollen grains that have survived in the peat provide a historical record of plantlife since the bog began to form. The best times to visit are between June and September.

Corrie Fee
Near: Kirriemuir, near Dundee Angus and Dundee
Map: 20, D3
Web: www.snh.org.uk
🆆🅲 ⓘ
Located in the south of the Cairngorms National Park, this reserve was sculpted thousands of years ago by ice which left behind corries, cliffs, moraines and a meandering river. The breathtaking landscape is a haven for scarce Arctic-alpine plants, birds and animals able to cope with the challenges of mountain life. Corrie Fee's newly-upgraded path is popular all year round with hill-walkers and crags here are well-known for winter climbing. Watch out for beautiful alpine flowers,

The power of nature

Well known as a treatment for depression, St John's wort grows wild throughout the UK in meadows, hedgerows and woodland. There are many varieties of the plant, all with five-petalled yellow flowers. Look for it on the Isle of Eigg or Marford Quarry in Wales.

Corrie Fee

demonstration of how readily native woodland of birch, alder, willow, rowan and oak recovers when the number of grazing animals is controlled.

Flanders Moss
Near: Thornhill, Argyll and Stirling
Map: 21, C1
Web: www.swt.org.uk
Flanders Moss reserve, lying in the broad flat valley of the Upper Forth, is a small part of a once extensive series of raised peat bogs. Roe deer and adders are common and there is a colony of blue hares. Many butterflies and moths can be seen here. Flanders Moss is one of Scotland's lowest heather areas, with typical moorland birds – grouse, curlew, stonechat and wintering hen harriers. It lies close to the Lake of Menteith which, in winter, attracts thousands of pink-footed geese to the area.

Glen Roy
Near: Fort William,
West Highlands
Map: 20, C3
Web: www.snh.org.uk
P
In 1970, part of Glen Roy was designated an NNR. The glen protects wildlife, including red deer, ravens, buzzards and occasional golden eagles, together with a flora, including pockets of native birch and oak woodland, and flowers, such as primrose and orchids in the meadows at Bohuntine.

Keen of Hamar
Near: Lerwick, Northern Isles
Web: www.snh.org.uk
P
It may look like a moonscape, but the bare stony scree of this reserve supports a unique collection of plants. Here, plantlife has adapted to survive on the rare serpentine rock found on Unst, the

rare mountain willows clinging to the crags, golden eagles and peregrines.

Corrieshalloch Gorge
Near: Ullapool, North Highlands
Map: 20, C1
Web: www.snh.org.uk
A suspension bridge allows you to look down into this spectacular, steep-sided slot gorge. Meltwaters created Corrieshalloch Gorge shortly before glaciers left the area. It's 60 metres deep with near vertical walls and in places it's very narrow, only 10 metres across at the

lip. The River Droma flows through the gorge in a series of waterfalls, the largest of which is the 46-metre Falls of Measach.

Creag Meagaidh
Near: Newtonmore, near Aviemore, West Highlands
Map: 20, D2
Web: www.snh.org.uk
P
The magnificent ice-carved crags of Coire Ardair are just one of the attractions of this varied reserve, stretching from loch shore to mountain top. It provides a vivid

most northerly island in Britain. The star attraction is Edmondston's chickweed, which is found nowhere else in the world. Several more common plants show peculiar serpentine growth forms. The best times to visit are between mid-May and early July.

Kirkconnell Flow

Near: Dumfries, Dumfries and Galloway
Map: 21, D3
Web: www.snh.org.uk

P 🚻

Kirkconnell is a classic example of the raised bogs that have developed on the flat coastal lands around the Solway Firth. Raised bogs form where the ground is poorly drained and represent some of our most ancient landscapes. Cranberry, bog rosemary, adder and large heath butterfly are among the species you can find on this reserve.

Knockan Crag

Near: Ullapool, North Highlands
Map: 20, C1
Web: www.snh.org.uk

P WC ℹ

This is one of the top earth-science sites in Scotland. It is recognised worldwide as the place where scientists first discovered a basic principle of geology. From studying Knockan Crag they realised that forces deep within the Earth can cause great masses of rock to slide up and over much younger rock.

Loch Druidibeg

Near: Lochmaddy, Western Isles
Map: 20, B2
Web: www.snh.org.uk

This reserve is an area of striking contrasts. The colourful flowery machair grassland on the Atlantic coast gradually gives way to the moorland of the interior. Quiet lochans

provide a haven for the distinctive plants and birds of the Uists, which include the corncrake with its persistent rasping call. Visit between May to June for breeding wildfowl, waders and corncrakes, and July for flowers.

Loch Maree Islands

Near: Kinlochewe, near Kishorn Northern Highlands
Map: 20, C2
Web: www.snh.org.uk

🚻

Three large islands and around 40 small ones make up this reserve. They support one of the most ancient and least disturbed fragments of native pinewood left in Scotland, with an unusual patchwork of

well-grown juniper scattered throughout. The islands also provide important breeding sites for black-throated divers. Best time to visit is between May and August. Boat trips operate during the summer.

Moine Mhor

Near: Kilmartin, near Tyvallich, Argyll and Stirling
Map: 21, B1
Web: www.snh.org.uk

P 🚻 🏕

The best views of this reserve are from the Crinan Canal near Bellanoch or the ancient hill fort of Dunadd. From here you can see the waterlogged system of pools and bogs alongside the gentle twists and turns of the River Add. Down at bog level, look out for hen

Glen Affric

Near: Inverness, East Highlands
Map: 20, D2
Web: www.forestry.gov.uk

P WC ℹ

Glen Affric is a very special place. It contains one of the largest ancient Caledonian pinewoods in Scotland as well as lochs, moorland and mountains. This wide range of habitats make Glen Affric a haven for wildlife. There are many rare and special birds, animals and plants found here. Among many others, look out for deer, Scottish crossbills, crested tits and – if you're very lucky – pine marten. Glen Affric has many designations – it is a Caledonian Forest Reserve, an NSA and has recently been chosen as an NNR. The reserve is also a great place for hillwalking, mountain biking on forest tracks, and open-water canoeing.

harriers and curlews, as well as an impressive range of dragonflies. The best times to visit are April to October.

Muir of Dinnet
Near: Aberdeen and Grampian
Map: 20, E2
Web: www.snh.org.uk

P WC ⓘ

Muir of Dinnet is a mosaic of reedbeds, woodland, bogs and heath with lochs Davan and Kinord at its centre. The reserve is home to otter, breeding birds, and wintering wildfowl. In the summer, the mires and bogs are carpeted with red and green sphagnum mosses and alive with dragonflies. You can visit the Vat, a giant pothole carved by a huge meltwater stream during the last Ice Age. The higher, drier slopes of Culblean Hill, along with some of the low-lying drier areas south of Loch Kinord are dominated by ling heather and bearberry heath. Visit in spring and winter for birds.

Rum
Near: Mallaig, Western Isles
Map: 20, B2
Web: www.snh.org.uk

Once the core of a volcano, Rum island was one of the earliest human settlement sites in Scotland. Rum was the base for reintroducing sea eagles to Scotland and, since the late 1950s, it has also been the setting for important red deer research and a native woodland restoration programme. Unusually, a colony of Manx shearwaters lives up a mountain here. Open all year, but the best times to visit for wildlife are between spring and autumn.

Silver Flowe
Near: Newton Stewart, Dumfries and Galloway

Horses playing at Rum

Map: 21, C3
Web: www.snh.org.uk

Visit in the summer for plants, birds and butterflies. Look out for the nationally rare azure hawker dragonfly which likes to sun itself during the summer. This dragonfly is at the most southern limit of its range here in Galloway. Large heath and Scotch argus butterflies can be seen as you walk through the forest tracks. On close inspection you may notice all three different forms of sundew. These plants survive the nutrient poor conditions by catching and digesting insects.

Whitlaw Mosses
Near: Selkirk, near Galashiels, Borders
Map: 21, D2
Web: www.snh.org.uk

P

Four wetland jewels make up Whitlaw Mosses deep in the Selkirk landscape. Each site has its own unique feel. They range from lichen-rich willow scrub to open moss carpets, feathery sedge swamps to sweet-smelling herb meadows and butterfly-favoured grasslands. The sites are

small and fragile, with moss surfaces that can be deceptive and dangerous.

BIRD RESERVES

Baron's Haugh
Near: Motherwell, North Lanarkshire
Map: 21, C2
Web: www.rspb.org.uk

P ♿ 🍽 🏠 🔭

Baron's Haugh is a mosaic of wetland, woodland, and parkland on the banks of the River Clyde. This wildlife gem is an excellent place for everyone to enjoy a range of wildfowl and woodland birds all year round. Four hides overlook the main pool providing good views of ducks and swans and, during a walk through the woods in the spring, you may see and hear woodpeckers, nuthatches and summer migrant warblers. The river often has goosanders and if you are lucky, the chance of seeing kingfishers and otters. During the autumn, there are often large numbers of passage waders, while the resident wildfowl are joined by flocks of wigeons and whooper swans in the winter.

Insh Marshes
Near: Inverness, East Highlands
Map: 20, D2
Web: www.rspb.org.uk
This is one of Europe's most important wetlands.
Around half of all British goldeneyes nest here in spring. You're also likely to see lapwing, redshank and curlew, as well as oystercatchers, snipe and wigeon. The marshes flood in winter and provide roosting and feeding for flocks of whooper swans and greylag geese. The best times to visit are between November and June.

Isle of May
Near: Anstruther, Forth and Borders
Map: 21, D1
Web: www.snh.org.uk
The Isle of May serves as an important research centre for breeding seabirds, such as puffins, guillemots and razorbills, as well as the grey seals that pup here in autumn. The reserve's wildlife are also stars of the big screen. A remote controlled camera on the island beams live pictures to the Scottish Seabird Centre in North Berwick.

Loch Garten, Abernethy
Near: Aviemore, Highland
Map: 20, D2
Tel: 01479 831476
Web: www.rspb.org.uk
Open: April to August, 10am to 6pm; also open for the capercaillie season
Admission: £2/£3
Loch Garten is the ancestral home of the osprey in Scotland. The Osprey Centre, set among the rare native caledonian pinewood of Abernethy Forest, overlooks the nest of these spectacular fish-eating birds of prey. A combination of binoculars, telescopes, CCTV cameras and expert staff help you enjoy the antics of these, most famous of Scottish birds.

DID YOU KNOW?
It is not uncommon to hear robins singing at night.

Loch of Strathbeg
Near: Fraserburgh, Aberdeenshire
Map: 20, E2
Web: www.rspb.org.uk
Open: daily (except 25 December and 1 January)
Admission: free
This wetland encompasses a range of habitats, including Britain's largest dune loch and its adjacent wetland habitats, superb coastal sand dunes, wet and dry grassland and woodland (both deciduous and conifer plantation). The reserve supports spectacular populations of over-wintering wildfowl, including a fifth of the world's population of pink-footed geese. There is also a huge variety and abundance of other wildfowl, including whooper swans, barnacle geese, wigeon and teal, as well as golden plovers and lapwings. In summer, breeding species, such as black-headed gulls, common terns, lapwings and redshanks, provide a noisy spectacle.

Lochwinnoch
Near: Paisley, Renfrewshire
Map: 21, C2
Web: www.rspb.org.uk
Situated within Clyde Muirshiel Regional Park, Lochwinnoch is one of the few remaining wetlands in west Scotland. The visitor centre, with its observation tower and telescopes, offers excellent views over the marshland and loch, where in the winter you may see a variety of wildfowl and waders. In the summer look out for broods of cygnets and ducklings, as well as otters slipping into the water.

Mersehead
Near: Dalbeattie, near Dumfries, Dumfries and Galloway
Map: 21, D3
Web: www.rspb.org.uk
Set between the beautiful Solway coastline and rolling heather-clad hills, this large reserve contains a variety of wildlife habitats, including wet meadows, saltmarsh, farmland and mudflats, on the north shore of the Solway. Birds found here include barnacle geese, lapwings, pintails, reed warblers and skylarks.

Montrose Basin
Near: Montrose, Angus and Dundee
Map: 20, E3
Web: www.montrosebasin.org.uk
From September onwards, several thousand pink-footed geese visit the reserve and in October and November, the numbers peak at more than 35,000 birds. The winter is also the best time to see all the over-wintering wildfowl – it is possible to see around 4,000 wigeon, pintail, mallard and eider ducks. Winter is also the best time to see waders, such as redshank, knot and oystercatcher.

Mull of Galloway
Near: Stranraer, Dumfries and Galloway
Map: 21, B1
Web: www.rspb.org.uk
Open: visitor facilities open from Easter to October
Admission: free

At the most southerly point in Scotland, there are stunning views in all directions. The lichen-encrusted cliffs are home to more than 3,500 nesting seabirds, such as puffins, guillemots, black guillemots, razorbills, kittiwakes and fulmars. The clifftops are covered with coastal heath, which, during the spring and summer, is alive with linnets, wheatears, stonechats and some precious butterflies. Through the summer months, there is a spectacular show of wildflowers: spring squill, sea campion, rock lavender and golden samphire.

Vane Farm
Near: Kinross, Perth and Kinross
Map: 21, D1

Web: www.rspb.org.uk
Open: Visitor centre, daily, 10am to 5pm; hides and trails, daily (except 25 and 26 December, and 1 and 2 January)
Admission: 50p/£3

Set in the beautiful Kinross countryside, only 30 minutes north of Edinburgh, Vane Farm nature reserve is an ideal day out for all ages, from the casual visitor to the enthusiastic birdwatcher. Its range of facilities, activities and wildlife experiences has made it one of the RSPB's most popular nature reserves in Scotland. The reserve is part of the Loch Leven NNR and it is to the loch and surrounding wet grassland that pink-footed and greylag geese, whooper swans and thousands of dabbling ducks are attracted each winter. In summer, ospreys fish in the loch and the grassland provides nesting sites for redshanks, snipe and lapwings.

FORESTS & WOODLAND

Abernethy Forest (including Dell Woods)
Near: Grantown on Spey, East Highlands
Map: 20, D2
Web: www.snh.org.uk

This is the largest native Scot's pinewood in Britain. It offers a unique mix of woodland and northern bog, with a great variety of homes for breeding birds such as capercaillie, crossbill, crested tit, osprey and goldeneye. Abernethy is also

It's all white in the winter...

The ptarmigan is a plump game bird, slightly larger than a grey partridge, that lives in the highest mountains of Scotland. In summer, it is a mixture of grey, brown and black above, with a white belly and wings but in winter, it becomes totally white except for its tail and eye-patch, which remain black. The colour change is caused by the shortening of days and happens even if there is no snow. Stoats and the Scottish Hare also change their colour to white during winter.

well known for its many rare northern insects. Best times to visit are April to July for birds, plants and insects.

Abriachan Wood
Near: Loch Ness, East Highlands
Map: 20, C2
Web: www.wt-woods.org.uk

The permanent streams provide for riparian woodland habitats and there are various heathland and grassland communities present.
There are at least 45 acres of felled pole stage exotic conifers that will provide an open ground habitat for small mammals, birds and woodland butterflies, such as the speckled wood, which is present throughout the site.

Ariundle Oakwood
Near: Acharacle, West Highlands
Map: 20, B3
Web: www.snh.org.uk

Ancient mossy oakwoods like this one were once widespread along the Atlantic coast. The trees are covered in a lush growth of mosses, ferns, liverworts and lichens, which thrive in this damp west coast climate. The woodland is also home to a wide variety of woodland birds. Now Scottish Natural Heritage cares for this vintage reserve, as modern guardian of an ancient place, where both wildlife and people have deep roots. Best times to visit are April to mid-August for tree mosses and ferns.

Balmacaan
Near: Drumnadrochit, near Inverness, East Highlands
Map: 20, C2
Web: www.wt-woods.org.uk

Birch, rowan, ash and alder are freely regenerating in scattered patches within the

Ayr Gorge Woodlands
Near: Failford Village, near Kilmarnock, Strathcylde and Ayrshire
Map: 21, C2
Web: www.swt.org.uk

Beneath the larger broad-leaved trees of this woodland, there is a sparse shrub layer of holly, hazel and rowan. In spring, large swathes of bluebells can be found. Kingfishers, spotted flycatchers and great spotted woodpeckers are regulars among the prolific birdlife. Summer months, from May to July, provide the best opportunity for seeing woodland plants such as wood sorrel, red campion and ransoms. It is also the best time for the woodland mammals – otter, badger, bats and roe deer. Autumn and winter provide views of the spectacular scenery, as well as a mosaic of reds, yellows and oranges as the leaves fall in the colder weather.

wood. There are also extensive areas of bluebells with some primrose, chickweed wintergreen, red campion, dog's mercury and herb robert also present. Wildlife you may see include roe deer and hares.

Butterdean Wood
Near: Edinburgh, Borders
Map: 21, D2
Web: www.woodland-trust.co.uk

A visit to Butterdean Wood might reveal birds, such as chiffchaff, wren, goldcrest, long-tailed tit and willow warbler. The wood provides cover for foxes and roe deer and look out for plants, such as three-leaved wood sorrel, honeysuckle, primrose and the notable bird's-nest orchid.

Cragbank Woods
Near: Hawick, Forth and Borders
Map: 21, D2
Web: www.snh.org.uk
This is the largest area of ancient ash, elm and hazel woodland left in the Scottish Borders. It forms a narrow band running across the steep slopes of Wolfehopelee Hill and has a rich variety of plants and butterflies. Visit in spring for woodland flowers.

Craigellachie
Near: Aviemore, East Highlands
Map: 20, D2
Web: www.snh.org.uk
Directly to the west of Aviemore is the hill of Craigellachie, the lower slopes of which are cloaked in mature birch woodland. Scenic trails through the birchwood provide fine views across Aviemore and Strathspey to the Cairngorms. You may even spot peregrine falcons, which regularly nest on the cliff here.

Crinan Woods
Near: Argyll, Argyll and Stirling
Map: 21, C1
Web: www.wt-woods.org.uk

The tree cover at Crinan Woods is predominately oak and birch with a hazel understorey. Ash, rowan, elm, beech and sycamore also occur. The oak is generally dominant on the eastern and main ridges, with the birch dominating on the western ridge. Ash, beech and elm are fairly scattered, with ash more plentiful on the main and eastern ridges, and beech, elm and sycamore concentrated mainly in the southern end of the wood.

Den Wood

Near: Oldmeldrum, near Aberdeen
Aberdeen and Grampian
Map: 20, E2
Web: www.wt-woods.org.uk

The site forms part of an undulating agricultural landscape of low rolling hills and ridges with occasional rocky outcrops. Buzzard, rabbit and roe deer are commonly seen in the woodland and evidence of the presence of badgers is extensive.

Foulshiels

Near: Stoneyburn, near Airdrie
Forth and Borders
Map: 21, C2
Web: www.wt-woods.org.uk

Foulshiels is a matrix of open ground, seasonal open water, open successional woodland, wet woodland and dense conifer. A wide range of mainly native broad-leaved species is represented with downy birch, willows (goat and grey) and rowan being the most common. Other species include common oak, silver birch, alder, aspen, beech and wild cherry.

Gight Wood

Near: Methlick, near Aberdeen,
Aberdeen and Grampian
Map: 20, E2
Web: www.swt.org.uk

The reserve today is largely a broad-leaved woodland. Tree species native to the area include oak, ash, elm, birch, rowan, bird cherry and wild cherry, which brightens the gorge woods with its wonderful spring blossom. Beneath the tree canopy there is hazel and blackthorn and the ground flora includes a number of locally uncommon plants. Many roe deer live in the wood and there are also fox, badger, red squirrel and hare. If you are very lucky you may see an otter or a heron. Visit April to June for spring blossom or October to November for autumn colours.

Glasdrum Wood

Near: Argyll, Argyll and Stirling
Map: 21, C1
Web: www.snh.org.uk

Mosses and lichens thrive at Glasdrum Wood in the moist Atlantic climate and acid and lime-rich rocks. There are plenty of flowers here, too, including bluebell, primrose, honeysuckle and bugle, whose deep blue blooms are a favourite nectar source for the rare chequered skipper butterfly. Few other places in Scotland can match Glasdrum for variety of butterflies. This mix of small creatures and lush plant growth makes it easy to see why Glasdrum merits special care.

Glen Finglas

Near: Stirling, Stirling and Argyll
Map: 21, C1
Web: www.wt-woods.org.uk

The Glen Finglas estate includes the glens of Finglas, Meann and Casaig, the southern slopes of Stuc Odhar

Know your muntjak

Muntjak deer were only introduced to Britain in the nineteenth century but they have succeeded in colonising large areas and are now probably the most widely distributed deer in England. Although they look as though their front legs are shorter than their back legs, this isn't actually the case it's just a hunkering position that they adopt when they move. They can be found at Whinny Hill Wood and Glencharnoch in Scotland, Broxbourne Woods in Hertfordshire, Whittle Dene in Northumberland and College Wood in Buckinghamshire.

(Lendrick Hill) and land around the village of Brig o' Turk and along the shore of Loch Venachar. The estate is situated in the Trossachs, a popular tourist area, within the Loch Lomond and the Trossachs National Park, on the southern edge of the Highlands and renowned for its mountain, loch and woodland scenery.

Glen Nant

Near: Oban, West Highlands
Map: 21, B1
Web: www.forestry.gov.uk

Glen Nant is a very special place, being a small remnant of the extensive native forests which once covered the Scottish Highlands. The mixed woodlands are dominated by oak and birch, but the more fertile, sheltered areas support ash, elm and hazel. There are rich communities of birds, mammals, insects and plants dependent on this moist sheltered environment.

Glencharnoch Wood

Near: Aviemore, East Highlands
Map: 20, D2
Web: www.wt-woods.org.uk

The field layer is dominated by a heather and blaeberry mosaic with a rich moss layer in places. The wet flushes, marsh areas and permanent streams provide variety with rushes and sedges present and seasonal pools provide additional interest. Wood ants (including the rare narrow-headed ant), red squirrel and roe deer are found within the wood, along with crossbills and crested tits.

Glencripesdale

Near: Loch Sunart, near Acharacle, West Highlands
Map: 20, B3
Web: www.snh.org.uk

It's a long way into this remote woodland on the shores of wild Loch Sunart, but you're rewarded with stunning views and you may even see otters. The damp, shady conditions of the broad-leaved woodland are ideal for a lush growth of ferns, mosses, liverworts and lichens.

DID YOU KNOW?

Hockey sticks, billiard cues and cricket stumps are traditionally made from the wood of the ash tree.

Ledmore and Migdale

Near: Spinningdale, Northern Hlighlglands
Map: 20, D1
Web: www.wt-woods.org.uk

The topography here is extremely diverse, including three distinct hills with slopes of all aspects with broad heath tops in some areas and some dramatic rock outcrops in others. Within the woodland boundaries are three SSSIs – Ledmore Oakwood, Migdale Pinewood and Spinningdale Bog – which contribute to a large and complex site of great value for nature conservation and amenity purposes and which supports a rich variety of flora and fauna.

Moncreiffe Hill

Near: Perth, Perthshire
Map: 20, D3
Web: www.wt-woods.org.uk

Moncreiffe Hill is an igneous escarpment, largely composed of andesite lava, which outcrops as cliffs along the steeper southern edge of the ridge. Roe deer, and red and grey squirrels are present within the wood, with red squirrels most frequently seen in the upper part of the wood,

although anecdotal evidence suggests that sightings of red squirrel have reduced in recent years. There are also foxes and smaller mammals and a range of birds. Rabbit populations are also growing in some areas. For plants and invertebrates, the crags and associated areas provide most interest and diversity.

Pease Dean

Near: Pease Bay, near Berwick-upon-Tweed, Forth and Borders
Map: 21, E2
Web: www.swt.org.uk

The best areas of the reserve for wildlife is where there's a mix of ash, oak and hazel with alders along the burnside. Beneath these trees, dog's mercury, an indicator of ancient woodland, is abundant and, in early summer, the air is thick with the garlic scent of ransoms. Primroses, bluebells and red campion add their colour to this thick layer of wildflowers. Great spotted woodpeckers, treecreepers, dippers and parties of long-tailed tits are regularly seen and marsh tits breed here. In summer, willow warblers, blackcaps, and white-throats fly in from their southern wintering areas.

Rassal Ashwood

Near: Kishorn, Northern Highlands
Map: 20, C2
Web: www.snh.org.uk

Rassal is one of Scotland's few natural ashwoods and the most northerly in Britain. The underlying limestone creates unusually fertile soils, which support many flowering plants. The woodland was once managed to provide feeding for grazing sheep and cattle, and many trees show signs of coppicing or repeated harvesting. The best times to visit are between April and June.

Taynish

Near: Tayvallich, Argyll and Stirling
Map: 21, B2
Web: www.snh.org.uk

P

The ancient deciduous woodland at Taynish is one of the largest in Britain. It lies on a scenic peninsula overlooking Loch Sween and has an atmosphere all of its own. The woodland's dripping ferns and mosses mingle with marshland and grassland to support more than 300 plant species and more than 20 kinds of butterfly. Look out, too, for the colourful marine life of the loch shores. Visit May to June for all woodland wildlife.

Uig Wood

Near: Portree, Skye, Western Isles
Map: 20, B2
Web: www.wt-woods.org.uk

P

The most striking physical attribute of Uig Wood is the steep gorge sides of the Rha and Conon Rivers. These form almost sheer cliffs in places with a spectacular waterfall in the Rha glen. The underlying geology of the area is igneous basaltic rock. This gives rise to a range of soils that are generally fertile. Soils on higher sloping ground are fairly free-draining while those lower down are damp.

Urquhart Bay

Near: Drumnadrochit, near Inverness, East Highlands
Map: 20, D2
Web: www.wt-woods.org.uk

P

Blackcap, willow and wood warbler, spotted and pied flycatcher are present during the summer months with great spotted woodpecker and buzzard all year round.

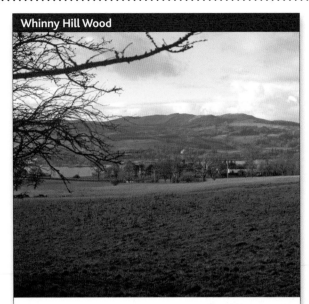

Whinny Hill Wood

Near: Loch Lomond, Balloch, near Dumbarton, Argyll and Stirling
Map: 21, C2
Web: www.wt-woods.org.uk

The woodland comprises largely mature conifer stands including sitka spruce, hybrid larch and Scot's pine, most of which were planted in the 1950s and 1960s. There are smaller stands of semi-mature broad-leaves including ash, beech, sycamore and birch, along with smaller groups of more mature, veteran trees, mainly ash and sycamore. A bird survey was carried out in May 1999. A total of 36 species were observed on the site over a two-day period. Many of these included rare species, on the RSPB conservation list, such as capercaillie, skylark, song thrush, linnet, reed bunting, oystercatcher, lesser black-backed gull (although not for breeding), swallow, blackbird and starling. A large number of rooks are present, although their rookery is not on the property. Buzzards are frequently seen on the site and may be breeding close by. There is an abundant presence of amphibia within the wet areas. Other fauna includes roe deer, rabbits, grey squirrels (which are causing considerable damage to pole stage beech and sycamore) and voles. It is likely that other common fauna are also present on site.

Hare and roe deer are resident in the wood. Important invertebrate species have been noted, including craneflies, snipe fly and hoverflies. European protected species found here include bats and otters.

COASTS, WETLANDS & WATERWAYS

Crinan Canal
From: Ardrishaig to Crinan
Map: 21, B2
Web: www.waterscape.com
Revelling in the title of 'Britain's most beautiful shortcut', the Crinan cuts through the Kintyre peninsula on the way to the Western Isles. Running for nine miles between Ardrishaig and Crinan, the canal was built to save sailing boats from the difficult passage around the Mull of Kintyre. Well used even today, the canal passes through wonderful Scottish scenery that is especially beautiful around the Crinan Basin.

Forth and Clyde Canal
From: Glasgow to Grangemouth and the Forth, near Glasgow
Map: 21, C2
Web: www.waterscape.com
As well as supporting the mute swan, mallard and moorhens, Dullatur Marsh beside the canal support breeding and visiting wading birds, water rail, wetland flowers and insects. Otters frequent the canal alongside pipistrelle and Daubenton's bats. The canal is also home to the extremely rare Bennett's pondweed, which is only found in the UK on the Forth and Clyde, and the rare tufted loosestrife.

Forvie
Near: Aberdeen
Map: 20, E2
Web: www.snh.org.uk
This huge area of sand dunes and coastal heath

Caledonian Canal

From: Fort William to Inverness
Map: 20, C2 and D2
Web: www.waterscape.com

The Great Glen, through which the Caledonian Canal runs, is a popular stop-off for migrating seabirds on their way between the Atlantic Ocean and the North Sea. Other birds spotted include buzzards, siskins and lesser spotted woodpeckers. More rarely you might catch sight of eagles and ospreys. On the ground, foxes and red squirrels might just cross your path – or even a wildcat. The red deer is still seen by locals and, sadly, considered rather a pest. Be careful not to dazzle one with your headlights. Many locations along the canal have been designated SSSIs. Some of the species you will spot along Glen Tarff SSSI include: unusual flowering plants, such as wood crane's-bill and greater wintergreen, and a rare insect called *Bolitophagus reticulates*. You might catch a glimpse of the shy sedge warbler or elusive reed bunting along South Laggan Fen SSSI. For approximately seven miles along the banks of Loch Ness, rare butterflies and birds inhabit the striking mix of trees that make up the Easter Ness Forest SSSI. You will also see juniper shrubs. Along Urquhart Bay Woods SSSI, alder tends to dominate the wetter ground while the variety of other species on the gently rising land include ash, gean, wych elm, white willow and bird cherry. Shrubs include sallow and blackthorn. In addition, there is a good woodland and wetland bird community and characteristic insect fauna. The gorge woodland of Inverfarigaig SSSI occupies a deep ravine cut through red sandstone rock and is home to a number of beetle species. The Beauly Firth has long been considered an important national site for its wildfowl and waders, while at low tide the sand banks within the firth are used for seals.

Loch Ness, one of the lochs making up the Great Glen

---

lies next to the Ythan Estuary. The estuary, riverside and seacliffs make this a particularly rich area for a variety of plants and wildlife. In particular, it supports the largest colony of breeding eider duck in Britain and attracts large numbers of geese and waders in winter.

Hermaness

Near: Baltasound, Northern isles
Web: www.snh.org.uk

ⓘ

Overlooking Muckle Flugga, Britain's most northerly point, Hermaness provides a wonderful haven for more than 100,000 seabirds. Some 16,000 pairs of gannets and more than 50,000 puffins come to nest each year on the dramatic seacliffs, offshore arches and stacks. Inland, the moors are home to the third-largest colony of great skuas in the world. The raucous cries and smell of birdlife provide an experience you're unlikely to forget in a hurry. The best times to visit are from mid-May to mid-July.

Loch a' Mhuilinn

Near: Ullapool, Highlands
Map: 20, C1
Web: www.snh.org.uk

Ⓟ

The most northern remnant of native oak woodland in Britain survives on this reserve. The stunting effects of westerly gales are clearly visible with some of the oaks reduced to a creeping form near the sea. Loch a' Mhuilinn also features grassland, peatbog, freshwater and seashore habitats, which help to attract a wide range of wildlife. The best times to

Falls of Clyde

Near: Lanark, Strathclyde and Ayrshire
Map: 21, D2
Web: www.swt.org.uk

[wc] [i] [icon]

Spring is a great time to visit Falls of Clyde if you want to join the ranger on badger watches as the cubs begin to emerge from their underground setts in spring. Early summer brings views of the young peregrines. The five species of bat residing at Falls of Clyde may be observed on evening strolls throughout the summer. The river's edge is an excellent place to see summer flowers, such as campions, water avens and marsh marigolds. You may also spot a dipper or a kingfisher. In autumn, the woodland is a mosaic of colours and a good time for fungal forays. With winter the sightings of resident otters increase.

visit are spring for woodland flowers or summer for the dragonflies.

Loch Ardinning

Near: Strathblane, near Glasgow, Argyll and Stirling
Map: 21, C2
Web: www.swt.org.uk

[icon]

The northern part of the loch is densely populated with reeds, rushes and sedges, the luxuriant growth resulting from the sheltered, shallow conditions. To the west of the loch lies a wet wood, consisting of mature willows, birch and alder. The loch is also a haven for a variety of over-wintering and breeding wildfowl. The water lobelia is a local speciality, flowering in the shallows in July. Visit May to July for wildflowers, insects and breeding birds and the rest of the year for wildfowl, moorland and woodland birds.

Loch Awe

Near: Kilchrenan, near Oban, Argyll and Stirling
Map: 21, B1
Web: www.loch-awe.com

Located in a stunning part of Scotland, the third-largest freshwater loch in Scotland blends in well with the unspoilt scenery. Loch Awe stands 117 feet above sea level in the charming and delightful county of Argyllshire. It is around 24 miles long, yet is surprisingly narrow. The loch is a haven for anglers and is renowned for its trout fishing. Salmon also pass through as they head to the River Orchy.

Loch Fleet

Near: Dornoch, near Spinningdale, northern Highlands
Map: 20, D1
Web: www.swt.org.uk

[P] [icon]

This reserve occupies a stunning coastal location where a river flows through a tidal basin. Common seals regularly haul out on the mudflats at low tide and you can enjoy great views of wildfowl and waders. Sand dunes and coastal heath are rich in wildflowers and the attractive pinewood plantations provide a home for flowers more usually seen in ancient native pinewoods. Visit all year round for birds and spring to summer for flowers.

Loch Katrine

Near: Stronachlachar, near Stirling, Argyll and Stirling
Map: 21, C1
Web: www.waterscape.com

Loch Katrine is located on the southern edge of the Highlands, contributing to the stunning scenery of the Loch Lomond and The Trossachs National Park. Take a trip on the *SS Sir Walter Scott*, the only surviving screw steamer in regular passenger service in Scotland, which has sailed this Loch for more than 100 years. Take in historic landmarks, such as Ellen's Isle, Silver Strand, Portnellan, the Royal Cottage and the Factor's Island, plus the breathtaking views of the backdrop of The Trossachs from the water.

Loch Leven

Near: Glasgow
Map: 21, C2
Web: www.waterscape.com

Golden eagles still soar above ancient woodlands which witnessed the life of Robert the Bruce and the imprisonment of Mary Queen of Scots. Loch Leven is a pleasure ground for the outdoors enthusiast. Everything from walking to rock-climbing, mountain-biking and canoeing can be enjoyed here. Even skiers and snowboarders find plenty to entertain them on the popular slopes of Glencoe. It is not surprising that this powerful landscape is so favoured by Hollywood – the blockbuster films *Highlander*, *Rob Roy* and *Braveheart* were all filmed here.

Loch Linnhe

Near: Fort William, Highlands
Map: 20, C3
Web: www.waterscape.com

Visitors to Loch Linnhe can't fail to notice the

Scotland

protective Ben Nevis standing tall along the head of the loch, dominating the rustic landscape. The southern end of the loch around Lismore is excellent for big pollack, giant skate, wrasse and conger. During summer months you can expect to find huge shoals of mackerel and see porpoises, dolphins and the occasional minke whale.

Loch Lomond
Near: Inchcailloch, near Glasgow, Argyll and Stirling
Map: 21, C1
Web: www.snh.org.uk

P WC ⚲

This loch is famous for its beautiful wooded shores and islands. Ancient woodland, including rowan, ash, oak, sycamore and beech, cloaks Loch Lomond and is a haven for wildlife, such as eagles, hawks and peregrine falcons. Wild deer can often be found swimming here. The forests provide cover for wildcats and there is even a colony of wallabies on one of the islands. Bluebells and wild garlic carpet the woodlands in spring, when migrant warblers, flycatchers and redstarts start to return. The reserve also includes the wetlands around the mouth of the River Endrick. These flood most winters and host good numbers of wildfowl. The best time to visit is between May and September for woodland wildlife, and autumn to spring for wildfowl.

Loch Tummel
Near: Pitlochry, Perthshire
Map: 20, D3
Web: www.waterscape.com
The outstanding landscape of Loch Tummel is in an area designated an NSA. Seen from the famous Queens' View (as in Mary of Scots and Victoria) it truly is a sight to behold.

Monach Isles
Near: North Uist, Western Isles
Map: 20, B2
Web: www.snh.org.uk
Every autumn these five islands play host to one of the most important breeding colonies of Atlantic grey seals in the world. The Monach Isles are also home to large numbers of seabirds, including black guillemots and terns, while the machair displays a rich variety of plants. The best time to visit for birds and flowers is May to August.

Noss
Near: Lerwick, Northern Isles
Web: www.snh.org.uk

WC ⓘ

Take a boat trip to this island where thousands of seabirds and wonderful scenery guarantee a memorable experience. Some 45,000 guillemots, 7,000 pairs of gannets and several thousand fulmars, kittiwakes and puffins crowd its noisy ledges during the breeding season. Look out for seals in the surrounding seas and marauding great skuas

Isle of Eigg

Near: Mallaig, Western Isles
Map: 20, B2
Web: www.isleofeigg.org

This is well worth a trip from the mainland. In spring, the hazel scrub woodland becomes home to a generous carpet of bluebells, wild garlic, wood anemone, wood sorrel and primroses. Further afield, golden eagles, buzzards and ravens can be seen. The summer months herald a whole new plantlife, with honeysuckle and enchanter's nightshade taking over in the woodlands. Bird visitors include cuckoo, whinchat, white-throat, willow warbler and twite, while 18 species of butterfly and many dragonflies and damselflies can regularly be seen. Between July and September, minke whales are also a frequent sight on the ferry crossings over to the island with as many as seven being seen at one time. As the days start to get shorter and the temperature cooler, great northern divers and jacksnipe can be spotted, as well as fieldfare, snow bunting and brambling.

PICTURED: Willow warbler

Scotland

in the moorland interior. Visit mid-May to mid-July for breeding seabirds. Seals, otters and flowers are best spotted before the end of August.

River Cart
Near: Paisley, Glasgow
Map: 21, C2
Web: www.waterscape.com
The River Cart into Paisley is navigable as a tributary of the Clyde. The White Cart flows from Castle Semple Loch and the Black Cart rises in East Renfrewshire. Further upstream, otters have recently been spotted.

River Clyde
From: Lanarkshire Hills through Glasgow to Atlantic Ocean
Map: 21, C2
Web: www.waterscape.com
Synonymous with Govan, which once produced a quarter of the world's ships, the Clyde's fortunes were largely based on the 29.5 miles from Cambuslang to Dumbarton. It derived much success from having a major European port facing the Americas. The Clyde is still a busy port area. The area around Glasgow has undergone much modernisation and is once more accessible by inland vessels following the restoration of the Forth and Clyde and Union Canals.

River Earn
From: Perth to Kinross
Map: 21, D1
Web: www.waterscape.com
The Earn is a tributary of the River Tay. There is good salmon and trout fishing to be found here.

River Leven
From: Loch Lomond to Glasgow
Map: 21, C2
Web: www.waterscape.com

River Forth
From: Stirling to the Sea
Map: 21, C1 to D2
Web: www.waterscape.com
The River Forth and borders are rich with a variety of wildlife and habitats. The fens have aquatic plants, such as water lilies and mare's-tails, vegetation in the form of creeping willow and black bay, a rare Scottish reed and the northern marsh orchid. Invertebrates like dragonflies and damselflies, as well as rosebay willowherb, roe deer, sparrowhawks, foxes and kestrels can be seen here. There are also more than 50 species of water beetles and flies, some unique to this area. The Forth estuary has more waders and wildfowl than any other estuary in Scotland. There is a large population of feeding river lampreys – adult and juvenile – in the Firth of Forth. Their existence helps to aerate and stabilise silt beds, and they are a food source for riverine birds, mammals and other wildlife. Grassland areas are awash with colour with the likes of lady's bedstraw, red fescue, cowslip, Scottish bluebells and various orchids, to name a few. Moorland and hills sport red grouse, snow bunting and golden plover, although sadly hen harrier and peregrine falcon numbers are on the decrease. Badgers and foxes dodge poisonous adders and woodlands here display all sorts of trees, from oak and hazel to birch and willow, towering above more than 300 species of plants.

The River Leven is Loch Lomond's connection to the Clyde. Though not currently navigable, it has been proposed for restoration.

River Nith
From: Dumfries to The Solway Estuary
Map: 21, D3
Web: www.waterscape.com
The River Nith, in Dumfries and Galloway, has superb salmon and trout fisheries. The upper reaches are accessible by canoe.

Rona and Sula Sgeir
Near: Butt of Lewis, Western Isles
Map: 20, B1
Web: www.snh.org.uk
Some 130,000 seabirds throng these remote islands during the breeding season, including storm petrel,

Leach's petrel, gannet and guillemot. Rona is also internationally important for its breeding grey seal population and there are many remains of former human settlements.

St Abb's Head
Near: Berwick-upon-Tweed, Forth and Borders
Map: 21, E2
Web: www.snh.org.uk
Visit this reserve for its stunning cliff scenery, which supports large colonies of breeding kittiwakes, fulmars, guillemots, razorbills, shags and puffins. Wonderful spring flowers form part of the rich but fragile coastal grasslands. The steep cliffs drop into the clear seawaters below, which support a varied marine life that attracts large numbers of underwater divers.

River Tay

From: Ben Lui to North Sea
Web: www.waterscape.com
Map: 21, D1

Renowned for its fantastic salmon fishing, the River Tay winds its way through varied countryside from its humble beginnings in the quaint village of Kenmore. Throughout its lengthy journey covering a total of 120 miles – making it the longest river in Scotland – the River Tay passes through lochs, meanders down hills and tumbles through villages and towns. An abundance of wildlife has made its home in or along the River Tay. Hiding below the bridges are grey wagtails, while the moorhen can be spotted along the river in the spring – an unusual sight as the birds are rarely seen in Scotland, Wales or northern England. A common sight along the Tay are the many species of swans, ducks and geese. Both black-headed gulls and herring gulls are often seen hunting and swooping for fish throughout the year. Visitors to the river will often see magnificent herons, standing motionless in the shallow water by the Tay islands, awaiting their next meal. Perhaps the most surprising inhabitant of the river is the seal, which has often been seen catching salmon throughout the winter along with otters which have been spotted on rare occasions.

River Tay

St Cyrus

Near: Montrose, Aberdeen and Grampian
Map: 20, E3
Web: www.snh.org.uk
WC ⓘ

The cliffs and dunes of St Cyrus support a distinctive range of plants, including many southern species. The reserve is also noted for its rich variety of insects, particularly butterflies and more than 200 kinds of moth. Breeding birds include stonechats and skylarks and you're also likely to see fulmars nesting on the cliffs. Best times to visit are in spring and summer for plants and breeding birds or in winter for wading birds.

Staffa

Near: Mull, Western isles
Map: 21, B1
Web: www.snh.org.uk

The uninhabited island of Staffa includes the famous Fingal's Cave. The island's distinctive six-sided columns of rock are formed from basalt, the same as the Giant's Causeway in Northern Ireland. During spring and early summer, the cliffs and grassy slopes provide nesting sites for various seabirds including guillemots, razorbills and puffins. The best times to visit are spring and summer.

Tentsmuir

Near: Tayport, near Dundee, Forth and Borders

Map: 20, D3
Web: www.snh.org.uk

The sand dunes and beach at the mouth of the Tay estuary are one of the fastest growing parts of Scotland. This dynamic coastline is important for seaduck, waders and wildfowl, along with the common and grey seals that haul out here. Inland, colourful butterflies light up the grassland and dunes in summer, while Morton Lochs attract ducks and waders. The best times to visit are spring to summer for flowers, and all year round for birds.

WWT Caerlaverock
Near: Dumfriesshire, Dumfries and Galloway

Map: 21, D3
Web: www.wwt.org.uk
P (££),

Open since 1970, Caerlaverock is famous for the thousands of Barnacle geese that arrive here from the Arctic each year. It is a wild reserve with 1,385 acres of high quality wetlands that play host to a wide range of waterbirds and the UK's most northerly population of natterjack toads.

NOT SO WILD

Auchingarrich Wildlife Centre
Address: Comrie, near Perth, Perthshire PH6 2JS
Map: 20, D3
Tel: 01764 679 469
Web: www.auchingarrich.co.uk
Open: daily, 10am to dusk
Admission: £4/£5.50
P (££)

Auchingarrich Wildlife Centre boasts wild animals, a wildbird hatchery and woodland walks. There is a deer park and creatures to be seen include otters, prairie dogs, coatamundis, swans, meerkats, peacocks, porcupines, crowned cranes, yaks, rabbits, racoons, pine martens and the elusive Scottish wildcat. In addition to the animals and birds, there is a collection of hens wandering around everywhere. Within Auchingarrich there is an enclosed falconry area.

Black Isle Wildlife and Country Park
Address: Drumsmittal, North Kessock, Ross-shire IV1 3XF
Map: 20, D2
Tel: 01463 731656
Web: www.visitscotland.com
Open: March to November, 10am to 6pm
P (inc),

If you are interested in animals and birds or just the countryside, you will enjoy a visit to this quiet corner of the Black Isle, an ideal place for all the family. Feed the friendly ducks, geese and swans on the many ponds. Make contact with goats and stroke the rabbits. Also resident are pot-bellied pigs and rare sheep and cattle.

Blair Drummond Safari Park
Address: Blair Drummond, Stirling FK9 4UR
Map: 21, C1
Tel: 01786 841 456
Web: www.safari-park.co.uk
Open: daily, 10am to 4.30pm
Admission: £6.50/£10

Blair Drummond Safari Park opened in 1970 in the grounds of Blair Drummond house. A visit to the park combines a mixture of driving through animal reserves, then parking and walking through pets farm, playing in one of the many adventure areas, taking in the sea lion and falconry displays and visiting chimp island. Wildlife to see includes lemur, elephants, tigers, chimpanzees, deer, meerkats and bison.

Camperdown Wildlife Centre
Address: Dundee, Angus DD2 4TF
Map: 20, D3
Tel: 01382 431806
Web: www.camperdownpark.com
Open: daily, 10am to 3.30/ 4.30pm
Admission: £2.50/£3

The wildlife centre is one of Dundee's most popular attractions and is home to around 50 species of animals, birds and reptiles. Meet the regular residents – Comet and Star, the European brown bears from the wilderness of Russia. Other highlights include lynx, wolves and one of Britain's rarest mammals – the pine marten.

Cowal Bird Centre

Address: Lochan Wood, Sandbank Rd, Dunoon, Argyll PA23 8QR
Map: 21, C2
Tel: 01369 707999
Web: www.cowal-dunoon.com
Open: daily, 10am to 6pm
Admission: £3/£4

Within one mile of Dunoon town centre on the Sandbank road, Cowal Bird Centre is a delightful place for both young and old. Here you will encounter many types of birds, such as peacocks, rheas, macaws, parakeets, ducks, geese, eagle owls and tawny owls, and much more. You will also see donkeys, goats, rabbits and deer.

Edinburgh Butterfly and Insect World

Address: Dobbies Garden World, Lasswade, Edinburgh EH18 1AZ
Map: 21, D2
Tel: 0131 663 4932.
Web: www.edinburgh-butterfly-world.co.uk
Open: daily, summer 9.30am to 5.30pm; winter 10am to 5pm
Admission: £3.60/£4.70

Whatever the weather, summer or winter, stroll through the wonderful world of an exotic rainforest, a landscape of tropical plants surrounding waterfalls and pools. You can marvel at the industrious leaf-cutting ants and handle weird and wonderful minibeasts (if you dare). Not to be handled, but fascinating to view, are a selection of deadly scorpions. At any one time, 30 to 40 butterfly species can be seen, from the brilliant blue of the South American morpho, to the transparent glasswing, to the scarlet, yellow and black postmen. On display are millipedes, crabs, spiders, scorpions and many types of insect. There are poison arrow frogs, various snakes, including royal pythons, tarantula and some large lizards. At regular intervals throughout the day, handling sessions are held, giving you the opportunity to get to grips with some of the animals.

Edinburgh Zoo

Address: Edinburgh EH12 6TS
Map: 21, D2
Tel: 0131 334 9171
Web: www.edinburghzoo.org.uk
Open: daily, April to September, 9am to 6pm; October and March, 9am to 5pm; November to February 9am to 4.30pm
Admission: £7/£10

Edinburgh Zoo, the largest managed wildlife attraction in Scotland, is committed to the highest standards of animal welfare, conservation and environmental education. In just one day, you can see more than 1,000 wonderful animals in a beautiful parkland setting on the outskirts of Edinburgh. Edinburgh Zoo is one of Europe's leading centres of conservation, education and research. There are a variety of amphibians, birds, fish, invertebrates, mammals and reptiles to see, including owls, eagles, penguins, tigers, polar bears, lions and jaguars.

Falconry Scotland

Address: Jedforest Falconry, 4 Mervinslaw Farm Cottages, Jedburgh, near Hawick TD8 6PL
Map: 21, D2
Tel: 01835 840393
Web: www.falconryscotland.co.uk
Open: daily, May to August, 10am to 5.30pm; September to 28 October, 11am to 4.30pm; other times by appointment
Admission: £2.50/£4

Falconry Scotland provides opportunities for handling falcons, hawks, owls and eagles. Coupled with the

---

Royal Botanic Garden Edinburgh

Address: Royal Botanic Garden Edinburgh, 20A Inverleith Row, Edinburgh EH3 5LR
Map: 21, D2
Tel: 0131 552 7171
Web: www.rbge.org.uk
Open: Daily, from 10am [except 25 December & 1 January]
Admission: Entry to the garden is free. Admission charge for Glasshouses £1/£3

RBGE's world-renowned living collection, around 16,000 species strong, is probably the second-richest collection of its kind in the world. It represents a number of families (such as Ericaceae, Gesneriaceae and Umbelliferae) and geographical regions (such as China, SE Asia, Chile and Bhutan). It is especially rich in rare and endangered plants, with 1,314 species of conservation importance. British plants are well represented, as are non-flowering plants: there's a Cryptogamic Sanctuary at Dawyck and complementary Bryophyte Sanctuary at Benmore. There are 62 Champion Trees in the collection. The landscapes at each of the four Gardens are both diverse and complementary.

---

experience of the deer herds and rare breeds of sheep, pigs, cattle, chickens, ducks and others at Jedforest Deer and Farm Park, this is a good family day out.

Galloway Wildlife Conservation Park

Address: Lochfergus Plantation, Kirkcudbright, Dumfries and Galloway DG6 4XX
Map: 21, C3
Tel: 01557 331645
Web: www.gallowaywildlife.co.uk
Open: weekends, December to January, 10am to 3pm
Admission: £3/£4.50
P (££), 🚻 🔧

Galloway Wildlife Conservation Park covers 27 acres of mixed woodland and is the wild animal conservation centre of southern Scotland. A varied collection of nearly 150 animals from all over the world can be seen within the peaceful and natural settings, where the woodland has been tailored to provide large and imaginative enclosures. There is a constant programme of construction and improvement to facilities for the animal, birds and visitors.

Highland Wildlife Park

Address: Kincraig, Kingussie, near Aviemore PH21 1NL

> ### DID YOU KNOW?
>
> A mole's tunnel can be up to 200m long.

Map: 20, D2
Tel: 01540 651270
Web: www.highlandwildlifepark.org
Open: daily, April to October, 10am to 6/7pm; November to March, 10am to 4pm
Admission: £6.75/£9.50
🚻 🖥

Highland Wildlife Park offers an opportunity to experience Scottish wildlife past and present. Here, you will see an amazing variety of animals including red deer and mouflon; after this you can step back in time and 'meet' the animals that our ancestors must have known hundreds, even thousands, of years ago. You can drive around the main reserve as well as explore the area by foot.

Knowetop Community Farm

Address: 113 Castlehill Road, Castlehill, Dumbarton, Strathclyde G82 5AT
Map: 21, C2
Tel: 01389 732734
Web: www.knowetopcommunityfarm.co.uk
Open: daily, 9am to 4pm (except 25 December)

Admission: free
🚻 🖥

Activities at Knowetop Community Farm include organic farming, animal husbandry, recycling, community composting, environmental awareness and vegetable growing using organic principles. Animals to see include sheep, pigs, ducks, chickens, goats, rabbits, guinea pigs and horses. There are also some rare animals like Guernsey goats, Aberdeen Angus cross heifers, Gloucester old spot pigs and an assortment of unusual poultry breeds.

Lamont Farm

Address: Barrhill Road, Erskine, near Paisley PA8 6BX
Map: 21, C2
Tel: 0141 812 5335
Web: www.erskinetown.org.uk
Open: 10.30am to 4.30pm

Among the many species at Lamont farm are Nigerian pygmy goats, Chinese geese and Vietnamese pot-bellied pigs. A weekly kids' club encourages children to get more involved with the running of the farm, helping with grooming, tree-planting and wildflower gardening.

Wales

So much of Wales is rural and relatively undisturbed by the invasion of man, that wildlife thrives here, and there are many fantastic settings in which to observe it.

Each area of the country has its own National Park, from the Brecon Beacons in the east, to the Pembrokeshire Coast in the west and Snowdonia in the north. Many other areas are designated AONBs, such as the Gower peninsula, south of Cardiff and the Wye Valley on the border with England. Wherever you go to watch wildlife, you'll be wowed by the views you find.

Habitats vary considerably throughout the country. In the high peaks of Snowdonia, for example, there are alpine plants and a Snowdon lily that is unique to the area. While down on the coast of Pembrokeshire, anemones, barnacles and seaweed thrive in the rockpools and seals are often sighted close to shore and even, on occasion, up on the beaches.

In between the high and low areas of the country there are mountain ranges such as the Clwydian Range that span all habitats from limestone grassland to heathland, woodland and river valleys. Each area has its own species of interest such as the orchids and rock-rose that grow in the limestone grassland and the upland birds such as stonechats and merlins that are found in the higher heathland.

A night-time walk around many lowland areas of Wales will often reveal glow worms, especially in June or July. These are also the best months for seeing puffins which are found at various sites in Wales such as Cardigan Bay, Holy Island and Skomer Island off the coast of Pembrokeshire.

Skomer Island is a little like the mini-Galapagos of Wales, as the stretch of water that separates it from the mainland means no predators such as dogs, cats, foxes or rodents live there and, as a result, it is a haven for ground-nesting birds. The island is covered with burrows of the manx shearwater. There are thought to be around 165,000 breeding pairs on the 730-acre island.

The variety of plants in Wales is vast, and a look through the entries for this region will

reveal the many interesting varieties to be found, such as the hoary rockrose on cliffs, and different types of moss in the area's many woodlands.

PICTURED: Left: Snowdonia
Above: A bottlenose dolphin

Not to be missed

● **Brecon Beacons**
Stunning scenery from mountaintops to river valleys and a wonderful variety of birds in one of Wales's most magical areas.

● **Dyfi National Nature Reserve**
With its wildfowl, birds of prey, mammals and unusual flora, this reserve is one you'll want to visit again and again.

● **Elan Valley**
Keep quiet around the riverbanks and you might spot otters, polecats, minks, stoats and a large population of reptiles and amphibians.

● **Gower**
This coastal corner in the south of Wales has habitats of heath, grassland, saltwater marsh, dunes and oak woodland and hundreds of birds to go with them.

● **National Wetlands Centre**
If you want one site that guarantees good hides and plenty of birdlife then the WWT's site in Wales is it – and there are plenty of themed events throughout the year.

● **Pembrokeshire Coast**
This spectacular landscape of rugged cliffs, sandy beaches, wooded estuaries and wild inland hills is one of Britain's jewels and quite simply nature at its best.

NATIONAL PARKS Brecon Beacons

Mid-Wales
Map: 22, C4
Web: www.breconbeacons.org

P WC ♿ ⓘ ✉ ⛲

Brecon Beacons National Park covers an area of 520 square miles and is the first national park in the UK to achieve Geopark status. All sorts of birds can be found here. In the west of the park you can see red kites wheeling overhead, and in the uplands there are red grouse in the heather. You can see golden plovers and curlews in the grasslands, with ring ouzels and peregrine falcons (pictured right) near the cliffs and crags. Skylarks, pipits, buzzards, bullfinch, spotted and pied flycatchers, yellow-hammers, barn owls, kingfishers, dippers and colonies of martins can also be spotted. Many of the reservoirs provide refuge for wintering wildfowl and waders, such as pintails, wigeon, teal, goldeneye and lapwings. Other wildlife includes otters, salmon leaping on the River Usk, bats on the canal and lizards on the heaths and grasslands. Alongside the purple heather you can find insectivorous plants such as sundew and butterwort.

Talybont Reservoir, Brecon Beacons

Pembrokeshire Coast
South-west Welsh coast
Map: 22, A4
Web: www.pcnpa.org.uk

Pembrokeshire is a spectacular landscape of rugged cliffs, sandy beaches, wooded estuaries and wild inland hills. Crab, dogwhelk, bladderwrack seaweed, anemone and barnacles can all be found on the beaches, and seals are known to come to the shore. Other key species include greater horseshoe bats, barn owls, seabirds, choughs, the marsh fritillary butterfly and golden-haired lichen, while the woodlands in north Pembrokeshire are home to dormice. The Gwaun Valley is home to a huge variety of birds, including redstarts, dippers, pied flycatchers, nuthatches, tree pipits, buzzards and sparrowhawks.

Snowdonia National Park
North-west Wales
Map: 22, B2 and C2
Web: www.eryri-npa.co.uk

Snowdonia is the second-largest national park in the UK after the Lake District. It covers 823 square miles and contains 17 NNRs. With its varied landscape and wide range of habitats, high mountains, wooded valleys, rivers, lakes and coastline, Snowdonia is populated by a wide range of wildlife, incuding chough, buzzard, marsh fritillary and otter. Among the Arctic-alpine plants found in the high peaks, the Snowdon lily is unique to Snowdon, so, too, is the Snowdon or rainbow beetle.

AONBs/AoHNEs

Anglesey (Ynys Mon)
Near: Bangor, Gwynedd
Map: 22, B2
Web: www.anglesey.gov.uk

The entire coastline of Ynys Mon is designated as an AONB. Some of the beaches are recognised as being among the best in Great Britain and Europe. Anglesey has a wealth of wildlife, such as choughs, grey seals, sea lavender and silver-studded

Snowdonia

blue butterflies. There are also many areas that are protected for their nature conservation value, such as Newborough Warren NNR.

Clwydian Range (Bryniau Clwyd)
Near: Prestatyn, Denbyshire
Map: 22, C1
Web: www.clwydianrangeaonb. org.uk

Clwydian Range is a 22-mile-long chain of hills between the vale of Clwyd to the west and the Dee Estuary to the east. Habitats, such as limestone grassland, heathland, woodland and river valleys, are special features of the AONB. Limestone grassland is a habitat with many wildflowers, such as cowslip, rockrose, autumn gentian and orchids. These in turn are home to a variety of invertebrates, including the common blue butterfly and

the red-spotted burnet moth. Heathlands are special places for upland birds, such as stonechat, tree pipit, hen harrier and merlin. Otters and water voles depend on the waterways. Among the mammals here are the brown hare, dormouse and bat, while lapwing, curlew and yellow-hammer are included in the birds.

Gower (Gwyr)
Near: Swansea
Web: www.swansea.gov.uk
Gower was the first AONB to be designated as such. It has a varied natural environment of heath, grassland, fresh and saltwater marsh, dunes and oak woodland and is a great place for birdwatching: species that can be seen include alpine swifts, ring-necked ducks, warblers (yellow browned, Cetti's and Dartford), velvet scooters, snow bunting, osprey and chough.

Lleyn (Llyn)
Near: Pwllheli, Caernarfonshire
Map: 22, B2
Web: www.wildaboutbritain.co.uk

Lleyn AONB is mainly coastal, but further inland its highest points are the north's volcanic peaks. The countryside has narrow lanes and white-washed farms and includes stretches of ancient open common. Ynys Enlli (Bardsey Island) is just one of Lleyn's many wildlife sites, home to the seabird sanctuary and grey seals. Lleyn also has family farms raising sheep and cattle.

Wye Valley (Dyffryn Gwy)
Near: Monmouth, Monmouthshire, and Ross-on-Wye, Herefordshire
Map: 22, C4
Web: www.wyevalleyaonb.org.uk
The Wye Valley is important for its rich wildlife habitats. Species include lesser horseshoe bats, peregrine falcons, ravens, rare white

Wildlife Britain **269**

Wales

beam, nightjar and lesser-known fish, such as shad and twaite. In September 2006, it was reported that one colony of lesser horseshoe bats in the area had reached record numbers, with some 890 bats in a small stone barn. This is believed to be one of the largest colonies of lesser horseshoe bats in Europe.

Delicate... in more ways than one

The marsh fritillary is one of Britain's most attractive butterflies with its orange and black markings that look like a leaded stained glass window. Sadly, it is also one of Britian's most threatened butterflies as loss of habitat causes rapidly declining numbers. Found at Butser Hill, south east, Pembrokeshire Coast, Wales and on Salisbury Plain in the south west.

NATURE RESERVES

Allt-yr-yn
Near: Newport
Map: 22, C5
Web: www.newport.gov.uk
P
This reserve has ancient woodland, meadows and five ponds. Species that have been recorded in Allt-yr-yn include butterflies and dragonflies, a variety of other invertebrates, smooth and common newts and flora, such as broad-leaved helleborines.

Bishops Wood LNR
Near: Caswell, Swansea
Map: 22, B5
Web: www.swansea.gov.uk
i
Bishops Wood covers 46 acres of woodland and limestone grassland. Guided tours can be arranged.

Blaen-y-Weirglodd
Near: Betwsy-y-Coed, Gwynedd
Map: 22, B2
Web: www.wildlifetrust.org.uk/northwales
Blaen-y-Weirglodd has a rich variety of colourful bog plants and supports snipe in winter. The 10-acre peat bog is a habitat once common in the valleys of Wales.

Burfa Bog
Near: Leominster, Radnorshire
Map: 22, C3

Web: www.radnorshirewildlife trust.org.uk
P P
In spring, Burfa Bog is carpeted by marsh marigold and in summer, the wet grassland contains marsh valerian, heath spotted orchid and ragged robin. Birds include spotted and pied flycatchers, redstarts and buzzards. In autumn, waxcap fungi, betony and devil's-bit scabious can be seen on dry grassland. Otters and water voles have been seen on the brook.

Cors Goch
Near: Bangor, Gwynedd
Map: 22, B2
Web: www.wildlifetrust.org.uk/northwales
P P
Cors Goch attracts a number of different birds, including snipe, hen and marsh harriers in the autumn and winter. From late spring, the site is filled with flowering orchids, such as early purple, green winged, marsh helleborine, early marsh, northern marsh fragrant and lesser butterfly, and more than 20 species of butterflies are attracted to the wildflowers.

Cors-y-Sarnau
Near: Bala, near Ruthin, Gwynedd
Map: 22, C2
Web: www.wildlifetrust.org.uk/northwales
P
Cors-y-Sarnau is a lowland valley mire, where a shallow lake has developed into different wetland mires and fens. This kind of habitat is rare in the UK.

Craig Cerrig Gleisiad
Near: Brecon, Powys
Map: 22, C4
Web: www.ccw.gov.uk
i
High in the Brecon Beacons, this reserve is home to rare Arctic-alpine plants and provides a safe nesting place for many birds. Scrub grows on and around its rocky outcrops and glacial debris is scattered across the area. The steep crags prevent sheep from nibbling rare vegetation such as purple saxifrage. A variety of upland birds can be seen here, including raven, peregrine and ring ouzel.

Cwm Idwal
Near: Mold, Gwynedd
Map: 22, C2
Web: www.ccw.gov.uk
P (ltd), WC
Cwm Idwal is one of the best places, and the most southerly

British place, to see plants that were very common during the cold glacial periods. Arctic-alpine plants such as moss campion and saxifrages can be seen in the cracks and crevices of the north facing slopes.

Dan-y-Graig
Near: Risca, near Newport, Gwent
Map: 22, C5
Web: www.wildlifetrust.org.uk/gwent
P

In spring, there is a good show of primroses, ramsons, hart's-tongue, male and shield ferns. Wild strawberry grows on the limestone grassland as well as scarlet pimpernel and pearlwort. The pond is home to water shrews, minnows and sticklebacks. In summer, a range of dragonflies can be seen on the pond and there are three species of primitive horsetail on the banks. Look out for slow worms.

Dingle LNR
Near: Anglesey
Map: 22, B1
Web: www.anglesey.gov.uk
P **&** (ltd)

Birds such as kingfishers, yellow wagtails, moorhens and wild ducks visit the river and lake, while treecreepers, blue tits and spotted woodpeckers inhabit the woodland. Dragonflies are also native to this reserve and, in spring, the ancient woodland is carpeted in bluebells and wood anemones.

Dolyth Hafren
Near: Newtown, Powys
Map: 22, C3
Web: www.montwt.co.uk
P

In winter, good numbers of goosander and curlew can be seen. In the warmer months look out for yellow wagtail, little ringed plover as well as redshank, oystercatcher, reed and sedge warblers and modwort. Mammals include otters and brown hares.

Elan Valley
Near: Llandrindod Wells, Powys
Map: 22, C3
Web: www.elanvalley.org.uk
P **i**

The Elan Valley is a haven for all kinds of wildlife. More than 180 species of bird have been seen including rarities such as roller, white stork and rosefinch. Ospreys are seen most years and, of the 80 regular breeding birds, pied flycatcher, redstart and wood warbler are found in the ancient oak woodlands, with red grouse, golden plover and dunlin on the high moors.

Elan Valley

Six British reptiles

There are six native British reptiles: the adder, the grass snake, the smooth snake, the sand lizard, the viviparous lizard and the slow worm. Of these, the smooth snake is the most rare and found only in heathland in Dorset, Hampshire and Surrey. Some sites do support all six reptiles, such as Studland in the South West, Drumburgh Moss in the North West and Bedford Purlieus in the East.

Pictured: Viviparous (common) lizard

Otters and stoats are often seen in the daytime especially in spring, while insects include the rare cardinal beetle, purple hairstreak butterfly and keeled skimmer dragonfly. The traditional hay meadows have butterfly and fragrant orchids and the very rare bog orchid is found in a few wet areas of the uplands.

Gilfach

Near: Llandrindod Wells, Powys
Map: 22, C3
Web: www.radnorshirewildlife trust.co.uk

P & (ltd), ⓘ ⌖ ⌂

Birds to see in spring include spotted and pied flycatcher, redstart and wood warbler. Early summer is a good time to see badgers with their cubs as well as wildflowers, such as mountain pansy and bitter-vetch. Salmon can be seen leaping up the waterfall in October and November.

Glaslyn

Near: Machynlleth, Gwynedd
Map: 22, B3
Web: www.montwt.co.uk

P

The lake is the main feature on the reserve and it attracts diving ducks in the winter. This reserve is also an important breeding ground for other birds, such as red grouse, skylarks, meadow pipits, merlins and red kite.

Gors Maen Llwyd

Near: Denbigh, Clwyd
Map: 22, C2
Web: www.wildlifetrust.org.uk/northwales

P WC ⓘ ⌂

Water voles live in the clear streams running through the peat and, in winter, wildfowl can be seen on Llyn Brenig. In the spring, red grouse start to breed and wheatear, skylark, chats, curlew, hen harrier and merlin are all common. The wet areas of the heath have more than 13 species of sedge and, in drier areas, mountain pansy, woodrush, harebell, heath speedwell and tormentil can be seen.

Gwaith Powdwr

Near: Porthmadog, Gwynedd
Map: 22, B2
Web: www.wildlifetrust.org.uk/northwales

P WC ⌖ ⌂

In spring, there are 35 breeding species of bird at Gwaith Powdwr. These include pied flycatcher, redstart, wood warbler, tree pipit, linnet and bullfinch. In summer, nightjar, roding woodcock, tawny and barn owls and six species of bat can also be seen. Reptiles include adder and grass snake, with various dragonflies among the invertebrates.

Maes Hiraddug
Near: Dyserth, near Prestatyn
Map: 22, C2
Web: www.wildlifetrust.org.uk/northwales
The Maes Hiraddug is a species-rich neutral grassland reserve that contains an excellent example of the type of wildflower meadow that occurred before modern agricultural land management. Look out for the spiny restharrow and greater butterfly orchid.

Magor Marsh
Near: Newport, Gwent
Map: 22, C5
Web: www.wildlifetrust.org.uk/gwent
P ℹ
In spring, you can see marsh marigolds on the whole reserve at Magor Mash and, in early summer, the hay meadows are a mass of thistle, yellow flag, yellow-rattle, ragged robin and lesser spearwort. In autumn and winter, the pond is a sanctuary for garganey and green sandpiper. Over-wintering birds include large flocks of teal and occasional spotted crake. Otters can also be seen here.

Marford Quarry
Near: Wrexham,
Map: 22, C2
Web: www.wildlifetrust.org.uk/northwales
P
The areas of open sand in this quarry are important for burrowing bees and wasps, which are one of the major features of the reserve. Ramsons and wood anemone grow in the wooded areas during spring and cuckoos

and woodpeckers are common at this time also. In summer, wildflower species include white mullein, pale St John's wort, wild liquorice and three types of orchids (common, spotted and pyramidal). The site is also home to 30 butterfly species and 39 moth species.

Mumbles Hill LNR
Near: Swansea, West Glamorgan
Map: 22, B5
Web: www.swansea.gov.uk
P ℹ
Mumbles Hill is home to more than 200 species of plants and fungi, 40 species of birds and hundreds of species of butterflies, bees and bugs. Small mammals, such as voles, foxes and shrews, can also be seen. Birds include green woodpecker, skylark and jay, while migratory birds include house martins, swallows and garden warblers.

DID YOU KNOW?
Unlike most reptiles which lay eggs, the viviparous lizard gives birth to live young.

Parc Natur Penglais
Near: Aberystwyth, Ceredigion
Map: 22, B3
Web: www.ceredigion.gov.uk
Public footpaths lead you through the reserve's woodlands, where oak, sycamore, cherry ash and Scot's pine grow. During the spring, the woods are carpeted with bluebells and other flowers. Blackcaps and jays can sometimes be seen and redwings visit in winter.

Parc Slip and Park Pond
Near: Bridgend,
Map: 22, B5
Web: www.welshwildlife.org.uk
P WC ℹ ✉ ⌂
Parc Slip covers 247 acres of land where sand martins

and lapwing can be seen. In summer, there are breeding teal, tufted duck, little grebe, small and dingy skipper butterflies and dragonflies. Autumn brings rare fungi and this is the time of year to see water voles and otters. Winter is good for wildfowl, with gadwalls and goosanders regular visitors.

Pendinas and Tanybwlch
Near: Aberystwyth, Ceredigion
Map: 22, B3
Web: www.ceredigion.gov.uk
Pendinas is the largest Iron Age hillfort in Ceredigion. The views from the fort can be spectacular. The whole of Cardigan Bay lies below and on a clear day, you can see the mountains of Snowdonia to the north and Pumlumon to the east. Tanybwlch is a shingle ridge beach tucked away round the corner from Aberystwyth harbour. Whimbrel and ringed plover can be seen here, as can the red kite. There have also been occasional sightings of polecat.

Penrhos
Near: Holyhead, Anglesey
Map: 22, A1
Web: www.anglsey.gov.uk
✉ ⌂
Birds to be spotted at Penrhos include divers, grebes, sea ducks, gulls, terns, auks, a large cormorant colony, pipits, warblers, chats and buntings. Rarities have included red-necked phalarope, Mediterranean and glaucous gulls, golden oriole, black redstart, and yellow-browed warbler.

Pentwyn Farm
Near: Monmouth, Monmouthshire
Map: 22, C4
Web: www.wildlifetrusts.org.uk/gwent
P

In spring, you can see early purple orchids and cowslips at Petwyn Farm, and it's also a good spot for migrant birds. In summer, there is a broader selection of flowers including orchids (greater butterfly, green winged, common spotted and common twyblade), oxeye daisy, yellow-rattle and eyebright. In autumn, dormice are common and the hedgerows provide food for over-wintering flocks of birds, such as fieldfares and redwings.

Flying high

You can spot a red kite from its reddish brown body, deeply forked tail and wings that are angled forward towards its head. Due to huge conservation efforts it has come back from the brink of extinction in Britain and there are now between 600-700 breeding pairs in the UK, most of them are in Wales but they're also seen at the College Lake Wildlife Centre in the south east and Eccup Reservoir in Yorkshire among other areas.

Pisgah Quarry
Near: Wrexham, Denbighshire
Map: 22, C2
Web: www.wildlifetrust.org.uk/northwales
Pisgah Quarry is a small reserve with a fascinating mixture of woodland, wildflower grassland and superb views over the Vale of Llangollen.

Pwll Y Wrach SSSI
Near: Talgarth, near Brecon, Powys
Map: 22, C4
Web: www.brecknockwildlifetrust.org.uk
Plants to be seen in spring include celandines, bluebells, early purple orchid, bird's-nest orchid, herb paris and toothwort. In the summer, lesser horseshoe, brown long-eared and pipistrelle bats fly through the trees and dormice climb onto the over-hanging branches. Birds to be seen all year round include dippers and buzzards. The waterfall occasionally freezes in winter.

Rhayader Tunnel
Near: Llandrindod Wells, Powys
Map: 22, C3
Web: www.brecknockwildlifetrust.org.uk
Birds on the site include red kite, buzzard, redstart, nuthatch, pied and spotted

flycatchers. In winter, the reserve is used as a bat roost and, in summer, wild plants include orpine, broad-leaved helleborine, wood bitter-vetch, knapweed, betony, great burnet and prickly sedge.

Roundton Hill
Near: Bishop's Castle, near Newtown, Montgomeryshire
Map: 22, C3
Web: www.montwt.co.uk
Ravens can be seen around the site in winter and, in summer, redstarts, willow warblers and pied flycatchers return to the oak woodland. The summer and autumn bring a wide range of fungi and, in spring, shepherd's-cress and common whitlow grass can be seen. Bats roost in disused mine shafts during the winter.

Snowdon
Near: Bangor, Snowdonia
Map: 22, B2
Web: www.eryri-npa.co.uk
Among the Arctic-alpine plants found in the high peaks, the Snowdon lily is unique to Snowdon, as is the Snowdon or rainbow beetle.

Vicarage Meadows
Near: Talgarth, Brecknockshire
Map: 22, C4

Web: www.brecknockshirewildlife trust.co.uk
The reserve consists of two fields separated by a line of beech trees. During spring, the second field is carpeted with bluebells and, in summer, the floral display includes dyer's greenweed, orchids and devil's-bit scabious. Small pearl-bordered fritillary butterflies are attracted to the wildflowers.

The Welsh Wildlife Centre
Near: Cardigan, Pembrokeshire
Map: 22, A4
Web: www.welshwildlife.org
The centre is a 264-acre nature reserve home to many species of wildlife. Located in the Ceredigion countryside along the banks of the River Teifi, the reserve has otters, badgers and many other mammals. Alongside these is a wide variety of birds, including kingfisher and red kite, as well as several butterfly species.

Wern Plemys
Near: Aberdare, Powys
Map: 22, B4
Web: www.brecknockshirewildlife trust.co.uk
Wern Plemys features both woodland and a wildflower

meadow. After winter, the chiffchaff is one of the first migrant birds to arrive and, in summer, buzzards fly overhead. Late in the year, flocks of tits inhabit the trees.

Withybeds and Wentes Meadow

Near: Llandrindod Wells, Powys
Map: 22, C3
Web: www.radnorshirewildlife trust.org.uk

In spring and summer, vegetation grows high at Withybeds and Wentes and a mass of meadowsweet gives the air a heady fragrance. The River Lugg borders the reserve and features brown trout, otter and damselflies. Harbour water voles and grass snakes can be seen moving through the tall vegetation around the small pond and watercourse.

BIRDWATCHING/ BIRD RESERVES

Conwy

Near: Conwy, Llandudno,
Map: 22, B2
Web: www.rspb.org.uk

The reserve has coastal lagoons and grassland alongside the Conwy Estuary with spectacular views of Snowdonia. Waders and wildfowl are the main interest, and more than 200 species have been recorded on the site. Birds to keep an eye out for include black-tailed godwit, lapwing, shelduck, skylark and water rail.

Gigrin Farm

Near: Llandrindod Wells, Powys
Map: 22, C3
Web: www.gigrin.co.uk

Gigrin Farm was Wales's first official red kite feeding centre. In summer, around 100 red kites can be seen during feeding time at the farm. Buzzards, goshawk and raven also join the daily feast. The farm has another feeding station where you can see brambling, yellow-hammers, siskin, redstarts and other smaller birds.

Lake Vyrnwy

Near: Oswestry, Powys
Map: 22, C2
Web: www.rspb.vyrnwy.org

Keep an eye out for the goosander, great crested grebe

and common sandpiper, as well as woodland birds such as the siskin and nuthatch. In addition, this reserve is home to a number of birds rarely found in other parts of the country, including the red grouse, merlin, hen harrier and black grouse. In the forest around Lake Vyrnwy, you can see several less common birds, such as goldcrests, coal tits, goshawks, crossbills, ravens and even the occasional nightjar.

Mawddach Valley

Near: Dolgellau, Gwynedd
Map: 22, B2
Web: www.rspb.org.uk

There are two reserves in the Mawddach Valley, Arthog and Coed Garth Gell. In the spring, pied flycatchers, wood warblers and redstarts can be seen and heard in Coed Garth Gell. Different types of warblers, reed buntings and water rails can be seen at Arthog. Ravens and buzzards occur all year round.

Ramsey Island

Near: St David's, Pembrokeshire
Map: 22, A4
Web: www.rspb.org.uk

Look out for the water voles

Immortalised as 'Ratty' in Kenneth Grahame's *Wind in the Willows*, the water vole is, sadly, another small mammal in declining numbers in the UK. They are active day and night, burrowing into riverbanks to make a nest that they then line with grass. You may see them swimming or scurrying around on riverbanks at sites such as Chobham Common, Howardian Hills, Alkincoates Woodland, Burfa Bog or the River Tweed.

Ramsey Island has 400-foot-high cliffs, which teem with thousands of breeding seabirds in spring and early summer. Chough, guillemot, peregrine, raven and razorbill are all common on the island. In autumn, breeding grey seals can be seen on the shingle beaches below the cliffs.

South Stack Cliffs

On: Holy Island
Map: 22, A1
Web: www.rspb.org.uk

In summer, more than 4,000 pairs of seabirds nest at South Stack Cliffs. From the visitor centre at Ellin's Tower you can watch puffins, fulmars and many others. Around 800 razorbills come to nest at South Stack. They start coming into the cliffs in January/February, but don't settle to lay eggs until May. South Stack has quite a small colony of razorbills and two pairs of peregrines. The peregrines are resident all year round, but settle in their nests in March/April. Guillemots are quite common. They are similar to razorbills, and nest on narrow ledges in front of Ellin's Tower.

Ynys-hir

Near: Machynlleth, Powys
Map: 22, B3
Web: www.rspb.org.uk

Set on the south side of the Dyfi Estuary, this reserve has both a Welsh oak woodland and the wet grassland and saltmarshes of the estuary. Lapwing, little egret, redshank, white-fronted goose and wood warbler are all common in Ynys-hir, as are greenshank, green sandpiper, peregrine barnacle goose, golden plover and red kite.

Go whalewatching... in Britain

Although whale and porpoise numbers are thought to be decreasing in British waters due to fishing practices, pollution and stress, it is still possible to see whales off the coast of Britain. Visit the Moray Firth for land or boat viewings, or Mull for minke whales and possibly orcas, short-beaked common dolphins and Risso's dolphins.

FORESTS & WOODLAND

Coed y Felin

Near: Hendre, near Mold, Clwyd
Map: 22, C2
Web: www.wt-woods.org.uk

Coed y Felin has rich woodland flora – this is the only site in North Wales which has the Deptford pink. From the main car park, a short section of wildflower grassland leads to an area of elder, hazel, dog rose, holly wych elm and young ash. Dog's mercury and ivy cover the woodland floor. Sweet chestnut, mosses and ferns also thrive in the woodland earth.

Coed Trellyniau

Near: Mold, Clwyd
Map: 22, C2
Web: www.wildlifetrust.org.uk/northwales

Coed Trellyniau is an ancient bluebell wood. There are splendid drifts of bluebells, while more plants are evidence of the wood's long history.

Croes Robert Wood

Near: Monmouth, Monmouthshire
Map: 22, C4
Web: www.wildlifetrust.org.uk/gwent
(££)

The wood has a thriving dormouse population. In spring, the woodland floor is carpeted with bluebells, wood anemone, yellow archangel and herb paris. In summer, you can see twyblade, common spotted orchid and enchanter's nightshade, as well as the white-letter hairstreak, silver-washed fritillary and white admiral butterflies. In autumn, fungi include stinkhorn, King Alfred's cakes, coral spot fungus, candlesnuff fungus and the goblet.

Cwm Clydach

Near: Craig Cefn Parc, Swansea
Map: 22, B5
Web: www.rspb.org.uk

The wood attracts many birds, including woodpeckers, nuthatch, sparrowhawk, kestrel, pied flycatchers, redstarts, buzzards and tawny owl. Clinging precariously to the cliffs are yew and whitebeam trees. There are many waterfalls within the reserve. Many species of moss can be found growing here and a huge variety of fungi.

Cwmcarn Forest

Near: Crosskeys, near Newport
Map: 22, C5
Web: www.forestry.gov.uk

Cwmcarn is a mature forest of larch and pine. Under the conifers, wood ant nests can be seen. Ponds thrive with water boatmen, diving beetles, tadpoles and newts. The raven is common to Cwmcarn Forest.

Cwmllwyd Wood LNR
Near: Swansea
Map: 22, B5
Web: www.swansea.gov.uk
The reserve consists mainly of oak trees which are around 100 years old and were planted after a previous clearance. There are also many birch, holly, willow and rowan trees as well as some large apple trees near the coal workings that may be the result of coal miners throwing away their apple cores.

Gwydyr Forest
Near: Betws-y-Coed
Map: 22, B2
Web: www.forestry.gov.uk
🅿 🆆🅲 ⓘ ⛲
Gwydyr Forest is located in the heart of the Snowdonia National Park. You can spot fallow deer or occasionally roe deer in the forest at dawn or dusk. You may also see black grouse in the Gwydyr South and Tyn y Cwm woodlands. These areas are the younger parts of the forest, where moorland meets trees, and are the habitats favoured by the grouse. The forest is also rich in raptors and buzzards, while goshawks, peregrines and merlin have all been sighted here. Butterflies and moths can be seen in the open areas within the woods.

Hiraethog Forest
Near: Ruthin, North Wales
Map: 22, C2
Web: www.forestry.gov.uk
🅿 🆆🅲 🅰
The conifer forest covers more than 15,000 acres and

is one of the few places in Wales where you can see the red squirrel. The goldcrest can be seen here as well as the black grouse.

> ### DID YOU KNOW?
> Clippings from the yew tree are used in some anti-cancer drugs.

Kilvey Community Woodland
Near: Swansea
Map: 22, B5
Web: www.forestry.gov.uk
Kilvey Community Woodland has a sculpture trail, woodland walks, Pluck Lake – a refuge for the blue-tailed damselfly and the emperor dragonfly – and great views over the city of Swansea.

Pembrey Forest
Near: Pembrey, near Llanelli, Carmarthenshire
Map: 22, B4
Web: www.forestry.gov.uk
🅿
Pembrey is one of Britain's sand dune forests, woodlands that are unusual and have become objects of great interest to naturalists. It is home to 35 species of butterfly, many migrant songbirds as well as birds of prey, including sparrowhawk and goshawk.

Pengelli Forest NNR
Near: Eglwyswrw, near Cardigan, Pembrokeshire
Map: 22, A4
Web: www.welshwildlife.org
🅿
This semi-natural woodland with streams and ravines covers 148 acres. In spring, you can see bluebells, migrant warblers and flycatchers. In summer, silver-washed fritillary butterflies and

bats are common. In autumn, dormice that feed on the hazelnuts.

Silent Valley
Near: Ebbw Vale
Map: 22, C4
Web: www.wildlifetrust.org.uk/gwent
🅿
There are large flocks of tits and finches passing through Silent Valley's woods in winter. In spring, bluebell flowers, lesser celandine, wood sorrel and golden saxifrage are common. Pied flycatchers and redstarts nest in the woods at this time. In summer, bats hunt for insects in the evenings and many species of fritillary can also be seen. Autumn is the best time to look for fungi in the woods. There is also the bonus of seeing the purple flowering heather on the hills above the reserve.

Wild Woods at Parkwood
Near: Swansea
Map: 22, B5
Web: www.forestry.gov.uk
🅿 (££)
Parkwood is a popular woodland situated on the Gower peninsula. The wood is home to a variety of birds, such as buzzards, woodpeckers and nuthatch, while you can see pheasants throughout the summer. There are two species of bat at Parkwood – the lesser and greater horseshoe bats.

COASTS, WETLANDS & WATERWAYS

Aberthaw Lagoon and Saltmarsh SSSI
Near: Cardiff
Map: 22, C5
Web: www.welshwildlife.org
🅿 ✉

Bottlenose dolphins

Aberthaw Lagoon is one of only four saline lagoons in Wales and is a top South Walian birding site. Autumn and winter bring migrant birds offshore and in summer the grassland is alive with orchids and insects, such as glow worms and the shiny emerald bombardier beetle.

Bala Lake (Lyn Tegid)
Near: Bala, Corwen, Gwynedd
Map: 22, C2
This lake is popular for all sorts of leisure pursuits inluding walking around its pretty perimeters. Down 80 feet below its surface lurks the gwyniad – a rare species of fish that survives from the time of the last Ice Age.

Bardsey Island
Near: Aberdaron
Map: 22, A2

Web: www.bardsey.org
Bardsey Island was declared an NNR in 1986. In the summer you can see cormorants, shags, manx shearwaters and curlews here. Grey seals also come to bask on the beaches and other unusual animals live on the island's mountain and grasslands.

Cardigan Bay
Near: Lynn and Pembrokeshire peninsulas
Map: 22, B2 and B3
Web: www.cardiganshirecoast andcountry.com
🅿 🆆🅲 ❶ ✉
Cardigan Bay is one of the most important locations off the British coast for bottlenose dolphins, with a population of approximately 127 living here. Cardigan Bay Marine Wildlife Centre in New Quay runs regular dolphin-watching boat trips.

Other marine mammals include harbour porpoises and Atlantic grey seals. Birds include the chough, peregrine falcon, gannet and puffin.

Ceredigion
From: Gwynedd to Carmarthenshire
Map: 22, B2 and B3
Web: www.tourism.ceredigion. gov.uk
🅿 🆆🅲 ❶ ✉
The Atlantic grey seal lives off the coast of Ceredigion and it is one of their favourite breeding grounds in the UK. You can also see bottlenose dolphins, harbour porpoises and starlings flocking in their thousands at Aberystwyth Pier. Other birds to see include guillemot, razorbill, gull, eider duck, puffin, tern, oystercatcher, ringed plover, chough and stonechat.

Dyfi National Nature Reserve

Near: Aberystwyth
Map: 22, B3
Web: www.ccw.gov.uk

The reserve is made up of three distinct areas: Dyfi Estuary Mudflats, Ynyslas Sand Dunes and Cors Fochno. The estuary is a vital feeding ground for large numbers of wildfowl and shorebirds, such as dunlin, oystercatcher, sanderling, tern and manx. Animals living in the dunes include the common lizard, stoats, polecats, rabbits and voles. The skylark, rare ringed plover and meadow pipit are also visitors. A variety of butterflies and moths can be seen, including the dark-green fritillary, gatekeeper butterfly, scarlet tiger moth and portland moth. The boardwalk path takes you past different types of marsh and bee orchids. Cors Fochno is home to several interesting plants, including sphagnum mosses and three species of carnivorous plant. Families of otters have made their home here and a small pack of Welsh mountain ponies lives on the bog. Red kites, buzzards, peregrine and harriers can be seen flying overhead.

Claerwen Reservoir

Near: Llandrindod Wells, Powys
Map: 22, C3
Web: www.waterscape.com

Claerwen is one of six reservoirs in this area. Great birdwatching is possible all year. You can spot red kites and buzzards in the area. Dolymynach is a special protection area under the European Wild Birds Directive – 180 species to date have been recorded here, of which 80 breed annually.

Dee Estuary

From: Mold to Liverpool Bay
Map: 22, C1 and C2
Web: www.deeestuary.co.uk

The Dee Estuary is one of the most important areas in the UK for wildfowl and waders – a typical winter's day holding 30,000 ducks and 100,000 waders. Species include sheldon, wigeon, teal, pintail, grey plover, dunlin, godwit, curlew and redshank, along with 500 grey seals. Common seals also turn up from time to time, as do the occasional porpoise and dolphin.

Flat Holm

Near: Cardiff
Map: 22, C5
Web: www.cardiff.gov.uk

Flat Holm is a haven for wildlife and home to one of the largest colony of gulls in Wales. There are many birds and animals to see, including shelduck, slow worms and wild tortoise. Spring and summer bring a profusion of rare and interesting wildflowers.

Gronant

From: Prestatyn, Denbighshire, to Gronant, Clwyd
Map: 22, C1
Web: www.prestatyn.org.uk

In winter, the lake and river can attract a good selection of ducks and the sand dunes hold a number of snow buntings and sometimes even shore larks. The wide sandy beach and sea beyond is always full of gulls, worth a good look for something out of the ordinary. The beach is also used as a roost for cormorants and several species of tern in summer and as a wader high tide roost in winter – particularly attractive to sanderling. The marsh contains large numbers of snipe, while little terns and rare ringed plover nest in the area.

Hilbre Island

Near: Birkenhead, the mouth of the Dee Estuary
Map: 22, C1
Web: www.hilbreisland.org.uk

Every autumn, Hilbre Island attracts thousands of oystercatchers, which come here to feed and rest. As well as oystercatchers, curlews also flock here in good numbers, generally to feed in the soft mud and sand of the estuary, but also, on occasion, among the rocks. The majority of the birds that come to Hilbre are migrating waders, but some smaller birds pass through too. As well as the 100,000 or so birds, there are also seals on the sand banks.

Menai Strait

From: Anglesey to mainland Wales
Map: 22, B1 and B2
Web: www.anglesey.gov.uk

The Menai Strait is one of Europe's most precious wildlife sites. The sheltered waters of the strait provide excellent conditions for growth of marine algae, sponges and other reef communities that rival those in tropical seas. Sheltered rocky areas act as homes for barnacles, marine snails and other molluscs, while there are mussel beds in the flatter areas. The waters of the strait feature bass, cod, conger eels and lobsters.

National Wetlands Centre

Address: Llanelli Centre, Penclacwydd, Llwynhendy, Llanelli SA14 9SH
Map: 22, B4
Tel: 01554 741087
Web: www.wwt.org.uk
Open: all year
Admission: £3.50/£5.50
P (££), WC 🅰 ❶
🎏 🏠 🅰 📷

The National Wetlands Centre is a prime location for birdwatching. Species include: great crested grebe, little grebe, mute swan, greylag goose, shelduck, mallard, gadwall, wigeon, teal, pintail, shoveler, tufted duck, pochard, red-breasted merganser, oystercatcher, lapwing, dunlin, curlew, black-tailed godwit, redshank, greenshank, spotted redshank and snipe. Other highlights include kingfisher, water rail, great spotted woodpecker, little owl, tawny owl, barn owl, hen harrier, merlin and peregrine.

Skomer Island

Near: Haverfordwest
Map: 22, A4
Web: www.welshwildlife.org
P ❶ WC 🅰

Skomer Island covers 759 acres and is 200 feet above sea level. The cliffs are home to thousands of migrant birds in spring, such as Manx shearwater, storm petrel, kittiwake, razorbill and guillemot. Through the year you can see bluebells, red campion and heather. The time to see puffins is in June and July and grey seals can be spotted all year round, or with their pups from the end of August until October.

South Gower Cliffs cSAC

Near: Port Eynon, near Swansea
Map: 22, B5
Web: www.welshwildlife.org
P WC 🖂

In spring, you can see Gower's famous yellow whitlow grass and spring cinquefoil and you may be able to spot the Dartford warbler. In summer, bloody crane's-bill, hoary rock-rose, spiked speedwell, stonechats and white-throats are everywhere. This is the premier site for the silky wave moth and 11 species of fungi have been recorded. During August and September, Port Eynon is the best site in South Wales for birdwatching: in winter, look out for choughs and marine birds offshore.

Spinnies, Aberogwen

Near: Bangor, Gwynedd
Map: 22, B2

Little egret, National Wetlands Centre

Newport Wetlands

Near: Newport
Map: 22, C5
Web: www.rspb.org.uk
P

Before the reserve was established at Newport Wetlands, the land used to hold only a small and decreasing number of farmland birds. Since 2000, there has been a big increase in the number of breeding lapwing, redshank, water rail, skylark, linnet and reed bunting. In winter there are large numbers of shoveler, pintail ducks, teal and wigeon. The reserve also provides safe roost sites for waders such as knot, dunlin, curlew, whimbrel and lapwing. A large area of wet grassland is a home for over-wintering shoveler, wigeon, breeding water rail, Cetti's warbler, marsh harrier, bittern and bearded tit. Other species include hares, water voles and great crested newts.

Web: www.wildlifetrust.org.uk/northwales
P (££), (ltd), 🏠 🏠 🏠

The main feature of this reserve is the coastal lagoon, which provides shelter and food for wildfowl and waders during spring and autumn. Red-breasted mergansers and great crested grebes can be seen from the reserve out to sea and winter species include kingfisher, surf scoter, spoonbill, greenshank and water rail.

Teifi Marshes

Near: Cardigan, Ceredigion
Map: 22, A4
Web: www.welshwildlife.org
P WC 🛈 🏠 🏠

In winter, wildfowl, including teal and wigeon can be seen here, with sand martin and chiffchaff, nuthatch, pied flycatcher, reed and sedge warbler here in the spring. At this time of year, the woodland is a mass of bluebells, campion, wood anemones, celandines, primroses and stitchworts. In autumn, many waders can be seen, as well as greenshank, godwit and migrating osprey. Kingfishers, red deer, otters and water buffalo are also common.

Valley Wetlands

Near: Caergeilliog, Anglesey
Map: 22, B1
Web: www.rspb.org.uk

The reed-fringed lakes of Valley Wetlands are one of the best places in Wales to see wildfowl all year round. Tufted ducks, pochards, shovelers, gadwalls and grebes all breed here and numbers swell in winter with the arrival of wigeon and goldeneye. In spring and early summer, the reedbeds are alive with reed and sedge warblers and you may be lucky enough to see water rails, marsh harriers and Cetti's warblers.

NOT SO WILD

Anglesey Sea Zoo

Address: Brynsiencyn, Anglesey LL61 6TQ
Map: 22, B1
Tel: 01248 430411
Web: www.angleseyseazoo.co.uk
Open: February to November, 10/11am to 4/6pm
Admission: £5.95/£6.95
P (££), (ltd), 🛈 ✉

The Anglesey Sea Zoo is Wales's largest marine aquarium. With more than 50 species, the sea zoo has recreated the habitats of the fauna and flora found around Anglesey and the North Wales coastline. From the invertebrates in the Bone-Free Zone, your tour takes you through a shipwreck, a walk over the shark pool and then on to the wonders of the open ocean. Tropical displays include piranhas, lobsters and seahorses, among others.

Bodafon Farm Park

Address: Bodafon Road, Llandudno Conwy LL30 3BB
Map: 22, B1
Tel: 01492 549060
Web: www.bodafonfarmpark.co.uk
Open: daily, 10am to 6pm
P WC 🚹

Bodafon is a real working farm where you can experience what it's like to work with animals. You can bottle-feed calves or help milk a cow. Other animals include sheep, goats, deer, llamas and alpacas in the farm's paddocks. In a move back to the olden days, shire horses work the fields and you can take a tractor ride round the grounds. The farm is also involved in an owl breeding programme and you can get up close to native and foreign species of owls and birds of prey.

Children's Farm Park and Slate Caverns

Address: Llanfair, Harlech, near Porthamadog LL46 2SA
Map: 11, B2
Tel: 01766 780247
Web: www.llanfairslatecaverns.co.uk
Open: May to mid-September, daily, 10am to 5pm
Admission: £3.30/£4
P WC 🚹

This working farm lets you get close to and feed its array of animals, including lambs, calves, goats, ducks and pigs. There is a small birds of prey centre and nature walks down to the lake and through the woods. Visitors can also investigate the slate caverns, learn about the industry and view the mine workings.

Conwy Aquatic Centre
Address: Glyn Isa, Rowen, Conwy, near Llandudno LL32 8TP
Map: 22, B1
Tel: 01492 650063
Web: www.conway.gov.uk
Open: Wednesday to Saturday, 7.30am to 5.30pm
Admission: free
🅿 WC ♿

Visitors can view the tropical, marine and cold-water fish in the extensive aquariums and the centre is currently involved in a breeding programme for the discus fish, so-called because it is flat and round. There are also opportunities to go coarse fishing in one of the four lakes or feed the ducks in the purpose-built pond.

Conwy Butterfly Jungle
Address: Bodlondeb Park, Conwy, near Llandudno LL32 8DU
Map: 22, B1
Tel: 01492 593149
Web: www.conwy-butterfly.co.uk
Open: April to September, 10am to 5.30pm; September to October, 10am to 3.30pm
🅿 WC

This large single-span greenhouse helps recreate a tropical atmosphere in the north-west of Wales. More than 400 tropical butterflies fly freely in and around the jungle plantlife, as do other insects. The tropical fish pool and jungle spring are accompanied by the noises of the jungle.

Foel Farm Park
Address: Brynsiencyn, Anglesey LL61 6TQ
Map: 22, B1
Tel: 01248 430646
Web: www.foelfarm.co.uk
Open: March to October (and February half term), 10.30am to 5.30pm

Admission: £3.95/£4.95
🅿 ♿

Tractor and trailer tours of the farm are available. There are also pony rides for smaller children during school holidays and at weekends. In spring and early summer you can have a hands-on experience, bottle-feeding the lambs or calves.

DID YOU KNOW?
There are 33 species of native British trees.

Henblas Country Park
Address: Bodorgan, Anglesey LL62 5DL
Map: 22, B1
Tel: 01407 840440
Web: www.parc-henblas-park.co.uk
Open: 24 March to 31 October, 10.30am to 5pm (closed Saturdays)
Admission: £4/£5
🅿 WC ♿

This country park is situated in the heart of Anglesey and offers families an insight into the workings of a farm. There are sheep-shearing and sheepdog demonstrations, as well as the opportunity to help feed lambs at Easter. There is also falconry, a duck display and stable block and both indoor and outdoor children's play areas.

The National Botanic Garden of Wales
Address: Llanarthne, near Llanelli, Carmarthenshire SA32 8HG
Map: 22, B4
Tel: 01558 668768
Web: www.gardenofwales.org.uk
Open: 30 October to 28 February, 10am to 4.30pm; 1 March to 31 October, 10am to 6pm
Admission: £8/£3
🅿 ♿ WC ♿ ♿

As well being a world-class botanic garden, The National Botanic Garden of Wales are

home to rare plants and fungi, such as greater butterfly orchid, whorled caraway and waxcap fungi, together with a large range of invertebrates, such as crickets, bugs, butterflies and moths. Badgers have been allowed to root among the mossy grassland for their main diet of earthworms, and otters hunt on the wet meadows for amphibians in spring. The estate has also retained pockets of diverse semi-natural woodland. Boggy, alder carr woodland near the Gatehouse contrasts with the drier oak and sweet chestnut woods of Pont Felin Gat in the northern end, where bluebell, anemone and golden saxifrage carpet the ground in spring. These, and small hazel coppices, are rich in birds, ferns, mosses, lichens and fungi. They also provide a home for dormice.

Pilipalas
Address: Menai Bridge, Anglesey LL59 5RP
Map: 22, B1
Tel: 01248 712474
Web: www.pilipalas.co.uk
Open: 10 March to 31 October, 10am to 5.30pm; 1 November to 24 December, 11am to 5.30pm
Admission: £4.50/£5.50
🅿 WC 🏠

Pilipalas lets visitors get close to our planet's smaller creatures. Both domestic and foreign species of butterfly cavort freely around the main palace, while children can find out more about such familiar little animals, such as hamsters, gerbils, mice, guinea pigs and rabbits, in the pets' corner. The Ant Avenue is home to the leaf-cutting *Atta acromirez* South American ants and the stick insects do their best to keep out of sight in the tropical hide.

Portmeirion Gardens
Address: Portmeirion, near Porthmadog, Gwynedd LL48 6ET

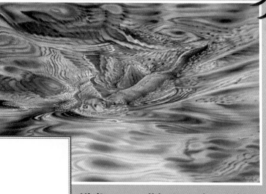

Map: 22, B2
Tel: 01766 770000
Web: www.portmeirion-village. com
Open: daily, 9.30am to 5.30pm (except 25 December)
Admission: £6.50/£3.50
🅿 ♿ 🆆🅲 & 🖼

These 70 acres of subtropical woodland gardens in and around Clough Williams-Ellis' Italianate village of Portmeirion, have been cultivated since Victorian times. Original specimen conifers, wellingtonia and Himalayan firs remain. Since 1980 a major renovation programme has been begun, with much clearing,

restructuring (especially the lakes, which have been re-dug and reshaped) and extensive replanting throughout the woods. The Gwyllts, a display woodland, was developed. Here you can find the major rhododendron, azalea and camellia plantings with a wide variety of trees.

Welsh Mountain Zoo
Address: Colwyn Bay Mountain Zoo, Flagstaff Gardens, Colwyn Bay, Conwy LL28 5UY
Map: 22, B1
Tel: 01492 532938
Web: www.welshmountainzoo.org
Open: daily, 9.30 to 4/5pm (except 25 December)

Admission: £5.50/£7.75
🅿 🆆🅲 &

The zoo is part of a programme to help safeguard the future of foreign species such as the Mongolian wild horses, Humboldt penguins and the white-fronted marmosets, as well as native red squirrels, otters and golden eagles. The reptile house is home to the only breeding pair of American alligators in the UK, while children can visit the smaller, friendly animals in pets corner. There is also the opportunity to watch the penguin parade, sea lion feeding displays and falconry.

Northern Ireland

Despite its small area, Northern Ireland has a great variety of scenic countryside, which reflects its contrasting geology and topography. The dramatic coastal landscape of county Antrim forms one of the most spectacular stretches of coastal scenery in the world, home of the famous Giant's Causeway with its celebrated basaltic columns and formations set in stunning cliff scenery. This whole stretch of coast is an NNR, providing a habitat for a diverse range of flora and fauna, and is a great place for birdwatching. A walk along the cliffs can give you a glimpse of buzzards, peregrine falcons and rare choughs, eider ducks and oystercatchers feed in the sheltered bays below.

In the north, the impressive Mourne Mountains rise up above Belfast, encompassed in the Mourne Mountains AONB. The landscape here is varied, ranging from mountains to farmed hill countryside and coastline. The Mourne mountain range affords not only spectacular views, but also an opportunity to spot some rare species, such as the peregrine falcon and Irish hare.

Situated as it is, Northern Ireland is also a great stop-off for migratory birds and it enjoys international recognition for its bird sanctuaries. North Strangford nature reserve attracts migratory wildfowl and waders in astounding numbers. A visit in September or October will coincide with thousands of migrating Brent geese – attracting a staggering 60 per cent of the world's population.

Further south and inland, the landscape changes into the sparse highlands and the lush river valleys of the Sperrin Mountains, where there are no end of beautiful places to explore. Heading south again takes you into Armagh, with its lakes and wetlands. There are a number of liquid trails to explore here, supporting unique flora and fauna, such as Oxford Island with its four miles of footpaths, birdwatching hides, woodland, ponds and wildflower meadows. This borders on Lough Neagh, the largest lake in the United Kingdom and home to a variety of bird life, including mallard, tufted duck, coot, large flocks of pochard, cormorants, goldeneye, little grebe and scaup in winter. In summer, grey herons, diving and nesting terns, gulls, mute swans, mallard, coot, shoveler and great crested grebe can all be seen here.

A visit to Northern Ireland is truly a unique experience. Its rolling hills and jagged indented coastline make for varied and exciting wildlife-watching opportunities.

PICTURED: The Carrick-a-rede rope bridge near Ballintony on the Causeway Coast

Not to be missed

● **Belfast Lough**
Perfect for the birdwatcher, with loads to see whatever time of the year, it's especially good in the summer for terns.

● **Castle Espie Wildfowl and Wetlands Centre**
Watch little egrets, shovelers, teals and shelduck from the comfort of a hide and, if you have any questions, the centre's staff are fonts of information.

● **Castlewellan**
Enjoy the majesty of the Mourne Mountains from this forest at their base – look out for red squirrels, pine martens and otters.

● **Causeway Coast**
The basalt columns of the Giant's Causeway are a huge attraction, but the rest of the coast with its abundant wildflowers and noisy seabirds is equally good for the wildlife watcher.

● **Lough Neagh Islands**
These hundreds of islands make wonderful, observation posts to see the many weary birds returning from across the Atlantic.

● **Straidkilly**
There is something very relaxing about a woodland with bluebells and wood anemones and the scent of wild garlic. Straidkilly is renowned for its fantastic display of butterflies.

AONBs

Binevenagh

Near: Magilligan and Portstewart, Co Londonderry
Map: 23, C1
Web: www.ehsni.gov.uk

Most available nooks and crannies in the cliffs are occupied by some kind of hardy plant. Two of the species at Binevenagh – moss campion and purple saxifrage – are rare in Northern Ireland. In early summer, harebells, thyme, kidney vetch, bird's-foot trefoil and many more take their turn to flower on the grassy slopes. Overhead you are likely to see kittiwakes, fulmars, buzzards and even a raven or peregrine falcon.

Bog Meadows

Near: Belfast, Co Down
Map: 23, D2
Web: www.ulsterwildlifetrust.org

Bog Meadows is the largest remaining piece of natural wild land in urban Belfast. Four spring-fed ponds attract a range of wildfowl including moorhen, coot, pochard, mallard and little grebe. A willow scrub area is a breeding site for willow, grasshopper and sedge warblers. In winter, wild duck and snipe are found in the marshes and ponds.

Glenarm

Near: Glenarm, Larne, Co Larne
Map: 23, E2
Web: www.ulsterwildlifetrust.org

During spring and summer, the woods are alive with songbirds, such as wood and garden warblers, and other birds at this time of year include dipper, grey wagtail, buzzard and raven. You can see butterflies, such as the wood white and silver-washed fritillary, in the warmer months, too – they are attracted to the site by toothwort and wood crane's-bill wildflowers. In autumn there are a variety of fungi and in winter, thrushes, crossbill and siskin are common. There are red squirrels present throughout the year.

Glendun Farm

Near: Cushendun, Co Antrim
Map: 23, D1
Web: www.ulsterwildlifetrust.org

P WC ☐

Look out for dippers and grey wagtail breeding along the river during spring, as well as ravens and buzzards overhead. Lambs and calves are common at this time also. Butterflies, dragonflies and bats can be spotted in the summer and in autumn there is a range of fungi present. In winter, fieldfares and redwings are common. Otter, red squirrel and red grouse can be seen all year round on the farm.

Lagan Meadows

Near: Belfast, Co Down
Map: 23, D2
Web: www.ulsterwildlifetrust.org

P

The meadows are grazed by cattle in the summer months, but late spring is the best time of the year to see meadow flowers such as the ragged robin, common-spotted orchid, large bittercress, whorl grass and wood club rush. The grasshopper warbler, sedge

Causeway Coast

Near: Bushmills, near Coleraine, Co Antrim
Map: 23, C1
Web: www.ehsni.gov.uk

P WC ❶

The Causeway Coast is a World Heritage site. It is 18 miles long and is made up of cliffs, headlands, fresh sandy beaches and dunes. The Giant's Causeway's spectacular basalt columns of different heights give shelter to a number of bays, while pavements of Causeway Stone march out in regular shapes from the foot of the cliffs towards the sea. The area is a home for sea birds, such as fulmar, cormorant, redshank guillemot and razorbill. The weathered rock has a number of rare and unusual plants and, in early summer, the ledges and cliff tops are carpeted with wildflowers such as bird's-foot trefoil, kidney vetch, spring squill and thrift. Watch out for buzzards, peregrine falcons and rare choughs around the cliffs. Eider ducks and oystercatchers feed in the sheltered bays below.

PICTURED Above: Giant's Causeway **Right:** Razorbill

warbler and reed bunting all breed in this area. Summer is also the best time to see butterflies, such as the wood white, and dragonflies, such as the banded demoiselle. During the colder months, you can spot fieldfares, redwings, jays and snipe.

Lagan Valley
Near: Belfast, Co Down
Map: 23, D2
Web: www.laganvalley.co.uk
Focused on the course of the River Lagan, the riverbank scenery, meadows, woods and pastoral land are home to a range of wildlife. You can see dabchicks or little grebes on the river, butterflies and damselflies alongside the towpath in the summer and jays feeding on acorns in the autumn.

Strangford Lough
From: Newtownards to Downpatrick, Co Down
Map: 23, E2 and E3
Web: www.ehsni.gov.uk
Strangford Lough is home to wintering wildfowl, while the shores, woodland, meadows, streams and marshes, together with the well-tended farmland, provide different views and great nature conservation interest.

Umbra
Near: Coleraine, Co Derry
Map: 23, C1
Web: www.ulsterwildlifetrust.org
P
In summer, you can see wildflowers, such as the marsh helleborine and grass of Parnassus, which attract dark-green, silver-washed fritillary and grayling butterflies. Peregrine falcons hunt overhead. The autumn brings fungi and migrant seabirds offshore such as the red-throated diver. Porpoises have been recorded offshore.

Mourne mountains

Newry and Mourne
Map: 23, C3 and D3
Web: www.mournemountains.com
ⓘ
This very large AONB has a range of habitats including mountains, coast, farmed drumlin and hill country, and so it is home to a great variety of wildlife. Inland areas provide shelter for hedgehogs, foxcubs, dragonflies, bluebells and foxgloves. The coastal regions are inhabited by snipe, oystercatcher, wheatears, sandwich terns, sand martins and common seals.

PICTURED: Mourne mountains

NATURE RESERVES

Altikeeragh NNR
Near: Articlave and Macosquin, near Coleraine, Co Londonderry
Map: 23, C1
Web: www.ehsni.gov.uk
In the wetter areas of Altikeeragh plants include sphagnum hummocks and flat waterlogged lawns with abundant bog asphodel and common cottongrass. The bog provides habitat for upland birds such as snipe, red grouse and raven.

Annagarriff and Mullenakill
Near: Dungannon, Co Tyrone
Map: 23, C2
Web: www.ehsni.gov.uk
P WC ⓘ
Annagarriff and Mullenakill nature reserves are found within Peatlands Park. Annagarriff has huge mounds of plant debris up to one metre high and two to three metres across. These hills have been built by wood ants and are the only Irish site for this species. Birds to see at Annagarriff include jays, sparrowhawks and long-eared owls. Mullenakill is raised bog and small lake, with large heath butterfly and snipe populations.

Ballynahone
Near: Knockloughrim, near Londonderry, Co Londonderry
Map: 23, C1
Web: www.ehsni.gov.uk
This nature reserve covers the southern part of Ballynahone Bog and provides a habitat for breeding birds, such as curlew and snipe, and birds of prey, such as hen harrier and merlin. The bog has one of the largest-known colonies of the large heath butterfly in Northern Ireland.

Ballyquintin Point

Near: Ards Peninsula, near Downpatrick, Co Down
Map: 23, E3
Web: www.ehsni.gov.uk

Plants to see at Ballyquintin Point include burnet rose and wind-dwarfed blackthorn. There is a patchwork of lichens, in shades of grey and sometimes yellow, on the cobbles. The gorse provides excellent cover and nesting opportunities for stonechats, white-throats and linnets. The point is a good spot to see Irish hares, which feed on the grassland and along the shoreline. Migrant butterflies such as red admirals cross the Irish Sea and can be abundant here in some years.

Belvoir Wood

Near: Belfast, Co Down
Map: 23, D2
Web: www.wt-woods.org.uk

The wildflower meadow at Belvoir Wood has burnet moths and orchids. A natural spring rises close to Belvoir Drive and forms the stream flowing though the centre of the site. The wood is one of the last heartlands for the red squirrel in Northern Ireland.

Brackagh Bog

Near: Craigavon, Co Armagh
Map: 23, D3
Web: www.ehsni.gov.uk

This cut-over fen scrub is rich in insects, including marsh fritillary and green hairstreak among the 17 species of butterfly. Dragonfly species include the rare Irish damselfly. Pike survive in many of the small pools where hunting mink or even an occasional otter may be spotted. You can see duck on the flooded areas in winter.

Castle Archdale

Near: Kesh, Co Fermanagh
Map: 23, B2
Web: www.ehsni.gov.uk

Castle Archdale is made up of small, hilly islands which are, in fact, the tops of drumlins. Open glades in the wood – with dense leafy areas of bracken, bramble, hawthorn and ivy – provide the ideal home for the garden warbler. This uncommon, small, brown bird nests close to the ground among the foliage.

> **DID YOU KNOW?**
>
> Oak trees can live up to 1,000 years or more.

Clements Wood

Near: Larne, Co Antrim
Map: 23, E2
Web: www.wt-woods.org.uk

Clements Wood has hazel copses, open spaces, and wet meadows situated between the Larne river and the disused Larne railway line. The best time to see wildfowers here is late summer and there are several interesting flower species in the hedges and copses.

Correl Glen

Near: Enniskillen, Co Fermanagh
Map: 23, B3
Web: www.ehsni.gov.uk

Correl Glen and the neighbouring Monawilkin are host to many species of butterfly and dragonfly. The silver-washed fritillary is the largest butterfly in Ireland and prefers shady clearings. The holly blue butterfly flies in May, while speckled wood butterflies are common throughout the summer. Also important to the reserve are the nesting curlews and meadow pipits that nest among tussocks or on moss hummocks from mid April to late June and July.

The Drum

Near: Cargan, near Ballymena
Map: 23, D2
Web: www.wt-woods.org.uk

Open areas at The Drum have plants, such as orchids and ragged-robin that are abundant in spring and also provide hunting territory for the many raptors that live here, such as sparrowhawk, kestrel and buzzard. Small pools in the wetland allow frogs to spawn in spring and are often black with tadpoles.

Britain's most endangered species

Of the 66 species of mammals that are found in the UK, the 10 that wildlife experts fear for the most are:

1 Water vole (pictured)
2 Red squirrel
3 Wildcat
4 Pine marten
5 Greater horseshoe bat
6 Barbastelle bat
7 Bechstein's bat
8 Bottle-nosed dolphin
9 Harbour porpoise
10 Northern right whale

Killard

cotton and yellow bog asphodel grow among heather. Small mammals include hares and stoats.

Kiltonga

Near: Newtownards, Co Down
Map: 23, E2
Web: www.ehsni.gov.uk
P

The lakes at Kiltonga nature reserve are managed for wildfowl, attract a wide variety of duck species and are regularly visited by gadwell. Bullfinch and song thrush have also been recorded here.

Lough Beg NNR

Near: Magherafelt,
Co Londonderry
Map: 23, C2
Web: www.ehnsi.gov.uk
Black-tailed godwit, green sandpiper, wood sandpiper, greenshank and knot are seen every year at Lough Beg. In early summer, the sky is alive with the calls of breeding waders. You can hear snipe, redshank and lapwing. The floods attract wildfowl.

Marble Arch

Near: Enniskillen, Co Fermanagh
Map: 23, B3
Web: www.ehsni.gov.uk
WC ⓘ 🖃

Wood goldilocks grow here, as do early purple orchid, birds'-nest orchid, bluebells and wild strawberry. You can also see red and grey squirrel in the tree canopies and feral goats can also be spotted.

Murlough

Near: Castlewellan, Co Down
Map: 23, D3
Web: www.ehsni.gov.uk
P ♿ (ltd), WC ⓘ 🏞

The varied habitats within Murlough reserve are home to a wide range of plants and animals, including badgers and stoats, as well as delicate flowers, such as the pyramidal

Killard

Near: Downpatrick, Co Down
Map: 23, E3
Web: www.ehsni.gov.uk
P 🚻

The abundant grassland flowers colour the landscape at Killard through the seasons. Species include spring squill, bulbous buttercup, kidney vetch, wild pansies, restharrow, centaury and pyramidal orchids. Knapweed, thyme and field scabious complete the picture. The banks in July and August are alive with butterflies – common blues, meadow browns and painted ladies abound. Notable birds include fulmars and sand martins on the cliffs and stonechats among the scrub.

Killykeegan and Crossmurrin

Near: Blacklion, Co Fermanagh
Map: 23, B2
Web: www.ehsni.gov.uk
P

Killykeegan and Crossmurrin's scrub is home to delicate woodland flowers, including wood sorrel and primroses. The cuckoo is frequently heard in May. Meadow pipits are mostly seen over the grassland. The grasses are grazed by sheep and this allows herbs, such as the colourful pink thyme, blue harebell and yellow bird's-foot trefoil, to flower and set seed. These herbs in turn provide food for insects, such as the common blue and peacock butterflies. In a patch of heath, bog orchid and carline thistle. There are also rare and colourful butterflies. The sea buckthorn attracts nesting willow warblers, white-throats and, in winter, thrushes, fieldfare and redwing. Many species of wader, duck and geese visit the estuary. From the beach, sea-watchers can observe more seabirds and, in the summer and autumn, both common and grey seals.

The Murrins
Near: Mountfield, Co Tyrone
Map: 23, C2
Web: www.ehsni.gov.uk
The Murrins is home to the red grouse. The small lakes,

known as kettle-holes, are the haunt of mallard, teal and the occasional nesting feral grey-lag goose. Around some of the lakes, green and blue damselflies dart among the swampy vegetation which includes the rare broad-leaved mud sedge. Hunting falcons are also in the area.

Quoile Pondage
Near: Downpatrick, Co Down
Map: 23, E3
Web: www.ehsni.gov.uk
P ♿ WC 🎣 ⓘ ⛱ 🏠
Marsh plants grow along the river fringes at Quoile Pondage, with reedbeds,

rushy grassland and willow scrub. Freshwater habitats are rich in insectlife, providing food for fish, such as rudd and eels, which in turn feed grey herons, cormorants and grebes. Otters are also occasionally seen here.

Randalstown Forest and Farr's Bay
Near: Antrim, Co Antrim
Map: 23, D2
Web: www.ehsni.co.uk
P 🚻 🏠
Randalstown Forest and Farr's Bay are two small adjacent nature reserves on the north shore of Lough Neagh. In winter, look out for mallard,

The beauty of bluebells

Bluebells are one of the marvels of spring, transforming forest floors into a lush carpet of green and purple. The UK native variety has drooping flowers that grow from one side of the stem only, while the invasive Spanish variety has flowers that grow all round the stem. Not all woodlands have bluebells, but those that do provide this quintessentially British spectacle in April and May each year. For the best displays visit: Little Acorn Wood, Brantwood or Coed Trellyniau.

PICTURED: Bluebells carpeting a woodland floor

Quoile Pondage nature reserve

teal and gadwall. In summer, great crested grebes, mute swans and coot nest in the reed-swamp fringe of the lagoon.

Slievenacloy
Near: Belfast, Co Down
Map: 23, D2
Web: www.ulsterwildlifetrust.org
Flower species recorded here include purple orchid, twayblade, greater and lesser butterfly orchid, frog orchid, northern marsh orchid and moonwort fern. The area is renowned for its variety of waxcap fungi present on the drier swards. Irish hares are regularly seen on the higher ground, while birds on the site include breeding curlew, snipe, lapwing, skylark, grasshopper warbler, reed bunting and meadow pipit. Marsh and dark-green fritillary butterflies have also been recorded. Dippers are regularly seen on the river and barn owls have been recorded hunting here.

Slieveanorra
Near: Ballymena
Map: 23, D2
Web: www.ehsni.gov.uk
The plantlife at Slievenorra varies from heather and deer grass in drier areas to damp patches where sphagnum moss, sedges and cotton grass grow. Bog asphodel, bog-bean and insect-eating sundews live on the edges of bog pools on Owennaglush. Hen harriers, merlins and red grouse can be seen in these upland areas.

BIRD RESERVES

Belfast Lough
Near: Belfast, Co Down
Map: 23, D2
Web: www.rspb.org.uk
On the harbour estate, there is a lagoon that has ideal conditions for birds including teal, black-tailed godwit lapwing and wigeon. From the observation room you

can see a wide variety of birds – waders and ducks in autumn and winter and terns in summer. Special feeders attract a host of small birds year round.

Lough Neagh Discovery Centre
Near: Craigavon, Co Armagh
Map: 23, D2
Web: www.oxfordisland.com
Open: weekdays, 9am to 5pm; weekends, 10am to 5pm
Birds to see at Lough Neagh Discovery Centre include mallard, tufted duck, coot, large flocks of pochard, cormorants, goldeneye, little grebe and scaup in winter and, in summer, grey herons, diving and nesting terns, gulls, mute swans, mallard, coot, shoveler and great crested grebe. In the Kinnegoe Meadows, wildflowers include colourful velches, trefoils and meadowsweet attracting common blue and wood white butterflies.

Portmore Lough

Near: Aghalee, Lisburn, Co Armagh
Map: 23, D2
Web: www.rspb.org.uk

P **WC** **ℹ**

The reserve at Portmore Lough consists of the lake (lough), the surrounding reedbeds and scrub and extensive meadows. In winter, greylag geese, whooper swans and wildfowl feed on the meadows and thousands of ducks can be seen from the hide on the lough edge. In spring, skylarks and wading birds breed on the meadows.

Rathlin – The West Light

Near: Ballycastle
Map: 23, D1
Web: www.rspb.org.uk

ℹ

From the RSPB West Light platform there are views of Northern Ireland's largest breeding seabird colony on the cliffs and offshore stacks. The colony is best seen between May and July, when there are large numbers of guillemot, razorbill, fulmar, kittiwake and puffin.

Collective nouns for British birds

- A flight of cormorants
- A gaggle of geese
- A murmuration of starlings
- A colony of gulls
- A congregation of plovers
- A cover of coots
- A murder of crows (pictured)
- A parliament of owls
- A watch of nightingales
- A piteousness of doves
- A convocation of eagles

FOREST & WOODLAND

Banagher

Near: Dungiven, Co Derry
Map: 23, C1
Web: www.ehsni.gov.uk

P

You can see drifts of primroses, bluebells, wood sorrel and wood anemone on the woodland floor at Banagher in spring. In early summer, the woods are filled with the silver-washed fritillary butterflies and common-hawker dragonflies. On most days you can see buzzards or sparrowhawks overhead and, on rarer days, a stoat or squirrel.

Bohill Forest

Near: Downpatrick, Co Down
Map: 23, E3
Web: www.ehsni.gov.uk

P

The reserve at Bohill Forest has a colony of holly blue butterfly. Red deer often pass through the woodland, their footprints, droppings and other signs revealing their presence. Many species of bird can be heard on the reserve. Jays, goldcrests and tits are joined by migrant summer visitors, such as the chiffchaff and blackcap.

Breen Oakwood

Near: Ballycastle, Co Antrim
Map: 23, D1
Web: www.ehsni.gov.uk

P

Ferns and mosses thrive in the damp, shady conditions at Breen Oakwood, while dragonflies, frogs and newts are attracted to the boggy pools. Tits and treecreepers are common and look for a sparrowhawk or buzzard hunting among the trees.

Carnmoney Hill

Near: Belfast, Co Down
Map: 23, D2
Web: www.wt-woods.org.uk

P **🚻**

The woodlands at Carnmoney Hill are a good place to see wildflowers, such as early purple orchids, wood anemone, wood sorrel, bluebells and primrose. There are also dog violet in the bracken fields above the wood.

Castlewellan Forest Park

Near: Castlewellan, Co Down
Map: 23, D3
Web: www.discovernorthern ireland.com

P **♿** (ltd), **🚻** **🍴**

Castlewellan Forest Park is located in the foothills of the Mourne mountains. Its huge forest park is a magnet for wildlife such as red squirrels, pine martens and otters. It is also home to the National Arboretum of Northern Ireland.

Drumlamph Woodland

Near: Magherafelt, Co Londonderry
Map: 23, C2
Web: www.wt-woods.org.uk

🚻 **P**

Rush Meadow, on Drumlamph Woodland's borders, has good invertebrate, butterfly, moth, small mammal and frog populations. Irish hares also use this area. In the north, the woodland has badgers and the river has otters.

Galgorm Wood
Near: Ballymena, Co Antrim
Map: 23, D2
Web: www.wt-woods.org.uk

Good place to see fungi.

Little Acorn Wood
Near: Ballymena, Co Antrim
Map: 23, D2
Web: www.wt-woods.org.uk
P 🐾 (ltd), 🏠
A range of flower species has been planted around the site, including bluebells, wild garlic, foxgloves, greater bird's-foot trefoil and ragged robin.

Rea's Wood
Near: Antrim, Co Antrim
Map: 23, D2
Web: www.ehsni.gov.uk
P 🏠
The woodland floor at Rea's Wood provides an ideal habitat for snails, slugs, hoverflies and beetles. There are swampy areas with sedges, marsh marigold, tall yellow flags and summer snowflake. The robin, wren and blackbird are common here, as well as the chiffchaff, blackcap and willow warbler.

Reilly and Gole's Wood
Near: Lisnaskea, Co Fermanagh
Map: 23, B3
Web: www.ehsni.gov.uk
P
Badgers can be seen in Reilly and Gole's Wood at dusk. Look out for the purple hairstreak butterfly, often found perched on the tops of oak leaves during July and August. Kestrels can be seen hovering high above the woodlands, while sparrowhawks weave through the trees below.

Rostrevor Oakwood NNR
Near: Kilbroney, Co Down
Map: 23, D3
Web: www.ehsni.gov.uk
Common woodland birds at Rostrevor Oakwood include blackcaps, willow warblers, chiffchaffs, jays and buzzards. Red squirrels and silver-washed fritillary butterflies are harder to spot.

Straidkilly
Near: Straidkilly Point, near Larne, Co Antrim
Map: 23, E2
Web: www.ehsni.gov.uk
P
In early summer, the woodland floor is carpeted with bluebells and wood anemones and there is a scent of wild garlic. Sunny glades within the woodland provide sheltered areas for insects and butterflies in particular. Look out for small coppers, common blue, speckled wood and tortoiseshell.

Creatures of the night

All 17 species of bat in the UK are protected. They are more often spotted in the summer than the winter and, although many live around buildings, the most likely feeding grounds are around water where the rich pickings of insects and moths can be found. Some places in Britian known for large bat populations include Skipton Woods, Yorkshire; Wild Woods at Parkwood, Wales; Grizedale Forest Park, Cumbria and Briddlesford Woods, Isle of Wight.

PICTURED: Lesser horseshoe bat

COASTS, WATERWAYS & WETLANDS

Bann and Lough Neagh
From: Toome, Co Antrim, to Portstewart, Co Derry
Map: 23, C1 and C2
Web: www.waterwaysireland.org
The Bann is a source of life to a wide variety of species, including cormorants, crows, grey herons, swans, spotted redshanks, mallard ducks, eels, salmon and pike.

Castle Espie Wetlands Centre
Near: Newtownards, Co Down
Map: 23, E2
Web: www.wwt.org.uk
P (££), 🏠 🏠
On the banks of Strangford Lough, this is a major site for birdwatching in Northern Ireland. Species to see include little egrets, shoveler, teal, wigeon, shelduck, spotted redshank, bar-tailed godwit, common guillemot, kingfisher and pale-bellied Brent geese.

Cloghy Rocks
Near: Downpatrick, Co Down
Map: 23, E3
Web: www.ehsni.gov.uk

P **ⓘ**

You can see both common and grey seals at Cloghy Rocks. Common seals favour the site for breeding, with pups being born in July. The variety of habitats, from rocks to fine mud are home to many small shellfish and worms, providing a rich feeding ground for shore birds. Oystercatchers, redshank and other wading birds are also common, as are grey herons, mute swans, sandwich terns and pale-bellied Brent geese.

Ecos Wood
Near: Ballymena, Co Antrim
Map: 23, D2
Web: www.ulsterwildlifetrust.org
P (££), **WC** **ⓘ** **☒**
The ECOS Millennium Environmental Centre is located in the floodplain of the River Braid. The lake is visited by large numbers of little grebe, greylag geese, teal, goldeneye, snipe, sedge and grasshopper warblers. Reed

bunting are found in the scrub and willow coppice and you can see sand martins flying over the site.

Granagh Bay
Near: Downpatrick, Co Down
Map: 23, E3
Web: www.ehsni.gov.uk
P
Edible crabs, squat lobsters and sea urchins are common at Granagh Bay, living beside starfish normally found in Arctic waters. Areas of soft mud and gravel are home to countless different worms, shellfish and sea cucumbers. Piles of seaweed, carried up by high tides and left to decompose on the strandline, attracts pipits, wagtails and wading birds that feed on the flies and other small animals living among the weeds. Teal and other wildfowl often gather here in winter. Both grey and common seals favour the rocks around the beacon.

Lough Neagh Islands
Southern Lough Neagh
Map: 23, D2
Web: www.ehsni.gov.uk
Around 80 of the islands in Lough Neagh are managed as part of the Lough Neagh NNR. Populations of breeding birds are monitored every year. On the islands as a whole, around 500 pairs of mallard, 300 tufted duck, 500 great crested grebes, 30,000 black-headed gulls, 150 common terns and 60 mute swans nest.

Magilligan Point
Near: Magilligan, Co Londonderry
Map: 23, C1
Web: www.ehsni.gov.uk
P **⌂**
Magilligan Point is one of the largest sand-dune systems in the British Isles. Butterflies, such as the common blue or meadow brown, are plentiful, as are six-spot burnet moths. There are good views of seabirds using the narrows

Brent goose

North Strangford Lough

and, in winter, of migrating waders and wildfowl.

Newry Ship Canal
From: Newry, Co Down, to Victoria Locks
Map: 23, D3
Web: www.discovernorthern ireland.com
Algae in summer improves roach and bream catches, while the colder waters of the winter months bring large pike to the canal. Anglers can also snare eels, perch and trout here.

North Strangford Lough NNR
Near: Newtownards, Co Down
Map: 23, E2
Web: www.ehsni.gov.uk
🅿 🆆🅲
North Strangford Lough is very rich in worms, shellfish and other small animals. This food resource attracts migratory wildfowl and

> **DID YOU KNOW?**
>
> Great crested grebes are clumsy on land because their legs are placed far back along their bodies.

waders. Eel grass is abundant and is the principal food source of the pale-bellied Brent geese, attracting more than 60 per cent of the world population. The spectacular presence of thousands of geese is best observed during September and October. During the summer months, Ogilby Island features as the Lough's breeding site for sandwich tern and includes a large population of black-headed gulls.

Portrush Nature Reserve/ Countryside Centre
Near: Portrush, Co Antrim
Map: 23, C1
Web: www.ehsni.gov.uk

Open: June to September, weekdays, 10am to 6pm; weekends, noon to 8pm
🅿 🆆🅲 ❶
Portrush is not only famous for its sticks of peppermint rock, but also for a small area of seashore rock which has helped us understand the way in which the Earth was formed. Rockpools are visible at low tide.

Roe Estuary
Near: Coleraine, Co Derry
Map: 23, C1
Web: www.ehsni.gov.uk
🅿
Hidden by the mud are lots of small seashore animals, such as lugworms, shrimps, ragworms and periwinkles. There are also large beds of mussels and extensive areas covered in eel grass. All these are food sources that act as a magnet for many of the thousands of migrating waders, ducks, swans and

geese that stop over on Lough Foyle each winter. Inside the railway bridge you can see the lapwing, curlew and the otter hunting crabs in the pools.

NOT SO WILD

Ballyarnett Racecourse Society – The Wildlife Sanctuary
Address: Amelia Earhart Centre, Ballyarnett Country Park, Derry BT48 7UF
Map: 23, C1
Tel: 028 71 354 040
Web: www.derry.goireland.com
Open: weekdays, 10 am to 8pm/ dusk; weekends, 10am to 6pm/dusk
ⓘ 🚻
This 45-acre wildlife park is found on the grounds of the former racecourse. The on-site farm has poultry, rabbits, budgies, pot-bellied pigs, emus, donkeys, ponies and sheep,

while the wildlife sanctuary is a home to minks, otters, wild ducks, geese, badgers and foxes. Amelia Earhart cottage is within walking distance of the farm.

Belfast Zoo
Address: Antrim Road, Belfast BT36 7PN
Map: 23, D2
Tel: 028 90776277
Web: www.belfastzoo.co.uk
Open: daily, 10am to 2.30/5pm (except 25 and 26 December)
Admission: £3.20/£6.30
P (££), **WC**
ⓘ 🖳 🚻
This world-class zoo acts as a safe haven for more than 160 species of rare and endangered animals. You can see gorillas, chimpanzees, birds, elephants, giraffes, penguins and sea lions here. New additions to the zoo include barbary lions, maned wolves, barn owls, cape porcupines and Moloch gibbons.

Exploris Aquarium
Address: The Rope Walk, Castle Street, Portaferry, Co Down BT22 1NZ
Tel: 028 4272 8062
Map: 23, E3
Web: www.exploris.org.uk
Open: weekdays, 11am to 6pm; weekends, times vary
Admission: March to September £3.80/£6.70; October to February £3.30/£5.40
P **&** (ltd), **WC** **ⓘ**
All local waterlife can be found at Exploris Aquarium. Species to see include bass, bib, starfish, cod, lobster, crawfish, cuttlefish, sea urchin, feather star, spider crab, hermit crab, octopus, long-spined sea scropion, lumpsucker, peacock worm, red mullet, turbot and wolf-fish. The adjoined seal sanctuary is for the rehabilitation and release of orphaned, injured and sick common and grey seals.

Maps

UNITED KINGDOM

MAP 20

SCOTLAND

MAP 21

MAP 19

NORTHERN
IRELAND

MAP 23

MAP 17

MAP 18

ENGLAND

MAP 13

MAP 15   MAP 14

MAP 12

MAP 22

MAP 16

WALES

MAP 6

MAP 7   MAP 2

MAP 1

MAP 9

MAP 5

MAP 8

MAP 4

MAP 10   MAP 3

MAP 11

N

100km

100miles

Key To Location Maps

	International border		M5	Motorway		Coastline
	Regional border		A30	Dual carriageway		Urban area
	County border		A39	Main road		

Maps © JP Map Graphics Ltd, based on XYZ Digital Map Company data

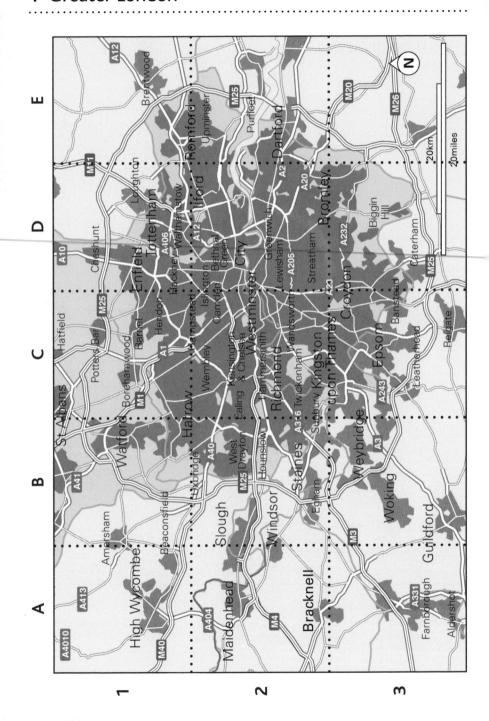

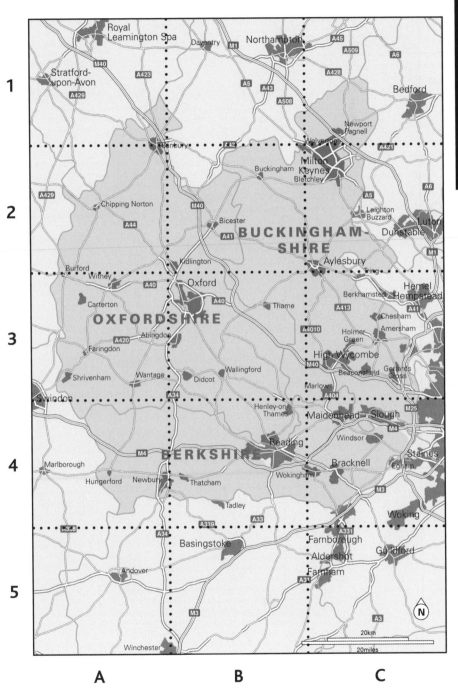

Royal Leamington Spa
Stratford-upon-Avon
Daventry
Northampton
Bedford
Newport Pagnell
Wolverton
Banbury
Milton Keynes
Bletchley
Buckingham
Chipping Norton
Bicester
BUCKINGHAM-SHIRE
Leighton Buzzard
Luton
Dunstable
Burford
Witney
Kidlington
Aylesbury
Tring
Hemel Hempstead
Berkhamsted
Carterton
Oxford
Thame
Chesham
Amersham
OXFORDSHIRE
Holmer Green
High Wycombe
Abingdon
Faringdon
Shrivenham
Wantage
Didcot
Wallingford
Beaconsfield
Gerrards Cross
Marlow
Swindon
Henley-on-Thames
Maidenhead
Slough
Marlborough
BERKSHIRE
Reading
Windsor
Bracknell
Staines
Egham
Hungerford
Newbury
Thatcham
Wokingham
Woking
Tadley
Basingstoke
Farnborough
Aldershot
Guildford
Andover
Farnham
Winchester

20km
20miles
N

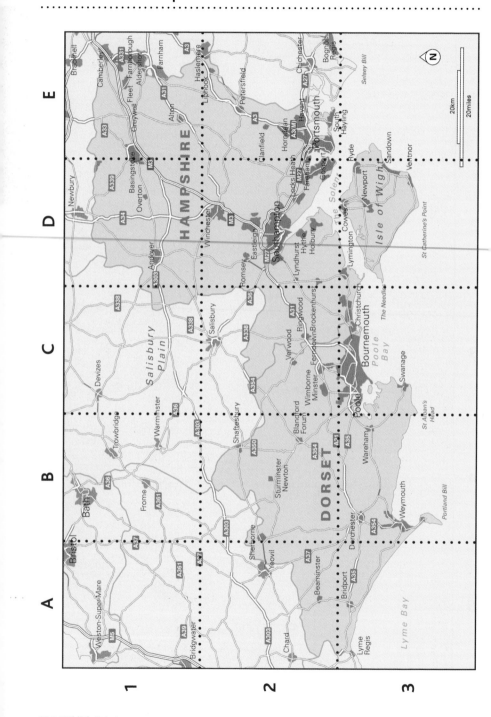

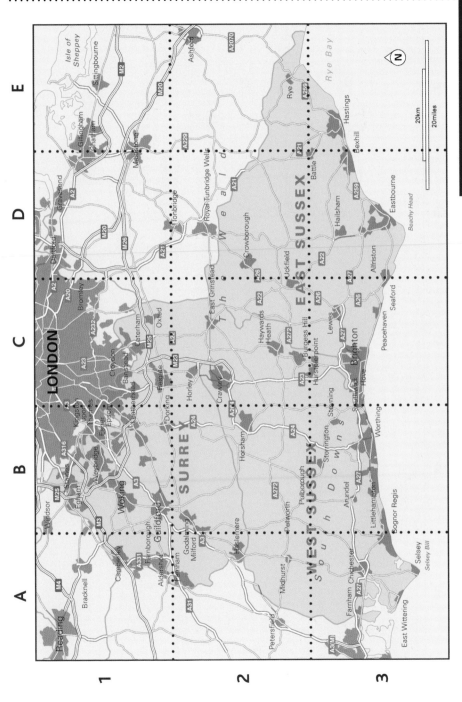

5 Kent

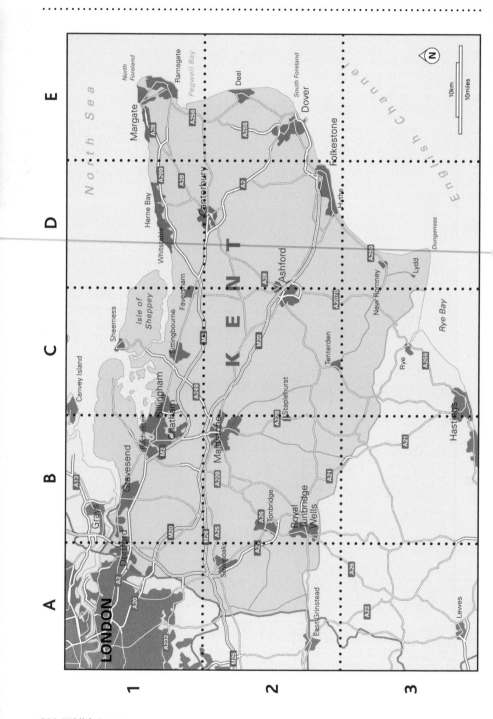

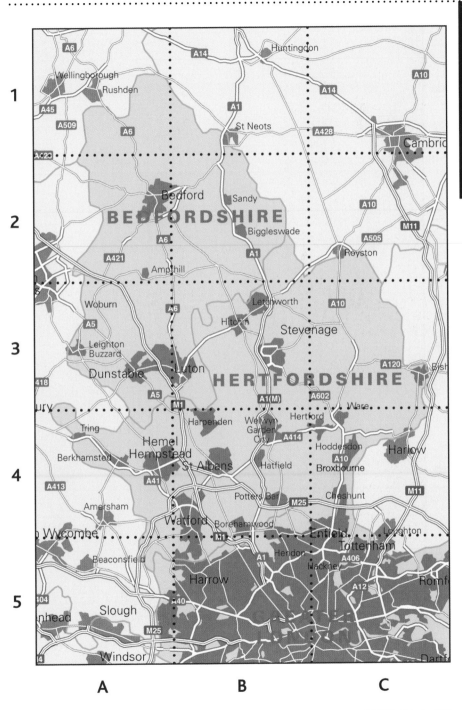

A   B   C

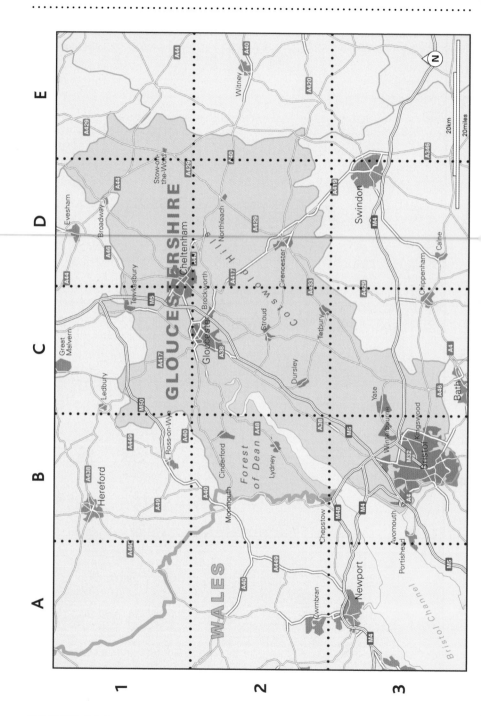

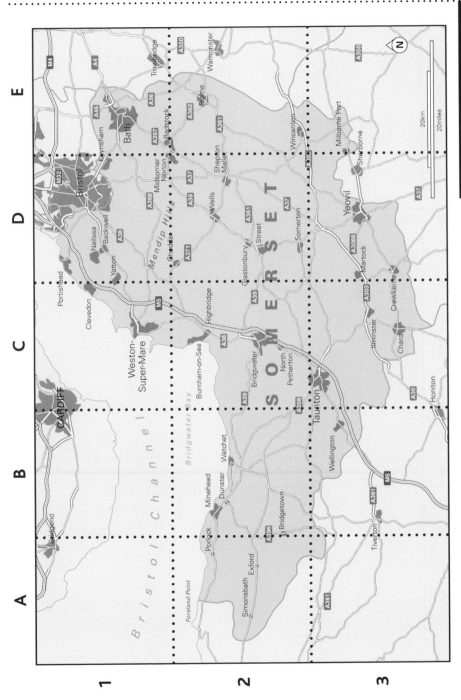

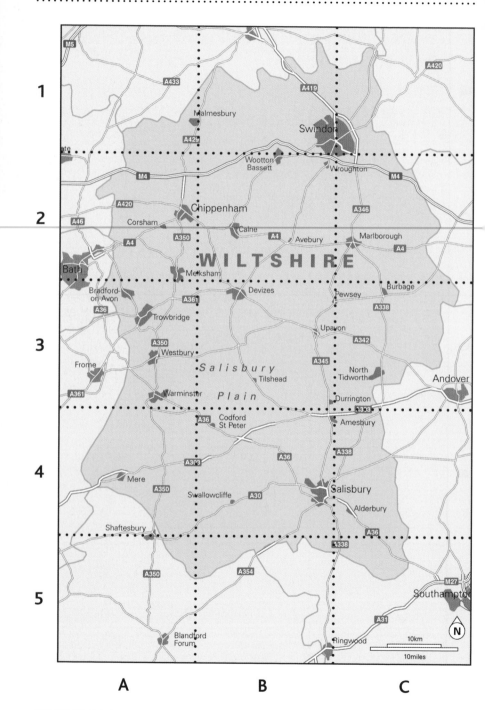

M5

A433

1

Malmesbury

A419

A429

Swindon

A420

Wootton
Bassett

Wroughton

M4

M4

A420

Chippenham

A346

2

A46

Corsham

Calne

A350

A4

Avebury

Marlborough

A4

Bath

W I L T S H I R E

Melksham

Bradford-
on-Avon

A361

Devizes

Pewsey

Burbage

A338

A36

Trowbridge

Upavon

A350

A342

3

Frome

Westbury

A345

North
Tidworth

Andover

Salisbury

Tilshead

A361

Warminster

Plain

Durrington

A303

A36

Codford
St Peter

Amesbury

4

A303

A36

A338

Mere

A350

Swallowcliffe

A30

Salisbury

Alderbury

Shaftesbury

A36

A338

A350

A354

5

M27

Southampton

A31

10km

N

Blandford
Forum

Ringwood

10miles

A

B

C

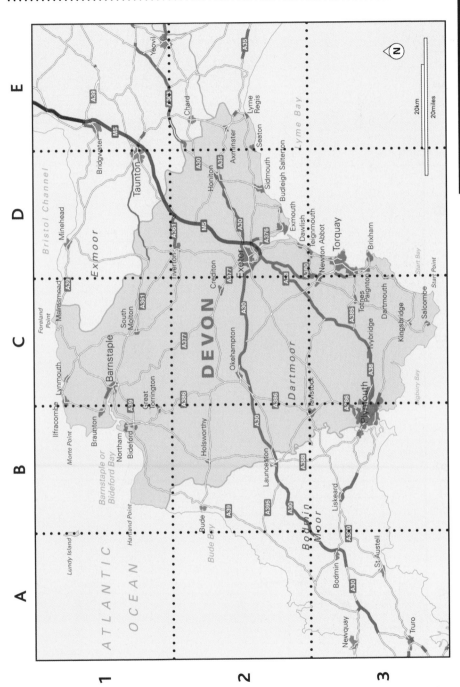

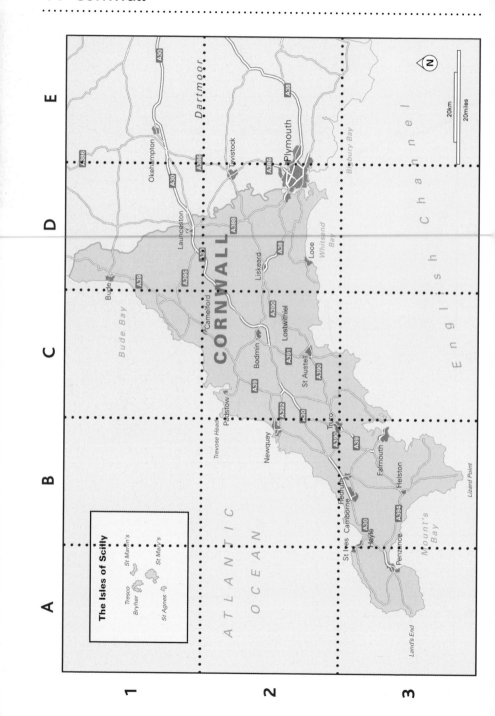

The Isles of Scilly

St Martin's
Tresco
Bryher
St Mary's
St Agnes

CORNWALL

Land's End
Penzance
Hayle
St Ives
Camborne
Redruth
Helston
Lizard Point
Falmouth
Truro
Newquay
Padstow
Trevose Head
Bodmin
St Austell
Lostwithiel
Camelford
Bude
Launceston
Liskeard
Looe
Plymouth
Tavistock
Okehampton

Bude Bay
Mount's Bay
Whitsand Bay
Bigbury Bay
English Channel
ATLANTIC OCEAN
Dartmoor

A30
A386
A388
A30
A386
A386
A38
A39
A395
A39
A30
A392
A39
A390
A391
A390
A390
A30
A394
A39
A388
A38

N

20km
20miles

A B C D E

1 2 3

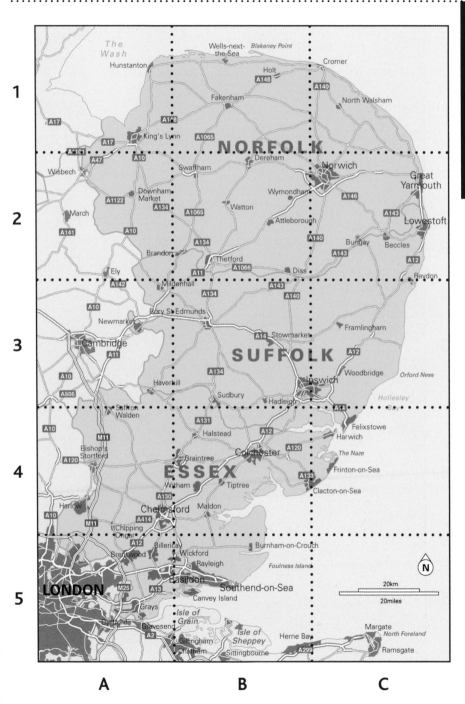

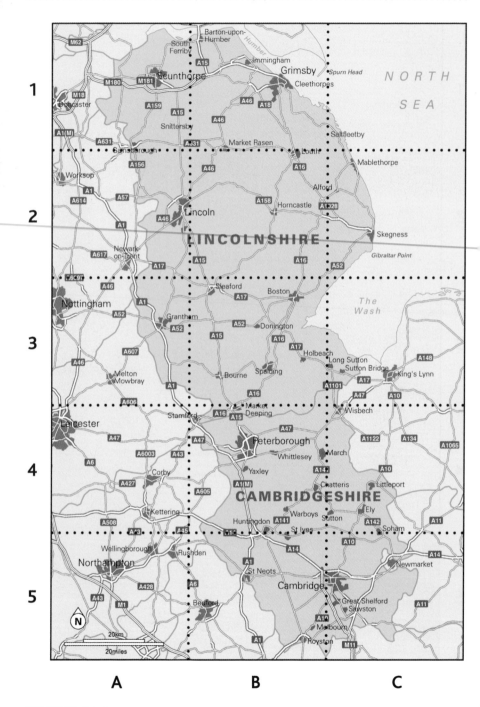

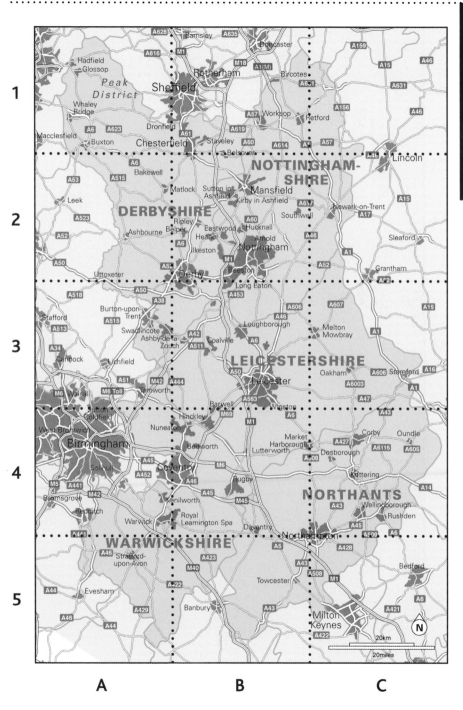

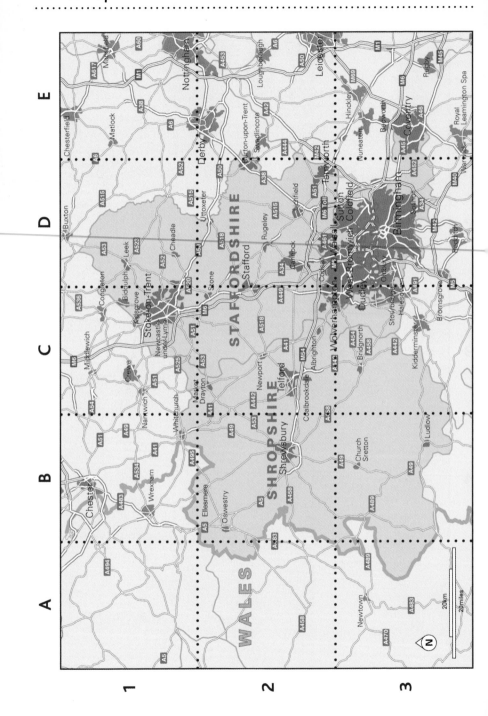

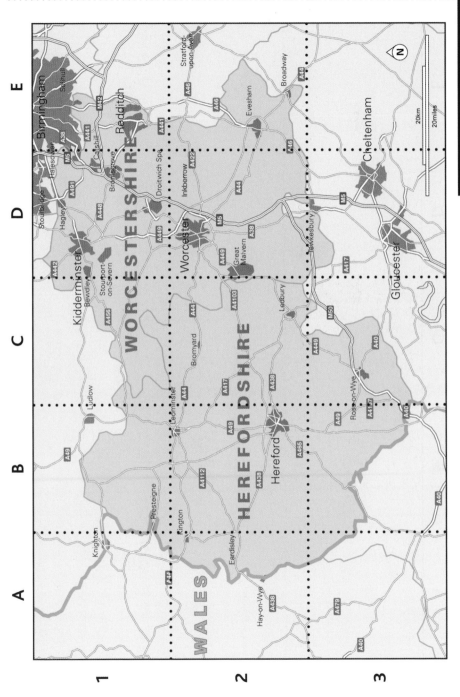

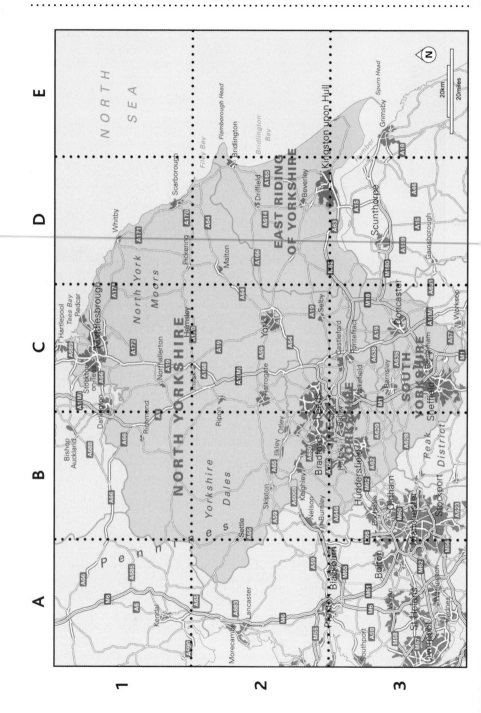

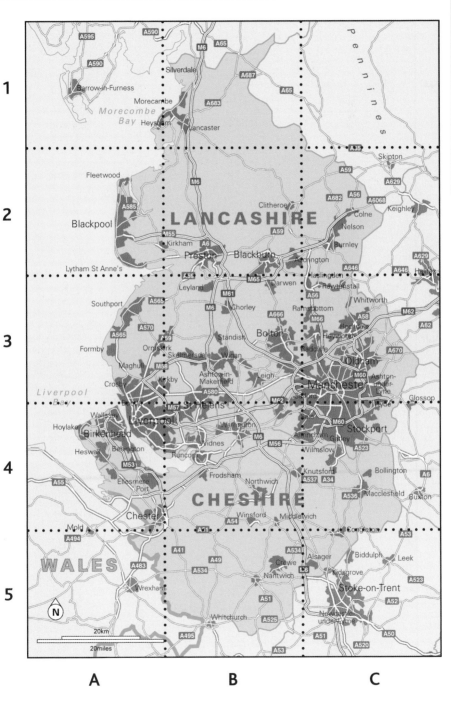

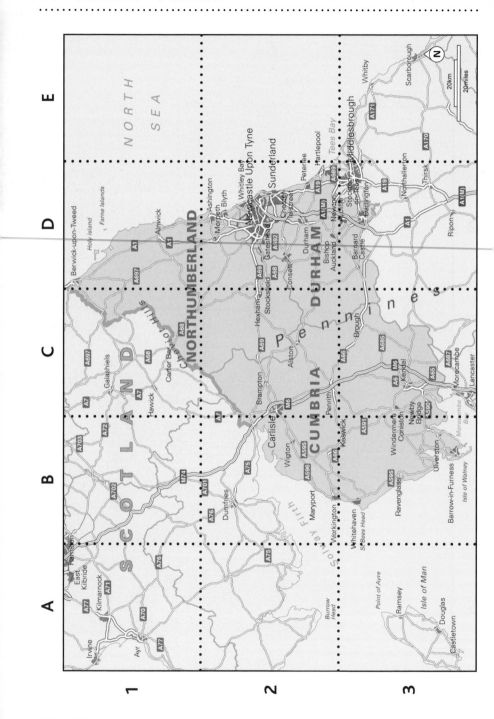

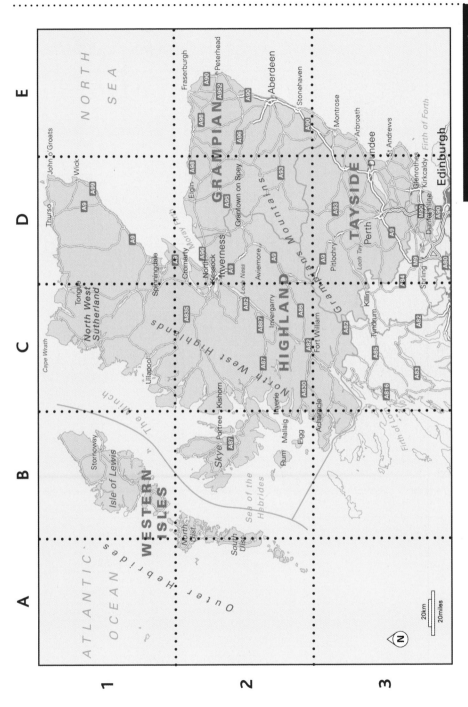

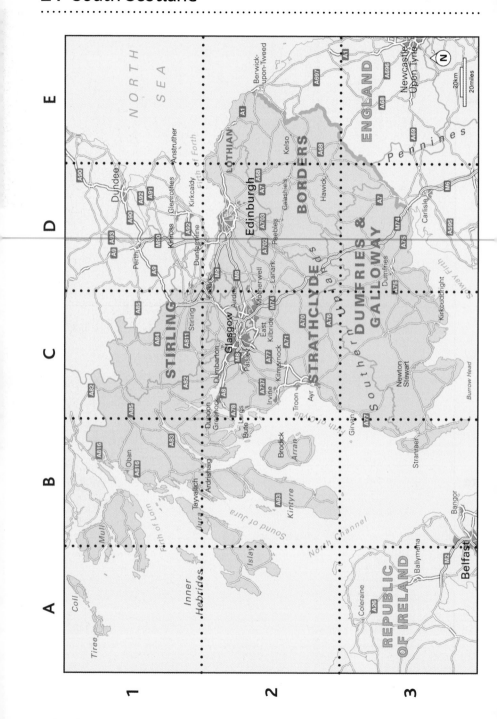

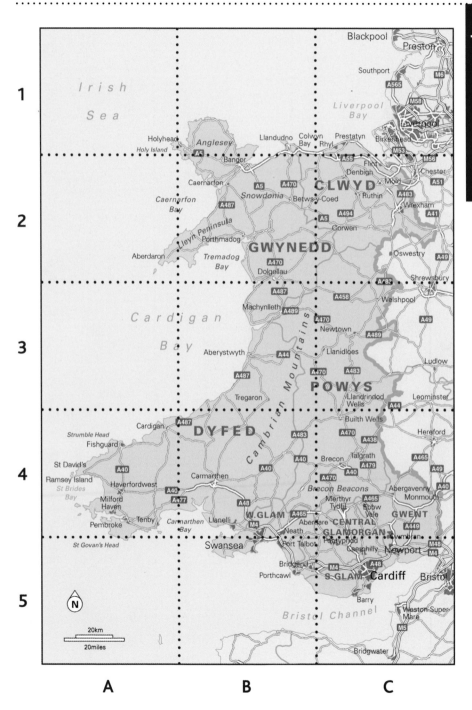

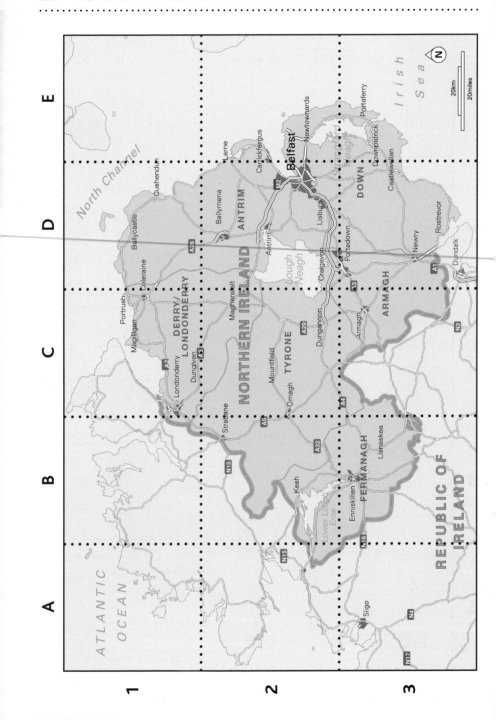

Directory of useful organisations

Association of National Parks Authorities – The ruling body for Britain's 14 National Parks.
Tel: 029 2049 9966
Email: c.marcus@anpa.gov.uk
Web: www.nationalparks.gov.uk

Buglife – The Invertebrate Conservation Trust. The first organisation in Europe devoted to the conservation of all invertebrates.
Tel: 01733 201 210
Email: info@buglife.org.uk
Web: www.buglife.org.uk

Butterfly Conservation – Works to safeguard the future of butterflies and moths through conservation work and managing reserves.
Tel: 0870 7744309
Email: info@butterfly-conservation.org
Web: www.butterfly-conservation.org

Countryside Council for Wales – The government body for rural affairs in Wales.
Tel: 08451 306 229
Email: enquiries@ccw.gov.uk
Web: www.ccw.gov.uk

CPRE – The Campaign to Protect Rural England.
Tel: 020 7981 2800
Email: info@cpre.org.uk
Web: www.cpre.org.uk

Defra – Department for Environment, Food and Rural Affairs. They bring together the interests of farmers and the countryside.
Tel: 08459 33 55 77
Email: helpline@defra.gsi.gov.uk
Web: www.defra.gov.uk

English Heritage – Protecting England's historic environment.
Tel: 0870 333 1181
Email: customers@english-heritage.org.uk
Web: www.english-heritage.org.uk

English Nature – (part of Natural England, see below)

Environment Agency – The leading public body for protecting and improving the environment in England and Wales.
Tel: 08708 506 506
Web: www.environment-agency.gov.uk

Environment Heritage Services Northern Ireland – Government agency for conserving the natural and built environment.
Tel: 028 9054 6545
Web: www.ehsni.gov.uk

Forestry Commission – Government organisation for conserving forests.
Tel: 0131 334 0303
Email: enquiries@forestry.gsi.gov.uk
Web: www.forestry.gov.uk

Marine Conservation Society (MCS) – The UK charity dedicated to caring for our seas, shores and wildlife.
Web: www.mcsuk.org

National Biodiversity Network – Bringing together all the biodiversity networks of the UK into one searchable database.
Tel: 01636 670090
Web: www.nbn.org.uk and www.searchbn.net

National Trust – A charity that looks after the national and built environments of England, Wales and Northern Ireland.
Tel: 0870 458 4000
Email: enquiries@thenationaltrust.org.uk
Web: www.nationaltrust.org.uk

Natural England – The new body created from English Nature, the Countryside Agency and the Rural Development Service to safeguard biodiversity, landscapes and wildlife.
Tel: 0845 600 3078
Email: enquiries@naturalengland.org.uk
Web: www.naturalengland.org.uk

Plantlife – The charity working to protect Britain's wild plants and the habitats in which they are found.
Tel: 01722 342730
Email: enquiries@plantlife.org.uk
Web: www.plantlife.org.uk

Pond Trust – The UK's leading centre for information and practical advice on the conservation of rivers, lakes, ponds, canals and drainage ditch systems.
Tel: 01865 483249
Web: www.pondstrust.org.uk

RSPB – The UK's charity for birds.
Tel: 01767 680551
Web: www.rspb.org.uk

RSPCA – The animal charity that can help injured or sick wild animals.
Tel: 24-hour national cruelty and advice line on 0870 55 55 999,

enquiries: 0870 33 35 999
Web: www.rspca.org.uk

Scottish Natural Heritage – The government body for national heritage in Scotland.
Tel: 01463 725000
Web: www.snh.org.uk

Visit Britain – Tourist information for all of Britain.
Web: www.visitbritain.com

Waterscape – Online guide to Britain's waterways.
Web: www.waterscape.com

Whale and Dolphin Conservation Society – Looking out for the habitats and treatment of cetaceans around the globe.
Tel: 0870 870 5001 **Email:** info@wdcs.org **Web:** www.wdcs.org

Wild Scotland – The Scottish Wildlife and Nature Tourism Operators Association, committed to delivering a first-class wildlife-watching experience.
Tel: 01463 723013
Web: www.wild-scotland.co.uk

Wildfowl and Wetlands Trust – Conservation charity for wetlands with a network of wetland reserves.
Tel: 01453 891900 **Email:** enquiries@wwt.org.uk **Web:** www.wwt.org.uk

The Wildlife Trusts – The UK's largest conservation charity with 47 local Wildlife Trusts.
Tel: 0870 036 7711
Email: enquiry@wildlifetrusts.org
Web: www.wildlifetrusts.org

Woodland Trust – Conservation charity for woodlands.
Tel: 01476 581135
Web: www.woodland-trust.org.uk

YPTENC – The Young People's Trust for the Environment charity aims to encourage young people's understanding of the environment and the need for sustainability.
Tel: 01460 249163
Email: ypteinfo@btconnect.com
Web: www.yptenc.org.uk

Zoological Society of London – Devoted to the worldwide conservation of animals and their habitats.
Web: www.zsl.org

Further reading

Complete British Animals
Paul Sterry
Collins, 224pp, 2005, £14.99
This photographic field guide to all mammals, reptiles and amphibians in Britain, is a comprehensive guide that allows the reader to identify species and their tracks and trails. Each animal has two pages of information that includes numerous photographs of the animal, its habitat and tracks as well as distribution maps and detailed text. Tips for the wildlife watcher on how to spot each animal are also included.

Collins Wild Guide: British Wildlife
Peter Holden
Collins, 512pp, 2005, £12.99
An introductory pocket-sized guide to 500 of the most common birds, wildflowers, trees, insects, mammals, fish, reptiles and amphibians that share the British Isles with us. Each page is devoted to a different species, with a detailed description, a full-colour photograph, a calendar guide for when it's around and an identification fact file for easy, at-a-glance reference. Additional artwork highlights identification features. The perfect companion for any budding naturalist.

Birds: A Complete Guide to all British and European Species
Dominic Couzens
Collins, 336pp, 2005, £30
This large-format, lavishly illustrated book is written in an engaging and entertaining manner providing fantastic insights into the secret lives of Britain and Europe's bird species. Over 450 birds are featured, each with a photo, a map showing where it's found, illustrations for different plumages and a comprehensive and authoritative text about the bird's behaviour. At-a-glance information panels give fast access to details on food, song, habitat, migration and breeding.

RSPB Birdwatching
Rob Hume
Dorling Kindersley, 226pp, 2006
Not just a guide to birds, but a guide to birdwatching, this book has sections on everything from attracting birds to your garden to how to identify them in the field and what equipment you'll need for birdwatching. It's comprehensive in coverage and concise in style with full-colour photography throughout. The guides to where to see birds in different European countries add an extra dimension to the book.

RSPB Handbook of British Birds
Peter Holden and Tim Cleeves
A&C Black Natural History, 304pp, 2006, £9.99
This revised and updated edition of the best-selling *RSPB Handbook of British Birds* provides a 'biography' of each of the 300 most common British bird species. It covers all aspects of field identification, using illustrations to show all common plumage forms. The text also covers behaviour, breeding biology, population, status, longevity and many other interesting facts. A detailed distribution map is provided for each species.

RSPB's Children's Guide to Birdwatching
David Chandler & Mike Unwin
A&C Black Natural History, 128pp, September 2007, £6.99
This new RSPB-endorsed book is a practical, exciting and comprehensive introduction to watching birds for children aged 8-12 years. Illustrated with full-colour photographs and paintings, it begins by discussing general birding – where to go and when, what equipment to take with you, tips on attracting birds to your garden, how to take field notes, etc. The second half is a field guide to over 130 species of birds found in Britain and Ireland. Each species is presented with clear illustrations backed up by concise, straightforward text describing key identification points, such as behaviour, voice and habitat.

Complete British Insects
Michael Chinery
Collins, 384pp, 2005, £16.99
This photographic field guide to 1,500 species of insects found in Britain includes all the common species and some unusual

ones, too. Each entry is illustrated with a clear photograph of the insect, details of its distribution and whether it is common or rare. The book also includes photographs on larvae and extra information on telling apart easily confused species.

Whales, Dolphins and Seals
Brett Jarrett & Hadoram Shirihai
A&C Black Natural History, 384pp, 2006, £12.99
This new field guide is a complete reference to every species of cetacean, pinniped and sirenian in the world, along with the marine and sea otters and the polar bear. Every species is illustrated with magnificent colour paintings and a stunning collection of photographs, chosen to illustrate the key field marks which can be used to separate each species in the field. This is a neat, practical field guide that will enable any observer to quickly identify any mammals they may encounter at sea.

Wild Flowers An Easy Guide by Habitat and Colour
Tracy Dickinson
Green Books, 208pp, 2003, £7.95
This full-colour guide to the wildflowers of Great Britain is designed to make wildflower identification as easy as possible. The flowers are categorised in eight sections based on habitat. Each habitat has a set of photographs for easy identification and essential information, which includes the botanical name, month of flowering and particular characteristics of the species.

Wild Flowers By Colour
Marjorie Blamey
A&C Black Natural History, 208pp, 2005, £9.99
An innovative and remarkably user-friendly guide to the identification of the flowers of Britain and north-western Europe. By organising the species by their colour group first (and by family within that colour group), this guide enables those less familiar with flower species to quickly and easily find what they are looking for. The lovely artwork by acclaimed illustrator Marjorie Blamey, with a neat, focused and simple text, makes this book a joy to use.

Wild Flowers of Britain and Ireland: A new guide to our wild flowers
Alastair Fitter, Marjorie Blamey & Richard Fitter
A&C Black Natural History, 482pp, 2003, £16.99
With over 2,000 detailed colour paintings and more than 800 maps, this is the most extensively illustrated wildflower guide to Britain and Ireland yet. Each entry includes specific details about the plant and a map to show the areas where it can be found. Coloured, boxed keys to plants in complex or difficult groups help with more complicated identifications.

Complete British Wild Flowers
Paul Sterry
Collins, 304pp, 2006, £15.99
A complete photo guide to all the wildflowers of Britain, from flowers and shrubs to aquatic plants, grasses, sedges and rushes.
A botanical hotspots section includes 100 rarer species while comparison pages show different leaf shapes and flower clusters, etc, so that you can quickly and easily navigate to the right section of the book to make an identification. Maps are included to show where all species can be found.

Complete British Trees
Paul Sterry
Collins, 288pp, 2007, £14.99
This easy-to-use guide covers the 360 species of tree that are found in Britain and Ireland. Each species is covered in detail with information on how to identify it, whether from a leaf, twig, bark or whole tree, plus extra information on where the tree grows (including a map), how high they grow, what uses it is put to and its place in history. Every species is also comprehensively illustrated with photographs of every useful feature – bark, leaf, seed, flower, twig and whole tree.

Index

Index

Index

PHOTOS

The photographs in this book are copyright of The Wildlife Trusts, Woodland Trust, RSPB, Natural England, Britain on View or the people or organisations listed. We would like to thank them for helping to make this book possible:

Woodland Trust (Keith Huggett, Richard Becker WTPL), RSPB (Nigel Blake, Jan Halady, David Tipling), Natural England (Peter Wakely, Peter Roworth, Pat Doody, Derek Ratcliffe, Paul Glendell, Julian Bateson), Britain on View (Alan Novelli, East Midlands Tourism/Daniel Bosworth, Martin H Smith/naturepl.com, John Cancalosi/naturepl.com, Richard Watson, Martin Brent, Duncan Shaw, David Sellman, John Mart, David Noton), Nature Picture Libray/Florian Graner, Isobel Cameron/Forestry Commissionn, George Adams, Ray Armstrong/Wye Valley AONB, Banham Zoo, Stephen Bedser – Eden Project, British Waterways Photolibrary, Laurie Campbell/SNH, Drusillas Park, Elan Valley Ranger Service, Forestry Commission/Isobel Cameron, Lorne Gill/SNH, John Harding, Mike Hartwell – EHSNI, Richard Taylor Jones, Selina Lane (PoetsLane), Paul Marsh/WWT, Muncaster Owl Centre, Norfolk Wildlife Trust – David Price, Northumberland National Park – Simon Fraser, Kevin Richardson – photowales.co.uk, Lady Scott/WWT, Martin Senior/WWT London Wetland Centre, Brian Sherwen, Shropshire Hills AONB Partnership, Shropshire Wildlife Trust, Mark Sisson, South Lakes Willd Animal Park, Staffordshire Wildlife Trust, Phil Sutton, The Berks, Bucks and Oxon Wildlife Trust, Nick Turner ©Brecon Beacons National Park Authority, Twycross Zoo – Press Association, Linda Wright/Wye Valley AONB, WWT

Observe and Record

Quickly. Easily. Precisely.

Welcome to the world of digiscoping! It's now possible to capture on camera unique observation experiences. The digital camera base from Swarovski Optik mounts your digital camera directly on to the telescope's eyepiece, simply converting the telescope into a telephoto lens. Photographs with astonishing pinpoint detail can be taken over long distances using your own camera. Recording the moment is simplicity itself thanks to the ability to switch between observation and photography modes in the blink of an eye.

SWAROVSKI
O P T I K

Swarovski U.K. LTD., Perrywood Business Park, Salfords, Surrey RH1 5JQ, Tel.01737-856812, Fax 01737-856885

www.swarovskioptik.c